Industry and Politics
in West Germany

A volume in the series

Cornell Studies in Political Economy

EDITED BY PETER J. KATZENSTEIN

A full list of titles in the series appears at the end of the book

Industry and Politics
in West Germany

Toward the Third Republic

Edited by
PETER J. KATZENSTEIN

CORNELL UNIVERSITY PRESS

Ithaca and London

Contents

CONTENTS

Contributors

CHRISTOPHER S. ALLEN is Assistant Professor of Political Science at the University of Georgia, Athens.

MARTIN BAETHGE is Professor of Sociology at the University of Göttingen and a Research Director of the Sociologisches Forschungsinstitut Göttingen (SOFI).

JOSEF ESSER is Professor of Political Science at the University of Frankfurt.

WOLFGANG FACH is Professor of Political Science at the University of Konstanz.

JOANNE GOWA is Associate Professor of Political Science at the University of Pennsylvania, Philadelphia.

JOST HALFMANN is Professor of Sociology at the University of Osnabrück.

GARY B. HERRIGEL is Fellow at the Center for European Studies, Harvard University, and Ph.D. candidate in Political Science at the Massachusetts Institute of Technology, Cambridge.

GERD JUNNE is Professor of International Relations at the University of Amsterdam.

PETER J. KATZENSTEIN is Walter S. Carpenter, Jr., Professor of International Studies at Cornell University, Ithaca, New York.

HORST KERN is Professor of Sociology at the University of Göttingen and President of the Sociologisches Forschungsinstitut Göttingen (SOFI).

HERBERT OBERBECK is a Research Director of the Sociologisches Forschungsinstitut Göttingen (SOFI).

MICHAEL SCHUMANN is Professor of Sociology at the University of Göttingen and a Research Director of the Sociologisches Forschungsinstitut Göttingen (SOFI).

WOLFGANG STREECK is Professor of Sociology and Industrial Relations at the University of Wisconsin, Madison.

Preface

The 1980s have been characterized by dynamic technological developments and the rise of new competitors in the international economy. The industrial system offers us a template for analyzing the political consequences of these rapid changes. Existing studies in political economy typically focus on one level of political action: the shop floor, or national politics, or the international system. The temptation is almost irresistible to magnify the importance of empirical findings at one level by extrapolating to the other two. This book differs from conventional studies in that it analyzes the implications of change at all three levels, ranging over a number of manufacturing and service sectors. Broadly speaking, it challenges the notion that the 1980s should be painted only in lively, bright hues—or, alternatively, only in brooding, dark colors.

This style of multilevel analysis should be applicable to all industrial states, but our focus here is the Federal Republic of Germany. The vexing problems of stability and change have been prime sources of concern for students of modern German history. Between the mid-nineteenth and mid-twentieth centuries dynamic changes transformed Germany but came into conflict with the international balance of power. This dynamism was a fundamental cause of two world wars. In the 1980s, this book argues, the political consequences of change in the heart of Europe are less ominous. Forty years after the founding of West Germany, we are witnessing a movement toward a third West German republic. The title of this book conveys the conviction that West German politics since 1949 should be viewed within a broad, comparative framework. Furthermore, changes in political regimes since 1949 merit closer attention than they have received from specialists preoccupied with comparing the Federal Republic to German regimes before 1945. In the

1980s West German politics appears to have evolved into a process of dynamic adjustment within stable institutions.

This book has two intellectual origins. Over the years my research and teaching had given me a substantial familiarity with the politics of industry in the United States and Japan; yet I knew very little about the same subject in West Germany. Furthermore, a frequent reaction of colleagues and German specialists to draft chapters of my *Policy and Politics in West Germany,* published in 1987, was general approval with the proviso that, of course, everything I had written about had changed in recent years. Since that book did not systematically cover developments in the 1980s, my analysis was dated even before publication. I was puzzled by this reaction, but it convinced me to think of a research project designed to deal with the consequences of change for West German politics in the 1980s, specifically the politics of industry, about which I wanted to learn more.

This project would have been impossible without financial and logistical support from a variety of sources. The German Marshall Fund of the United States and the Volkswagenwerk Foundation jointly financed a workshop and a conference that provided the opportunity to discuss drafts of chapters. Cornell University's Center for International Studies and the Wissenschaftszentrum Berlin hosted these two meetings and provided the necessary logistical and administrative support. I thank, in particular, Kay Rice of Cornell and Gernot Grabher of the Science Center, without whose generous and efficient help I could not have organized the two meetings. The German Academic Exchange Service (DAAD) awarded me a "Study Visit to the F.R.G." grant, which supported an exploratory trip in 1985.

Project participants benefited greatly from critical comments and suggestions of scholars invited to attend the two meetings. The Cornell workshop was attended by Steven Caldwell, Alice Cook, Michael Goldfield, Gernot Grabher, Stephen Hamilton, Michael Hannan, Sheila Jasanoff, Peter Johnson, Harry Katz, Herbert Kitschelt, Ikuo Kume, David Patton, T. J. Pempel, Jonas Pontusson, Simon Reich, Charles Sabel, Sidney Tarrow, Norbert Walter, and Lynne Wozniak. The conference in Berlin was attended by Elmar Altvater, Alice Cook, Christopher Deutschmann, Hans-Jürgen Ewers, Gernot Grabher, Hansjörg Herr, Peter Johnson, Ulrich Jürgens, Herbert Kitschelt, Hans Maier, Jürgen Müller, Frieder Naschold, Joachim Niebuhr, Bernhard Roth, Ronald Roth, Manfred Schmidt, Georg Voruba, and Norbert Walter.

One of the intentions of this project was to provide an American audience with a political assessment of West Germany's political economy in the 1980s. My West German colleagues thus committed themselves to producing final drafts in English. Preparation of the manuscript for publication was a particular challenge for some of them and required special care in the editorial process. I thank Ruth Crowley, Trudie Calvert, and Emily Wheeler for their remarkable translation and editorial skills, which were essential for getting the manuscript ready so quickly. At Cornell University Press, Roger Haydon supervised the review and production process with his customary efficiency and good humor.

This project has taught me that collaborative, interdisciplinary, and international research has intellectual rewards that far outweigh the time unavoidably invested in getting a project off the ground and seeing it through to completion. I hope such research will become more common so that authors on both sides of the Atlantic can learn more from one another and so that interested audiences can become acquainted with analyses that challenge the accepted view of what political life across the Atlantic is really like.

PETER J. KATZENSTEIN

Ithaca, New York

Part I

INTRODUCTION

CHAPTER ONE

Industry in a Changing West Germany

PETER J. KATZENSTEIN

For a generation West Germany has enjoyed spectacular success in dealing with economic and social change. The 1950s witnessed a "miracle" of economic reconstruction and social consolidation. With some justification an astute observer of the 1950s called the Federal Republic the "Fourth and Richest Reich."[1] In the 1960s, the Federal Republic managed the transition to lower economic growth rates in an increasingly liberal international economy. It adjusted so well to the economic turbulence of the 1970s that West Germany was often referred to as a "model."[2]

But the prolonged worldwide recession after the second oil shock of 1979 changed our political assessments. Balance-of-payment deficits in the early 1980s, sharp increases in unemployment, a deterioration in the political climate between business and labor, the rise of new social movements, and a sharp pruning of the welfare state by 1983 had undermined West German self-confidence and dampened foreign admiration. In its infatuation with new Asian competitors the American business press, for example, was all but writing off West Germany and with it all of Western Europe. West Germans themselves became deeply

For their comments, criticisms, and suggestions on several drafts of this chapter I thank the authors in this volume, as well as Michael Goldfield, Peter Hall, Jeremy Rabkin, Sidney Tarrow, and the members of the seminar "State and Capitalism since 1800" at the Center for European Studies at Harvard University.

1. Edwin Hartrich, *The Fourth and Richest Reich* (New York: Macmillan, 1980).
2. Peter J. Katzenstein, "Problem or Model? West Germany in the 1980s," *World Politics* 32 (July 1980): 577–98; Andrei S. Markovits, ed., *The Political Economy of West Germany: Modell Deutschland* (New York: Praeger, 1982).

3

worried over lagging too far behind the United States and Japan in the development of critical high-technology products and production processes.[3] In 1984 a cover of *The Economist* made fun of the West Germans by asserting that "Germans do get so glum."[4] The weekly *Der Spiegel* ran a series on the arteriosclerosis of the West German economy.[5] And in a very critical, scholarly study Bruce Scott concluded that "Germany has lost relative market share in the high technology categories. . . . In addition the Germans appear to be losing relative strength in passenger cars, machine tools, construction equipment and rubber products. The German portfolio appears to be deteriorating to a striking degree, a phenomenon that could have unfavorable future implications for their capacity to earn their standard of living in the years ahead."[6] The German miracle and model, it appeared, had become the German muddle.

Yet by 1986, despite stubbornly high unemployment, the Federal Republic was once again brimming with self-confidence. With one of the lowest inflation and highest growth rates in the Organization for Economic Cooperation and Development (OECD), the Federal Republic took a leading role in helping bring down international interest rates, thus spurring international growth. Its trade surplus was running at record levels of about DM 100 billion despite a sharp appreciation of the deutschmark. That year the Federal Republic was the largest exporter in the world. Some analysts pointed to the perfectionist strain of West German business, with its striving for technical excellence; others pointed to its tradition of specialization and complex subcontracting arrangements.[7] The technical competence of its work force was again mentioned frequently. In late 1986 *The Economist*'s survey of West Germany was titled "the right to smile."[8] Amplifying on the shift in the economic and journalistic climate, Peter Drucker published a substantial article in the *Wall Street Journal* titled "What We Can Learn from the Germans."[9]

3. Bruce Nussbaum, *The World after Oil: The Shifting Axis of Power and Wealth* (New York: Simon & Schuster, 1983).
4. *The Economist*, 1–7 December 1984. See also, in a similar vein, Alan Reynolds, "Germany: Focusing on the Supply Side," *Wall Street Journal*, 1 June 1988, p. 27, and Josef Joffe, "Lack-lustre Wunderkind at 40: Warning Signs in the German Economy," *German Tribune*, 5 June 1988, p. 5.
5. *Der Spiegel* 39 (25 March 1985): 100–112, and (1 April 1985): 98–112.
6. Bruce R. Scott, "National Strategies: Key to International Competition," in Scott and George C. Lodge, eds., *U.S. Competitiveness in the World Economy* (Boston: Harvard Business School Press, 1985), pp. 71–143.
7. Peter Lawrence, "Some German Business Neuroses Yield Good Dividends," *Wall Street Journal*, 28 November 1984, p. 31; Charles F. Sabel and Gary B. Herrigel, "Losing a Market to a High-Wage Nation," *New York Times*, 14 June 1987, sec. 3, p. 2.
8. *The Economist*, 6 December 1986.
9. Peter Drucker, "What We Can Learn from the Germans," *Wall Street Journal*, 6 March 1986, p. 24.

These rapid swings in the journalistic assessment of West Germany's economic and political fortunes resemble the fever chart of the doctor more than that of the patient. Since we distinguish only dimly between transient and enduring change and do not think systematically about the cumulative or canceling effects of change, such rapid swings in the political assessment of West German developments are probably inevitable. But they are not a sound intellectual foundation on which to base our judgment about the future development of the West German political economy.

WEST GERMANY'S THREE REPUBLICS

The title of this book differs in two ways from titles of other volumes dealing with contemporary West Germany. It substitutes "West Germany" for "Bonn" and thus sidesteps the comparison of Bonn with Weimar. And it talks about the "Third Republic" rather than the "Third Reich," thus avoiding the exclusive preoccupation with German exceptionalism, military aggression, and the Holocaust. Instead of the deeply ingrained historical anchors for the interpretation of German politics I chose a title that would convey reference points dealing with the present and future, not the past, one that stresses the comparability rather than the exceptionalism of West Germany. This is not to argue that the West Germans or students of Germany should either forget the past or stop worrying over the possibility that, in a different guise, it could repeat itself. But forty years after the founding of the Federal Republic it is time to consider the pattern of change of Germany's longest experiment with democracy. Compared to France, since 1949 that pattern has been marked by the absence of dramatic changes. Chancellor Helmut Schmidt was no Napoleon III. The newspapers did not send us reports of any "Bonn Commune." But considering the violent changes they have created and endured in this century, West Germans recognize small signposts. This book hopes to avoid the temptation of an ahistorical historicism, of constantly comparing West German democracy to the past without recognizing how West German democracy itself has changed since 1949.

Such recognition is essential if we want to put West Germany's recent political evolution into a perspective that points out its politically significant features in the 1980s. I have not chosen to focus on aspects of implied significance which are probably familiar to the readers of this book: the preoccupation with Germany's division in the heart of Europe or the fixation on the inherent instabilities of capitalism. I do not wish to deny that these are two important features of West German politics. But within the framework of this book, the first is too specific and the second

5

too general. Furthermore, for a very simple reason neither one is very helpful for bringing the changes of the 1980s into focus. Germany remains divided, and capitalism continues to thrive in the Federal Republic. Yet West Germany is somehow changing.

To label that change is a necessary first step for beginning to think more systematically about it. West German politics in the 1980s is not merely an extension of the principles of Social Democracy of the 1970s. Nor is it a return to the principles of Christian Democracy of the 1950s. It is of course, to some extent, both of these. But at the same time in two specific ways it is also different and new. First, a change in the partisan composition of the federal government is juxtaposed with an institutional stability that is remarkable by the standards of other states. Second, a noteworthy continuity in the national institutions is accompanied by widespread experimentation in less visible arenas of politics.

I have analyzed elsewhere the convergence between changes in political coalitions and continuities in national policies.[10] Based on the evidence provided by the authors in this book, my two essays focus on what appears to me to be distinctive about West German politics in the 1980s, the compatibility of institutional stability in national politics with widespread experimentation. This balance between continuity and change in West German politics is novel and deserves the attention of those who wish to understand what the Federal Republic can and what it cannot accomplish in the 1980s and 1990s.

I have chosen here to claim that West Germany has three different republics in part because I want to draw attention to the need for a perspective on West German politics that is uncommon, especially in the United States. The precise dating of each of West Germany's three republics is a matter of convenience. Indeed, some may prefer to talk about different phases in the evolution of West German democracy since 1949. Dietrich Thränhardt, for example, in his recent history of the Federal Republic distinguishes between a first period of economic reconstruction and a chancellor democracy (1949–61), a second period of political reform in domestic and foreign policy (1962–73), and a third period of crisis management in a turbulent global economy since 1974.[11] This periodization has some appeal. It takes account of major international developments such as the Berlin Wall of 1961, the Cuban missile crisis of 1962, and the oil shock of 1973. It points to an era of West German reform starting in 1967 and lasting through the early 1970s that

10. Peter J. Katzenstein, *Policy and Politics in West Germany: The Growth of a Semisovereign State* (Philadelphia: Temple University Press, 1987).

11. Dietrich Thränhardt, *Geschichte der Bundesrepublik Deutschland* (Frankfurt: Suhrkamp, 1986). See also Karl Dietrich Bracher et al., eds., *Geschichte der Bundesrepublik in fünf Bänden* (Stuttgart: Deutsche Verlagsanstalt, 1981–87).

was crucial in the evolution of the Federal Republic. And it highlights important continuities in the policies pursued by Chancellors Schmidt and Helmut Kohl since 1974. At the same time this periodization is imprecise. Did the Adenauer era stop in 1959 when the grand old man of West German politics first accepted and then withdrew from candidacy for the office of president; in 1961 when the Liberals (F.D.P.) extracted from Konrad Adenauer and the Christian Democrats (CDU) the concession that he would serve as chancellor for no more than an additional two years; or in 1963 when Ludwig Erhard replaced him? Thränhardt's periodization is also implausible in characterizing the Erhard interregnum between 1963 and 1966 as an era of reform, small though significant changes in foreign policy to the contrary notwithstanding. Furthermore, this view of West Germany's postwar history slights the changes that are making the 1980s a decade in some respects significantly different from the 1970s. Finally, Thränhardt's periodization underestimates the role of political parties, arguably the most important actors in what is often referred to as West Germany's "party state."

Realizing that the precise demarcation between the different republics is arbitrary, I argue that 1949–52 was a prelude to the First Republic, which ended in 1966; that 1966–69 was a prelude to the Second Republic, which ended in 1980; and that the 1980s are a decade of movement toward the Third Republic. Early in the decade power gradually slipped from the Social Democratic party (SPD)–F.D.P. coalition government and then, by conscious choice, it was not fully exercised by the CDU/Christian Social Union (CSU)–F.D.P. coalition.

The First Republic (1949–66) was a conservative welfare state centered around distributing the dividends of economic growth as they trickled down. Governed by Chancellors Adenauer and Erhard through center-right coalition governments, the First Republic developed the institutional practices that gave life to the constitutional provisions of the Basic Law of 1949. It consolidated the hold of democratic parties on West German politics. Its foreign policy agenda was dominated by Western integration, rearmament, and the failure to move closer to the goal of national reunification. The domestic agenda was shaped by the creation of West Germany's social market economy. Generous welfare programs, including the first system of inflation-indexed pensions in any capitalist state, were instituted under the political leadership of the CDU/CSU and its smaller political allies. And West German economic policy successfully enshrined market competition rather than state intervention as the central principle informing government policy. Significantly, despite the opposition of the SPD, the unions and other groups representing working-class interests were well entrenched in the institutions of the First Republic.

The Second Republic (1969–80) brought to power a center-left coalition of the SPD/F.D.P. intent on consolidating a major institutional overhaul, begun in the brief era of the Great Coalition (1966–69) between the CDU/CSU and SPD, and embarking on new policy initiatives. In foreign policy that initiative was Chancellor Brandt's Eastern policy. Carried by the emergence of détente between the two superpowers, Willy Brandt's foreign policy succeeded in normalizing the relations between the Federal Republic and its Eastern neighbors including the Soviet Union and the German Democratic Republic. On the question of domestic reform the record was much more mixed. The attempt to extend social citizenship by creating equal opportunities for disadvantaged social groups, especially in the fields of education and vocational training, was blocked by a conservative opposition well placed in the institutions of the Second Republic. But after the oil shock of November 1973 the inclusionary character of West German institutions was essential for maintaining international competitiveness. The major producer groups, senior civil servants, and political leaders collaborated in a variety of ways, rarely free from conflict, in seeking to bolster West Germany's competitive position in international markets.

The 1980s are witnessing movement toward the Third Republic. Established ways of political bargaining proved to be not fully suited to dealing with a more hostile international context marked by rapid swings in the relations between the superpowers and sharp changes in oil prices and interest rates. Having won the election of 1980 handily, the SPD/F.D.P. coalition had an extremely difficult time forming a new government. Mounting economic problems and the eventual change in government were accompanied by a growing chorus of political commentators talking about "the Big Change" (*die Wende*). Yet in the 1980s the position of none of the major political forces was drastically altered. There was no large-scale attack on the programs of the welfare state or the position of the unions. The SPD's electoral position was weakened by the rise of the Greens; yet the potential for new alliances forged around new issues still offered prospects for returning to power. And the complex conflicts between CDU, CSU, and F.D.P. were partly immobilizing some of the political resources the new coalition government had been able to concentrate in its hands.

In the years 1984–85 the possibility arose that major changes might transform West German politics. A bitter strike over the introduction of the thirty-five-hour workweek in 1984 and heated discussions over changes in the rules governing strikes and lockouts in 1985 signaled a sharp deterioration in the country's political climate.[12] The West Ger-

12. Stephen J. Silvia, "The West German Labor Law Controversy: A Struggle for the Factory of the Future," *Comparative Politics* 20 (January 1988): 154–74; Alfred Klein-

man Left grew increasingly apprehensive that a change in government
and the political climate in the country might lead to a major overhaul of
key institutions with the intent of dramatically weakening the position of
the labor movement. A variety of smaller political conflicts raised the
possibility that conservative political interests might try to use their
temporary political strength to create large-scale institutional transformations. But the metalworkers union succeeded in rallying its unenthu-
siastic rank and file for a bitter strike that, whatever its economic merit,
served the political purpose of sending a clear signal to business not to
underestimate union power and reminded especially large corporations
of the great importance of social peace.

That movement toward the Third Republic is bringing many changes
this book's authors illustrate. That the big change in institutional design
or national public policy cannot be found among them is, as I argue in
the conclusion, one of the most distinctive political characteristics of
contemporary West German politics. Movement toward the Third Republic reveals hidden flexibility within stable institutions. It is too early
to say anything definitive about precisely how flexibility and stability are
connected. But they include, for example, political action groups with
informal ties to established parties, social self-help groups that are often
linked to the state's social service delivery agencies, and "alternative"
culture and youth groups that often rely on public subsidies. These
diverse groups signal some of the changes that affect West Germany in
the 1980s. And the institutional links between them and the state as well
as its ancillary, large private bureaucracies are a distinctive political
feature of movement toward the Third Republic. Indeed, conventional
distinctions between state and society are of little use if we want to
capture the interpenetration and coordination so typical of West Germany's political economy. But at this early date it is difficult to identify
more precisely other political characteristics of the emerging Third
Republic. It is easier to define these characteristics negatively. Movement toward the Third Republic is not a return to West Germany's
chancellor democracy of the 1950s. It is not a return to the corporatist
arrangements of peak level association bargaining of the 1970s. And it is
not an embodiment of the alternative politics which the new social
movements tried to define and implement in 1980.

As the chapters in this book illustrate, movement toward the Third
Republic occurs within the well-established, major institutions of the
Federal Republic. They include not only federalism, the major political
parties, and interest groups operating on the national stage but also a
differentiated system of industrial relations, parapublic institutions, and

---

knecht and Tom van Veen, eds., *Working Time Reduction and the Crisis in the Welfare State*
(Maastricht: Presses Interuniversitaires Européennes, 1986).

a vocational training system which are less visible but not necessarily less important.

Territorial decentralization is one of the hallmarks of West German politics. Among the major capitalist states West Germany's federal arrangements resemble those of the United States and Canada more than those of its more centralized West European neighbors. The West German states exercise primary responsibility in such important areas as environmental policy, education and cultural policy, law enforcement, and the supervision of local government. Furthermore, West Germany's public bureaucracy is decentralized. Only a very small number of civil servants work in the federal capital, Bonn. The vast majority is employed by state and local governments. This federal system is of great significance in an era of sharply growing concern over environmental issues and substantial shifts in the growth poles of the West German economy from north to south.

The three major political parties, the Christian Democrats (CDU), Social Democrats (SPD), and Liberals (F.D.P.), have had a preeminent political position in the institutional life of West Germany's three republics. Until the advent of the Greens in the late 1970s, they had succeeded in reducing to insignificance all other parties espousing political causes that deviated from their centrist solutions. Middle-of-the-road party politics results from two distinct features of West Germany's political parties. The two major parties are umbrella organizations for divergent social interests. Strong political elements within the CDU/CSU and the SPD make very difficult any significant departure from the political center. Although the F.D.P. subscribes to positions to the right of the CDU/CSU on a number of economic issues, on virtually all other questions it holds the middle ground between the two large parties. Since the F.D.P. knows that its survival depends largely on its ability to hold this middle ground, its policies tend to reinforce the move to rather than away from the political center. In the 1980s the Greens succeeded in establishing themselves as a second, small party on a national scale. Their political position is to the left of the established parties on virtually all major issues. But they have been unwilling to contemplate seriously participating in coalition governments in national politics. They have thus not been able to shake the centrist tendencies of a system that relies on government by coalition.

West German interest groups are large, centralized, and encompassing. The "peak associations" of business and labor, in particular, have been central actors. West German business makes its presence felt through three major institutions. With a membership of about 80 to 90 percent of all firms, organized in a complex system of more than five hundred branch and regional associations, the Federation of German

Industry (BDI) is the central vehicle for representing the general policy objectives of business. The collective bargaining strategy of business is defined and carried out by the Federation of German Employers' Associations (BDA). More than 80 percent of all West German employers belong to one or several of the more than eight hundred branch or regional associations. Finally, the Diet of German Industry and Commerce (DIHT) represents the interests of small business and the crafts, especially on a regional basis. The dense network of local chambers as well as other institutions is of particular importance in an era of rapid economic and social change. But the chambers with their compulsory membership are also involved in organizing West Germany's vocational training program and other important activities.

After 1945 West Germany's trade unions chose a united, industrywide form of organization that includes about 40 percent of the work force. Under the umbrella of the Federation of German Trade Unions (DGB) seventeen unions organize more than 7 million workers along industry lines. Independent unions for white-collar employees and civil servants also exist. Most important among all the industrial unions is the metalworkers' union, IG Metall. With about 2.5 million members, it is the largest industrial union in any democratic, capitalist state. Its demands—the extension of codetermination, humanization of work, and a thirty-five-hour workweek—have always been important parts of West Germany's public agenda. Although West German unions are in many ways a model of strength for other labor movements, in the 1980s they have been on the defensive. They have been unable to propose convincing programs that could reduce unemployment, which has hovered around the 2 million mark since the early 1980s. And stopping short of radical demands for deregulation and privatization, the center-right coalition of CDU/CSU and F.D.P. nonetheless has created an adverse political climate for union policy preferences and initiatives.

West Germany's industrial relations system is politically perhaps less visible but nonetheless of great importance to the nation's politics. Through the institution of codetermination, joint decision making both at the workplace and in corporate boardrooms, labor is intimately linked to the requirements of capitalist production and international competition; business cannot neglect the consequences of its investment decisions on employment and social welfare. In industrial relations West Germany has a dual system of representing the interests of workers: in industrial plants through works councils and in collective bargaining through unions. In the 1970s only one-sixth of West Germany's 22 million workers, laboring in small firms with fewer than five employees, were not covered by this dual system of representation. Worker participation in works councils or boardrooms probably has pacified labor by instilling a sense of participation, and it has not interfered with the technical or economic efficiency of West German firms. Conversely, employers have adjusted to the institutional presence and demands of worker representatives. On balance, West Germany's complex industrial relations system has had a stabilizing effect on the political fabric of the three republics.

The same is true of a wide range of other parapublic institutions, such as the Council of Economic Experts, the social security funds, private welfare associations, the churches, and the vocational training system. Parapublic institutions figure prominently in virtually all policy sectors. Some have a long history; others were created only after 1945. Some are political actors in their own right; others are political arenas. But all of them provide strong links between the public and private sectors. The density of the institutional life of the Federal Republic reinforces its social peace and stability. Under the general auspices of the state, parapublic institutions provide the key for a relatively quiet process of policy formulation and implementation. To many Americans, they are a suffocating blanket of institutional growth that kills social spontaneity and entrepreneurial drive. But to the West German elite of virtually all political persuasions they are the institutional anchors that reduce risk, increase expertise, share information, and channel otherwise unpredictable actions.

West Germany's vocational training system is a good example of one of these parapublic institutions. General education is provided only by public schools, but public and private actors collaborate in the provision of vocational training.[13] For about 60 percent of West German teenagers that training occurs in a dual system. Public vocational schools teach for a day or two each week general subjects and some theoretical aspects of occupational training. The rest of the workweek apprentices acquire practical skills at the workplace, primarily in the ongoing work process. Completion of the program takes about three years. Business and unions negotiated detailed regulations for more than four hundred recognized training programs backed by state law and supervised by the Chambers of Commerce. The program is funded by both the state and private business. Although it is the site of inevitable and often prolonged political conflicts, the policy process reveals a strong commitment of all the major actors—business, the unions, the chambers, the Länder, and the federal bureaucracy, among others—to make the system responsive to the technological and demographic changes of the 1980s and 1990s. New production technologies are making it necessary to redefine the

13. Wolfgang Streeck et al., *The Role of the Social Partners in Vocational Training and Further Training in the Federal Republic of Germany* (Berlin: European Centre for the Development of Vocational Training, 1987).

required skill profile of large numbers of occupations, and between 1973 and 1984 the number of training contracts issued increased by half a million to 1.8 million.

THREE MAJOR CHANGES

Three prominent changes are transforming the context in which West Germany now operates: new production technologies in industrial plants, new social movements in national politics, and new political currents in the international economy. These changes are testing the political limits of an industrial system of mass production and a Keynesian welfare state operating in a liberal international economy.[14] In the 1950s and 1960s firms produced ever larger quantities of standardized goods with increasingly specialized machines. Government policy helped in supporting mass consumption through Keynesian-style economic policies that justified further investments to expand capacity. Interest groups and political parties organized electoral politics. Finally, the compatibility between mass production and mass consumption was reinforced by a liberalization of the international economy that separated economic from political issues and gave room to West Germany's strategy of export-led growth. Production occurred at a rate that institutions at the level of the industrial plant in national politics and in the international system could absorb.

Since the mid-1970s the economic and political climate in the Federal Republic has changed. Pioneered by American corporations for the American market, mass production has to some extent become a norm even though West German industry retains a strong crafts legacy.[15] But West German industry, especially heavy industry, can no longer expect stable markets shielded from foreign competitors that frequently have more advanced plants, cheaper labor costs, or both. Social movements organized around the issue of nuclear power, peace, and the environment have formed a political party that has already had a strong impact on West German society, whatever its fortunes in federal, state, and local elections. In the international economy protectionist pressures and se-

14. Fritz W. Scharpf, *Sozialdemokratische Krisenpolitik in Europa* (Frankfurt: Campus, 1987); Christopher S. Allen, "The Underdevelopment of Keynesianism in the Federal Republic of Germany," in Peter Hall, ed., *The Political Power of Economic Ideas: Keynesianism across Nations* (Princeton: Princeton University Press, 1989).

15. Heinz T. Thanheiser, "Strategy and Structure of German Industrial Enterprise," diss., Graduate School of Business Administration, Harvard University, 1972; Peter Lawrence, *Managers and Management in West Germany* (New York: St. Martin's, 1980); Stanley Hutton and Peter Lawrence, *German Engineers: The Anatomy of a Profession* (Oxford: Clarendon, 1981); Volker R. Berghahn, *The Americanisation of West German Industry, 1945–1973* (Cambridge: Cambridge University Press, 1986).

curity concerns have, for example, made foreign trade and technology-transfer policies highly charged political issues. Oil shocks and debt crisis have reinforced the impression of a volatile international economy open to disruption. In these new conditions established institutions such as firms, unions, parties, and governments struggle to retain profitability, employment, legitimacy, and autonomy.

Since the publication of Horst Kern and Michael Schumann's important and widely noted book *Das Ende der Arbeitsteilung?* West German industrial sociologists have been deeply divided in their debate of the thesis that a profound change is affecting West Germany's industrial plants.[16] In the United States Michael J. Piore and Charles F. Sabel's *Second Industrial Divide* has elicited a similar though far weaker echo.[17] Kern and Schumann's thesis is prospective in emphasizing tendencies toward flexible specialization. It interprets the intensification of the rationalization of production methods in West Germany's industrial plants as a potentially fundamental break with the Fordist paradigm of mass production. New production technologies apparently often require a process of reskilling that enhances the value, autonomy, and political power of workers. Few West German industrial sociologists deny that computer-aided design and manufacturing production technologies are transforming some segments of West German industry. Strong disagreement exists, however, on the pervasiveness of such changes throughout all spheres of production and on whether this development is likely to lead to a paradigm shift in West German labor relations.[18]

16. Horst Kern and Michael Schumann, *Das Ende der Arbeitsteilung? Rationalisierung in der industriellen Produktion* (Munich: Beck, 1984); Klaus Düll, "Gesellschaftliche Modernisierungspolitik durch neue 'Produktionskonzepte'?" *WSI-Mitteilungen* 1985, no. 3: 141–45; Peter Brödner, *Fabrik 2000: Alternative Entwicklungspfade in die Zukunft der Fabrik* (Berlin: Sigma Bohn, 1986); Rudi Schmidt, "Zu den arbeitspolitischen Chancen und Grenzen neuer Produktionskonzepte. Einige Ammerkungen zum Konzept Horst Kerns und Michael Schumanns einer industriellen Modernisierung als gesellschaftlichem Projekt," *WSI-Mitteilungen* 1985, no. 3: 146–50; Michael Hartmann, "Dequalifizierung oder Requalifizierung der Arbeit?—Über das Theorem der rellen Subsumtion," *Leviathan* 13 (1985): 271–90; Rudi Schmiede and Bodo van Greiff, "Industriesoziologie als Geschichtsphilosophie? Über die 'Trendwende' in der Industriesoziologie und den Begriff der 'rellen' Subsumtion," *Leviathan* 13 (1985): 291–306; Thomas Malsch and Rüdiger Seltz, eds., *Die neuen Produktionskonzepte auf dem Prüfstand: Beiträge zur Entwicklung der Industriearbeit* (Berlin: Sigma Bohn, 1987); Mario Helfert, "Chancen neuer Produktionskonzepte. Zur Kontroverse um die neue Studie von Horst Kern und Michael Schumann," *WSI-Mitteilungen* 1985, no. 3: 136–40; Fred Manske, "Ende oder Wandel des Taylorismus. Von der punktuellen zur systemischen Kontrolle des Arbeitsprozesses," *Soziale Welt* 1987, no. 2: 166–79.

17. Michael J. Piore and Charles F. Sabel, *The Second Industrial Divide: Possibilities for Prosperity* (New York: Basic Books, 1984).

18. Hans-Willy Hohn, "Interne Arbeitsmärkte und betriebliche Mitbestimmung-Tendenzen der 'Sozialen Schliessung' im 'dualen' System der Interessenvertretung," *Discussion Paper* IIM-LMP (Wissenschaftszentrum Berlin, 1983); Hohn, *Von der Einheitsgewerkschaft zum Betriebssyndikalismus: Institutionelle Determinanten der Gewerkschaftlichen*

A second change affecting West Germany is the emergence of new social movements in the 1970s. They have established relatively strong political footholds in the major urban areas and have had variable success in state and federal politics. Fed by diverse sources of support, environment and peace became a potent combination of issues that galvanized a broad coalition of West Germans into a range of political action that was not restricted to electoral politics.[19] Few deny the importance of the new social movements for West German politics. Corporatist bargaining among party elites, interest group leaders, and civil servants over economic and social issues had been a central characteristic of West Germany's semisovereign state in the 1960s and 1970s.[20] But since the late 1970s it has been complemented by a new politics that often favors new issues and new methods of political action. Sociologists are divided in their assessment of the capacity of existing institutions to absorb the substantive demands of new social movements and to adjust to new styles of political action. They are genuinely uncertain how the "politics of consumption" that often characterizes the new social movements conditions or transforms the "politics of production" of traditional group and party politics.[21]

Finally, West German politics is also affected by a politicization of international economic relations during the last decade.[22] Great instability in the price of oil, the debt crisis, and creeping protectionism

Krise (Berlin: Internationales Institut für Management, 1984); Eva Brumlop, *Krise der analytischen Arbeitsbewertung? Skizze einer Umbruchsituation am Beispiel der Volkswagenwerke AG* (Frankfurt: Campus, 1986).

19. Karl-Werner Brand, *Neue Soziale Bewegungen* (Opladen: Westdeutscher Verlag, 1982); Brand, ed., *Neue Soziale Bewegungen in Westeuropa und den USA: Ein internationaler Vergleich* (Frankfurt: Campus, 1985); Brand, Detlev Busser, and Dieter Rucht, *Aufbruch in eine andere Gesellschaft: Neue Soziale Bewegungen in der Bundesrepublik* (Frankfurt: Campus, 1983); Horst Mewes, "The West German Green Party," *New German Critique* 28 (1983): 51–86; Herbert Kitschelt, "Between Movement and Party: Structure and Process in Belgian and West German Ecology Parties," paper presented at the Conference of Europeanists, Washington, D.C., 18–20 October 1985; Kitschelt, "Political Opportunity Structures and Political Protest: Anti-Nuclear Movements in Four Countries," *British Journal of Political Science* 16 (January 1986): 57–86; Ferdinand Müller-Rommel, "New Social Movements and the Smaller Parties: A Comparative Perspective," *West European Politics* 1985, no. 1: 41–54.

20. Katzenstein, *Policy and Politics in West Germany*.

21. Jost Halfmann, "Soziale Bewegungen und Staat: Nicht-intendierte Folgen neo-korporatistischer Politik," *Soziale Welt* 35 (1984): 294–312; Halfmann, "Industrial Modernization and Social Conflict: New and Old Social Movements in the United States of America and the Federal Republic of Germany," manuscript, Osnabrück, 1985; Halfmann, "Risk Avoidance and Sovereignty: New Social Movements in the United States and West Germany," *Praxis International* 8 (April 1988): 14–25.

22. Wolfgang Streeck, "Neo-korporativistische Kooperation und weltwirtschaftliche Konkurrenz," in Forschungsinstitut der Friedrich-Ebert-Stiftung, "Pluralismus unter Konkurrenzdruck," *Analysen aus der Abteilung Entwicklungsländerforschung*, nos. 101–2 (Bonn, 1982): 11–28; Peter J. Katzenstein, *Small States in World Markets: Industrial Policy in Europe* (Ithaca: Cornell University Press, 1985).

PETER J. KATZENSTEIN

during the 1970s drastically transformed the global economic environment in which the Federal Republic must operate. Politics has intruded into international economic affairs because governments have become central players in a broad range of economic arenas. With new competitors moving more quickly into mass markets, West Germany's business, labor, and political elites agree that international competitiveness can be maintained only by producing knowledge-intensive, sophisticated, high value-added products that are tailored to particular market niches and require a highly skilled labor force as well as flexible business strategies. Since some areas of its electronics industry in particular are lagging behind American and Japanese producers, West Germany's race for high-profit niches in quality markets may be vulnerable to interruptions in the transfer of technological know-how. West German fears of a long-term change in American technology-transfer policy stem from the more recent, explicit politicization of an aspect of international economic relations that heretofore had been only implicitly politicized by the research and development policies of all of the major OECD countries. Furthermore, by 1987 West Germany and the United States were in sharp disagreement on how to narrow the American trade deficit and check the fall of the dollar.

What are the political implications of change affecting West German politics at different levels: industrial plants, national politics, and the international system? American scholarship on these changes in West Germany is virtually nonexistent. In the early 1980s two edited volumes investigated the foundations of the German model.[23] Informed by West Germany's evolution in the 1970s, these volumes appeared just as the three changes I highlight here were becoming more important. More recently, a number of books have been published, but they are typically macroscopic and retrospective in trying to offer an overall assessment of West Germany's political evolution since 1945.[24]

West German scholarship is richer but also surprisingly fragmented. Industrial sociologists in Göttingen, Frankfurt, Berlin, and Munich have done a substantial amount of theoretically sophisticated and empirically rich work at the plant level, often designed to capture differences between industrial sectors. But these studies pay virtually no attention to national and international developments. A growing number of sociolo-

23. William E. Paterson and Gordon Smith, eds., *The West German Model: Perspectives on a Stable State* (London: Cass, 1981); Markovits, ed., *Political Economy of West Germany*.

24. Charles Burdick, Hans-Adolf Jacobsen, and Winfried Kudszus, *Contemporary Germany: Politics and Culture* (Boulder: Westview, 1984); James Cooney et al., eds., *The Federal Republic of Germany and the United States* (Boulder: Westview, 1984); Henry Ashby Turner, Jr., *The Two Germanies since 1945* (New Haven: Yale University Press, 1987); John Ardagh, *Germany and the Germans: An Anatomy of Society Today* (New York: Harper & Row, 1987); Edwina Moreton, ed., *Germany between East and West* (Cambridge: Cambridge University Press, 1987).

16

gists and political scientists have mapped West Germany's social movements, building up a substantial data base from which to formulate middle-level theories about the origins and consequences of different movements. But with few exceptions they fail to relate their descriptions to changes under way in the industrial and international realms. And West German economists, Keynesian and monetarist alike, view changes in international markets as automatically forcing structural changes on West German producers. Their interpretation largely blocks out important political changes in the international economy. Commissioned by the federal government and issued by the five major economics research institutes in 1980 and 1984, two sets of structural reports are a gold mine of economic data.[25] But they do not permit us to probe the causes and consequences of the politicization of the international economy.

The extent and eventual effect of the three sets of changes on the stability of West German politics is very much an open question. Focusing on one of the three levels, optimists typically assume that developments left unexamined but presumed to be favorable to enhance stability at the other two levels will consolidate West German politics again along the axes that organized the West German "model" in the 1960s and 1970s. For example, the reskilling of labor required by the rationalization of industrial production, the accommodative tendencies of federal institutions (parties, interest groups, and government bureaucracies) to new social movements, and the broad range of West Germany's response to the race for profitable market niches all point to a reconsolidation of West Germany's corporatist political arrangements.

Pessimists, on the other hand, reach the opposite conclusion by extrapolating developments unfavorable to stability at one level to the other two. The incipient segmentation of the West German labor force is being reinforced by a new technology push that creates a small labor aristocracy supervising extensive automation of production and a deskilling of substantial numbers of skilled or semiskilled workers; the conflict of values that the new social movements have introduced into West German politics is fundamental and will split West German society more deeply over time; finally, the intensification of international competition in a new international division of labor will squeeze West Germany out of global markets because its wage levels are too high, its fringe benefits too generous, and its innovative and adaptive capacities too sluggish.

It appears improbable, though not impossible, that the changes now affecting West Germany's political economy are cumulative and interlocking and that West Germany's future will either see merely a recon-

---

25. Bernhard Gahlen, ed., *Strukturberichterstattung der Wirtschaftsforschungsinstitute: Analysen und Diskussion* (Tübingen: J. C. B. Mohr [Paul Siebeck], 1982).

solidation of old political arrangements or a fundamentally new segmentation of society and politics. More probable is a pattern of change
that is more complex. Tendencies toward reconsolidation and segmentation are linked, I shall argue in the conclusion, in the form of a
dynamic equilibrium. This makes plausible small changes (*die Wende im
Kleinen*) precisely because big changes (*die Wende im Grossen*) are so
unlikely.

THREE INDUSTRIAL SECTORS

How we interpret the changing contexts of West German politics
obviously depends on the terrain we investigate. General speculation
will not advance our insights. Only by answering these questions in
specific settings can we hope to discern the fault lines where changes are
likely to occur first or have their greatest impact. Focusing on industrial
sectors is one promising way for seeking to answer the question of how
West Germany copes with different changes in the 1980s. Among all of
the major industrial democracies West Germany has, in relative terms,
the largest industrial sector. In 1985, 41 percent of the civilian working
population was employed in industry.[26] Industrial production is the
core of West Germany's export-oriented economy and thus the foundation of its national prosperity. And industry occupies a central place on
West Germany's political agenda. Although other aspects of the Federal
Republic could have been selected as windows through which to analyze
continuity and change in West German politics, we hardly can go wrong
in picking this one.

This book analyzes the consequences of economic and social change
for West German politics in three different industries.[27] In Joseph
Schumpeter's perspective on industrial change, policy debates in West
Germany as well as in the United States and elsewhere are often cast in
terms of sunrise, sunset, and core industries. In three core industries—
chemicals, automobiles, and machinery—West Germany has largely
retained its competitiveness in world markets and is prospering. In old

26. Organization for Economic Cooperation and Development, *Historical Statistics,
1960–1985* (Paris: OECD, 1987), p. 36.
27. Peter J. Katzenstein, "Research Design: Comparative Analysis of Economic and
Foreign Economic Policies of Advanced Industrial States," unpublished paper, Ithaca,
Cornell University, 1977; James R. Kurth, "The Political Consequences of the Product
Cycle: Industrial History and Political Outcomes," *International Organization* 33 (Winter
1979): 1–34; Lee Preston, "A Perspective on MesoEconomics," *Discussion Paper* IIMV
(Wissenschaftszentrum Berlin, 1984); Christian Deubner, "Change and Internationaliza-
tion in Industry: Toward a Sectoral Interpretation of West German Politics," *International
Organization* 38 (Summer 1984): 501–35.

18

sectors (such as shipbuilding and steel) and in new industries (for example, electronics and biotechnology) West Germany is slipping either in absolute or relative terms. With a few exceptions, federal and state governments have stayed clear of the three core sectors. But in either nursing or in nurturing them, these governments have become more closely linked to the fate of lagging and leading industries.[28]

Industrial sectors are statistical artifacts. To delimit them carefully by product or product line is a difficult task for students of industrial organization and international trade. For this book, however, the difference between the nature of industrial products is less important than are the relations between different actors (workers, businessmen, politicians) and different institutions (unions, firms, interest groups, political parties, and government bureaucracies). Across different industrial sectors the key actors and the relationships among them differ significantly. In declining industries unions and government are trying to defend existing jobs or create new ones. In growth industries corporations, universities, and government—but not the labor movement—are the

28. Andrew P. Black, "Industrial Policy in West Germany: Policy in Search of a Goal?" *Discussion Paper* IIM (Wissenschaftszentrum Berlin, n.d.); Volker Hauff and Fritz Scharpf, *Modernisierung der Volkswirtschaft: Technologiepolitik als Strukturpolitik* (Frankfurt: Europäische Verlagsanstalt, 1975); Boston Consulting Group, *A Framework for Swedish Industrial Policy: Appendix 12—German Industrial Policy* (Stockholm: Departementens Offsetcentral, 1979); Harvard Business School, *Germany (B): The Uncertain Stride of a Reluctant Giant* (Boston, 1980); Erwin von den Steinen, "Industrial Policy in the Federal Republic," unpublished paper, Washington, D.C., U.S. Department of State, 1980; Stephen Woolcock, "Industrial Policy in the European Community" M.Phil. diss., University of Edinburgh, 1980; Klaus-Werner Schatz and Frank Wolter, "The Federal Republic of Germany," in Geoffrey Renshaw, ed., *Employment, Trade and North-South Cooperation* (Geneva: ILO, 1981), pp. 181–208; U.S. Congress, Joint Economic Committee, *Monetary Policy, Selective Credit Policy, and Industrial Policy in France, Britain, West Germany and Sweden* (Washington, D.C.: U.S. Government Printing Office, 1981); Wyn Grant, *The Political Economy of Industrial Policy* (London: Butterworths, 1982); Ernst-Jürgen Horn, *Management of Industrial Change in Germany* (Sussex: Sussex European Research Center, 1982); Ira C. Magaziner and Robert B. Reich, *Minding America's Business: The Decline and Rise of the American Economy* (New York: Harcourt Brace Jovanovich, 1982); Gerard F. Adams and Lawrence Klein, eds., *Industrial Policies for Growth and Competitiveness: An Economic Perspective* (Lexington, Mass.: Lexington Books, 1983); Michael M. Atkinson and William D. Coleman, "Corporatism and Industrial Policy," unpublished paper, Florence, EUI, November 1983; Robert A. Isaak, "The German Industrial Mode: Under Siege," *Adherent* 10 (Spring 1983): 2–14; Geoffrey Shepherd, François Duchêne, and Christopher Saunders, *Europe's Industries: Public and Private Strategies for Change* (Ithaca: Cornell University Press, 1983); John Zysman and Laura Tyson, eds., *American Industry in International Competition: Government Policies and Corporate Strategies* (Ithaca: Cornell University Press, 1983); Douglas Webber, "The Framework of Government-Industry Relations and Industrial Policy Making in the Federal Republic of Germany," unpublished paper, University of Sussex, 1985; Jeffrey A. Hart, "German Industrial Policy," in Claude E. Barfield and William A. Schambra, eds., *The Politics of Industrial Policy* (Washington, D.C.: American Enterprise Institute, 1986), pp. 161–86; Wolfgang Neumann and Henrik Uterwedde, *Industriepolitik: Ein deutsch-französischer Vergleich* (Opladen: Leske and Budrich, 1986).

central actors, bargaining about subsidies and the opportunities for economic growth. In core industries business and labor hold center stage with the federal government, some exceptions to the contrary notwithstanding, relegated to its ideologically acknowledged role of establishing only the framework for market competition.

What are the effects of these differences on the actors and on the character of their relations with others, for the erosion or consolidation of political arrangements, and for the political response adopted at the level of the plant, nationally and internationally? Sectors are both an arena in which we can study empirically the manifestations of economic and social change and a heuristic device for tracing the consequences of change on the strategy of actors and on the structure of West German politics.[29]

This perspective on industry differs significantly from that of West German scholars and journalists. Economists, for example, in the structural reports which the five research institutes periodically issue, look at various measures of market share and competitiveness to gauge the economic viability of different industrial sectors, sector segments, and product groups. In contrast, industry is viewed here as both a political arena and a heuristic device in which one can analyze the political consequences of change.

Political scientists, on the other hand, analyze problems of industrial change either from a territorial perspective, for example, the shifting economic power from north to south, or they select individual policy sectors (such as technology or environmental policy) and industries (such as steel or automobiles) for detailed investigation. Some excellent work has been done along these lines. Typically, though, it does not incorporate both the micro-level concerns of the industrial sociologist and macro-level developments in the global economy.

Journalists, too, view this topic skeptically. *Der Spiegel,* for example, published two major essays on German industry, in late December 1983 and in late December 1984.[30] The topic of industrial change, it seems, is covered extensively only between Christmas and New Year's Eve when all other copy has run out. And books written for the broader public on the question of West Germany's competitiveness typically lack a perspective that permits a focus on how the recent changes affect West German politics.[31]

29. Peter J. Katzenstein, *Corporatism and Change: Austria, Switzerland, and the Politics of Industry* (Ithaca: Cornell University Press, 1984).

30. *Der Spiegel* 37 (26 December 1983): 19–29, and 39 (31 December 1984): 36–51.

31. Wilhelm Hankel, *Der Ausweg aus der Krise* (Dusseldorf: Econ, 1975); Herbert Giersch, ed., *Wie es zu Schaffen ist: Agenda für die deutsche Wirtschaftspolitik* (Stuttgart: Deutsche Verlagsanstalt, 1983).

Core Industries

The chemical industry in many ways is prototypical for the stable core of West German industry.[32] The industry is capital-intensive, invests heavily in research and development, experiences a rapid turnover in product lines, and has developed sophisticated production technologies. It is distinguished by a great diversity in production lines, the convergence of firm concentration with strong competition, and relatively low political visibility. The West German chemical industry is broadly based. Besides the three successor firms to IG Farben, it also features numerous medium-sized and small firms that are highly competitive and innovative. During the last fifteen years the three industrial giants have rapidly expanded their operations worldwide. This move was spurred by a number of developments abroad and at home: American protectionism in the form of the American Selling Price (ASP), changes in the availability and price of critically important raw materials, the appreciation of the deutschmark, and the increase in wage levels. A highly skilled West German work force has been successful in achieving sharp wage increases through skillful though nonmilitant collective bargaining. Between the late 1970s and the mid-1980s economic prospects have been dim. Only since 1984 have industry spokespersons sounded somewhat more optimistic about an easing of the pressures of excess capacity, uncertainties about the cost and availability of petroleum as the industry's basic raw material, and the lagging introduction of new products and technologies.

A second economic core of the Federal Republic is the automobile industry.[33] More than any other, this industry typifies the Fordist model

32. Sandra E. Peterson, "Structural Continuity and Industrial Strategies: The Case of the German Chemical Industry," B.A. thesis, Cornell University, 1980; Giovanni Rufo, *Technical Change and Economic Policy: Sector Report, the Fertilizers and Pesticides Industry* (Paris: OECD, 1980); Bruna Teso, *Technical Change and Economic Policy: Sector Report, the Pharmaceutical Industry* (Paris: OECD, 1980); Thomas L. Ilgen, "Chemicals in the World Economy," *International Organization* 37 (1983): 647–80; Christopher S. Allen, "Structural and Technological Change in West Germany: Employer and Trade Union Responses in the Chemical and Automobile Industries," diss., Brandeis University, 1983; Wyn Grant, William Patterson, and Colin Whiston, "Government-Industry Relations in the Chemical Industry: An Anglo-German Comparison," unpublished paper, 1985; Manfred Groser, "Die Organisation von Wirtschaftsinteressen in der pharmazeutischen Industrie der Bundesrepublik Deutschland," *Discussion Paper* IIM-LMP (Wissenschaftszentrum Berlin, 1985); Stephen Wilks and Maurice Wright, eds., *Comparative Government-Industry Relations: Western Europe, the United States, and Japan* (Oxford: Clarendon, 1987); "Germany Beats World in Chemical Sales," *Wall Street Journal*, 3 May 1988, p. 26; Volker Schneider, *Politiknetzwerke der Chemikalienkontrolle: Eine Analyse einer transnationalen Politikentwicklung* (Berlin: de Gruyter, 1988).

33. Wolfgang Streeck, "Industrial Relations and Industrial Change: The Restructuring of the World Automobile Industry in the 1970s," *Economic and Industrial Democracy* 8 (1987): 437–620; Eckart Hildebrandt, "Der VW Tarifvertrag für Lohndifferenzierung,"

of production. It is capital-intensive, has traditionally been organized to increase economies of scale, specializes in a myriad of process innovations, and relies on sophisticated marketing. In the Federal Republic the industry features both domestic (Volkswagen and Daimler) and foreign (Ford and General Motors), mass (VW, Ford, GM), and specialty producers (BMW, Porsche, Audi). After strong growth in the 1950s and 1960s, West Germany's automobile industry also did very well, by the standards of most of its industrial competitors, after VW had mastered its crisis in the mid-1970s.[34] Since the late 1970s the industry has confronted new challenges to which it is responding vigorously. The revolutionary impact of microelectronics on production technology, advances in the organization of the production process made by the Japanese, the growth of new competitors among the newly industrializing countries, the spread of protectionism, and the sharp recession of the early 1980s have created a new and uncertain environment. Undoubtedly in the 1980s that uncertainty has been reinforced by the intensification of conflict between employers and the powerful metalworkers union (IG Metall).

Machinery is a third core industry.[35] It is a sprawling and hetero-

Discussion Paper IIVG (Wissenschaftszentrum Berlin, 1981); Reinhard Doleschal and Rainer Dombois, eds., Wohin läuft VW? Die Automobilproduktion in der Wirtschaftskrise (Reinbeck: Rowohlt, 1982); Allen, "Structural and Technological Change"; Eva Brumlop and Ulrich Jürgens, "Rationalisation and Industrial Relations in the West German Automobile Industry: A Case Study of Volkswagen," Discussion Paper IIVG (Wissenschaftszentrum Berlin, 1983); Daniel T. Jones, "Motor Cars: A Maturing Industry?" in Shepherd et al., Europe's Industries, pp. 110–38; Peter Cowhey and Edward Long, "Testing Theories of Regime Change: Hegemonic Decline or Surplus Capacity?" International Organization 37 (Spring 1983): 158–88; Andreas Hoff, "Assessing Investment-Related Medium-Term Manpower Needs: A Case Study from the German Automobile Industry," Discussion Paper IIM-LMP (Wissenschaftszentrum Berlin, 1984); Ulrich Jürgens, Knut Dohse, and Thomas Malsch, "New Production Concepts in West German Car Plants," Discussion Paper IIVG (Wissenschaftszentrum Berlin, 1984); Knut Dohse, Ulrich Jürgens, and Thomas Malsch, "Reorganisation der Arbeit in der Automobilindustrie," Discussion Paper IIVG (Wissenschaftszentrum Berlin, 1984); Thomas Malsch, Knut Dohse, and Ulrich Jürgens, "Industrieroboter im Automobilbau," Discussion Paper IIVG (Wissenschaftszentrum Berlin, 1984); Wolfgang Streeck, Industrial Relations in West Germany: A Case Study of the Car Industry (New York: St. Martin's, 1984); Streeck, "Introduction: Industrial Relations, Technical Change and Economic Restructuring," in Streeck, ed., "Industrial Relations and Technical Change in the British, Italian, and German Automobile Industries: Three Case Studies," Discussion Paper IIM-LMP (Wissenschaftszentrum Berlin, 1985); Werner Olle, "Internationalisierungsstrategien in der deutschen Automobilindustrie," unpublished paper, Berlin, Forschungsstelle Sozialökonomik der Arbeit, FU Berlin, 1985; Ulrich Jürgens, "Entwicklungstendenzen in der Weltautomobilindustrie bis in die 90er Jahre," Discussion Paper IIVG (Wissenschaftszentrum Berlin, 1986).

34. Streeck, Industrial Relations in West Germany.

35. Wolfgang-Ulrich Prigge, "Bargaining Systems and Employers' Organizations in British and West German Engineering Industry," Discussion Paper IIM (Wissenschaftszentrum Berlin, 1979); Bernard Real, Technical Change and Economic Policy: Sector Report, the Machine Tool Industry (Paris: OECD, 1980); National Economic Development Office, Toolmaking: A Comparison of UK and West German Companies (London, 1981); Gary B.

geneous sector consisting of thirty-seven recognized industry segments including machine tools. Machine tools are the "reproductive center" of the economy. They reproduce both themselves and other capital goods. Their level of technological development affects the efficiency with which capital equipment is produced and thus the competitive position of all industries. The machinery industry is highly cyclical, with both profit and employment levels varying disproportionately over the business cycle. Although the pace of technological product innovation has been rapid, the development and international competitiveness of some segments of West Germany's machinery industry, including machine tools, has been held back by lower investments than in Japan but also by considerable resistance to introducing integrated numerically controlled manufacturing units, as distinct from individual numerically controlled machine tools. For a while West German producers saw their position slip in international markets. But this stronghold of West German engineering also showed in the 1980s that it was able to stage a strong comeback, regaining international market share in the process.

Old Industries

In West Germany as elsewhere steel has become a political symbol of the decline of one of the foremost industries in any mature economy.[36] In the 1950s and 1960s this industry experienced medium rates of econo-

Herrigel, "Economic Crisis and Industrial Adjustment: A History of the West German Machine Tool Industry, 1945–Present," research proposal, MIT, 1983; Daniel T. Jones, "Machine Tools: Technical Change and a Japanese Challenge," in Shepherd et al., *Europe's Industries*, pp. 186–208; Hajo Weber, *Die Organisation von Wirtschaftsinteressen im Maschinebau, 1. Version* (Bielefeld, October 1983).

36. Gerhard Ollig, "Steel and the State in Germany," *Annals of Public and Cooperative Economy* 51 (1980): 423–37; Josef Esser, Wolfgang Fach, and Kenneth Dyson, "Social Market and Modernization Policy: West Germany," in Kenneth Dyson and Stephen Wilks, eds., *Industrial Crisis: A Comparative Study of the State of Industry* (New York: St. Martin's, 1983); Josef Esser, Wolfgang Fach, and Werner Väth, *Krisenregulierung: Zur politischen Durchsetzung ökonomischer Zwänge* (Frankfurt: Suhrkamp, 1983); Patrick Messerlin and Christopher Saunders, "Steel: Too Much Investment Too Late," in Shepherd et al., *Europe's Industries*, pp. 52–81; Peter A. Johnson, "Twilight of the Idols: The Decline of German Steel since 1977," unpublished paper, Ithaca, Cornell University, 1984; Joachim Müller, Heinz-Dieter Loeber, and Günther Dey, *Krise in der Stahlindustrie*, 2 vols. (Oldenburg: Bibliotheks- und Informationssystem der Universität Oldenburg, 1984); Wolfgang Streeck, "Neo-Corporatist Industrial Relations and the Economic Crisis in West Germany," in J. H. Goldthorpe, ed., *Order and Conflict in Contemporary Capitalism* (Oxford: Clarendon, 1984), pp. 291–314; Streeck, "Co-Determination: The Fourth Decade," in Bernhard Wilpert and Arndt Sorge, eds., *International Perspectives of Organizational Democracy*, vol. 2 of the International Yearbook of Organizational Democracy (New York: Wiley, 1984), pp. 391–422; Josef Esser and Werner Väth, "Overcoming the Steel Crisis in the Federal Republic of Germany, 1975–1983," in Yves Mény and Vincent Wright, eds., *The Politics of Steel: Western Europe and the Steel Industry in the Crisis Years (1974–1984)* (Berlin: de Gruyter, 1987), pp. 623–91.

mic growth in stable domestic markets, which only in recent years have been exposed to serious import competition from low-cost producers. The steel industry is typically dominated by a few (frequently nationalized) large corporations often linked in cartel-like arrangements and has well-organized labor unions. The enormous investment programs in the steel industry make corporations depend on external sources of capital provided by either governments or banks. Large steel corporations often dominate trade associations and national interest groups. Because it diversified early out of basic steel production, West Germany's steel industry traditionally has enjoyed a strong competitive position in European and world markets. But since the mid-1970s competition from low-cost producers, a collapse in demand for steel products, and extensive government assistance of its European competitors have forced West Germany's steel industry on the defensive. The crisis of steel has spread from the Saar to Germany's industrial heart, the Ruhr, which is now suffering from the ills familiar to America's industrial heartland in the early 1980s: excess capacity, regionally concentrated unemployment, and in the early 1980s uncertain prospects of how to diversify the region's economic base. West Germany's governments, both state and federal, have become directly involved in the industry's fortunes through participation in the Davignon Plan of the European Community, the granting of subsidies, and an ill-fated attempt to spur a reorganization of the industry, in short through a variety of measures that are reactive and bear the stamp of improvisation.

Shipbuilding is a second declining industry that has suffered a fate little short of disaster.[37] The fortunes of this industry are tied closely to the same structural changes in the global economy that are affecting the steel industry. One-half of all bulk freight is accounted for by the two most important raw materials of the steel industry: iron ore and coal. A crisis in steel thus translates quickly into a crisis of this segment of the shipbuilding industry. New competitors both in the Eastern bloc and among the newly industrializing countries have created large excess

37. Alan Peacock et al., *Structural Economic Policies in West Germany and the United Kingdom* (London: Anglo-German Foundation, 1980); Robert Kappel and Detlev Rother, *Wandlungsprozesse in der Schiffahrt und im Schiffbau Westeuropa's: Möglichkeiten einer Beeinflussung* (Bremen: Institut für Seeverkehrswirtschaft, 1982); Michael Greve, "The Limits of Statist Policy-Making: Ship-building in West Germany and Japan," unpublished paper, Ithaca, Cornell University, 1983; Heiner Heseler and Hans Jürgen Kroger, eds., *"Stell Dir vor, die Werften gehörn uns . . ."*: *Krise des Schiffbaus oder Krise der Politik* (Hamburg: VSA, 1983); Peter Mottershead, "Shipbuilding: Adjustment-Led Intervention or Intervention-Led Adjustment?" in Shepherd et al., *Europe's Industries*, pp. 82–109; Kooperation Universität/ Arbeiterkammer Arbeiterverein "Use Akschen," *"Irgendwie musste es ja weitergehen": 4 Jahre nach Schliessung der AG "Weser"* (Hamburg: VSA, 1987); Heiner Heseler, *Europäische Schiffsbaukrise und lokale Arbeitsmärkte: Eine Untersuchung über die Folgen von Betriebsschliessungen in Schweden, der Bundesrepublik Deutschland und Dänemark* (Bremen: Universität Bremen, Forschungstransferstelle des Kooperationsbereichs Universität/Arbeiterkammer Bremen, 1987).

capacities. And the instabilities in the price of oil, the severe recessions of the mid-1970s and early 1980s, and lessening dependence of the industrial economies on petroleum have had a disastrous effect on the tanker market. For West Germany specifically, in its contribution to employment, exports, and industrial production, the shipbuilding industry pales in comparison to steel. But West Germany's shipyards are concentrated in four states within close reach of the Baltic and North seas: Schleswig-Holstein, Lower Saxony, Hamburg, and Bremen. Furthermore, shipbuilding has strong links to other industries, such as machinery. In the 1950s and 1960s West Germany's strategy of export-led growth required a modern merchant fleet that contributed greatly to the growth of the industry, aided by special investment incentives provided by the government and, since the early 1960s, limited subsidies. But spurred by extensive government assistance in other countries, international competition created an increasingly severe crisis, deepening government involvement in the industry and, with the collapse of the world demand for ships after 1977, mass unemployment because of the closure or conversion of German shipyards.

New Industries

The industrial complex centering around advances in electronics—computers, semiconductors, and telecommunications—has experienced high economic growth in rapidly expanding domestic and international markets.[38] The leading position of the United States has been undis-

38. Mick McLean, *Technical Change and Economic Policy: Sector Report, the Electronic Industry* (Paris: OECD, 1980); Peacock et al., *Structural Economic Policies*; Bundesministerium für Forschung und Technologie, *Forschungsbericht Datenverarbeitung: Die Entwicklung der Datenverarbeitung in der Programmbewertung der DV-Förderung des BMFT 1967 bis 1979* (Bonn: BMFT, 1982); Cecile Babcock, "West Germany: The Impact of Domestic Structure on the Semiconductor Industry," unpublished paper, Ithaca, Cornell University, 1983; Giovanni Dosi, "Semiconductors: Europe's Precarious Survival in High Technology," in Shepherd et al., *Europe's Industries*, pp. 209–35; Dirk de Vos, *Governments and Microelectronics: The European Experience* (Ottawa: Science Council of Canada, 1983); Rob van Tulder and Eric van Empel, "European Multinationals in the Semiconductor Industry: Their Position in Microprocessors," unpublished paper, Amsterdam, 1984; Richard R. Nelson, *High-Technology Policies: A Five-Nation Comparison* (Washington, D.C.: American Enterprise Institute, 1984); K. P. Friebe and A. Gerybadze, eds., *Microelectronics in Western Europe: The Medium Term Perspective, 1983–1987* (Berlin: Erich Schmidt, 1984); Gerd Junne, "Multinationale Konzerne in 'High Technology'–Sektoren. Oder: Wie gut ist die Strategie vom guten Zweiten," in Peter H. Mettler, ed., *Wohin expandieren Multinationale Konzerne?* (Frankfurt: Haag and Herchen, 1985); Margaret Sharp, ed., *Europe and the New Technologies: Six Case Studies in Innovation and Adjustment* (Ithaca: Cornell University Press, 1986); Kevin Morgan and Douglas Webber, "Divergent Paths: Political Strategies for Telecommunications in Britain, France and the Federal Republic of Germany" (N.p., n.d.); J. Nicholas Ziegler, "The Hare and the Tortoise Revisited: Political Strategies for Technological Advance in the French and West German Semiconductor Industries, 1972–1985," unpublished paper, Cambridge, Mass., Harvard University, Department of Government, 1987.

puted in all segments of these industries until the very recent Japanese challenge in supercomputers and some segments of the semiconductor market. In this global race European producers, including West Germany's industrial giant, Siemens, have fallen behind in relative terms while enjoying substantial absolute growth. This industrial complex is dominated by large multinational corporations and national champions, enterprises especially favored by national governments, that sometimes play an important role in trade associations and national business federations. No "national champion" firm in the computer industry has achieved significant success outside its own borders. Even in their own countries, only ICL in Britain and the major Japanese mainframe companies have been able to achieve a significant market share. Some "specialty producers" such as West Germany's Nixdorf, however, have fared well without government assistance. The investment needs of the large corporations are typically met through retained earnings or borrowing on international capital markets; corporations in this industry thus operate relatively autonomously from the state bureaucracy and the national banking community. Rapid economic growth rates, a high degree of internationalization of production, and financial autonomy give giant corporations such as West Germany's Siemens great influence, especially when they demand government subsidies for expensive research and development programs. In the mid-1980s the ESPRIT program of the European Community and ambitious corporate investment projects (such as Siemens's attempt to market a megachip by the late 1980s) are, in the eyes of American and Japanese observers, the final and probably unsuccessful attempt to reverse a prolonged period of West Germany's and more generally Western Europe's relative decline in this dynamic complex of growth industries.

The biotechnology industry promises future growth. It involves a number of activities and techniques developed over the last decade that use the natural processes of living organisms to manufacture commercial products.[39] In this industry the impetus for rapid development originated in the United States, but fast parallel developments are now taking place in Japan and Europe, including West Germany. This industry is

---

39. Sheila Jasanoff, "Public and Private Sector Activities in Biotechnology: The Federal Republic of Germany," unpublished paper, Washington, D.C., Office of Technology Assessment, 1982; U.S. Congress, Office of Technology Assessment, *Commercial Biotechnology: An International Analysis* (Washington, D.C.: U.S. Government Printing Office, 1984); Gerd Junne, "Auswirkungen der Biotechnologie auf den Welthandel und die internationale Arbeitsteilung," unpublished paper, Amsterdam, University of Amsterdam, 1984; Gerd Junne, "European Multinationals in Biotechnology," unpublished paper, Amsterdam, 1984; "West German Biotech Industry Comes to Life in Spite of Itself," *Genetic Engineering News* 4 (September 1984): 1, 36–37; Sheila Jasanoff, "Technological Innovation in a Corporatist State: The Case of Biotechnology in the Federal Republic of Germany," *Research Policy* 14 (1985): 23–38.

founded on scientific progress which greatly expands the range of application of molecular and cellular manipulation of life processes. Equally critical is the increased confidence of private firms in their ability to patent life forms and processes. This new-found ability sustains the expectation that biotechnology will reinvigorate the flagging economic prospects of the petrochemical and, to a lesser extent, pharmaceutical industries. Depending on their resource endowments and product mixes, different countries and companies adhere to different strategies. As it has with the electronic industries, the West German government has been actively assisting the evolution of biotechnology since the early 1970s. But the character of West Germany's scientific institutions—laboratories in the universities and in industry or government-sponsored research centers—appears to be inimical to the industry's dynamic development. When in 1981 Hoechst decided to invest heavily in Boston's MGH rather than in any of West Germany's labs, the crisis of this nascent industry became a highly publicized political event. Developments since then do not suggest any great change in the problems this West German industry faces compared to its American and Japanese competitors.

This book's focus on industry, some American readers may argue, is outmoded. After all, are not all industrial economies pulled by post-industrialism and pushed by deindustrialization toward a service economy? On closer inspection the question is framed incorrectly in general and inappropriately applied in this particular case. It is incorrectly framed because it presumes a split between industrial manufacturing and vast stretches of the modern service economy which does not exist.[40] And it is inappropriately applied because, as I have argued, in West Germany industry looms so large. Nevertheless, even in the Federal Republic the size of the manufacturing sector is shrinking. Establishing a fundamental similarity in the consequences of economic and social change between industry and the West German service economy thus would broaden and consolidate this book's argument. This is one of two reasons for including a case study of the banking industry. The second reason is that in virtually all major writings on West Germany's political economy since 1945 the role of finance and the large banks figures prominently.[41] Yet there is a dearth of careful, detailed analysis of

40. U.S. Congress, Office of Technology Assessment, *International Competition in Services*, OTA-ITE-328 (Washington, D.C.: U.S. Government Printing Office, 1987); Stephen S. Cohen and John Zysman, *Manufacturing Matters: The Myth of the Postindustrial Economy* (New York: Basic Books, 1987).

41. Andrew Shonfield, *Modern Capitalism: The Changing Balance of Public and Private Power* (London: Oxford University Press, 1965); Kenneth Dyson, "The State, Banks and Industry: The West German Case," in Andrew Cox, ed., *State, Finance and Industry: A Comparative Analysis of Post-War Trends in Six Advanced Industrial Economies* (New York: St. Martin's, 1986), pp. 118–41.

trends in the financial sector.[42] Arguably West Germany's most important service industry, banking is included here to shed a different light on a core sector of its contemporary economy.

This book seeks to analyze the political responses of different industries to the changes now under way in the Federal Republic. Part II analyzes three major changes that are affecting West German politics in the 1980s: changes in West Germany's international setting, new social movements, and new production technologies in factories. Part III analyzes core as well as lagging and leading sectors of West Germany's manufacturing and service economy. Economic sectors are the research sites in which this project proposes to trace empirically the political consequences of change. The concluding essay in Part IV elucidates further the complex relations between stability and flexibility in the emerging Third West German Republic.

The main conclusion of this book takes issue with views about West Germany's future prevailing on both sides of the Atlantic. In the 1980s in the Federal Republic the Right was unrealistic in its optimism, the Left excessive in its pessimism. By contrast, American conservatives were too skeptical and liberals too admiring of West Germany. The West German future can be painted in bright pink or brooding black only if we assume that the current changes in West German factories, articulated by new social movements and discernible in the international system, are forming a cumulative and interlocking pattern. That assumption is probably mistaken. This book offers evidence and insights that challenge thinking in stark alternatives.

For many West Germans the fortieth anniversary of the Federal Republic is a fitting occasion to celebrate or criticize but in any case to reminisce as they evaluate the last four decades. This exercise in collective retrospection offers strong support for a major premise of this book. West German democracy has existed sufficiently long to invite sustained thought about the continuities and discontinuities in its political structures and strategies. This book tries to peer into the future. The intent is to be prospective rather than retrospective. This volume advances some guesses about the future, based on concrete developments in the very recent past. At the same time the essays that follow seek to avoid unprofitable speculation about West Germany's future.[43]

42. Martin Baethge and Herbert Oberbeck, *Zukunft der Angestellten: Neue Technologien und berufliche Perspektiven in Büro und Verwaltung* (Frankfurt: Campus, 1986); Stefan Welzk, *Boom ohne Arbeitsplätze* (Cologne: Kiepenheuer & Witsch, 1986).

43. G. Erman, "Deutschland im Jahre 2000," *Deutsche Schriften für nationales Leben* 1, 4 (Kiel: Lipsius and Tischer, 1981), pp. 5–40; Herman Kahn and Michael Redepenning, *Die Zukunft Deutschlands: Niedergang oder neuer Aufstieg der Bundesrepublik* (Stuttgart: Poller, 1982).

How West Germany will deal with changes affecting it in the 1990s is a timely and important subject. The First West German Republic experienced reconstruction, growth, and consolidation; the Second Republic experimented with halting political reforms, followed by successful crisis management and resigned retrenchment. Arguably, in the 1980s the Federal Republic has moved toward the Third Republic defined by new challenges and opportunities both at home and abroad. This book focuses on the analysis of adjustment in different industries. Since West Germany's political fortunes are so closely tied to its industrial prowess, these studies are important in their own right. But they command our attention also because they offer an opportunity for a better comprehension of the particular political structures and distinctive political responses to the changes that the Federal Republic is likely to confront in the 1990s.

PART II

THREE TYPES
OF CHANGE

CHAPTER TWO

Bipolarity and the Postwar
International Economic Order

JOANNE GOWA

Several essays in this volume record an apparently extraordinarily successful adaptation by major West German industries to the economic dislocations of the last fifteen years. Conspicuous among these success stories are those of machinery, automobiles, and chemicals in which the ability to export freely to world markets plays a critical role.[1] An implicit but nonetheless integral element of these analyses, therefore, is an assumption that the international foundations of West German industrial recovery are secure.

The importance of world markets to the Federal Republic of Germany (FRG) extends beyond particular industrial sectors. More so than other advanced industrialized countries in the postwar period, the FRG has relied on expanding international markets to regulate both its political and economic development. Its growth strategy has been distinguished by an emphasis on exports, and its political conflicts have been constrained by the need to maintain the price competitiveness of German products on world markets.[2] Thus both the relatively strong macro-

For comments on an earlier version, I am grateful to Peter J. Katzenstein and Norbert Walter. For bibliographic assistance, I am indebted to Eileen Crumm.

1. The machinery industry exported 62.5 percent of its output in 1985 (Gary B. Herrigel, "Industrial Order and the Politics of Industrial Change: Mechanical Engineering"); the automobile industry exported 61.6 percent of its output in 1986 (Wolfgang Streeck, "Successful Adjustment to Turbulent Markets: The Automobile Industry"); "roughly 50 percent" of the chemical industry's output is exported (Christopher S. Allen, "Political Consequences of Change: The Chemical Industry"), all in this volume.
2. For a good analysis of German macroeconomic policy during the postwar period see Frank Wolter, "From Economic Miracle to Stagnation: On the German Disease," in Arnold C. Harberger, ed., *World Economic Growth* (San Francisco: Institute for Contemporary Studies, 1984), pp. 95–122.

33

economic performance and the comparatively apolitical "politics of productivity" of the Federal Republic reflect and depend on the liberal international economic regimes that were political constructions of the early postwar period.[3]

Recent press reports and academic analyses suggest, however, that the international foundations of German economic prosperity and political stability may be weakening. Journalists and scholars document their fears of a serious erosion in the commitment of the industrialized nations to a liberal world economic order. They point to the rapid proliferation of nontariff barriers (NTBs) to trade; to periodic outbreaks of mini–tariff wars among the advanced countries; and to the failure of the core Group of Five states (Britain, France, Germany, Japan, and the United States) to coordinate their fiscal and monetary policies to secure the essential foundations of an expanding world market economy. Echoes of the 1930s resound in these and other references to conflicts among states whose cooperation is essential to the survival of the postwar regimes.

If these observations accurately represent threats to the existing order, the story of German adaptation to the economic problems of the recent past is destined to end unhappily. Even a shadow of the economic disarray that characterized the interwar years would undercut West Germany's relatively impressive recovery from the stagflation of the 1970s.[4] A country in which international trade contributes roughly a quarter of gross domestic product (GDP) is highly vulnerable to international developments over which it has little control.[5] If the future begins to resemble the past, the German success story of the 1980s will quickly unravel.

This chapter argues, however, that there is very little resonance between the contemporary system and that of the 1930s. Arguments to the

3. As in recent international political economy literature, an international regime is defined here as a set of "implicit or explicit principles, norms, rules, and decision-making procedures around which actors' expectations converge in a given area of international relations." See Stephen D. Krasner, "Structural Causes and Regime Consequences: Regimes as Intervening Variables," in Krasner, ed., *International Regimes* (Ithaca: Cornell University Press, 1984), p. 3.

4. West Germany has made more progress on inflation than on unemployment, however. While inflation has been restored to low levels, unemployment remained above 8 percent in the mid-1980s. Low in comparison to other major European countries, unemployment in West Germany remains high in historical perspective and is characterized by wide regional variations. See "West Germans Are Doing Nicely as They Are, Danke," *The Economist*, 7 December 1985, pp. 75–76.

5. In 1980, total West German imports were 22.7 percent of GDP; exports totaled 23.4 percent of GDP. Corresponding figures for the United States were 9.3 and 8.5 percent, for Japan 13.6 and 12.5 percent. See A. M. El-Agraa, "The Basic Statistics of the EC," in El-Agraa, ed., *The Economics of the European Community*, 2d ed. (New York: St. Martin's, 1985), p. 60.

contrary betray a fundamental misapprehension of the importance to the economic order of the sea change in world politics that occurred in the wake of World War II. The transformation of a multipolar to a bipolar distribution of international power profoundly affected the economic relationships among several of the great powers of the prewar years. In particular, it imparted to those relationships an imperative for cooperation that will endure for the foreseeable future: that imperative derives from a security alliance dictated by rivalry for influence limited primarily to the United States and the Soviet Union.

To support its argument, this chapter compares the contemporary to the interwar period. It first briefly reviews the responses of the industrialized countries to the economic difficulties that began early in the last decade and points out that these responses varied widely from those that followed the advent of the Great Depression. The next section explains these differences as the product of the bipolar international political system that emerged after 1945, advancing the argument that the postwar system, unlike its multipolar predecessor, offered strong incentives to a core group of advanced industrialized states to engage in sustained economic cooperation.

The remainder of the chapter assesses the impact of changes in the postwar balance of power on economic cooperation among the principal members of the Western alliance. It argues that recent intra-alliance economic conflicts can be understood as the result of stability at the core but changes at the margins of the international distribution of power: enduring bipolarity ensures that the core of the postwar regimes will remain intact; stabilization of the balance of power within Western Europe, however, provokes U.S. demands that its allies assume some responsibility for regime management. An extended discussion of the "locomotive" dispute illustrates the argument that the transition to multilateral leadership will be prolonged but not destructive of the existing order: in particular, a "Fortress Europe" is a highly unlikely outcome even of the current push within the European Economic Community to dismantle all barriers to trade among its members by 1992.[6]

In sum, this chapter provides explicit support for the optimism about the international foundations of recent German industrial recovery that is an implicit theme of other essays in this volume. Its optimism is tempered, however, by its analytic boundaries: as is made clear in the conclusion, the analysis here emphasizes the constraints imposed by the

6. In his 1984 *World Politics* article, Glenn H. Snyder attributes the stability of the NATO alliance to the bipolar distribution of power. He argues that bipolarity has thus empowered the members of NATO to disagree with each other about alliance security policies without fears that their disagreements will fracture the alliance. The argument here owes much to Snyder's formulation. See his "The Security Dilemma in Alliance Politics," *World Politics* 36 (July 1984): 461–95.

bipolar international political system on individual state actions deleterious to free trade. Its argument, therefore, necessarily remains vulnerable to charges that the international system and its constituent free-trade regimes are only as resilient as the intrastate forces that support them.

RECENT RESPONSES IN HISTORICAL PERSPECTIVE

Relatively high levels of growth characterized much of the industrialized world for most of the three decades that followed World War II. Given the relationship of macroeconomic conditions to pressures for protection,[7] it is not surprising that in this period international trade expanded rapidly relative to world production: between 1948 and 1973, world trade increased at an average annual rate of 7 percent, and world production grew at an average rate of 5 percent.[8] Beginning in the early 1970s, however, the world economy became less congenial to a rapid expansion of international trade: between 1974 and 1980, for example, world production increased at an average annual rate of 3 percent and world trade at a rate of 4 percent.[9] The sharp increase in world oil prices, the ensuing stagflation in the industrialized countries, and a changing division of international labor combined to slow progress toward lower barriers to trade.

In an international economic environment already subject to strong inflationary pressures, the Organization of Petroleum Exporting Countries (OPEC) raised oil prices from $3.60 to $9.60 per barrel in early 1974, thereby effecting an income transfer to it from the oil-importing countries of $90 billion during that year alone and roughly double that during 1980.[10] The terms of trade of the industrialized countries shifted sharply against them: without a corresponding increase in demand for their exports, the sharp rise in oil prices implied a deterioration in the standard of living in the advanced countries.

Adjustment to the oil shock was complicated in many countries by domestic labor markets that had become increasingly rigid as the postwar period progressed. Adaptation, therefore, was characterized by a

7. For an explanation and survey of empirical studies of the relation between economic cycles and demands for protection, see Bruno Frey, "The Political Economy of Protection," in David Greenaway, ed., *Current Issues in International Trade: Theory and Policy* (New York: St. Martin's, 1985), pp. 139–58.

8. Robert Reich, "Beyond Free Trade," *Foreign Affairs* 61 (Spring 1983): 778.

9. R. C. Hine, *The Political Economy of European Trade: An Introduction to the Trade Policies of the EEC* (New York: St. Martin's, 1985), p. 260.

10. Richard N. Cooper, "Managing Risks to the International Economic System," in Richard J. Herring, ed., *Managing International Risk* (Cambridge: Cambridge University Press, 1983), p. 44.

sharp rise in both prices and unemployment throughout the industrialized world. Averaging 6.7 percent in the early 1970s, inflation in the advanced countries jumped to 11.5 percent between 1973 and 1975 and remained above 10 percent through 1981. Unemployment doubled over the same period: from 2.5 percent in 1971–73, it reached 5.0 percent later in the same decade.[11]

Changes in the pattern of international trade exacerbated pressures for protection stemming from widespread increases in unemployment. When trade expands along intraindustry lines, as it did among the industrialized countries for much of the postwar period, resource shifts among industries are minimized: gains from trade accrue from each country's specialization within a given industry.[12] Interindustry trade, however, is increasingly evident in the recent entry of the newly industrialized countries (NICs) into world markets. As Albert Bressand observes, the implications of this shift are profound: "Rather than the fairly manageable pattern of two-way trade within a given sector which has been at the center of transatlantic and, even more, intra-European relations, Japan and the NICs will present the challenge of intersectoral trade shifts. Following the free trade recipe would not mean therefore trading Renault cars for Mercedes cars: whole lines of products would have to be abandoned. Regional and sectoral impacts will be much more visible."[13] The more radical resource shifts and unemployment effects associated with inter- rather than intraindustry trade also imply a rise in demands for protection in the advanced countries.

These macro- and microeconomic pressures on employment are reflected in the proliferation of NTBs in the industrialized world in the 1970s and 1980s. Assuming a variety of forms, the NTBs cover a wide range of imported products.[14] Since 1980, for example, the United States has imposed orderly marketing agreements (OMAs) on Korean and Taiwanese exports of nonrubber footwear; placed safeguards on

11. Michael Bruno and Jeffrey D. Sachs, *Economics of Worldwide Stagflation* (Cambridge, Mass.: Harvard University Press, 1985), p. 2.

12. Estimates are that intraindustry trade represents more than one-half of Organization of Economic Cooperation and Development trade in manufactures and has increased steadily as a percentage of total trade during the postwar period. See Gilbert R. Winham, *International Trade and the Tokyo Round Negotiation* (Princeton: Princeton University Press, 1986), p. 51.

13. Albert Bressand, "Mastering the World Economy," *Foreign Affairs* 61 (Summer 1983): 753.

14. The ratio of consumption of restricted products to total consumption of manufactured goods is estimated to lie between 15 and 25 percent in the major industrialized countries. See Bela Balassa, *Change and Challenge in the World Economy* (New York: St. Martin's, 1985), p. 438. As Balassa cautions, however, though such measures "show the proportion of imports or consumption subject to non-tariff barriers, they do not provide an indication of the extent to which imports have been reduced as a result of their imposition" (ibid., p. 440).

imports of color televisions, citizen band radios, porcelain-on-steel cookware, high-carbon ferro-chromium, industrial fasteners, clothespins, specialty steel, and motorcycles; and negotiated voluntary export restraints (VERs) on Japanese automobiles and European Community (EC) carbon steel products.[15] The European Community has imposed OMAs on jute products and on iron and steel. It has also reached agreement with Japan on export restraints for video recorders and large color television tubes and on "surveillance" of Japanese exports of hi-fi equipment, quartz watches, forklift trucks, light vans, and motorcycles. NTBs have been deployed in France, in Italy, and in the United Kingdom against cars, radios, televisions, and communication equipment. West Germany and the United Kingdom have restrained imports of Japanese flatware.[16] The United States and the EC have also cooperated in imposing restraints on textile and clothing imports via the Multifiber Arrangement (MFA).

The rapid spread of NTBs, however, is not by itself an accurate indicator of the overall reaction of the industrialized states to stagflation. Tariff levels, for example, reflecting diverse economic interests with a stake in free trade, continued their postwar decline through the conclusion of the Tokyo Round of trade negotiations in 1979.[17] Although it is difficult to assess rigorously the net effects of increasing nontariff and decreasing tariff barriers to trade, the judgment rendered by two observers in 1983 seems reasonably accurate: "On balance," they comment, "while there has been a resurgence of non-tariff protectionism in the 1970s, the liberal gains of earlier decades have not been destroyed."[18] Thus the responses of the advanced countries to the economic dislocations of the last fifteen years do not appear to have seriously eroded the foundations of the postwar international economic order.

15. Restrictions on some of these products have been lifted, for example, nonrubber footwear, televisions, automobiles, and Japanese specialty steel.

16. All information on trade restraints is from Balassa, *Change and Challenge in the World Economy*, pp. 435–39.

17. The conclusion of the Kennedy Round of tariff negotiations under the General Agreement on Tariffs and Trade (GATT) in the early 1960s resulted in average tariffs on manufactured products, weighted by total imports, of 7.0 percent in the United States, 8.3 percent in Europe, and 10.0 percent in Japan. With the implementation of the Tokyo Round cuts, the corresponding figures will be 4.9 percent in the United States, 6.0 percent in the EC, and 5.4 percent in Japan (see ibid., pp. 428, 430). This trend reflects a variety of free-trade interests: exporters, banks with outstanding loans to Third World countries, consumers aware of the high costs to them of import restraints, and decision makers sensitive to the dangers to national competitiveness inherent in protection. For a historical analysis of the changes in national competitiveness that ensue when countries respond differently to pressures for protection, see Victoria Curzon Price, "Recessions and the World Economic Order," in Susan Strange and Roger Tooze, eds., *The International Politics of Surplus Capacity* (London: Allen & Unwin, 1981), pp. 46–56.

18. Helen Hughes and Jean Waelbroeck, "Foreign Trade and Structural Adjustment," in Hans-Gert Braun et al., eds., *The European Economy in the 1980s* (Aldershot, Eng.: Gower, 1983), p. 6.

The restraint apparent in these responses is even more striking when compared with the wave of economic nationalism that swept across the major industrial countries at the onset of the Great Depression. Although the depression of the 1930s delivered a much stronger blow to the world economy than did the stagflation and slow growth of the 1970s and 1980s,[19] there were few sustained attempts at international cooperation to contain its effects.[20] Instead, "beggar-thy-neighbor" policies became the modal response, as major countries engaged in an ultimately futile effort to export unemployment to others.

The United States initiated this process in 1930, when it raised its tariffs to a level unmatched either before or since: the Hawley-Smoot Tariff Act levied an average tariff of 60 percent on dutiable imports.[21] The reaction abroad was predictable: France introduced quotas; Britain expanded its imperial preference system and increased its tariffs; and Germany sought protection via a system of elaborate exchange controls.[22] Along with a precipitous drop in real income and in prices, the increase in barriers to exchange took a major toll on world trade, which declined between 1929 and 1933 by 66 percent.[23]

The trend toward protection begun by the Hawley-Smoot Tariff Act was the product of several important factors other than strict reciprocity. Among these were a widespread shortage of foreign exchange and the absence of a variety of now familiar domestic relief mechanisms.[24] Also absent was a strong constraint on protection that evolved only after World War II: the transformation of the multipolar to a bipolar international political system.

MULTIPOLARITY, BIPOLARITY, AND INTERNATIONAL ECONOMIC COOPERATION

The distribution of power in the international system most conducive to extensive free trade among states is a controversial issue in the con-

19. Between 1929 and 1932, for example, U.S. national income declined by 38 percent. See W. Arthur Lewis, *Economic Survey, 1919–1939* (London: Allen & Unwin, 1949), p. 52.
20. For a description of cooperation and conflict among the major countries in the interwar period, see Kenneth A. Oye, "The Sterling-Dollar-Franc Triangle: Monetary Diplomacy, 1929–1937," *World Politics* 38 (October 1985): 173–99.
21. I. M. Destler, "Protecting Congress or Protecting Trade?" *Foreign Policy*, no. 62 (Spring 1986), p. 100.
22. Price, "Recessions and the World Economic Order."
23. In the judgment of Richard N. Cooper, tariffs were "no doubt the least important" of these three causes of the decrease in world trade ("Managing Risks to the International Economic System," p. 27).
24. Foreign exchange problems were the result of the imbroglio over reparations and war debts, the collapse of foreign lending, and the disintegration of the gold-exchange standard. Domestic substitutes for trade barriers that were largely unavailable in the 1930s include demand stimulus programs, unemployment insurance, agricultural support pro-

temporary international relations literature. Recently, several scholars have argued that a small group of relatively powerful states can organize and maintain an international system of free trade.[25] Yet small-group arguments are silent before a question at the core of both international relations research in general and this chapter in particular: given that the great powers of any international system are always few in number, what explains wide variations in the capacity of such systems to organize and support market exchange among their constituent states?

As evidenced by the contrast between the interwar and postwar systems, a great deal of this variation can be explained by the overarching patterns of either the great power rivalries that divide or the alliance ties that bind states that are potential members of any small group. Thus what seems to be relatively little variation in numerical terms between a multipolar and a bipolar system can produce a great deal of variation in the probability that an international system of free trade will result. That both the interwar and postwar systems are small-number systems, in short, betrays a much more fundamental difference between them.

The small group of states that could potentially form the core of a liberal international economic order in the interwar period includes the great powers of the security system among its members; the potential core of the postwar system does not. Embedded within the trade conflicts of the interwar period, as a result, are the more severe conflicts that typically divide the great powers of any international security system from each other. The postwar system, in contrast, effectively isolates international trade and security conflicts from each other. This difference is fundamental to an understanding of why the organization of economic systems was so disparate in the two periods.

The Interwar System

The legacy of World War I was an international political system in which each of the great powers remained almost exclusively concerned with its own interests and power. It was a system that was wholly devoid of genuine commitments to or concerns about collective security. Even had the United States adhered to the Treaty of Versailles, the unwillingness of any great power to commit itself to the security of others would have crippled the League of Nations. Myopic interpretations of self-

---

grams, and lenders of last resort or other analogs of the U.S. Federal Deposit Insurance Corporation.

25. See, for example, Robert O. Keohane, *After Hegemony: Cooperation and Discord in the World Political Economy* (Princeton: Princeton University Press, 1984); and Duncan Snidal, "Limits of Hegemonic Stability Theory," *International Organization* 39 (Autumn 1985): 579–614.

interest would also thwart efforts to reconstruct the prewar system of trade and finance.

Irreconcilable differences among the great powers on the issue of European reconstruction after World War I reflected sharp conflicts of political and security interests. Britain and the United States viewed the economic recovery of Germany as the cornerstone of a restoration of European political stability. The Anglo-American emphasis on the economic rehabilitation of Germany reflected the interests of both countries in minimizing their Continental responsibilities.[26] Preoccupied by domestic political and economic problems, neither state was willing to commit itself deeply to the task of maintaining the European balance of power.

France viewed the problem of reconstruction very differently. Any initiatives to restore Germany to economic prosperity—particularly any revision of the reparations settlement—represented a security threat to the French. In the absence of either British or U.S. guarantees of French security against a resurgent Germany, France was determined to block any economic accords that might advantage the country it viewed as the principal threat to its security. France's clear priority in negotiations over the economic reconstruction of Europe was to keep Germany economically and therefore militarily weak.

Thus attempts to reconstruct Western Europe to provide a basis for rebuilding prewar systems of trade and finance foundered over the inability of the great powers to reach consensus on the political foundations of those systems. Under these conditions, the prevailing distribution of international power could produce only deadlock: none of the major states alone was powerful enough to force other states to accept its preferred solution to European problems; each state retained sufficient power to veto any solution with which it disagreed.

When the Great Depression confronted the industrialized states with an urgent need for cooperation, therefore, it was within a political environment extremely hostile to any form of sustained economic co-

26. With respect to the United States, Melvyn P. Leffler observes: "American officials did not consider the nation's vital interests, either strategic or economic, to be at stake in Europe. With Germany's military power emasculated, policymakers saw no imminent strategic threat to America's national security and did not wish to become embroiled in disputes over such matters as the Rhineland occupation and the Polish corridor." See Melvyn P. Leffler, *The Elusive Quest: America's Pursuit of European Stability and French Security, 1919–1933* (Chapel Hill: University of North Carolina Press, 1979), p. 363. Of Britain in the same period, as Paul Kennedy notes, "splendid isolation was still the preferred policy." Paul Kennedy, *The Realities behind Diplomacy: Background Influences on British External Policy, 1865–1980* (London: Allen & Unwin, 1981), p. 272. Cooperation in the defense of allies, Kennedy adds, rated a poor fourth in a ranking of British security objectives, trailing behind the security of Britain itself and that of its trade routes and empire.

operation. The combination of highly individualistic definitions of national interest and an unstable European balance of power transformed a situation that might otherwise have been perceived as an opportunity for joint gain into a zero-sum or total conflict situation. Because each state viewed any gains to others as a potential threat to its own security, the distribution of gains assumed precedence over the opportunity to realize a net gain for all: economic nationalism was the inevitable result. Responses to the Great Depression mirrored responses to interwar security problems.

The Postwar System

In the postwar world most of the prewar great powers could no longer hope to defend their vital interests independently. France was not powerful enough either to dictate or veto nor Germany to revise the terms of the postwar settlement; even Britain had only a secondary role in influencing its terms. Nor did these prewar rivals any longer define their interests in a way that rendered their independent pursuit compelling; in the context of a global struggle for influence between the United States and the Soviet Union, their joint interest in opposing the extension of Soviet influence was clear.

Nor could the United States hope that the European balance of power would stabilize without its sustained intervention. In contrast to the 1930s, there was no possibility that the United States might free ride on either British or French efforts to maintain Continental stability.[27] No longer was the United States one among several great powers able to influence the balance of power in Europe in a way that would protect U.S. interests: it was the only one capable of doing so.

The particular form of intervention the United States pursued reflected its interpretation of World War II. In analyzing the outbreak of that war, U.S. decision makers emphasized the breakdown of international trade and capital flows in the wake of the Great Depression. They viewed the widespread turn toward higher tariffs, the organization of preferential trading arrangements, and the failure to restore a sound international monetary system as precipitants of the breakdown of the international political order. As Cordell Hull, secretary of state in the Roosevelt administration, put it: "If goods can't cross borders, soldiers will."[28] In the minds of American policy makers, conflict over

27. Barry Posen interprets the interwar system as a Prisoners' Dilemma in which each of the major powers sought to free ride on the security efforts of others, thereby guaranteeing the insecurity of all. See his *The Sources of Military Doctrine: France, Britain, and Germany between the World Wars* (Ithaca: Cornell University Press, 1985).

28. Quoted in Barry Buzan, "Economic Structure and International Security: The Limits of the Liberal Case," *International Organization* 38 (Autumn 1984): 599.

trade, reparations, and exchange rates inhibited the restoration of a stable peace in Europe in the wake of World War I.

Thus the U.S. attempt after 1945 to ensure that intra-European tensions would never again become a source of systemic war assumed a strong economic cast. To pursue what had become an inescapably vital interest in a Continental balance of power conducive to its own security, the United States sought the economic integration of the West European countries within a larger transatlantic political and economic alliance. To this end, the United States strove to break down barriers to trade and capital flows within Western Europe and across the Atlantic. The stillborn International Trading Organization, its partial resurrection in the General Agreement on Tariffs and Trade (GATT), and the Bretton Woods system of fixed but adjustable exchange rates all reflect this U.S. objective.

It is reflected as well in the measures the United States took in the immediate postwar period to ensure that foreign exchange shortages would not interfere with its plans. Its efforts in this sphere differ markedly from those it undertook in the same area after World War I: the U.S. effort in the interwar period was characterized by a strong reluctance to make concessions on war debts and by an equally strong insistence that private capital flows bear the burden of reconstruction.[29] After World War II, however, the U.S. government moved aggressively to lower foreign exchange barriers to free trade: it virtually canceled Britain's Lend Lease debt, extended to Britain a $3.75 billion loan,[30] initiated the Marshall Plan and the Organization for European Economic Cooperation (OEEC), and enforced a devaluation of several European currencies in 1949.[31]

When the Soviet-American struggle for power and influence intensified and the Cold War began, U.S. interest in supporting reconstruction in Western Europe and in tying the European economies to its own intensified as well. Viewing Western Europe as the pivotal element in the evolution of the postwar balance of power between East and West, the United States was determined to keep Western Europe within its camp. It was determined to prevent West European development as an autonomous political and economic actor potentially capable of forming

29. For a detailed explanation and account of U.S. policy in the interwar period, see Leffler, *Elusive Quest.*
30. Kennedy, *Realities behind Diplomacy*, p. 318.
31. As was true after World War I, domestic and congressional politics were hostile to the extension of economic aid to Western Europe. The Truman administration, however, embarked on a determined and ultimately successful campaign to overcome this opposition. For an excellent account of the course and implications of its effort, see Richard Freeland, *The Truman Doctrine and the Origins of McCarthyism: Domestic Politics, Internal Security, and Foreign Policy, 1946–1948* (New York: Schocken, 1974).

an independent relationship with the Soviet Union and of disrupting the worldwide balance of power.

Thus for two decades after the end of World War II, its interests and power led the United States to assume both the tangible and intangible costs of providing the institutional and other foundations of an open-market transatlantic trading system. It supplied sufficient foreign exchange to enable the European states to begin to orient their economies toward such a system. It assumed the costs of organizing several institutions that remain as bulwarks of the current international economic regime: the GATT; the International Monetary Fund (IMF); and the OEEC, the predecessor of the Organization for Economic Cooperation and Development (OECD).

It became, in addition, the implicit enforcer of multilateral tariff accords, as well as the key currency state and "nth" country of the international monetary system.[32] It sanctioned the formation of the European Community despite its implied threat of lower barriers to intra-European than to transatlantic trade.[33] Until 1958, in addition, it was willing to ratify de jure reciprocal exchanges of tariff concessions that concealed de facto unilateral U.S. concessions: European markets remained protected by a network of exchange controls.[34]

THE EVOLUTION OF BIPOLARITY:
THE RESTORATION OF A EUROPEAN BALANCE OF POWER

The stabilization of the postwar balance of power within Western Europe freed the United States from its role as the only available guarantor of a Continental balance favorable to Western interests. As a result, U.S. willingness to support unilaterally the postwar economic order gave way to demands that the major European states, particularly Germany, accept responsibility for several aspects of that order: the management of world macroeconomic stability, the reconciliation of inconsistent balance-of-payments targets, and the absorption of the trade-diverting effects of the EC.[35]

32. For an analysis of the postwar monetary system and an interpretation of the transatlantic political and economic bargain behind it, see Benjamin J. Cohen, *Organizing the World's Money: The Political Economy of International Monetary Relations* (New York: Basic Books, 1977).

33. Almost all empirical studies conclude that the trade-creating effects of the EC have exceeded its trade-diverting effects by a wide margin. Some also conclude that U.S. exports have actually benefited as a result of the EC's formation. See Hine, *Political Economy of European Trade*, p. 52.

34. Wolfgang Hager, "Germany as an Extraordinary Trader," in Wilfrid L. Kohl and Georgio Basevi, eds., *West Germany: A European and Global Power* (Lexington, Mass.: Lexington Books, 1980), p. 16.

35. The most recent U.S. efforts to reduce the impact of the EC on its exports focus on agricultural products. Press reports suggest that a global reduction of agricultural sub-

The evolving balance of power, however, has not been especially conducive to a smooth transition to multilateral leadership. In one sense, it has enhanced the leverage of the United States over its European allies by making it possible for the United States to issue a reasonably credible threat to withdraw from Western Europe if its demands are not met.[36] The enduring bipolarity of the international system, however, makes it difficult for the United States to exploit fully this threat: the continuing Soviet interest in European instability makes it obvious to all that vital U.S. interests remain at stake on the European continent.[37]

In the context of the growing economic power of the European states, the net effect of the stabilization of the European balance of power and of enduring systemic bipolarity is clear: it is an intra-alliance stalemate on a series of economic issues that occurs within a larger consensus on the importance of maintaining intact the core of the postwar order. Whether the issue is the Soviet gas pipeline, EC agricultural support programs, or a locomotive for the world economy, a similar pattern is evident. Sharp conflicts of economic interests, the absence of a decisive power advantage for either side, and a strong common interest in the preservation of the Western alliance preclude both a clear resolution of any given issue and its escalation to the level of a serious threat to the economic order.[38]

This pattern is illustrated here by a detailed analysis of the locomotive case, chosen because of its centrality to recent debates over regime management and the salient role in it played by West Germany. The case engages a principal support of the postwar economic order: the provision of global macroeconomic stability. Since 1977, the United

---

sidies will be a major target of the United States during the forthcoming Uruguay Round of GATT negotiations. See, for example, *New York Times*, 6 July 1987, p. 1.

36. No credible threat in reality attached to Dean Acheson's warning that an "agonizing reappraisal" of U.S. interests in Western Europe would follow any failure to realize a European defense community. In the context of growing Soviet power and a still unstable Continent, U.S. security would have been endangered had the United States executed its threat.

37. As Chancellor Helmut Kohl's reaction to it indicates, the recent Soviet-American agreement to eliminate medium-range nuclear missiles does not reflect a change in the U.S. commitment to European stability. Kohl described the agreement as "a great success for the Atlantic alliance." See *The Week in Germany*, 11 December 1987, p. 1.

38. A discussion of recent conflicts over economic issues within the alliance should not obscure the relatively long history of these conflicts. As early as 1962, for example, West Germany and the United States opened the "chicken war," in which the United States responded to the FRG's increase in duties on poultry by withdrawing tariff concessions it had made under the GATT on a set of imports equivalent in dollar volume to its poultry exports to the FRG. See Winham, *International Trade and the Tokyo Round Negotiation*, p. 153. Similarly, the recent imbroglio over pipeline exports to the Soviet Union echoes— albeit with a very different outcome—the pipeline controversy that erupted during the Kennedy administration. See Bruce W. Jentleson, "From Consensus to Conflict: The Domestic Political Economy of East-West Energy Trade Policy," *International Organization* 38 (Autumn 1984), pp. 625–60.

States has sought to persuade Germany and Japan to assume responsibility for world economic reflation. Its efforts reflect the disincentives that inhibit any one country from acting alone in pursuit of domestic economic expansion,[39] as well as changes in the postwar balance of economic power that render unilateral U.S. expansion less effective and more costly than it was at one time.[40]

Clear evidence of these changes was provided by the balance-of-payments deficits that followed the U.S. macroeconomic expansion of 1977–78. The Carter administration responded to the deficits by urging both Germany and Japan to expand as well. A positive response by Japan left Germany as the principal target of the administration's efforts. At the 1978 Bonn summit meeting, Germany agreed to stimulate its domestic economy by up to 1 percent of its GNP in exchange for a U.S. pledge to decrease its oil imports and raise its oil prices.[41] The coincidence of German reflation and a sharp increase in oil prices in 1979, however, produced that country's first current account deficit since 1965 and an inflation rate that exceeded 5 percent.[42] As a consequence, Germany has resolutely resisted subsequent U.S. requests that it stimulate its economy in the interest of reviving world economic growth. After the stock market fall of "Black Monday," as before, West Germany insisted that fundamental changes in its macroeconomic policy could not substitute for a U.S. refusal to pursue a stable domestic economic policy of its own.[43]

39. The following are among the obstacles to macroeconomic expansion in only one country: (1) A relatively small and open economy will see a large proportion of the stimulus it applies leak abroad. Thus its expansion of demand will have small effects on its own economy. If several countries expand simultaneously, however, the leakages will be contained within the group so that macroeconomic expansion will remain effective. (2) Absent coordinated expansion, any country attempting to stimulate its own economy threatens to depreciate its currency and thus to affect its own terms of trade adversely; again, macroeconomic coordination neutralizes this effect. See Richard N. Cooper, "Global Economic Policy in a World of Energy Shortage," in Joseph Pechman and N. J. Simletz, eds., *Economics in the Public Sector* (New York: Norton, 1982), pp. 104–5; see also Randall Hinshaw, ed., *World Recovery without Inflation?* (Baltimore: Johns Hopkins University Press, 1985), pp. 23–52.

40. The U.S. traded goods sector has expanded: in 1950, for example, U.S. exports and imports were 8.3 percent of gross national product (GNP); in 1985, however, they accounted for 23.2 percent of U.S. output. Moreover, as Western Europe and Japan recovered economically from World War II, the size of the U.S. economy relative to that of the rest of the world declined: in 1950, U.S. GNP was 33 percent of world GNP; by 1986, the corresponding figure was 23 percent. See Alan J. Stogh, "If America Won't Lead," *Foreign Policy*, no. 64 (Fall 1986), pp. 80–81, 88.

41. By mid-1978, Germany also had strong domestic economic and political reasons to turn toward expansion. For an analysis of the Bonn summit, see Robert D. Putnam and Nicholas Payne, *Hanging Together: The Seven-Power Summits* (Cambridge, Mass.: Harvard University Press, 1984).

42. George deMenil, "From Rambouillet to Versailles," in deMenil and Anthony M. Solomon, eds., *Economic Summitry* (New York: Council on Foreign Relations, 1983), p. 26.

43. Germany did, however, undertake several small changes in its economic policy in late 1987 in apparent response to U.S. pressure. The Bundesbank lowered the key

The net result of the locomotive debate has been a continuing political deadlock on the issue of global economic expansion. The deadlock reflects the inconsistent effects of the changing postwar balance of power. While empowering the United States to demand that its allies assume some responsibility for the steady growth of world demand, the restoration to Western Europe and Japan of political and economic stability has also enabled its allies to resist its demands that they do so. Apart from their divergent preferences with respect to macroeconomic expansion, both Germany and Japan prefer to continue to free ride on the global effects of U.S. expansion.[44]

The deadlock, however, is less important in and of itself than for its implications for the future of the liberal international economic order as a whole. The locomotive debate has remained self-contained; it has not spilled over into other issues equally central to the future stability of the postwar economic order. Thus neither the Tokyo Round of GATT negotiations nor preliminary negotiations over the opening of the Uruguay Round seem to have been adversely affected by the continuing controversy over global reflation. Nor has there been any apparent weakening of the commitment to the larger regime of any of the countries either directly or indirectly engaged in the locomotive debate.

The course and outcome of the locomotive debate are typical of intraalliance disputes. After the Europeans made several apparently minimal concessions to its requests, the Reagan administration in November 1982 lifted the embargo it had imposed less than six months before on the export by U.S. subsidiaries and licensees of pipeline equipment to the USSR.[45] Similarly, the sharp conflict of interests between the EC and the United States on trade in agricultural products, reflecting the U.S. comparative advantage in that sector, was papered over during the Tokyo Round by an agreement to establish a consultative council on improving trade in agricultural goods.[46] Conflicts over trade in more restricted product ranges—as in the case of steel, for example—have

---

discount rate to 2.5 percent as of 4 December, and the government increased its interest rate subsidy to and the lending capacity of its Reconstruction Loan Corporation and also raised investment in the postal service. For more detailed information about these and other measures of similar scale, see *The Week in Germany*, 4 December 1987, p. 5.

44. Not even all academic observers are convinced that there are great benefits to coordinated expansion by the United States, Germany, and Japan. For a skeptical view, see Gilles Oudiz and Jeffrey Sachs, "Macroeconomic Policy Coordination among the Industrial Economies," *Brookings Papers on Economic Activity*, 1984 no. 1: 1–75. As Oudiz, Sachs, and their critics note, however, there are a variety of reasons to believe that the gains from coordination may be much larger than the calculations in the article admit.

45. For a discussion, see Putnam and Payne, *Hanging Together*, chap. 10. For an interesting analysis that emphasizes the benefits to West German industry of the U.S. attempt to impose export embargoes on the USSR, see Gerd Junne, "Competitiveness and the Impact of Change: Applications of High Technology," in this volume.

46. See Winham, *International Trade and the Tokyo Round Negotiation*, chap. 4.

also been resolved without significant escalation,[47] and the United States and its European allies have sometimes found common cause in the restriction of trade in other products.[48]

Thus it seems improbable that any fundamental threat to the international economic order will develop out of existing intra-alliance economic conflicts. In particular, it seems very unlikely that the EC will act on suggestions that it surround itself with an economic "fortress."[49] The history of the European Monetary System (EMS) since its inception in 1979 is less an indication of a transition than a suggestion of the formidable barriers that lie in the path of any attempt to create a European fortress as a substitute for the existing international economic order.

Among these barriers are the costs it would impose on competitive industries within the EC and on the constituent member states of the European Community. In the long run, efficient EC industries would be neither willing nor able to support the continued subsidization of inefficient industries within Western Europe. Moreover, only approximately half of the trade of the larger EC members is intra-EC trade; the potential for trade wars, therefore, is another significant deterrent to the formation of an EC trading bloc.[50] The highly unequal distribution of budgetary burdens within the EC also argues against a substantial increase in EC barriers to outside trade.[51]

47. For a discussion of the EC-U.S. steel controversy, see Marina v. N. Whitman, "Persistent Unemployment: Economic Policy Perspectives in the United States and Western Europe," in Andrew J. Pierre, ed., *Unemployment and Growth in the Western Economies* (New York: Council on Foreign Relations, 1984), pp. 14–52.

48. Textiles is perhaps the most notable example, but there are other less obvious cases in which producers in both importing and exporting countries have apparently profited from the continuation of import restraints. For a history of cooperation in the imposition of barriers to textile imports, see Vinod K. Aggarwal, *Liberal Protectionism: The International Politics of Organized Textile Trade* (Berkeley: University of California Press, 1985). For a very brief discussion of the willingness of Japan to maintain export controls on autos and of Korea and Taiwan to maintain controls on footwear after the United States was willing to allow them to expire, see Vinod K. Aggarwal, Robert O. Keohane, and David B. Yoffie, "The Dynamics of Negotiated Protectionism," *American Political Science Review* 81 (June 1987): 358, 362.

49. Contending that the European welfare state cannot survive increasing export competition from the United States, Japan, and the NICs, Wolfgang Hager argued in 1982 that a resort to protection at the European Community level was the only alternative to either a revival of class warfare or an erosion of the EC itself. See Hager's "Little Europe, Wider Europe and Western Economic Cooperation," *Journal of Common Market Studies*, September–December 1982, pp. 171–97, and "Fortress Europe: A Model?" in Stephen A. Musto and Carl. F. Pinkele, eds., *Europe at the Crossroads: Agendas of the Crisis* (New York: Praeger, 1985), pp. 65–76.

50. For West Germany in 1981, for example, imports from other EC countries stood at 48.2 percent of total FRG imports; other EC countries absorbed 46.9 percent of West Germany's exports. See El-Agraa, "Basic Statistics of the EC," p. 62.

51. Germany remains "by far the biggest 'net contributor' in the Community; thus it financed almost two-thirds of the transfer of resources effected through the Community budget in 1983" ("The Financial Relations of the Federal Republic of Germany with the European Communities since the Beginning of the Eighties," *Deutsche Bundesbank Monthly Report*, August 1985, p. 44).

Nor should the survival of the EMS to date be interpreted as strong evidence of an emerging European bloc; that survival reflects several serendipitous developments conducive to the fixed-rate exchange rate agreement. The long-term survival of the EMS as a support for any Fortress Europe depends on the inclusion of all EC members in it and on a convergence of macroeconomic policy that remains problematic. Even the EC's highly publicized commitment to dismantle all internal trade barriers by 1992 should be treated with some skepticism. In 1970 and again in 1972, for example, EC members agreed on 1980 as the deadline for economic and monetary union. Moreover, as Willy de Clerq, the EC's commissioner of external relations, recently observed, there is no necessary relationship between lowering internal and raising external barriers to EC trade.[52]

International and alliance politics also argue strongly against any resort to autarky by the EC. The continuing bipolarity of the international system drives Western Europe, Japan, and the United States together in a defense of their common interests against the Soviet Union. Particularly in an era of intense congressional concern about American competitiveness, it is unlikely that the U.S. commitment to West European security would survive intact the challenge to U.S. economic interests implied by the creation of Fortress Europe.

The advent of bipolarity largely eliminated the great power rivalry that deterred an effective international response to the Great Depression. Because only the United States among them now ranks as a great power, the members of the small group of industrialized states that form the core of existing international economic regimes are no longer as inhibited as they were in the interwar period by concerns about the distribution of gains from economic exchange. Although each state would prefer a larger to a smaller share, the absence of any security implications attached to any given distribution renders the issue much less politically divisive than it was earlier. Thus states belonging to the Western alliance are now free to focus on the absolute gains that accrue to each of them as the consequence of economic cooperation.

The transformation of the international system from multipolarity to bipolarity also offers these states an incentive to avoid the economic nationalism that marked their responses to the Great Depression. It has led members of the Western alliance to recognize that their power and security are inextricably linked. This recognition, in turn, strongly encourages each state to forego efforts to export unemployment. When the exported costs are borne by allied states, the induced reduction in their welfare also reduces the welfare of the would-be exporter. Analo-

52. *New York Times*, 31 July 1988, sec. 4, p. 1.

gously, the incentive to lower barriers to trade is strengthened when the benefits of such action accrue primarily to allied states.

Thus because bipolarity links the security interests of a core group of industrialized states to each other, it diminishes the significance of the inherently zero-sum issue of the intragroup division of gains from cooperation. It also internalizes within the group both the benefits of free trade and the costs of efforts to export unemployment. As a result, it imposes fairly narrow boundaries on the extent to which existing international economic regimes are likely to degenerate into a series of nationalistic actions by states at the core of these regimes. Indeed, the bipolar distribution of international power offers a compelling explanation for the virtual absence during the last fifteen years of challenges to basic premises of the postwar regimes, as well as an explanation of those changes that have occurred.

The international foundations of the recent return to prosperity of much of German industry seem secure. Because the postwar international economic regimes are inextricably tied to systemic politics, only a fundamental disruption of the international political system is likely to lead to their disintegration. Such a disruption, however, is unlikely. Inherent in a bipolar distribution of international power are substantial safeguards against any breakdown of the international order. In the 1930s, an Adolf Hitler could exploit the gaps in systemic security left by multipolarity: the expansion of Nazi Germany was the product at the international level of attempts by each of the major status-quo states to shift the burden of maintaining the balance of power to others. The postwar system of bipolarity leaves much less room for error: the tacit division of much of the globe into U.S. or Soviet spheres of influence suggests that one of the two superpowers is very likely to respond forcefully to any attempt to challenge the existing order.

That a bipolar system seems relatively secure against the forces of disequilibrium that inhere in a multipolar system is not necessarily a blanket guarantee of the stability of the contemporary international political system or of its constituent economic regimes. The maintenance of a bipolar system does not depend only on the ability of its two great powers to deter third states from threatening that order; it also depends critically on the willingness and ability of those great powers to remain great powers. Thus the current international political system remains as vulnerable to significant change as there are ways in which domestic political and economic patterns can depart from the interests of states as international actors.

CHAPTER THREE

Social Change and Political
Mobilization in West Germany

JOST HALFMANN

Social movements not only respond to pressing social problems, they actively define them. Social movements spring up when social institutions perpetuate manifest injustices[1] or when "collective goods" are no longer unequivocally acknowledged as benefits. Protesting against the deployment of Euromissiles in the early 1980s, the West German peace movement claimed that the missiles reduced West German security rather than restoring a credible system of deterrence. Albert Hirschman points to the potential for disagreement over definitions of collective goods, especially when they are provided by the government: "He who says public goods, says public evils. . . . What is a public good for some— say a plentiful supply of police dogs and atomic bombs—may well be judged a public evil by others in the same community."[2] Social movements articulate social problems by defining and dramatizing issues that hitherto were not considered issues. The women's movement of the nineteenth century started from the observation that a blatant discrepancy existed between the egalitarian pathos of bourgeois society and the exclusion of women from political (especially electoral) participation. The early women's movement fought against the established male belief that female sovereignty had to stop short of the political sphere.

As long as there are social problems in a society and space to define

1. Barrington Moore, *Injustice: The Social Bases of Obedience and Revolt* (White Plains, N.Y.: Sharpe, 1978).
2. Albert O. Hirschman, *Exit, Voice and Loyalty* (Cambridge, Mass.: Harvard University Press, 1970), p. 101. For an illuminating discussion of the role of public goods for the emergence of social protest, see William A. Gamson, *The Strategy of Social Protest* (Homewood, Ill.: Dorsey, 1975), chap. 5.

and interpret them, there will be social movements. This truism needs no further elaboration. It is interesting, however, to ask whether and how social movements are capable of affecting existing institutions or elite modernization strategies. Not all social movements pursue radical political goals, and not all historical political configurations allow for major social change.

The history of the Federal Republic of Germany abounds with social movements and protest activities. The 1950s and 1960s were full of political turbulence: the mine workers in the Ruhr area staged large demonstrations in the late 1950s when coal extraction was reduced in the wake of cheap oil imports from the Near East; a succession of peace movements accompanied the formation of the West German army in the mid-1950s (the *ohne-mich* movement) and the deployment of American atomic weapons on West German soil (the Kampf dem Atomtod movement); the student movement of the 1960s nearly managed to build a coalition with some unions and the Social Democratic party in an attempt to prevent the Emergency Powers Act from being ratified by the West German parliament.

But during these turbulent periods no serious observer of West Germany concluded that social movements were causing the Federal Republic to deviate from a course of stable growth, moderate political change, and low-profile foreign policy. Only since the 1970s have social movements affected the political system; such movements found maneuvering space when formerly stable relationship between voters and parties partially disintegrated.[3]

Whereas in the 1950s and 1960s social movements rarely received recognition from the established parties, media, and cultural elites, today hardly anyone publicly opposes ecological considerations in industrial modernization or equal civil rights for women. The social movements of the 1970s and 1980s have succeeded in gathering mass support of proportions unprecedented in the history of West Germany. The antinuclear movement, aided by the nuclear accidents at Harrisburg and Chernobyl, nearly succeeded in convincing a stable majority of the West German population of the risks of nuclear energy;[4] the peace movement drew up to three hundred thousand protesters at the height of the demonstrations against the deployment of the Cruise and Pershing II missiles in 1983. The squatters movement created serious strife within the city governments of Berlin (in 1983–84) and Hamburg (1987) over how to act vis-à-vis massive seizures of empty and unused housing space. The environmental movement can claim to have pushed

3. Max Kaase, "The Challenge of the 'Participatory Revolution' in Pluralist Democracies," *International Political Science Review* 5 (1984): 299–318.

4. Emnid-Institut, "Umfrage zur Kernenergie," *Der Spiegel* 20 (1986): 28–32.

the government toward measures stricter than in any other European country. And the women's movement is strong enough to prevent Helmut Kohl's coalition government of Christian Democrats and Free Democrats from revising abortion laws that were liberalized under the Schmidt government in the mid-1970s.

The history of these social movements raises several questions. First, can the wave of social protest in the 1970s and 1980s be related to social and economic changes in the Federal Republic? Second, are these movements significantly different from earlier movements? And, third, can we conclude from some spectacular events—for example, huge anti-nuclear demonstrations or coalition pacts between the SPD and the Greens party to form a government in the state of Hesse—that these movements have made some impression on the political or industrial elites? Social movements and new political parties like the Greens in West Germany do not seem to be a transient phenomenon of advanced industrial societies. New political parties with ecological and so-called left-libertarian programs have appeared on the political stage in several European countries.[5] These movements and parties are an expression of social, economic, and political changes whose unresolved consequences provide the fertile soil from which organized social conflict emerges.

Social movements and left-libertarian parties in West Germany are particularly interesting because the country shares many economic and social features with other smaller and medium-sized northern European welfare states, yet it is apparently deviating from its own history of high institutional stability and strong voter affiliation to political parties. Among the features that favor the emergence of social movements and new parties is the expansion of the educational system, which since the school and university reforms of the 1960s has provided more opportunities to women and working-class youths. The ensuing mobilization of large parts of the population has not only encouraged more critical attitudes toward traditional lifestyles and values but also fueled demands that go well beyond the interest in material well-being. The quest for better quality of life, protection from technological risks, or less competitive forms of social relations has diffused from small professional elites with so-called postmaterial values into the larger populace.

Another source of dissatisfaction is the way social services are provided by the welfare state: discontent with the bureaucratic nature and the alienating effects of many social services has led to organized protest by groups as diverse as the old and the handicapped. A third cause for concern among many citizens is the pursuit of technological projects

5. Herbert Kitschelt, "The Rise of Left-Libertarian Parties in Western Democracies: Explaining Innovation in Competitive Party Systems," Working paper no. 8, Duke University Program in International Political Economy (Durham, N.C., 1986).

53

whose undesirable consequences are only hesitantly acknowledged by the public authorities; spectacular technological accidents as well as damage to the environment have increased resistance and skepticism toward the established course of industrial and social modernization.

The feminist, the self-help, and the antinuclear movements are thus offsprings of the economic and social changes that many advanced industrial nations faced after World War II. Yet the emergence of social movements is not a simple result of the emergence of problems; these movements are an outgrowth of the economic and social modernization that confronts varying segments of a population with contradictory options. Existing social and political institutions do not seem to these segments to provide satisfactory solutions to current problems.

This double perspective—the social and economic changes that prompt social movements to emerge and the impressions these movements make on the social and political institutions—are the focus of this chapter. The specific German ingredient in this general northern European phenomenon is the relatively sudden development of these movements as a result of the removal of ideological and sociostructural barriers to social conflict in the late 1960s and early 1970s. After twenty years of Christian Democratic rule, the Social Democrats assumed power in 1969. Subsequently the reform programs of the Brandt government opened the floodgates for political expression and social demands that the Social Democrats neither expected nor were willing to satisfy.[6] For social movements and their perception of the West German society a new phase of the political and social process opened in the 1970s.

SOCIOECONOMIC CHANGE AND SOCIAL MOVEMENTS

Sociostructural Developments and Social Movements

Social movements become visible in society when social problems accumulate and the political opportunity structure allows them to intervene. When the 1970s opened, these two (relatively independent) developments coincided in the Federal Republic. The effects of social and economic changes became visible at the same time that the ideological and institutional rigidity of the political sphere of the 1950s and early 1960s began to relax.

In retrospect, the early 1970s seem a watershed for West Germany. In 1969 a Social Democratic government took over for the first time in postfascist history. The student movement had just introduced radical democratic demands into the political process, and many people viewed

6. Andrei Markovits and Jost Halfmann, "The Unraveling of West German Social Democracy," in Michael K. Brown, ed., *Remaking the Welfare State: Retrenchment and Social Policy in America and Europe* (Philadelphia: Temple University Press, 1988), pp. 183–226.

Willy Brandt's government as an initiator of social and political reforms. But the economic recessions of 1966–67 and 1969 had already signaled the decline of the economic miracle that had brought unprecedented wealth to many West Germans. Until around 1970 the Federal Republic seemed to be a model of economic reconstruction following the far-reaching destruction of material and social assets during World War II. The economic history of postwar Germany was characterized by the conjuncture of several favorable conditions.[7] Although much production equipment was destroyed during the war, some intangible assets of the West German economy were quickly restored for peacetime use: the quality of the labor potential remained high despite wartime casualties, and financial support and political integration by the Western allies gave West Germany quick access to international markets. Thus West Germany profited from a variety of favorable factors that drove the German economy to a high level of output, productivity, and income until the late 1960s.[8] The recessions of the late 1960s indicated that material well-being and social peace would no longer necessarily result from hard work, cooperative industrial relations, and paternalistic welfare state policies. The international conditions of national industrial policies and economic development also grew more restrictive and unstable.[9] Thus the end of the German miracle was signaled well before it became obvious in the mid-1970s.

Labor markets have changed significantly during the last forty years of West German history if we are to believe Burkart Lutz's theory of the "territorial annexation" (*Landnahme*) of traditional sectors by industrial capitalism. Among other factors, Lutz states, the economic miracle of West Germany in the 1950s and 1960s was based on the successful removal of barriers in the traditional sectors against the full inclusion of the work force in the labor market. Only after World War II was industrial capitalism able to absorb idle workers in the agricultural subsistence sector as well as in small manufacturing; similar developments took place in households. Between 1950 and 1970 more than 3.5 million workers moved from the agricultural sector into the industrial one. In private households the number of domestic help personnel shrank from six hundred thousand in 1950 to one hundred thousand in 1970. During the same period the number of employed women grew from 4 million to 7 million.[10] Women experience the most dramatic social consequences of this modernization process because productive and

7. Wolfgang Abelshauser, *Wirtschaftsgeschichte der Bundesrepublik Deutschland, 1945–1980* (Frankfurt: Suhrkamp, 1983).

8. Dirk Ipsen, *Die Stabilität des Wachstums* (Frankfurt: Campus, 1983).

9. Michael J. Piore and Charles Sabel, *The Second Industrial Divide* (New York: Basic Books, 1984), chap. 7.

10. Burkart Lutz, *Der kurze Traum immerwährender Prosperität* (Frankfurt: Campus, 1984), pp. 221–22.

reproductive activities, work and family life, are potentially contradictory options. The share of married women who also work outside the home rose from 34.6 percent in 1950 to 60.9 percent in 1975.[11] The integration of women into the labor markets was paralleled and supported by the educational mobilization of substantial numbers of women. In the 1970s and 1980s young women have entered the educational institutions in large numbers, and they are advancing further in the system than ever before in West German history. The share of female high school (*Gymnasium*) students rose from 36.5 percent in 1960 to 49.7 percent in 1981; the percentage of women students in universities rose from 23.9 percent in 1960 to 37.6 percent in 1981.[12]

Employment figures and educational levels notwithstanding, female equality has not been achieved, nor have women become fully integrated into all the professions. Women compete mostly with women in the labor markets and displace other women with lower qualifications; women have not entered top positions in industrial corporations, high courts, or universities to a degree commensurate with the number of formally qualified women in the work force.[13] Women are, however, threatened more severely by unemployment than are men. According to Ulrich Beck, "In 1983 more than 50% of the 2.5 million unemployed were women even though they contribute 30% fewer members to the work force."[14]

Education and salaried work have made traditional forms of marriage and partnership unattractive to many women. Younger women no longer want to be like their mothers but strive for the material autonomy of their fathers.[15] Marriage becomes less and less frequently a *Versorgungsgemeinschaft* (community of caring) with the male in the breadwinning role and the female in the child-rearing role; and more women than men have sought divorce in the recent decades. On the one hand, the traditional family is eroding; on the other, the nature of the standard (male) employment pattern is still inimical to female expectations of combined salaried work and child-rearing. Women are drawn into the labor markets, but they are among the first to lose their jobs when labor markets contract. Socioeconomic change has produced contradictory options for women and at the same time blocked the possibility of return

11. Elisabeth Beck-Gernsheim, "Vom 'Dasein für andere' zum Anspruch auf ein Stück 'eigenes Leben,'" *Soziale Welt* 3 (1983): 316, n. 42.

12. Ibid., p. 312.

13. Ulrich Beck, *Risikogesellschaft: Auf dem Weg in eine andere Moderne* (Frankfurt: Suhrkamp, 1986), pp. 166–67.

14. Ibid., p. 168.

15. Christel Eckart, "'Es führt kein Weg zurück': Historische Veränderungen der Existenzsicherung von Frauen durch Ehe und Erwerbstätigkeit," *Kommune* 5 (1986): 23–30.

to the traditional family. Thus many women are forced to shuttle between labor market and family.[16]

The Federal Republic had been pursuing the technology of civil nuclear energy in the 1950s, long before a significant social movement began to emerge. By the 1960s politicians, scientists, and industrialists became concerned about the huge technology gap between Europe and the United States. Energy producers and plant manufacturers seriously engaged in developing nuclear energy plants around 1967 when the third atomic program of the federal government was launched.[17] Ironically, during this period, when industrialists and politicians were busy switching from the experimental to the commercial stage in nuclear energy, the public took almost no interest in changes in domestic energy provision. Traditionally the general public had seen nuclear energy as a military issue. It had not been a political issue since the campaigns against the deployment of American nuclear weapons on West German territory during the 1950s had ended and the threat of a military confrontation between the superpowers had receded. In addition, the West German unions dropped their early support of the struggle against the deployment of nuclear weapons in Germany and came out strongly in favor of nuclear energy, a position fully in line with their positive attitude toward technological progress.[18]

The antinuclear movement emerged after the decision to expand the system of nuclear power plants had been made and construction had begun. The movement began to flourish in the early 1970s, when the economy was shaken by external shocks. The oil crisis of 1973 brought nuclear energy into the limelight as the cheapest (and cleanest) solution to rising fuel costs. For reasons independent of the economic climate, however, critics who noted safety problems in nuclear power plants were suddenly taken seriously. Concerns about containment during meltdowns, protection against sabotage, the prevention of proliferation, and thermic effects of the cooling systems used by power plants were publicly discussed; slowly the general indifference or optimism about nuclear energy was transformed into serious concern and resistance. Growing concerns with the nuclear community spilled over into the public at a moment when the general trust in the stability of the Modell Deutschland began to erode. Again, protest was stirred and magnified by contradictory signals and by a loss of confidence among the political, scientific, and industrial elites. The trade-offs between the (alleged) cost-

---

16. Christel Eckart, Ursula Jaerisch, and Helgard Kramer, *Frauenarbeit in Familie und Fabrik* (Frankfurt: Campus, 1980).

17. Joachim Radkau, *Aufstieg und Krise der deutschen Atomwirtschaft, 1945–1975* (Reinbek: Rowohlt, 1983), pp. 216–17.

18. Ibid., pp. 431–33.

effectiveness of nuclear energy and the risks of radiation began to split West Germany into different ideological camps.

Social Movements and Sociocultural Change

Social movements are not simply a product of social and economic change, they are also a genuine source of social change. Two examples will elucidate how social movements have shaped cultural habits and social perceptions. Typically, social movements do not simply deny old views but produce ambivalence by interpreting such views in new ways and by forcing social actors to integrate potentially controversial interpretations into a functioning perceptional structure.

The environmental movement grew out of various unconnected citizens' resistance to such diverse projects as highway and airport construction, chemical spills, and industrial emissions. One of the first influential coalitions of citizens' initiatives was the Bundesverband Bürgerinitiativen Umweltschutz (Federal Association of Citizens' Initiatives for Environmental Protection), founded in 1972.[19] Ecological protests became organized when wine growers in the Wyhl area protested the construction of a nuclear power plant.[20] In the 1970s, opposing the West German nuclear power program took most of the environmental movement's attention. Its greatest successes, however, were symbolic and cultural. Joseph Huber aptly sums up the prevailing public mood of the 1970s and 1980s: "Nobody can and will afford to be against ecology."[21] The environmental movement dramatized the negative effects of big industry on the environment and appealed to moral concerns about the exploitation of nature. Despite early resistance to the movement's doomsday prophesying and millenarianism among the media and political leaders, ecological concerns are now acknowledged as public responsibilities and as a stimulus for social and industrial innovations.

The influence of the environmental movement on public opinion shows even in the assessment of ecological demands among people whose livelihood depends on production activities that carry environmental risks. In a study based on interviews with unemployed workers, skilled workers in a chemical factory, and workers in environmentally neutral firms, Hartwig Heine and Rüdiger Mautz of the Sociological Research Institute (SOFI) in Göttingen have found that only a small percentage (around 14 percent) of those interviewed rejected ecological

19. Karl W. Brand, Detlef Büsser, and Dieter Rucht, *Aufbruch in eine andere Gesellschaft. Neue soziale Bewegungen in der Bundesrepublik* (Frankfurt: Campus, 1983), p. 93.

20. Dieter Rucht, *Von Wyhl nach Gorleben. Bürger gegen Atomprogramm und nukleare Entsorgung* (Munich: Beck, 1980).

21. Joseph Huber, *Die verlorene Unschuld der Ökologie. Neue Technologien und superindustrielle Entwicklung* (Frankfurt: Fischer, 1982), p. 14.

considerations and that almost 50 percent of all workers considered themselves more or less determined environmentalists.[22] Unemployed workers more strongly rejected the ecological agenda because it conflicted with their interest in getting a job. Most surprisingly, skilled workers in a big chemical factory shared the environmental concerns of other workers, although they were less willing to believe that their company posed a risk to the environment. Despite this difference in the group-specific risk assessment, Heine and Mautz believe that the chemical workers they sampled were sensitive to ecological problems because the company that employed them was committed to environmental awareness. Consequently, health and safety issues were taken seriously in the company, and workers took pride in supporting this policy. The main result of this study is that awareness of ecological risk is not subordinated to concerns about job security among a significant number of skilled chemical workers. There seems to be little doubt, the authors conclude, that the public criticism of risk technologies has transformed the perceptions of management and workers within such industries toward more proenvironmental attitudes.

The influence of social movements on cultural habits and perceptions can also be seen in the effect of the women's movement on men's perceptions of gender relations. The social mobilization of women in the postwar period has stimulated women to take an active stance in public life and to redefine their social relationships with men. Married women seek paid work more out of a desire for increased independence than for financial reasons.[23] One would expect men's traditional self-perceptions to be affected by such a development.

In 1986 Sigrid Metz-Göckel and Ulla Müller conducted a study of German men between twenty and fifty years old. Their questionnaire focused on issues central to the new women's movement: abortion, violence against women, division of household work, and comparable worth. The responses of men in 1986 differ in many respects from the responses of men in the mid-1970s when Helge Pross conducted a similar study. Pross concluded that German men still had a conservative attitude toward women. Men saw themselves as breadwinners and women as housewives. Today, because of female mobilization men take ambivalent positions vis-à-vis female emancipation. Only a small minority of men still believe that breadwinning is an exclusively male privilege. Yet the majority of men reveal a discrepancy between preference and prac-

22. Hartwig Heine and Rüdiger Mautz, "Haben Industriefacharbeiter Probleme mit dem Umweltthema?" *Soziale Welt* 39 (1988): 123–143. Since the authors interviewed only 117 workers and could not check their results against a randomly selected control group, they do not make strong claims concerning the representativeness of their findings.

23. Sigrid Metz-Göckel and Ulla Müller, "Partner oder Gegner? Überlebensweise der Ideologie vom männlichen Familienernäher," *Soziale Welt* 38 (1987): 9.

tice in their attitudes toward female employment. More than 80 percent of the men think that women with small children should stay at home while their partners work, but only 50 percent of the men would personally pursue such a strategy.[24] Almost 60 percent of the men with employed female partners, but only 40 percent with nonemployed female partners, believe that their own jobs could be done by women.[25] The authors find a "subdued conservatism" among German men, who tend publicly to accept but personally oppose the major demands of the new women's movement.

Rights, Risk, and Reciprocity

The relations between social and economic change and social movements are complex and difficult to discern. What share in men's attitudinal changes toward women can be attributed to the new women's movement? How important is evolution or generational change? Demands that older men may conceive of as an assault on established privileges, the next generation of men may consider normal. In addition, established social actors such as parties, unions, professional associations, and the media set their own agendas and often try to absorb and modify the positions initially introduced by social movements.

The only viable strategy for deciding these questions is to identify issues that were first raised or rediscovered and dramatized by a social movement and to relate them to the interests and strategies of the established institutions and actors. The fault lines along which new demands and resistance to them converge will be the starting point for the analysis of social movements; the changes in perceptions and attitudes of the established actors and institutions can then be understood as the impact of the social movement.[26] The following classification is meant systematically to relate social and economic change to the emergence and contents of social movements. The distinction between different types of social movements will help to identify types of social protest which are historically new and to distinguish them from those activities which seem to be modified versions of traditional forms of social conflict.

I suggest using a definition of social movements which is general enough to include many different movements but strict enough to distinguish social movements from interest groups, formal organizations, citizens' initiatives, or political parties. Social movements are triggered by social problems whose solution is envisaged in the context of a

24. Ibid., p. 20.
25. Ibid., p. 25.
26. Social movements also change in this process; but in this chapter emphasis will be on the changes they accomplish.

more or less complex future institutional reorganization of society; social movements pursue activities that are geared toward increasing public support and participation and discrediting social institutions or elites that are viewed as causing the social problems; social movements are characterized by loose organizational structures, informal membership roles, and little hierarchical differentiation.[27] The development of (utopian) concepts of institutional rearrangement distinguishes social movements from citizens' initiatives, which usually pursue single issues. The organizational structure sets social movements apart from formal organizations; and the attempt to delegitimize established practices, institutions, or elites separates social movements from interest groups.

I propose to distinguish between three themes in contemporary social movements: rights, risk, and reciprocity.[28] Rights movements continue the tradition of struggle for civil, economic, and social rights. They seek full inclusion in the political and social process. Their strategic goal is equality, justice, and the removal of delegitimized privileges. I will include the equality-oriented goals of the women's movement ("equality-feminism") and the civil and welfare rights movements in this group.

Risk movements oppose critical developments in the realm of risk technologies and risk policies. Military rivalries have increased the potential for catastrophic consequences of such technologies as atomic weapons; and in civil nuclear energy and genetic engineering the relations of science and technology to society seem to have changed. Scientific and technical experiments are no longer confined to the laboratory; instead whole societies have become the testing ground for new knowledge. Some technologies (nuclear energy, nuclear weapons, genetic engineering, toxic chemicals) contain a high catastrophic potential.[29] Risk movements oppose risk technologies and policies and attempt to control the collective goods that these movements see as monopolized by the state. The goal of these movements is independence from the state and control over such collective goods as peace, personal health, and the environment. The main representatives of risk movements are the peace movement, the antinuclear movement, the environmental movement, and the anti-gene-splicing movement.

The reciprocity movements focus on social interaction. In all ad-

27. For a similar definition see Norbert F. Schneider, *Ewig ist nur die Veränderung: Entwurf eines analytischen Konzepts sozialer Bewegungen* (Frankfurt: Peter Lang, 1987).

28. For reasons of clarity in the presentation of contemporary social movements I will equate themes with specific types of movements. This strategy extinguishes overlaps and ambiguities in social movements; the women's movement in West Germany, for instance, is not clearly divided into rights- and reciprocity-oriented parts. But by highlighting certain themes in social movements rather than concentrating on the concrete appearance of these movements it is possible to assess the implications of their goals and demands for social change.

29. Charles Perrow, *Normal Accidents: Living with High Risk Technologies* (New York: Basic Books, 1984).

vanced industrial-capitalist nations modernization has resulted in re-structuring of the social division of labor and the relations between labor and leisure time, wage earners and "gratis" workers (such as unpaid household workers), men and women. The dissolution of traditional social ties; the absence of a sense of belonging in class milieus, professional groups, or family structures; the growing risk of unemployment (a permanent threat to growing numbers of people throughout their working lives); and the intellectual mobilization through lifelong requirements for continuous education have produced a social climate in which life is full of risks and responsibility for each individual faces these risks; individualism (or rather, privatism) has expanded beyond the realms of markets and politics. The reciprocity movements comprise the radical feminist part of the women's movement ("equity-feminism"), the alternative movement, and the self-help movement. Risk and reciprocity movements and rights movements differ mainly in their goals. The former anticipate social utopias in which the community has tamed the drives toward more risk taking and the dissolution of social ties; the latter struggle for inclusion in existing social institutions. They want to perfect, not abolish or drastically remodel, these institutions.

Rights Movements

The emergence of rights movements—or rather, the transformation of revolutionary movements into rights movements—is a result of the politics of inclusion by the state and the ruling elites, according to T. H. Marshall.[30] By granting civil, economic, and social rights in successive stages, the political elites of the eighteenth and nineteenth centuries pacified the (potentially) revolutionary zeal of the poor and gradually allowed the political system to be transformed into the modern welfare state. Contemporary rights movements are concerned with completing the goal of including all adult members of a society into the welfare state: civil rights movements and welfare rights movements[31] as well as the equality-oriented women's movement[32] struggle for unrestricted recognition of individual rights of inclusion. The inclusion of all citizens in the political process has been institutionalized as participatory democracy, and it is built on the disappearance of the earlier revolutionary concept of democracy as participation of the citizens in all societal affairs.

The establishment of a societal collectivity (and the semantics of democracy that accompanies this process) put the state in a central position

30. T. H. Marshall, "Citizenship and Social Class," in Marshall, *Class, Citizenship and Social Development* (Chicago: University of Chicago Press, 1977), pp. 71–134.

31. Frances F. Piven and Richard A. Cloward, *Poor People's Movement* (New York: Vintage Books, 1979), chap. 4.

32. Ethel Klein, *Gender Politics* (Cambridge, Mass.: Harvard University Press, 1984).

of societal development. The state has become the main modernization agency and the central addressee for complaints about endangered collective goods. Ironically, the interventionist state and welfare capitalism, developed as solutions to the social problems of nineteenth-century capitalism, have led to new social problems: the collective disadvantages of capitalism threaten to undermine the fabric of the social consensus, and the modernization drives of public bureaucracies and private entrepreneurs cut deeply into established modes of interaction. The risks of modernization and the disappearance of established ligatures have stimulated the emergence of risk and reciprocity movements.

Risk Movements

Modern social movements differ from traditional movements in their concept of a collective good. Whereas rights movements conceive of the democratic political community as allowing the execution of individual rights, new social movements emerge because of the individual and collective abuse they perceive of collective goods like peace, the environment, and health. New social movements emerge because the pursuit of individual rights and participation in representative democracy do not seem to provide a solution to the problems incurred by risk technologies and privatism.

Risk movements are concerned with "dread risks"; their strategic goal is sovereignty rather than liberty or participation. Risk movements want access to decision making about technologies and policies that contain catastrophic potential and are more or less created and regulated by the state.

This definition of risk movements has four implications.

First, risk movements address the catastrophic potential of risk technologies and policies. Some modern technologies are qualitatively different from older technologies in their potential for global, irreversible, and universal catastrophes. Social movements make risk an object of concern when dread is involved: the distinction between tolerable and intolerable risks[33] depends on whether risks can be controlled, whether they are involuntary or unequally distributed, and whether they will increase over time.

Second, risk movements confront the risky effects of technologies on collective goods. High-risk technologies threaten people directly, but protection from these risks is not fully within the reach of individuals. One can stop smoking (although the dangers of passive smoking teach a lesson about the limits of individual preventive strategies), but one

33. Paul Slovic, Baruch Fischhoff, and Sarah Lichtenstein, "Facts and Fears: Understanding Perceived Risk," in Richard C. Schwing and Walter A. Albers, eds., *Societal Risk Assessment: How Safe Is Safe Enough?* (New York: Plenum Press, 1980), pp. 181–212.

cannot stop eating (when all food is contaminated by a nuclear plant accident). Social movements dramatize the irony that the achievement of physical well-being is a highly individualized endeavor but, at the same time, increasingly dependent on collective provisions.

Third, some of these new collective goods (like health) have become public goods. The preservation of personal health or physical identity is becoming more and more dependent on physical, monetary, and legal provisions of the state. When many collective goods are public goods and risks surrounding their quality increase, social movements have to address the state rather than other individuals, interest groups, or private enterprises.

Finally, risk movements emerge because people learn that the individual pursuit of interests cannot guarantee avoidance of the feared risks. Risk movements aim at controlling decisions about collective goods. Unlike rights movements, they try to achieve control over collective goods by circumventing the state or disassociating themselves from it: declaring "autonomous zones" or secluding themselves from political and social life (by founding communes, for example) are some ways in which they attempt to realize the metagoal of sovereignty to which participatory strategies like litigation, bargaining, and lobbying are considered complementary activities rather than political goals in their own right.

In new social movements we witness the revival of the idea that Thomas Hobbes criticized vehemently in his *Leviathan*: the polity consists of two sovereign bodies, the ruler and the people who engage in a social contract. Since Hobbes, European political thought has been overwhelmingly influenced by the notion that there can be only one source of sovereignty—the people—and only one locus of executing sovereignty—the state. Modern societies are based on this division between the provision and the execution of sovereignty.[34] New social movements—when focusing on technological risks or the strain of individualism—wish to enhance the role of the community by trying to restrict state sovereignty in decision making and policy executing. The most extreme version of this attempt might be the separation of the community or parts of it from the state. This is the idea behind some (sectarian) North American communes in remote areas of the United States.[35] Less radical forms of enhancing the role of the community against the state

34. Francis H. Hinsley, *Sovereignty*, 2d ed. (Cambridge: Cambridge University Press, 1986), p. 222.

35. Mary Douglas and Aaron Wildavsky, *Risk and Culture: An Essay on the Selection of Technological and Environmental Risks* (Berkeley and Los Angeles: University of California Press, 1983); Jost Halfmann, "Risk Avoidance and Sovereignty: New Social Movements in the United States and West Germany," *Praxis International* 1 (1988): 14–25.

are demands for strengthening the plebiscitarian element in the constitution.[36]

Reciprocity Movements

Modernization of industrial-capitalist and democratic societies has led to the formation of social systems based on media of communication (truth, power, money) rather than on consensus, convention, or tradition. Ralf Dahrendorf has tried to capture the consequences of this form of modernization for the social actors in the two categories of dissolving ligatures and expanding options.[37] Life chances are individualized, ligatures (direct social ties) no longer facilitate lifestyle decisions, and the growing options have to be negotiated with those institutions and bureaucracies which—as agents of the welfare state—have helped dissolve the ligatures.[38] Social movements that address the risks of identity center around motives of community and reciprocity. There are three contemporary reciprocity movements: the alternative, the self-help, and the equity-oriented part of the women's movement.

The alternative movement highlights the risks of the individualization of a working life. Since the original desires of past social movements for protection against the hazards of wage labor have been transformed into rights to health, unemployment, and accident insurance, wage earners no longer address the welfare state as members of a collectivity but as individuals. Under conditions of the deregulation and erosion of the standard employment pattern,[39] social actors experience individualism and privatization not only as personal risk but also as subtle exclusion from the community of respected citizens. The flexibility of labor markets and the deregulation of the legal provisions for a "normal" employment pattern tend to erode the established model of community, namely, the participation of the employed (as holders of certain rights) in the community of the welfare state. When these ties disappear, individualism becomes alienation, and no subsidiary structures compensate for the loss of participation in the community of holders of social rights. When risks in the work life become entirely privatized, resistance to the system

36. For a discussion of this issue see Bernd Guggenberger and Claus Offe, *An den Grenzen der Mehrheiktsdemokratie. Politik und Soziologie der Mehrheitsregel* (Opladen: Westdeutscher Verlag, 1984).

37. Ralf Dahrendorf, *Lebenschancen* (Frankfurt: Suhrkamp, 1979).

38. Life chances are a function of options and ligatures, as Dahrendorf argues. Options and ligatures create potentially contradictory demands for individuals. "Ligatures create references and as a consequence foundations for action; options demand decisions and as a consequence openness for the future" (ibid., p. 51).

39. Martin Osterland, "Deregulation and Erosion of the Standard Employment Pattern: The Spread of Gray-Zone Work in the Federal Republic of Germany," paper presented at the Center for European Studies, Harvard University, 1986; see also Beck, *Risikogesellschaft*, chap. 6.

of individualized risk management becomes likely. Attempts at acquiring alternative forms of employment emerge which not only provide the means for a living but also offer some form of a (less formal) community. The alternative movement creates an informal sector of the economy in which nonstandardized forms of work are combined with cooperative forms of social organization.[40]

Similarly, the emergence of the self-help movement is a result of the standardization and juridification of human services. Again, the bureaucratic management of social services extracts clients from their social milieus and individualizes them. Such bureaucracies may ultimately undermine their own model of rationality: increasing control over the clients by standardizing services and individualizing claims may increase clients' needs for services, which may in turn push the bureaucracies to their limits. In the end, the clients may lose control over their lives and the bureaucracies over their resources.[41] Efforts to rationalize costs in the administration of social services may then lead clients to regain some autonomy by providing themselves with the necessary services.[42] The self-help movement originates in this interaction between individual clients and a human services bureaucracy that expands and contracts depending on its position in its own self-induced rationalization cycle.

The women's movement, especially when it pursues the theme of equity, owes its growth and importance (but not necessarily its origin) to the consequences of individualization of female life chances. Social inclusion in the welfare state and the political system created the basis for full citizen status. The attrition of the family and the massive inclusion of women in the labor process, however, created major contradictory options and expectations for women. The traditional form of marriage and the family, which institutionalized women's mothering and child-rearing roles, exacted a price from women by making them dependent. Since the "desertion" of men and women from traditional marriages[43] and the full inclusion of women in the political system and the labor markets, the formal inequality of gender relations is diminishing, although no social institution replaces marriage as the realm for child-rearing.

The lack of modern institutional provisions for child-rearing and the model of individualized pursuit of life chances stimulate resistance in

40. Rolf G. Heinze and Thomas Olk, "Selbsthilfe, Eigenarbeit, Schattenwirtschaft," in Frank Benseler, Rolf G. Heinze, and Arno Klönne, eds., *Zukunft der Arbeit* (Hamburg: VSA, 1985), pp. 13–29.

41. Klaus P. Japp, *Wie psychosoziale Dienste organisiert sind. Widersprüche und Auswege* (Frankfurt: Campus, 1986).

42. Jost Halfmann and Klaus P. Japp, "Grenzen sozialer Differenzierung—Grenzen des Wachstums öffentlicher Sozialdienste," *Zeitschrift für Soziologie* 10 (1981): 244–55.

43. Barbara Ehrenreich, *The Hearts of Men* (Garden City, N.Y.: Doubleday, 1983).

women, who struggle to reach a collective solution to the problem of child-rearing. It is in this context that "female values" of reciprocity and a "female concept of identity" as compassion are brought forward as alternatives to the (male) concept of identity as separateness.[44] The metagoal of this movement is reciprocity, a model of interaction based on the idea of community as compassion and responsibility. Since this idea of community is not restricted to child-rearing and family life, equity-feminism proposes a system of social organization which is counter to the established mode of individualized competitiveness.

SOCIAL MOVEMENTS AND POLITICAL CHANGE

The 1970s: The Political Arena Expands

In the last two decades social movements have received a great deal of attention and influenced public awareness with considerable success. Opinion research polls have discerned that up to 20 percent of the West German population has expressed disenchantment with the political performance of the government; a large share of this population segment can be regarded as the potential reservoir for social movements and new parties like the Greens.[45] The rise of social movements in West Germany has surprised observers as well as supporters of these movements because the political system in the Federal Republic has long been regarded as inaccessible to those with unconventional demands.[46]

Most contemporary social movements in West Germany date back to the end of Christian Democratic rule. The student movement that laid much of the groundwork for the new social movements flourished during the Grand Coalition of Christian and Social Democrats between 1966 and 1969. The Social Democratic party became the dominant political force in 1969. The decade that followed brought not only political changes and institutional reforms but also a general climate of cultural and political liberalization. The Social Democrats seemed to be able to provide solutions to the recessions of 1966–67 and 1969. Chancellor Willy Brandt's foreign policy of détente and reconciliation with Eastern Europe as well as his domestic reforms (the Works Constitution Act, the divorce and abortion laws, the university reforms) tackled

44. Such values stem from a socialization oriented toward caring for others; see Carol Gilligan, *In a Different Voice: Psychological Theory and Women's Development* (Cambridge, Mass.: Harvard University Press, 1982).

45. Helmut Kistler, *Bundesdeutsche Geschichte. Die Entwicklung der Bundesrepublik seit 1945* (Stuttgart: Bonn Aktuell, 1986), p. 357.

46. Herbert Kitschelt, "Political Opportunity Structures and Political Protest: Anti-Nuclear Movements in Four Democracies," *British Journal of Political Science* 16 (1985): 57–85.

JOST HALFMANN

pressing problems. In addition, the Social Democratic government initiated administrative reforms (introducing planning staff in the federal ministries, emphasizing interdepartmental coordination) that provided institutional answers to the problems of increased welfare state intervention[47] and as an unintended side effect removed the air of the *Obrigkeitsstaat* that characterized the German state under conservative rule. For even more influential than the administrative and political reforms and the material benefits of expanded welfare programs was the impression many West Germans had of a growing democratic political culture that stimulated them to increased political participation.

The strength of the West German system rests primarily on the interplay of interest groups and voluntary associations. Peter Katzenstein argues that the stability and continuity of West Germany relies equally on state institutions and what he calls parapublic institutions: the social welfare funds, the Labor Office, the Federal Reserve, and media such as public television and radio.[48] The installation of the political institutions in the two German states was a product of the victors. The Western allies were strongly in favor of the decentralization of state power. The installation of the federalist principle, the delegation of political authority to the states (*Länder*) was meant to weaken the traditional power of the German centralized bureaucracies. The "demontage" of the strong state, the "loosening" of the relations between civil society and state power, came about in Germany not as a result of social movements but as an intervention by the victors after World War II. But in the course of West German history decentralization became a problem for effective government. The Social Democratic attempt at social and institutional reforms ran into serious difficulties in the mid-1970s. Under Chancellor Helmut Schmidt the coalition government of Free and Social Democrats abandoned the reformist ambitions of the Brandt period and subsequently implemented severe cuts in the "social net" that had been built and expanded in the years before.[49] But despite reduction in material welfare, social contestation remained strong, and some legal and political measures that contrasted markedly with the reform spirit of the early Social Democratic rule intensified the mobilization from below. The "Radicals' Decree" of 1972, for instance, which attempted to restrict the access of "enemies of the constitution" to the civil service was bitterly resisted throughout the 1970s. The abortion laws prompted similar reactions within the women's movement. Political debate and conflict

47. Peter Katzenstein, *Policy and Politics in West Germany: The Growth of a Semisovereign State* (Philadelphia: Temple University Press, 1987), pp. 259–63; Fritz W. Scharpf, *Planung als politischer Prozess* (Frankfurt: Suhrkamp, 1973).
48. Katzenstein, *Policy and Politics in West Germany,* pp. 58–76.
49. Markovits and Halfmann, "Unraveling of West German Social Democracy."

continued through the 1970s. It is a curious fact of West German history, however, that only after the reform period and the emergence of social movements did the public become aware that West Germany provided political space for diverging political interests and claims.

Social movements have effectively undermined the myth of the strong German state. Social movements seem capable of influencing input in the policy process: in the 1980s the Social Democratic party adopted some of the concepts of the peace movement when it proposed a plan to establish a nuclear-free zone in Europe; some of the ideas from the ecology movement are found in the SPD's most recent program for the ecological modernization of the economy; a Green party representative was nominated minister of the environment in Hesse; some grievances of the antinuclear movement have entered the political system and led to improved legal provisions and safety measures in nuclear power plants. But the persistent reluctance of West German governments to implement reform policies may undermine the advantages that social movements gain by capturing public attention.

The irony of the growing opportunity for social movements to influence the political agendas of parties and governments may be that the arena in which these movements have established themselves—high-level politics—may not be the most efficient level at which to transform social demands into functioning politics. Successes in high politics may distract from the fact that in the areas where social movements seek change—for example, work regulations that allow women to care for their children, compliance with environmental protection regulations by specific firms in specific towns, cancellation of drilling projects that explore possible underground deposits for nuclear waste—local and regional decision-making procedures and informal arrangements among established interest groups may block outsiders from participating directly in policy implementation. The potential for change in high-level politics may be undercut by the relative impermeability of the institutions in low-level politics.

The Effects of Social Movements on High-Level Politics

It is difficult to assess the impact of social movements. William Gamson has examined many protest groups and suggests that their success be defined in terms of their acceptance by their adversaries and the advantages they gain for their constituents. Gamson concentrates on gains made by protest groups.[50] In the context of this study, however, success needs to be assessed in terms of the impression a movement

---

50. Gamson, *Strategy of Social Protest*, pp. 28–29.

makes on its adversary. How do social movements change strategies of modernization, if at all? How do they succeed in delegitimizing elites and policies which they think increase social risks? What effects do movements have even when they do not achieve their metagoals?

Obviously, the impact of social movements depends on the openness of the society to the actions of unexpected and even unlicensed actors and policies that may be unusual, illegitimate, or even illegal. I suggest that the more complex the social change these movements hope to effect and the more institutions need to be remodeled, the less impact the movements will have, at least in the short run. Conversely, the more the demands of these movements can be transformed into incremental change and small innovations, and the less these innovations collide with the strategic thrust of the institutions that are addressed, the greater the impact of social movements will be. If these institutions or policies are already in flux, social movements have a real chance to determine their future development. The impact of social movements on society will be very different in the realms of high- and low-level politics. In high-level politics—the realm of institutionalized political participation and decision making, political parties, and the state—the impact of the West German social movements seems most spectacular: they and the Green party have achieved a major realignment and dealignment of voter behavior. The Green party may significantly influence the spectrum of political choices if it survives. But success in the electoral process does not necessarily mean real change in political practices and institutions. Therefore, low-level politics—the realm of public opinion and informal decision making in the gray zones between civil society and the state—is the political ground on which the flexibility of a society and the impact of social movements will be tested. The rise of new social movements has disproved the popular belief that West Germany is a nation with extremely stable political cleavages.[51] Next to the Netherlands, West Germany is the country with the highest degree and potential to mobilize social movements in Europe.[52] The most visible effect of contemporary social movements in Europe is the rise of new parties that differ significantly from established parties in the political goals they pursue, the form of organization they adopt, and the relations they establish with their constituency. These new parties may signal a realignment among voters. The emergence of a new party like the Greens in West Germany was made possible by three developments. First, established social cleav-

51. Joachim Hirsch, *Der Sicherheitsstaat. Das "Modell Deutschland," seine Krisen und die "neuen sozialen Bewegungen"* (Frankfurt: Europäische Verlagsanstalt, 1980).

52. Nicholas S. Watts, "Mobilisierungspotential und gesellschaftspolitische Bedeutung der neuen sozialen Bewegungen. Ein Vergleich der Länder der Europäischen Gemeinschaft," in Roland Roth and Dieter Rucht, eds., *Neue soziale Bewegungen in der Bundesrepublik Deutschland* (Frankfurt: Campus, 1987), pp. 47–67.

ages gradually lose significance for voters. Protestant workers, for example, no longer automatically vote for the SPD, and Catholic civil servants no longer unequivocally adhere to the CDU. Earlier regimes from Adenauer to Erhardt built their politics on well-entrenched sociostructural bases and sociopolitical interests and kept the opposition in check by denouncing its lack of competence and trustworthiness in the pursuit of the "common welfare."[53] The rise of the Social Democrats to power in the 1970s indicated a changed sociostructural and political scenario according to which political parties slowly but steadily witnessed the dissolution of clear-cut cleavages. Party loyalty has declined among West German voters since the 1970s: during the federal elections of 1976 only 25 percent of SPD supporters and 35 percent of CDU supporters stated that "under no conditions" would they vote for the major competitor.[54] The switch votes have grown to unprecedented dimensions. During the federal elections of 1987 28 percent of the voters changed their party preference; switch had grown by 6 percent since the elections of 1983.[55] The decreasing traditional party loyalty is also expressed in the growth of votes cast for small parties. In 1976 the big parties (CDU/CSU and SPD) attracted 91.2 percent of the vote and the small parties only 8.8 percent; in 1987 the big parties received 81.3 percent and the small parties 18.7 percent.[56] No doubt, traditional cleavages still ensure the established parties a large share of the votes,[57] but the switch votes will become increasingly important in determining which party will govern and with which coalition partner. Growing uncertainty about the number of loyal voters forces the big parties to pay attention to the small parties in order either to (re)gain their constituency or to qualify for a coalition with a smaller party.

A second factor behind the emergence of the Greens is that as voters' loyalty to parties decreases, the core constituencies of the parties are shrinking. In the course of industrial modernization, the share of industrial workers (a stronghold for the Social Democrats) among the working population has decreased from 51.0 percent in 1950 to 42.2 percent in

53. Gabriel Almond and Sidney Verba, *The Civic Culture* (Princeton: Princeton University Press, 1965); Juan Linz, "Cleavage and Consensus in West German Politics: The Early Fifties," in Seymour M. Lipset and Stein Rokkan, eds., *Party Systems and Voter Alignments: Cross-National Perspectives* (New York: Free Press, 1967), pp. 283–321.

54. David P. Conradt, "Changing German Political Culture," in Gabriel Almond and Sidney Verba, *The Civic Culture Revisited* (Boston: Little, Brown, 1980), p. 236.

55. Ursula Feist and Klaus Liepelt, "Modernisierung zu Lasten der Grossen. Wie die deutschen Volksparteien ihre Integrationskraft verlieren," *Journal für Sozialforschung* 3 (1987): 281.

56. Ibid., p. 277.

57. Manfred Berger et al., "Stabilität und Wechsel: Eine Analyse der Bundestagswahl 1980," in M. Kaase and Hans-Dieter Klingemann, eds., *Wahlen und politisches System. Analysen aus Anlass der Bundestagswahl 1980* (Opladen: Westdeutscher Verlag, 1983), pp. 22–57.

1981; similarly, the independent entrepreneurs, among them many small farmers (traditionally supporters of the CDU/CSU), have declined from 28.3 percent in 1950 to 11.7 percent in 1981; during the same period civil servants and clerical employees more than doubled their share of the working population from 20.6 percent to 46.1 percent.[58] This development has created serious concern among the major political parties about how to guarantee *Mehrheitsfähigkeit* (the capacity to attract the majority of the voters). In a research report for the executive committee of the SPD, the growth of *Wechselwähler* (switch votes) is considered the most important factor in the electoral process.[59] The competition among the major political parties will be focused on the two voter milieus in which most vote switching occurs: the so-called technocratic-liberal milieu (professionals, higher civil servants, clerical workers, and medium and small entrepreneurs), which presumably constitutes 11 percent of the population, and the upwardly mobile milieu (skilled workers and middle management), which supposedly constitutes 21 percent of the population. The size of these milieus and the reluctance of their members to develop party loyalty make political coalitions necessary and prevent the programmatic stagnation of the big parties.

The large number of independent voters has created serious problems in some states about how to build a government with a sufficient majority. During the 1987 state elections in Schleswig-Holstein, for instance, the CDU and the F.D.P. (today coalition partners on the federal level) together won 47.8 percent of the votes, while the SPD and the Greens (who did not qualify for representation in parliament with 3.9 percent of the votes) received 49.1 percent.[60] Since 1986 the CDU/F.D.P. coalition in Lower Saxony has governed with a one-vote majority. Election outcomes in the states of Hesse and Hamburg stalled effective government between 1983 and 1987. The common cause for these tendencies toward ungovernability is that despite the dependability of a certain level of voter support for the big parties, the attainment of the additional 5 percent (with a small coalition partner) to 10 percent (without a small coalition partner) illustrates the increasingly intractable problem of *Mehrheitsfähigkeit*.

Third, a significant number of citizens believe that political parties and governments do not provide solutions to the threats of social and technological risks. New social movements can be regarded as defining a new cleavage oriented toward soft modernization strategies (avoiding risk and emphasizing community) as opposed to hard modernization

58. Ibid., p. 27.
59. SPD, "Planungsdaten für die Mehrheitsfähigkeit der SPD. Ein Forschungsprojekt der SPD," mimeo, Bonn, 1984, p. 8.
60. *Frankfurter Allgemeine Zeitung*, 15 September 1987.

strategies (growth-oriented and geared toward international competi-tiveness). Joachim Raschke calls this new cleavage postindustrial.[61] This new cleavage has had two effects on the established party system in West Germany. First, the Green party, a "postindustrial framework party," is neither a "voter-maximizing" nor a traditional "integration" party, but a loose representation of claims by marginalized strata of society and of allegedly marginalized social problems (risks and individualism).[62] Sec-ond, the cleavage that is opened by new social movements cuts into at least one of the major parties. The SPD is confronted with an important ideological problem as it struggles to integrate the interests of clerical and industrial workers and those of the postmaterialistic professionals. The supporters of the new party, educated professionals in the service sector, will back the SPD only when postindustrial issues are included in its program and politics. Traditional loyalties to their working-class con-stituency (which holds materialist rather than postmaterialist values), however, will prevent the Social Democrats from adopting these new issues.

According to a representative study by a survey research institute, Infas, in 1986 approximately 15 percent of West Germans held post-materialist convictions and favored personal freedom, more democracy, and more social equality over law and order and a Protestant work ethic.[63] If parts of this segment continue to opt for a new party like the Greens, social movements and new parties may increase the costs of governability and *Mehrheitsfähigkeit* for the established parties, which may find it necessary to reconcile soft modernization alternatives and postmaterialistic claims with the demands of their traditional constituen-cies.

The Impacts of Social Movements on Low-Level Politics

Social movements develop complex expectations about the future re-organization of institutions. They not only pursue multiple-issue strat-egies, but in many cases they wish to replace their adversaries. New and old social movements differ, however, with respect to the depth of social change they desire. Rights movements may not wish to remodel institu-

61. Joachim Raschke, "Soziale Konflikte und Parteiensystem in der Bundesrepublik," *Aus Politik und Zeitgeschichte*, B 49/85 (1985): 22–39.

62. For a more detailed description of the characteristics of new parties, see Herbert Kitschelt, "New Social Movements and the Decline of Party Organization," paper pre-sented at a conference on "New Social Movements," Florida State University, Tallahassee, Florida, 2–4 April 1987.

63. Ursula Feist and Klaus Liepelt, "Modernisierung zu Lasten der Grossen. Wie die deutschen Volksparteien ihre Integrationskraft verlieren," *Journal für Sozialforschung* 3 (1987): 281.

tions but to replace those in privileged positions, to be included in established institutions, and to have the benefits reaped by those belonging to such institutions redistributed. Some factions within equality-feminism, for example, have demanded pay for housework (a redistribution of income) and the abolition of barriers to women's access to privileged positions. Risk movements, on the other hand, want more complex and radical social changes. The ecology movement, for instance, envisages a remodeling of big industry into small production units and of exploitive relations to nature into benign relations. The realization of such a utopia would require major institutional changes such as the demise or modification of growth-oriented market capitalism. Yet the complexity of movements' goals is not necessarily an obstacle to success, as Gamson shows convincingly.[64] The main problem for social movements lies somewhere else: "What really stands in the way of success for the ambitious challenger is not diffuse objectives but targets of change who are unwilling to cooperate in their own demise."[65] Not only adversary elites but the structure of institutions stand in the way of success for social movements. Meeting the demand of equity-feminism for a feminization of society (a social structure centered around values that are reproductive rather than productive) would entail not only changing men's perceptions of women and the family but also reformulating the distinctions between private and public life and between work and nonwork.

The success of a social movement can be assessed in the strategic as well as the symbolic dimension. Movements that change institutions produce strategic results. Movements that change public belief and established interpretations produce symbolic results. The most successful social movements can establish both strategic and symbolic dominance. Among the spectrum of social movements in West Germany presently one can observe five types of success, each of which involves different strategic and symbolic effects: coexistence, blocking, attention, adaptation, and colonization.

Coexistence denotes one extreme on a scale of possible interventions; as a strategy it comes close to having very little impact on the process of modernization and the institutions that implement modernization. Movements like the alternative movement that practice this strategy achieve acceptance from the established elite because they help solve social problems for which no standard solution is available. The movement has had little effect either strategically or symbolically. The other extreme on the scale of interventions is colonization, which involves a thorough change of existing policies and institutions; the self-help

64. Gamson, *Strategy of Social Protest*, pp. 38–54.
65. Ibid., p. 49.

movement belongs in this category. Colonizing movements have high strategic and symbolic impact. In between are three other types of impacts. Blocking—the contribution to the breakdown of an elite modernization policy without fully changing the philosophy and the program of the elites—describes the activities of the antinuclear movement. The impact of the peace movement can be put in the category of attention. Almost everyone embraces the goals of this movement, but it has hardly changed the institutions and policies that triggered its formation. The peace movement has had a low strategic effect and medium symbolic effect. Adaptation, finally, is characterized by medium strategic impact and high symbolic impact. Equality-feminism and the ecology movement are unchallenged in the symbolic realm, but existing institutions allow only selective and incremental changes.

Colonization: The Self-Help Movement

The self-help movement challenges two pillars of the German social service system: professionalism and paternalism. Many social service organizations started as volunteer organizations with strong religious or class bases but were transformed by public welfare legislation into quasi-state institutions with hierarchical organizational features and paternalistic bureaucratic relations to the clients.[66] The antiauthoritarian wave of the 1960s launched the self-help movement, which established alternative organizations with more democratic structures and stronger emphasis on lay and semiprofessional help.[67] Self-help is the provision of noncommodified goods and services.[68] Self-help movements view the public management of social problems as a source of the social problems: professionalism and bureaucraticism are viewed as putting the clients under tutelage. The self-help movement in West Germany concentrates on those areas of public social services typified by low levels of professionalism and bureaucratic procedures: services characterized by intensive interaction. These are typically rehabilitative services. Self-help groups concentrate on rehabilitation groups, Alcoholics Anonymous, handicapped groups, and cancer rehabilitation groups.

The activities of the West German self-help movement have changed the public provision of social services. Its success was facilitated by the conservative government of Helmut Kohl, which for financial and ideo-

66. Dietrich Tränhardt, "Established Charity Organizations: Self-Help Groups and New Social Movements in West Germany." Discussion Paper in Political and Administrative Science, Institut für Politikwissenschaft, University of Münster, 1987.
67. Alf Trojan, ed., *Wissen ist Macht. Eigenständig durch Selbsthilfe in Gruppen* (Frankfurt: Fischer, 1986).
68. Peter Gross, "Der Wohlfahrtsstaat und die Bedeutung der Selbsthilfe-Bewegung," *Soziale Welt* 33 (1982): 28.

logical reasons proposed to strengthen the subsidiary support systems.[69] Conservatives as well as progressives embrace the goals of the self-help movement, albeit for different reasons. The Christian Democrats view self-help as a means of unburdening public welfare budgets and taking the state out of social services. The Social Democrats believe that solidaristic practices will restore the self-esteem of the client vis-à-vis an overwhelming bureaucracy.[70] In any case, drastic cuts in welfare budgets facilitated institutional reforms that reduced the weight of professionals and administrative agencies in social services. The self-help movement of the 1970s and 1980s met a service bureaucracy on the retreat and could thus develop ideas of a solidaristic community of the helpless without alienating existing institutions.

Strategically, the self-help movement has entered the organizational framework of the charity system under the umbrella of the smallest and least hierarchic of the established charity organizations. This development has "resulted in an intensified competition between the various welfare organizations forcing all groups to be more open to self-help activities."[71] The self-help movement has succeeded in part because of the flexibility of the system of intermediary institutions. "The characteristically prominent position of the peak organizations in social welfare and their continuous mediating role allow for an easier integration of 'grass-roots' movements than in the social sector of those countries which lack these intermediary organizations and which are dominated by centralized bureaucratic structures."[72]

The success of the self-help movement is a result of a process common to low-level politics: adaptation to modernization via decentralization and self-regulation. But, decentralization will not necessarily lead to overall solidaristic forms of organization; in this sense the deeper goals of the self-help movement—the organization of all institutions around reciprocity and a concern for community well-being—are not met by the present institutional reforms. Colonization does not mean the transformation of the target institutions but, rather, the successful implantation of symbolic and organizational motives of the movement into established institutions.

Adaptation: Equality-Feminism and the Environmental Movement

The women's movement of the 1970s and 1980s has raised a variety of issues: the liberalization of abortion laws, comparable worth, improved

---

69. Heiner Geissler, ed., *Verwaltete Bürger—Gesellschaft in Fesseln* (Darmstadt: Ullstein, 1978).

70. Adrienne Windhoff-Héritier, "Selbsthilfe-Organisationen—Eine Lösung für die Sozialpolitik der mageren Jahre?" *Soziale Welt* 38 (1982): 54.

71. Tränhardt, "Established Charity Organizations," p. 20.

72. Rolf G. Heinze and Thomas Olk, "Die Wohlfahrtsverbände im System sozialer Dienstleistungsproduktion—Zur Entstehung und Struktur der bundesrepublikanischen Verbändewohlfahrt," *Kölner Zeitschrift für Soziologie und Sozialpsychologie* 33 (1981): 111.

access to professional positions (via hiring quotas in favor of women), and recognition of work done in the home as productive work. West German equality-feminism and equity-feminism are not as organizationally distinct as they are in the United States, but it seems reasonable to uphold this distinction because of the vastly different institutional impact each strand has had. The revival of feminism dates back to the student movement. The female dissidents in the Sozialistischer Deutscher Studentenbund (Socialist German Student Union, SDS) attempted to organize separately because of the different goals of women in the SDS and of the organization as a whole. The abortion campaign of the early 1970s marks the beginning of the new women's movement. Many women came to view antichoice laws as part of a larger scheme in which women's civil, social, and economic rights were not equal to those of men. The claim that women have the right to full control over their bodies was extended to demands for equal educational opportunities, equal pay on the job market, and compensation for household work.[73] In each case the slogan of the new women's movement was "the personal is political." Equality-feminism struggled for full inclusion for women in public life and in labor markets. The growth of public support for the women's movement was accompanied by organizational endeavors: *Frauenzentren* (women's centers), *Frauenhäuser* (houses for battered women), women's bookstores and publications (like the magazines *Emma* and *Courage*), and the Berlin Women's Summer University, which has taken place each year since 1976. The inclusion of women in labor markets was the most significant demand of equality-feminism. The specific working conditions that women demanded to accommodate their roles as childbearers have contributed heavily to erosion of the standard employment pattern that unions and management had developed for male workers in the preceding decades.

The environmental movement has had tremendous symbolic success. It has denounced some technologies as wasteful and dangerous, but it has also given rise to new technologies that previously seemed irrelevant. The catalytic converter is an example of an adaptation effect of a social movement. The environmental movement was among the first to point to the close connection between toxic emissions from cars and conventional power plants and the decay of the forests. It rallied behind the installation of filters in power plants and for a major reduction in private use of automobiles. In the early 1980s legislation was passed which required newly built cars to be equipped with catalytic converters and granted tax reductions to owners of cars with these filters. Although the positive effect of catalytic converters on the environment has not been

73. Leonore Knafla and Christine Kulke, "15 Jahre neue Frauenbewegung. Und sie bewegt sich noch!—Ein Rückblick nach vorn," in Roland Roth and Dieter Rucht, eds., *Neue soziale Bewegungen in der Bundesrepublik Deutschland* (Frankfurt: Campus, 1987), pp. 89–108.

completely demonstrated, the West German car industry, which originally vehemently resisted catalytic converters, has emerged as a major winner in this affair. Since similar legislation in other European countries is lagging behind, West German car manufacturers have gained a competitive advantage in this technology. Adaptation, as this case shows, does not necessarily mean that the social movement has come much closer to its goals; but it has taken the initiative and proved that pressure in the symbolic realm can influence the strategic dimension.

Symbolic pressure has not had similar strategic success in the peace movement. Its attempt to influence industrial investment decisions and the government's industrial policy was directed toward stopping the manufacture of military goods. The Green party has adopted this goal in its program "Reconstruction of Industrial Society."[74] Military conversion is part of a triple concept: conversion of nuclear into solar energy, conversion of "hard" into "soft" chemistry (chemistry that includes ecological criteria in its production), and conversion of military into civilian products.[75]

The Federal Republic is among the five biggest manufacturers and exporters of military goods in the world, but only 20 percent of its military products are exported. The bulk of military hardware is acquired by the Bundeswehr, the German army.[76] Peace and Third World groups have persistently protested the generous export policy of the West German government with respect to weapons manufacturers. Despite strict laws that prohibit the export of weapons into crisis areas, West German weapons appear on many battlefields. Recent scandals involving a German submarine producer who was suspected of having illegally channeled know-how and submarine equipment into South Africa have shed light on the lax export controls. The call for conversion, however, has found little resonance among larger interest groups such as unions. The lack of a military-industrial complex in West Germany makes military markets rather unstable and creates some economic risks for weapons producers. As a consequence, employment in this sector is not guaranteed. Unions, however, have not adopted conversion arguments. A small number of metal union members in weapons-manufacturing firms like Messerschmitt Bölkow-Blohm and Krupp have founded conversion circles that cooperate with peace groups.[77] But these activities

74. Die Grünen, *Umbau der Industriegesellschaft. Programm zur Überwindung von Erwerbslosigkeit. Armut und Umweltzerstörung* (Bonn, 1986).

75. Sarah Jansen, Uwe Lahrl, and Barbara Zeschmar, "Chemische Industrie und Grüne," in Projekt Grüner Morgentau, eds., *Perspektiven ökologischer Wirtschaftspolitik* (Frankfurt: Campus, 1986), pp. 115–34.

76. Eckart Hildebrandt, "Rüstungskonversion, alternative Produktion und Gewerkschaften in der Bundesrepublik," in György Széll, ed., *Rüstungskonversion und Alternativproduktion*, Argument Sonderband 118 (Berlin: Argument Verlag, 1987), p. 50.

77. Hildebrandt, "Rüstungskonversion," p. 50.

have had no impact on union policies or on the decisions of corporate management.

Attention: Equity-Feminism and the Peace Movement

Equity-feminism differs from equality-feminism in the depth and scope of its strategic goals. A feminist revolution would pursue three goals, according to Herrad Schenk: "the abolition of the gender-specific division of work in the family, the dissolution of the psychic foundations of different gender roles, and the feminization of the societal system of norms and values."[78] Equality-feminism defines male domination of women as exclusion from full citizenship. Inclusion in the system of social rights would reduce the relevance of gender differences. Equity-feminism, however, takes subjugation of women as a starting point for designing a feminist counterculture in which the differences between men and women are to be upheld. Equity-feminism attempts to develop institutional preconditions against the individualization of female life chances which is the (unintended) outcome of the struggles of equality-feminism. Feminization of society would require major institutional changes that would have to start with the revision of the present institution of reproduction, the family. Up to now, equity-feminism has not significantly changed prevailing social institutions. Instead, this movement has developed an institutional structure of a feminist counterculture.

The peace movement, although very different in scope and content from equity-feminism, has had a similar fate in the 1970s and 1980s. The emergence of the peace movement in the 1980s was associated with the resurgence of high tension between the United States and the Soviet Union. Many West Germans perceived the changes in the nuclear strategy of the North Atlantic Treaty Organization (NATO) and the increasing tensions between the superpowers after the Soviet invasion of Afghanistan as a threat to the achievements of détente.[79] Anxiety was heightened by U.S. plans to deploy medium-range missiles in West Germany and other European countries following the so-called double-track decision of 1979. In the four years that followed, a wave of anti-missile protests rolled through West Germany the size and intensity of which were unprecedented in its history. The peace movement's activities included a wide range of interventions, from "legal forms of noncooperation" (refusing military service or proclaiming nuclear-free zones) to civil disobedience (the besieging of the Bundestag in 1983 or the blocking of access roads to missile facilities) and also to violent re-

78. Herrad Schenk, *Die feministische Herausforderung. 150 Jahre Frauenbewegung in Deutschland* (Munich: Beck, 1981), p. 204.
79. Joyce M. Mushaben, "Cycles of Peace Protest in West Germany: Experiences from Three Decades," *West European Politics* 8 (1985): 24–40.

sistance (attacking military installations or cementing launching equipment).[80] The strategic impact of the peace movement was very low. It was unsuccessful in preventing the deployment of the Euromissiles; it could not persuade the West German government to contribute to a less—as the peace movement saw it—aggressive NATO strategy; nor did it come close to achieving goals such as establishment of a nuclear-free zone in European countries that are not atomic powers or withdrawal from the NATO defense pact and pursuit of a neutral foreign policy.

Symbolically, however, the peace movement was fairly successful. It caused a split within the Social Democratic party, which had initiated the double-track decision under the Schmidt government, and divided the party over the issue of nuclear weapons. "Atlanticists" like Helmut Schmidt emphasized the need for unity within NATO and argued against "decoupling" from the United States; "Europeanists" like Egon Bahr (the military policy expert in the SPD) were very concerned about preserving détente with the East and strengthening the European position within NATO.[81] The lasting consequence of the movement is that the Social Democrats became highly supportive of the "denuclearization" of Europe.

The other thematic impact of the peace movement lies in the impression it made on public opinion. Support for the peace movement has risen steadily since 1979 and reached a high shortly before the deployment of the Euromissiles, when 66 percent of those interviewed opposed deployment, 15 percent favored deployment, and 18 percent were undecided.[82] The peace movement also intensified the postindustrial cleavage. Attitudes toward the peace movement are shaped in part by party affiliation. It receives strong support from members of the Green and the Social Democratic parties; its opponents show more sympathy for the Christian Democrats or the Free Democrats.[83]

Blocking: The Antinuclear Movement

The antinuclear movement is the only new social movement in West Germany that has had considerable influence on the strategy and per-

---

80. Joyce M. Mushaben, "Grassroots and Gewaltfreie Aktionen: A Study of Mass Mobilization Strategies in the West German Peace Movement," *Journal of Peace Research* 23 (1986): 141–54.

81. Jost Halfmann and Rolf Wortmann, "Das Sicherheitsdilemma. Dimensionen einer revidierten Sicherheitspolitik," *Sozialismus* 1 (1985): 29–38.

82. Karl H. Reuband, "Issueorientierung und Nachrüstungsprotest," in Jürgen W. Falter, Christian Fenner, and Michael T. Greven, eds., *Politische Willensbildung und Interessenvermittlung* (Opladen: Westdeutscher Verlag, 1984), pp. 589–601.

83. Rüdiger Schmitt, "Was bewegt die Friedensbewegung? Zum sicherheitspolitischen Protest der achtziger Jahre," *Zeitschrift für Parlamentsfragen* 18 (1987): 110–36.

formance of a specific industry. The antinuclear movement and the electricity utility companies and power plant manufacturers were not direct opponents. The antinuclear movement considered the state to be the true promoter of atomic energy policy and the energy companies merely instruments of the government.[84]

The atomic power program of West Germany came to an almost full halt by the mid-1980s.[85] The contribution of the antinuclear movement to its stoppage is hard to assess. The movement was able to retard licensing procedures for power plants by filing legal objections. According to some public figures, the antinuclear movement prevented possible investment in nuclear technology up to about a billion deutschmarks.

The antinuclear movement was partly responsible for raising safety standards in nuclear power plants. To prevent risks of sabotage, nuclear meltdown, operator error, and so on, utilities were forced to raise construction costs to increasingly prohibitive levels. The public campaigns of the antinuclear movement in conjunction with the nuclear accidents at Three Mile Island and Chernobyl have influenced (but not fully convinced) the general public of the danger of nuclear energy. Polls conducted by the opinion research company Emnid showed the following views regarding nuclear energy: in April 1980, pro 56 percent, contra 42 percent; in October 1981, pro 52 percent, contra 46 percent; in March 1982, pro 52 percent, contra 46 percent; in May 1986, pro 29 percent, contra 69 percent.[86] The relationships between the antinuclear movement and the unions exemplify the difficulty a social movement has in achieving symbolic impact. Unlike their relation with industry, new social movements either compete or cooperate with unions. Unions represent yesterday's social movements and pursue general social goals more or less openly, even though they seem to restrict their scope of activity to distributional politics. New social movements see themselves as competing with unions for control of the future organization of the economy and society. Unions in West Germany have been strong supporters of growth economics, technological progress, and parliamentary democracy. New social movements (and the Green party) pursue a policy of nongrowth or so-called qualitative growth, of grass-roots democracy and risk-free "soft" technologies. The history of the relations between

84. Radkau, *Aufstieg und Krise.*
85. For the development up to 1984, see Kitschelt, "Political Opportunity Structures," p. 78.
86. Emnid-Institut, "Umfrage zur Kernenergie"; for more on attitudes to nuclear energy and risk assessment see Haus Kessel, "Environmental Awareness in the Federal Republic of Germany, England and the United States—Current Status and Changes," *Discussion Paper* IIUG (Wissenschaftszentrum Berlin, 1984); O. Renn, *Risikowahrnehmung der Kernenergie* (Frankfurt: Campus, 1984).

new social movements and unions originates in this conflict. Underlying the conflict is the belief shared by unions and the environmental movement that employment and environmental protection are mutually exclusive goals. Up to the mid-1970s the environmental movement was not visible in West Germany. Therefore, the union's position on energy and employment remained unchallenged within the labor force. After the protest against the construction of nuclear power plants in Wyhl (1975), Brokdorf (1975), and Grohnde (1977), the Deutsche Gewerkschaftsbund (the federal trade union association) issued statements supporting nuclear energy and even organized a counterdemonstration in 1977.

Antinuclear demonstrations were at their height between 1977 and 1982. The Gorleben demonstration in 1979 (after the Three Mile Island accident) attracted several hundred thousand demonstrators; in 1981 one hundred thousand came together to protest against the Brokdorf construction. Toward the end of the 1970s, the Green party emerged and started to compete with the Free Democratic party for the position of third strongest force in politics. Union members began to have more sympathy with environmental goals. The proenvironmental protection circle within the unions, Arbeitskreis Leben, was founded in more than forty cities.

Since then relations between the DGB and the antinuclear movement and the Greens have become somewhat less antagonistic. Heinrich Siegmann gives three reasons for this rapprochement: "The change in Bonn [in 1983] aided the labor-environmentalist rapprochement in several ways. It enabled the SPD and labor to shift their position on important issues closer to the Greens" (issues including not only environmental protection but also industrial policy, the thirty-five-hour work week, and social policy).[87] Since the labor unions are strongly attached to the SPD, a political change in the SPD directly affects the unions' attitudes. In addition, Heinrich Siegmann continues, "the electoral shifts to the Greens and the goal of the SPD to make up the loss of power in Bonn by maintaining and strengthening its position at the state and local levels fostered cooperation between environmentalists and labor interests."[88] The coalition pact between the Greens and the SPD in Hesse from 1983 to 1987 was the most interesting sign of this change. Finally, "public awareness of the degradation of the natural environment has grown to the point where environmental policies have become extremely politically sensitive. Moreover, (structural) unemployment levels have remained so high that labor has come to recognize environmental protec-

---

87. Heinrich Siegmann, *The Conflicts between Labor and Environmentalism in the Federal Republic of Germany and the United States* (Aldershot: Gower, 1985), pp. 20–21.
88. Ibid., p. 21.

tion as one, if not the area with a very high potential for creating new jobs."[89]

Coexistence: The Alternative Movement

The alternative movement emerged in West Germany in the 1970s when the era of postwar prosperity came to an end and intensified economic modernization began to contract the labor markets, weigh on the social security system, and change the system of professional qualifications. A diversity of communal projects in agriculture, small manufacturing cooperatives, networks of food coops, and counseling projects sprang up throughout the Federal Republic. This movement was embedded in changing lifestyles and values that promised to alleviate the effects of increased privatism and the experience or anticipation of unemployment in the formal sector. The movement was also accompanied by the growth of a critical counterculture that expressed itself in an alternative press; the Berlin-based *TAZ* for example, a leftist daily newspaper, was founded in 1979 and is a small but respected publication.[90] Joseph Huber estimates that in 1980 about eighty thousand people worked in the alternative sector and that three to four hundred thousand actively sympathized with alternative activities.[91] Alternative enterprises are characterized by three principles: identity, the principle that those who work own the enterprise; democracy, the principle that all members in a firm have equal votes in decisions; and subsistence, the principle that revenues should be sufficient to support the owners of the enterprise. Wolfgang Beywl estimates that in 1987 about fifteen to eighteen thousand people were able to support themselves in the alternative economy.[92] The majority of alternative enterprises are engaged in services and trades; only about 25 percent belong to the manufacturing sector.

The alternative movement was not conceived of as a strategic alternative to capitalist production methods and hierarchic business organizations, and therefore its strategic impact on the capitalist system has been very low. The alternative movement coexists peacefully with market capitalism and offers little challenge to conventional notions of organi-

89. Ibid.

90. Roland Roth, "Neue soziale Bewegungen in der politischen Kultur der Bundesrepublik," in Karl W. Brand, ed., *Neue soziale Bewegungen in Westeuropa und den USA* (Frankfurt: Campus, 1985).

91. Joseph Huber, *Wer soll das alles ändern. Alternativen der Alternativbewegung* (Berlin: Rotbuch Verlag, 1980), p. 29.

92. Wolfgang Beywl, "Alternative Ökonomie—Selbstorganisierte Betriebe im Kontext neuer sozialer Bewegungen," in Roland Roth and Dieter Rucht, eds., *Neue soziale Bewegungen in der Bundesrepublik Deutschland* (Frankfurt: Campus, 1987), p. 195.

zational efficiency, investment, or ideology. Rather, the experiments it has conducted are considered potentially viable solutions to the problems of shrinking labor markets and decreasing welfare budgets. Rolf Heinze and Thomas Olk believe that the alternative economy might even intensify the segmentation of the labor market into core and peripheral workers.[93] If this hypothesis turns out to be true, the alternative movement would face the trade-off between enjoying the benefits of self-determination and decentralization and suffering the costs of low revenues and economic marginalization.

The symbolic impact of the alternative movement is rather low. Early reactions by the media and the social and political elites pointed toward outright rejection because the alternative movement was looked at as subverting the prevailing (Protestant) work ethic in the formal sector. Currently it seems that less militant attitudes prevail; members are carrying out some innovative experiments in small-scale ecological farming and traditional high-quality craft production. In this sense, the alternative movement is seen as enriching the German social and political culture and as providing solutions to social problems for which the state may no longer wish to be held responsible. Table 3.1 presents the impact of social movements in a schematic form.

Table 3.1. Impact of social movements

		Symbolic impact		
		high	medium	low
Strategic impact	high	self-help movement	antinuclear movement	
	medium	equality-feminism; environmental movement		
	low		peace movement; equity-feminism	alternative movement

Contemporary social movements are an expression of fundamental changes in modern societies in general and in West Germany in particular. These movements seem to be more sensitive to critical consequences of modernization processes than are established actors and social systems. The beginning of the 1970s marked a turning point in the political and cultural history of West Germany. The economic recessions of the late 1960s undermined the "dream of everlasting prosperity" (as Burkart Lutz called his book on West German postwar economy) and at the same time opened up the political space to diverging political interests

93. Heinze and Olk, "Selbsthilfe, Eigenarbeit, Schattenwirtschaft," p. 22.

and expressions. "The march through the institutions"—the slogan with which the student movement challenged the established elites—started in the streets, but in the course of the 1970s and 1980s the social movements reached and changed institutions with varying success and depth. The system of political party representation was most visibly changed as a result of the formation of a new party. In intensifying the dissolution of established cleavages in high-level politics, social movements encouraged new voting alignments; they also introduced new issues such as ecological modernization into the political landscape.

Institutions that suffered financial cutbacks in the late 1970s, like the social services bureaucracies, were most deeply impressed by the new social movements. Other institutions with a longer and more complex history of attrition, like the traditional small family, were shaken further by the women's movement. Without an alternative institution in sight, the consequences of the women's movement are unclear and will be difficult to grapple with. Finally, those institutions that manage the implementation of political decisions and the adaptation to changes in the economic, social, and international environment of West Germany—the intermediary and parapublic institutions—seem to be least affected by the challenges of the social movements. Unions still resist the modification or dissolution of the standard employment pattern, despite growing pressure from women's organizations. Citizens' initiatives and social movements have not yet become accepted partners in low-level politics: when local governments negotiate with industry about the ramifications of new industrial parks, environmentalists or concerned citizens still have to fall back on the traditional tactics of outsiders, demonstration and petitions.

Ironically, by advocating decentralization of the political decision-making processes, social movements may inadvertently strengthen the process of self-regulation and informal decision making among the established social actors. But even though these movements will probably not achieve their metagoals of sovereignty or reciprocity, they will gain more maneuvering space for further activities. Contemporary social movements seem to have little influence on the international performance of West Germany. The nuclear power plant industry has complained that the antinuclear movement has prevented West German firms from investing in promising reactors that would have given them a competitive edge on international markets against French or American firms. It is more plausible, however, to assume that the West German nuclear industry made the wrong choices with respect to reactors and lost markets because it failed to produce state-of-the-art power plants.[94]

94. Otto Keck, *Der schnelle Brüter. Eine Fallstudie über Entscheidungsprozesse in der Grosstechnik* (Frankfurt: Campus, 1985).

In only one area may a West German social movement have some future impact on the country's international involvement: the peace movement. Though the movement failed to prevent the deployment of Euromissiles in 1984, its demands for the denuclearization of West Germany and parts of Europe have received new stimulus from two unlikely sides: the United States and the Soviet Union. The Geneva Accord on Intermediate Nuclear Forces will lead to the scrapping of those Euromissiles that the peace movement resisted in the early 1980s. Since the United States seems to be pursuing a strategy of nuclear disengagement from Europe and the Soviet Union seems ready to reduce military pressure on Europe for internal economic reasons, the West German government must decide on new defense options. The traditional policy of reliance on the American nuclear shield can no longer be pursued unconditionally. The United States and the Soviet Union have contributed to the Europeanization of Europe, which parts of the peace movement have proposed since the early 1980s. This constellation improves the chances for political actors who opt for further denuclearization and détente in Europe. Whether the peace movement will be capable of intervening in this process will depend on its ability to regain active support among the populace and to win over coalition partners like the Greens and the Social Democrats.

Obviously, the social movements have not exhausted their strategic and symbolic efforts, which is one reason why they will remain part of the political future of the West German Republic.

Chapter Four

New Concepts of Production in West German Plants

Horst Kern and
Michael Schumann

As West German industry attempts to survive increased international competition and to gain a favorable position in the international market, a turning point appears to be at hand. Although West German enterprises still aim to make a substantial profit, they are changing the way they put that goal into practice. The philosophy of mass production now involves new strategies characterized by product innovation—that is, a shift to products of high quality, high technology, and great variety. The new strategies, also known as "concepts of production," are supported by new technologies. "Flexible automatization" has become a technical possibility and promises to make high productivity compatible with small-scale manufacturing. The new strategies are also based on a new attitude toward the work force. Today management considers the worker a person endowed with wide-ranging abilities and a great capacity for growth, one who is most efficient when his or her full potential is involved.[1]

These new concepts of production are affecting both the product and the manufacturing process. The concepts are founded on a redefinition and an unorthodox combination of product philosophy, manufacturing technology, work design, and personnel policy. The main variables in these new concepts of production are a "menu" that offers diversified products of high quality; a manufacturing process characterized by flexible automatization; integration of the functions of production, maintenance, and quality control; and modes of recruiting and training

1. See Horst Kern and Michael Schumann, *Das Ende der Arbeitsteilung?* (Munich: Beck, 1984).

which encourage the development of the highly skilled blue-collar worker.

Within West German industry many enterprises are adopting these concepts and altering their strategies for using capital. That the number of enterprises adopting the new concepts is growing cannot be disputed. Despite the restrictions, asymmetries, and contradictions involved, the new concepts of production are coming into fashion.

New Concepts of Production

Mass production in industry was developed near the end of the nineteenth century. It soon became the general model of capitalist modernization. In all variants of this model workers have been considered an obstacle to production which should be replaced by technological means as much as possible. Yet some jobs could not be done by machines, and because management viewed workers who filled those jobs as a possible source of trouble, they were treated mainly from the perspective of control. Management attempted to organize work restrictively. Designers and users of machinery gave this attitude toward workers the status of a technological paradigm and envisioned the automated, unmanned factory.[2]

At present, an entire social class may be abandoning patterns of behavior and perception it has held for generations. To accommodate the new concepts of production, capitalist management is changing its vision of mass production in industry, a vision that has until recently been crucial to its identification and orientation. This change is not a sudden leap but a fluid process. Discontinuity and friction between retarding and propelling forces may be essential in such a period of transition.

The rapidity and consistency with which this new vision is adopted depends on several factors. The attitudes toward change of those involved are influenced by six factors. (1) Of great importance is the historical stage in the process of rationalization which a given enterprise or industry has reached, in particular, the degree to which it has been able to establish the principles of mass production during the past eighty years. The less successfully it has adopted mass production techniques in the past, the less rigid it is and the more easily management can adopt the new concepts of production. (2) Changes in production depend also on the ability and readiness of management to abandon the established modus operandi and to explore unconventional opportunities.

2. See Michael Piore and Charles Sabel, *The Second Industrial Divide* (New York: Basic Books, 1984).

The more qualities such as technological imagination and a sound business instinct management derives from education and experience, the stronger will be the desire for innovation. (3) The degree to which capital and labor are used to compromise and cooperate even in areas sensitive to both also matters. The more used to combining bargaining and cooperation both parties are, the more willing they will be to accept "live-and-let-live" arrangements and to abandon restrictive practices that hinder change. (4) Implementation of the new vision depends further on the volume and structure of the work force, specifically, the availability of highly qualified workers with multiple skills. The more qualified workers there are, the easier it is to ensure that there will be enough workers to apply the new concepts of production. (5) A political regime that strives for a strategic consensus among government, business, and unions on basic economic issues will also be helpful to the introduction of new production concepts. The more stable the mechanisms of tripartite economic integration, the smaller the probability that social conflicts will occur during implementation of new concepts of production, and the more effectively the state can apply its financial and planning resources to support innovations without creating tension between one or the other party. (6) Finally, the extent to which the economic participants are integrated into the world market also matters. Involvement in the international economy must be matched by the effort to secure international competitiveness and, at the same time, the drive to develop new concepts of production that will allow enterprises to supply products with specifications, qualities, and prices that are superior to those of international competitors. As data from West German industry in the 1980s show, in many cases the prerequisites have been met for applying the new concepts of production.

Although many German technicians and entrepreneurs greatly admired the concept of mass production, historical circumstances prevented them from adopting it completely. In numerous industries requiring craftsmanship, qualified and fairly well-organized workers remained skeptical of the benefits of mass production. Cutbacks in mass production were also necessary because German industry traditionally specialized in producing sophisticated items. Traditional and patriarchal habits, characteristic of Germany's small and middle-sized enterprises, could also have inhibited the process.[3] On the whole, German industry adapted itself imperfectly to mass production. At the turn of the century, among industries in the dominant metal sector the electric industry

3. Up until recently 95 percent of German plants had a work force of less than five hundred people; these small plants employed 50 percent of the total work force (*Industrieberichterstattung des Statistischen Bundesamtes*, series 4, subseries 4.1.2 [Stuttgart/Mainz: Kohlhammer, 1985]).

used the mass production system most extensively, and it has continued to do so. The automobile industry remained primarily a machine-building industry until the 1950s, when it embraced mass production. The machine tools industry continued to favor diversified products of high quality and, because of that, could only stumble toward mass production. Finally, the chemical industry in Germany traditionally combines big industry in management with decentralization in production; it thus approximates mass production only imperfectly.

Those who were influential in the rise of German industry usually had technical or scientific backgrounds. Werner Siemens and Robert Bosch, Gottlieb Daimler and Carl Friederich Benz, Carl Duisberg and Carl Bosch were already central figures at the genesis of the electric, automobile, and chemical industries. Also essential were the innumerable mechanics who, with their "mechanicus inventions" (little improvements on the shop floor), influenced the development of the machine tools industry. When as a result of capital accumulation, enterprises were forced to rely on the capital market and, sometimes, to change their organization (for example, by turning into joint-stock companies), managers with a nontechnical, juridical, or commercial background often gained more influence. In general, however, German management maintained a strong technical bias. Managers were normally educated at one of the many technical colleges founded in the early 1900s. Some commercial training was included in their college education, but they gained most of their business skills on the job. The high competitive pressure West German industry faces today has forced these technicians to acknowledge that economic success presupposes the compatibility of technical perfection and economic efficiency. West German management does not represent an ideal combination of technical competence and entrepreneurial spirit, but there are in West Germany today many people who are capable of finding new solutions, who meet high technical standards in designing and manufacturing without ignoring economic feasibility.

Creating an ideology from the social system of the factory along the lines of an industrial community or plant family is a tradition deeply rooted in German history and national character. Even if the union movement has barely accepted this tradition, it has coexisted with the reformist attitude German unions exhibited from the very beginning. After Nazism, when ideologies in general had lost credibility and the social climate demanded secularization, it became easier to find a common denominator for employers' and unions' interests. Promoted by economic recovery and prosperity, which deemphasized the allocation of economic rewards, and sponsored by legislation and jurisdiction, a system of industrial relations was established in which each party tries to

fulfill its particular interests by a combination of pressure and cooperation. In West Germany today we often observe an integrative style of
control on the side of management and a preference for negotiation
rather than open conflict on the side of workers. Naturally other patterns of behavior are also possible (for example, despotic, patriarchal,
bureaucratic, or confrontational management styles, and submissive or
aggressive labor responses), but the established modes balance mutual
interests.

Because of long reverence for the artisan, many industries in Germany initially relied on the traditional qualification of craftsmen. But by
around 1910 industries adopted the idea of training personnel by apprenticeship. Under pressure from the unions and regulated by the
state, which passed legislation governing vocational training and absorbed some aspects of it in its compulsory school system, most future
blue-collar factory workers received their training through apprenticeships. Of course, the profile of apprentices has changed through time.
Management often tried to abandon vocational training when mass
production reduced the demand for qualified workers. Yet ultimately
the vocational training system remained in force, and many new apprenticeships have been established to replace antiquated ones.[4] The
process of vocational training is currently being put in place or updated
in the most dynamic industries. New training methods attempt to produce workers such as the mechanic in the automobile industry and the
skilled worker in the chemical industry who are able to implement the
new concepts of production. Furthermore, even the machine tools industry, in which training has always been of high quality, is reforming
and intensifying its activities. In this way, the skill level of blue-collar
workers needed to support a shift in manufacturing methods is guaranteed.

The conservatives who ruled during the first stage of the Federal
Republic were antistatist in theory. In reality, however, they not only
maintained a large sector of publicly owned enterprises (the few examples of reprivatization can be overlooked here), but they also undermined the self-government and responsibility of capital and labor, the
two "partners in social life," by employing subsidies and asserting the
state's influence in subsystems that provided training and retraining,

4. About 60 percent of the young generation pursues and completes an apprenticeship. Only about 10 percent has little or no vocational training. The rest pursue some form
of higher education (Heinz Stegmann and Hermine Kraft "Ausbildungs- und Berufswege
von 23–24 jährigen. Methode und ausgewählte Ergebnisse der Wiederholungserhebung
Ende 1985," *Mitteilungen aus der Arbeitsmarkt- und Berufsforschung,* 1987, no. 2, p. 147). Most
members of each generation of blue-collar workers become workers via apprenticeships
(perhaps three-quarters of them favoring modern training as mechanics, electricians, and
the like).

social support, and so on. The social-liberal coalition legalized, enlarged, and perhaps even radicalized the role of the state in the economy and tried to integrate business and labor with government according to a strategy of macroeconomic stabilization. Even if the coalition's attempt to realize coordinated actions on a macro level failed in the long run, many tripartite institutions for enacting industrial policy and binding business and labor were stabilized or established in the subsystems. By combining this regulatory power with the direct economic influence of the state, through its own enterprises and its power to subsidize, the government could create and support a climate favorable for technical change. The social liberals, fascinated by technological progress, used this opportunity as long as they were in power. The "new area" in West German politics, once the Social Democrats were ousted from power, seems in this respect to be anything but a change.

Because of shortages of raw materials and narrow internal markets, the West German economy is in many areas linked with the international economy. International competitiveness is the non plus ultra of prosperity.[5] It is thus hardly astonishing that many of the activities of West German industry support our contention that new concepts of production are becoming widespread. It seems plausible to call this change a new mode of economic reproduction within the industrial system of West Germany.

Whether the new concepts of production must be perceived as a particular phenomenon of national capitalist subeconomies, or whether they indicate a general development of the total capitalist system is not the focus of this chapter. Our impression is that, as a result of the increasing integration of national subeconomies into the world market, a long-term process of homogenization is occurring. The new concepts of production seem to be crossing the borders between nations.[6] We view this as a preliminary and provisional conclusion which further research should examine.

Changing Position of Labor in the Plants

From a sociological point of view, it is remarkable that the new concepts of production are causing the idea of the unmanned factory to lose its appeal. Enterprises cannot base their hopes only on new technology because labor remains a central element of the production process.

5. See Joanne Gowa, "Bipolarity and the Postwar International Economic Order," in this volume.
6. Horst Kern and Michael Schumann, "Die neuen Produktionskonzepte im internationalen Vergleich," in *Festschrift für Dieter Mertens*, forthcoming.

They know it is imperative to keep the work process open to change and innovation.

Despite the microelectronic revolution, complete, consistent automation remains a dream (or a nightmare, depending on one's point of view). Recently, many factories were heavily fined for moving too fast toward development of a technological autonomous production process. Plant managers have had to accept the limitations of mathematical models for controlling manufacturing processes and to acknowledge the technical redundancy required to guard against breakdowns. Difficulties increase when the range of the technical system is enlarged. Therefore, work and work organization remain relevant parameters in concepts of production.

Work today has a very different function than it did with traditional manufacturing processes. Human work no longer involves more or less direct contact with materials and products. Instead, it encompasses activities such as planning, regulating, and controlling in which humans handle technical systems rather than make commodities. This work resists division. It is most efficient if it is combined with functions such as planning and preparing the work, upkeep and repair of the machinery, and inspection of the finished product. The traditional logic of rationalization holds that these functions should be separate from the manufacturing process. This new, more synthetic approach redefines factory jobs, making them less fragmented and more complex. Integrating the functions and reducing the division of labor are now the fashion.

In fieldwork in a great number of West German plants (information concerning our sample is given in the Appendix) we have seen several such redefined workplaces. In many, direct labor (the handling of material, observing, regulating, and so on) integrates traditionally separate functions; sometimes there are few demarcations between direct and indirect labor (maintenance, quality control, and the like).

From our observations of West German workplaces we can characterize the new worker. He or she is not semiskilled as would have been true of a traditional machine system (for example, a transfer machine in a mechanical department of an automobile plant). The need for theoretical competence is too high for on-the-job training. Professional training, in the form of a modernized apprenticeship, is necessary. Models of such apprenticeships have been implemented in many German industries, leading, for example, the skilled process worker in the chemical industry to acquire additional skills in mechanics and electronics; or the new mechanic in the automobile industry to acquire maintenance skills; or the metal-cutting specialist to combine traditional metalworking skills with competence in operating numerically controlled machines. However qualified this modern worker may be, he or she is not a technician or an engineer but a kind of scout: sensitive to breakdowns, with quick reactions and the ability to improvise and take preventive action. This worker needs empirical knowledge gained by working directly with machinery and materials and the behavioral skills to be able to close the technological gaps in the machinery. Finally he or she is not the traditional craftsperson but is less materials-oriented and more concerned with technical and organizational procedures. Moreover, in contrast to traditional craftspeople, modern skilled workers are not masters of the work process. Others such as scientists or engineers define the layout of the technical system and hence decide when and what human intervention is necessary. The new worker has less autonomy than the traditional craftsperson but more than workers during the reign of mass production.

Even in the automobile, chemical, and machine-building industries in which the new concepts of production are centered, only parts of the total work force perform functions characteristic of the new concepts of production (see Figure 4.1). The shift toward the new form of work is ongoing, but a complete change is still in the future. Ours is a transition period. Can the new concepts be generalized in these industries. If so, in what forms? When will this happen? Can structural or mental barriers against the new concepts be removed or will they grow stronger? All these questions have yet to be answered.

That many industries are in flux is reflected in the appearance of new divisions in the labor force of the modernizing industries. One group that reflects the new concepts is highly skilled blue-collar workers and maintenance specialists, or those who have the potential to move into such positions. They are the winners in rationalization. They have become accomplices to further rationalization and are protagonists in the reorganization of their firms. Their status within the firm is high and they are awarded bonuses. Once the new concepts of production have been implemented, these workers could emerge with increased power.

Another group consists of workers in traditional jobs in these industries who, because of personal characteristics—advancing age, lack of multiple skills—are apparently not attractive for employment under the new concepts. Their behavior is most likely that of tolerators of rationalization. True, their jobs are protected by wage agreements, and their working conditions are defined by collective bargaining. But the safety of their interests is questionable, for their jobs could be phased out.

There is a final group of workers: those who are not considered candidates for any jobs in the new workplaces, who are, in fact, on the point of being let go. They are the losers. In the total work force in the most actively modernizing industries, this third group is a minority. Yet many losers, as we shall see, can be found outside these industries. Although we want to emphasize the transitory character of the changing

94

Figure 4.1. Structure of the German work force in selected industries

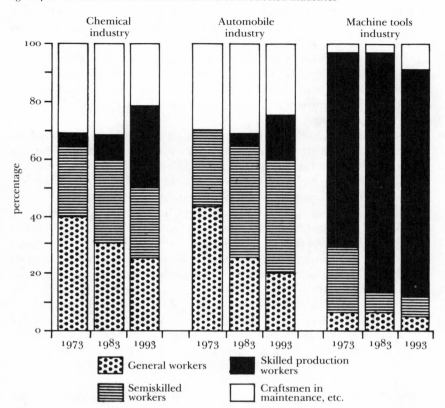

COMMENT: The diagram takes into account only blue-collar workers, i.e., it neglects the white-collar workers who on average make up a third of the industrial work force. Because West German official statistics do not give a satisfactory report on industrial work, we can only give estimated figures based on our case studies. The given figures are fairly reliable and valid for the whole branch in the instance of the machine tools industry. We are doubtful about the other figures (rough estimates are valid only for the three largest chemical companies and only for eleven plants producing motor cars). The figures given for the year 1993 are estimates based on our information about the structures and the planning of the companies.

labor force, clearly in modernizing factories labor is generally not unskilled and is becoming more highly skilled. If we look only into these parts of the economy, there is reason to be optimistic.

MASS UNEMPLOYMENT

Although the rationalization of production has changed the way the human work force is used, there is no guarantee that the new technologies will enable West German capitalism to overcome the great social challenge posed by the inhumanity of capitalist industrial production. Insofar as plants are changing the techniques of producing commodities and services, capitalist modes of production may be "deproblematized." But the deproblematization observable in the work processes is connected to increasing social problems outside the field of work. Deproblematization and problematization are thus linked; both are to varying degrees influenced by those changes that we call the new concepts of production.

One drastic piece of evidence that highlights the externalization of the problems inherent in new developments within West German plants is the unemployment rate, which has been high for fifteen years. West German society seems to have become accustomed to living with mass unemployment. Since 1983 the number has stabilized: there are more than 2 million registered unemployed workers (not including the counted reserve of the labor market, which is calculated to be more than a million).[7] The rate of registered unemployment totals almost 10 percent.

No one can predict exactly how long West Germany's unemployment problem will last. But all prognoses show the gap between the size of the labor market and the demand for workers increasing until the beginning of the 1990s and not closing until the turn of the century. Even the most optimistic projections of the Institute for Surveys on Labor Market and Occupation (IAB), perhaps the most competent observer of the labor market,[8] forecasts 2.2 million registered unemployment by 1990 and 0.8 million by 2000; a forecast of 2.4 million for 1990 and 1.4 million for 2000 is considered more realistic.[9]

West Germany's unemployment problem is influenced by the spread of the new concepts of production. It would not, however, be correct to attribute high unemployment to increases in productivity resulting from implementation of these concepts. The "technological unemployment" argument, which ascribes joblessness to improvements in technology, is too simple to be valid for the present situation. According to the results of studies on this subject, a positive correlation exists between the adoption of new technologies and the increase of productivity on the one side

7. Statistics of West German unemployment include only those unemployed persons who report to the Unemployment Office. Persons who are looking for jobs but who do not officially register with the exchange because they have no claim on state subsidies or because they grow resigned to the bad labor market are considered part of the counted reserve.

8. The Institute for Surveys on Labor Market and Occupation (Institut für Arbeitsmarkt- und Berufsforschung, IAB) is the research department of the West German Unemployment Office.

9. Wolfgang Klauder, Peter Schnur, and Manfred Thon, "Arbeitsmarktperspektiven der 80er und 90er Jahre. Neue Modellrechnungen für Potential und Bedarf an Arbeitskräften," *Mitteilungen aus der Arbeitsmarkt- und Berufsforschung*, 1985, no. 1, pp. 60–67.

New Concepts of Production

and the stability, perhaps even the increase of employment, on the other.[10] In other words, industries that use the new concepts of production offer fairly stable jobs; industries that are too weak to adopt these new concepts are mainly responsible for the reduced demand for labor.

An industrywide comparison of rates of stable employment supports this conclusion.[11] Employment is most stable in the power industry, banks and insurance, the chemical, metal-producing, machine-building, automobile, and shipbuilding industries. Remarkably, all branches that lead in implementation of the new concepts belong to this group.[12]

We can conclude that such sectors of the West German economy which are able to adopt the new concepts of production can achieve sufficient economic expansion to prevent their increases in productivity from destabilizing employment. But their expansion is inadequate to absorb the workers who have already lost their jobs in declining industries. The total demand for labor is decreasing instead of increasing. And the economic expansion of "sunshine" industries like electronics is too small to employ additions to the work force caused by changing demographic factors (increasing birth rates) and changes in the working population (addition of women to the work force).[13] These forces have resulted in such a high level of unemployment that their political regulation is called for. Government has intervened to an extent, but it has not counteracted the crisis effectively.[14]

Looking more closely not only at the amount but also at the structure of unemployment, we gain some additional information about the mechanisms of externalizing which characterize the West German labor market. Which workers will probably confront unemployment? The risk of becoming unemployed is especially high for those who lack occupational training and seniority. For example, the average unemployment rate is 8 percent among the generation of current twenty-five-year-olds, whereas

10. Wolfgang Klauder, "Technischer Fortschritt und Beschäftigung: Zum Zusammenhang von Technik, Strukturwandel, Wachstum und Beschäftigung," *Mitteilungen aus der Arbeitsmarkt- und Berufsforschung*, 1986, no. 1, p. 5.

11. Ulrich Cramer, "Zur Stabilität von Beschäftigung," *Mitteilungen aus der Arbeitsmarkt- und Berufsforschung*, 1986, no. 2, 248. The "rate of stable employment" means the proportion of employees with uninterrupted employment to the total number of employees (in percent). The year of reference is 1981.

12. The metal-producing and the shipbuilding industries, both of which are declining, are also within that group. Notwithstanding their overall character, employment in these industries was stable in the year of reference (1981).

13. Klauder, Schnur, and Thon, "Arbeitsmarktperspektiven der 8oer und 9oer Jahre," p. 44.

14. These government interventions provided financial incentives for foreign workers to leave Germany and for early retirement of employees and promotion and financial support for the training and establishment of jobs for the long-term unemployed. Of further measures based on agreements between unions and employers, the most important were regulations for early retirement and the reduction of weekly or annual work time.

it is much higher (18 to 23 percent) for those who have not finished their schooling and have little or no vocational training.[15] Even those young people who have completed vocational training risk unemployment because they lack seniority; on average 14 percent are unemployed directly after finishing their training, are unemployed for fourteen weeks, and are finally forced to take jobs below their level of education.[16] Together with those members of their generation who do not have any formal qualification, they replenish the buffer sector of the labor market.[17] If the economy expands, unskilled jobs are filled by workers from the buffer sector. Should a plant develop excess capacity, general workers who lack seniority would be the first to be let go.

This reserve army is obviously not being recruited to fill the jobs that are being redefined and stabilized as new concepts of production are implemented. The personnel backbone of the new strategies is made up primarily of skilled, middle-aged West German nationals who already are employed in the company (in some industries males have an advantage). Only those who have successfully completed professional training have access to the attractive jobs. Statistics reflect this situation. Male West German employees between the ages of thirty and fifty with a solid educational background and formal professional training usually monopolize secure positions (their rate of stable employment is about 75 percent).[18] Young people who have completed professional training in a typical plant of a sunshine industry will likely experience relative economic security. Rates of acceptance,[19] 48 percent on average, are extremely high in such industries: for example, the chemical industry, 73 percent; banks and insurance, 68 percent; the automobile industry, 67 percent. Only the machine-building industry at 45 percent is on a lower level because of its structure and vocational tradition. Finally, workers without formal qualification, who in the past have had the highest unemployment rates, fear increasing unemployment as a result of future reductions in the demand for unskilled workers. (The IAB, in its middle-of-the-road scenario for the period 1982–2000, forecasts a de-

15. Heinz Stegmann and Hermine Kraft, "Ausbildungs- und Berufswege von 23–24 jährigen. Method und ausgewählte Ergebnisse der Wiederholungserhebung Ende 1985," *Mitteilungen aus der Arbeitsmarkt- und Berufsforschung*, 1987, no. 2, p. 146.
16. Ibid., p. 123.
17. 12 percent; ibid., p. 147.
18. Ulrich Cramer, "Zur Stabilität von Beschäftigung: Erste Ergebnisse der IAB-Stichprobe aus der Beschäftigungs-Statistik," *Mitteilungen aus der Arbeitsmarkt- und Berufsforschung*, 1986, no. 2, p. 251.
19. Hans Hofbauer and Elisabeth Nagel, "Mobilität nach Abschluss der betrieblichen Berufsausbildung," *Mitteilungen aus der Arbeitsmarkt- und Berufsforschung*, 1987, no. 2, p. 61. The "rate of acceptance" is defined as the proportion of qualified skilled blue-collar workers who remain in the plant where they received their training to all workers qualified in the particular plant in one year. The figures given are for 1984.

crease in demand of about 3.2 million unskilled workers and an increased demand for 3.5 million formally qualified workers.)[20]

All available information indicates that the influence of new concepts of production is gradually giving unemployment the status of a negative career. A particular group is precluded from joining the work force because its members do not have the qualifications and attributes prerequisite for employment in a modern plant. These persons risk becoming unemployed, and they must fear long-term unemployment sooner or later. Although after a period of unemployment they may find a new job, they cannot enter the core of the modern production process; they must remain on the periphery. Former unemployment and their marginal social position add to the negative attributes they already exhibit. A vicious circle of cumulative unemployment is established. Escaping from it becomes more and more difficult because the experience of unemployment, particularly when repeated, may injure self-confidence and give the unemployed worker a sense of paralysis.[21] "Once a loser, always a loser," as the novelist Hans Fallada put it in his book *Wer einmal aus dem Blechnapf frisst.*

These processes segment the West German work force. One of these segments is made up of well-situated employees in sunshine industries—the winners in the process of implementing the new concepts of production. Diametrically opposed are the poor, chronically unemployed, who are fired and denied access to the functioning centers of the economy. Meanwhile, the ghetto of long-term unemployed in West Germany includes 0.65 million persons (32 percent of all unemployed).[22] The proportion of people with negative attributes and qualifications is much higher within the sample of long-term unemployed than within the average population. Being old or handicapped dramatically increases the probability of falling victim to discrimination in the labor market, and being uneducated reinforces this likelihood.[23]

Even if this rigid segmentation results from various causes, the personnel policy practiced by sunshine sectors also influences the misery of long-term unemployment. This is not to say that the increase in productivity reached in these sectors is directly responsible for the tension in the

20. Volkmar Gottsleben, "Randgruppe in der zertifizierten Arbeitsgesellschaft? Zur abnehmenden Bedeutung der nicht formal Qualifizierten (NFQ) am Arbeitsmarkt," *Mitteilungen aus der Arbeitsmarkt- und Berufsforschung,* 1987, no. 1, p. 10.

21. See Christoph F. Büchtemann and Bernhard von Rosenbladt, "Kumulative Arbeitslosigkeit," *Mitteilungen aus der Arbeitsmarkt- und Berufsforschung,* 1983, no. 3, p. 273.

22. As long-term unemployed are counted, registered unemployed persons who are without work for more than one year without any interruption (see also the more differentiated analysis of Günter Buttler, "Zur mittleren Dauer der Arbeitslosigkeit," *Mitteilungen aus der Arbeitsmarkt- und Berufsforschung,* 1987, no. 2, p. 213).

23. Here we use the official statistics of the German Labor Exchange.

external labor market. The potential negative effects on the labor market of increased productivity are often compensated for by an expanding volume of production, which is also a result of the new concepts. Neither can it be said that the powerful modernizing sectors create external unemployment by means of vertical centralization, that is, by forcing their suppliers to diminish capacity and thus reduce jobs. Some examples of increased vertical centralization do exist; however, some of the most modern plants pass on to suppliers operations that do not fit their own new concepts of production.

When discussing the involvement of the sunshine industries in the scandalous long-term unemployment in West Germany, we refer mainly to the personnel policy of these industries, which follows the principle of splendid isolation. These modernizing sectors tend to use their expansion mainly to stabilize the employment of their own cadres and seldom hire from the ranks of the unemployed. However innovative and farseeing these protagonists of modernization may be in some areas, their hiring policies remain very exclusive. By scrupulously avoiding drawing on the segment of long-term unemployed, the prosperous industries further darken the hopeless situation of the wretches of the labor market.

ENVIRONMENTAL MOVEMENTS AND NEW SOCIAL ALIGNMENTS

The dangers posed by the use of the new technologies (and, indirectly, the new concepts of production) have raised an explosive new issue: ecology. Activists in the ecology movement cite as examples of these dangers the chemical emissions that are ruining nature, gene splicing and biotechnological manipulation of human beings, and the civil and military use of nuclear energy, which, they believe, endanger the liberty of the community and the survival of mankind. Those in charge of the manufacturing process do not acknowledge that natural resources are limited; the industrial designers do not concern themselves with industrial waste; and manufacturers are indifferent to the dangers of some of their products. The ecological crisis resulting from the dangers generated by the new technologies marks a new social and political reality in West Germany.

The theoretical approach to this crisis which categorizes the situation in West Germany today as "perilous," interprets subjection to ecological risks as the characteristic feature of modernity.[24] It also stresses the vulnerability of all members of society to these risks, for they ignore traditional demarcations between the classes. This approach is to some

24. Ulrich Beck, *Risikogesellschaft* (Frankfurt: Suhrkamp, 1986).

extent plausible because new social structures are in fact emerging. Conflicts between the traditionally separated capitalists and laborers have softened, and new conflicts have superseded the old. These new conflicts are generated by the different positions of those who produce the new social perils.[25] Today industries causing the risks battle against industries bearing the risks (power, chemical, and automobile industries versus agriculture, the food industry, and tourism). Traditional class conflicts are subsumed by the common interests of capital and labor in dangerous industries to preserve their investments and workplaces.

If one agrees with the thesis of the perilous society, workers who benefit from rationalization may be seen as the main ally of insecure businesses. Such businesses could win the support of these workers in the fight against ecologists. Not only are their jobs and their newly acquired professionalism at stake but also their rank in society. By problematizing the usefulness and the advantages of technologically advanced products, ecologists undermine the consensus that the most sophisticated products contribute the most to social progress. The current debate about ecology stigmatizes the products of industrial work as dangerous for human beings and nature because the old argument that the disadvantages of these products are compensated by their beneficial attributes is no longer considered valid. Allying themselves to business against attacks from the outside thus probably seems justifiable to these workers insofar as they see themselves defending social progress and refusing to be blamed for destruction. In West Germany forerunners of such a new political bloc were already present in 1986, when employers and employees of the nuclear power stations jointly defended the official energy policy. More than crude bargaining for particular interests underlies such coalitions. The ecological crisis is reorganizing the defenders and supporters of the social system, and there is some reason to believe that the most resolute defenders are involved with the new concepts of production.

But even if that new coalition has already become visible in West Germany, we must be cautious in drawing conclusions. Recent investigations by Hartwig Heine and Rüdiger Mautz at the Sociological Research Institute Göttingen show that even workers in industries under attack from ecologists such as the chemical industry typically do not react in a narrow-minded manner.[26] The probability that a major environmental

25. Ulrich Beck, "Arbeit und Ökologie," in *Göttinger Sozialwissenschaften heute* (forthcoming).
26. See Hartwig Heine and Rüdiger Mautz, "Industriefacharbeiter im Spannungsfeld zwischen Arbeitsplatzinteresse und soziologischer Sensibilisierung," *Soft-Mitteilungen* 13 (1986): 1; Heine and Mautz, "Haben Industriearbeiter besondere Probleme mit dem Umweltthema? Vorlaufige Ergebnisse einer empirischen Untersuchung," *Soft-Mitteilungen* 15 (1988): 16.

hazard will affect everybody, including these workers, and the general awareness of ecological problems in West Germany make it difficult for any social group to ignore ecological questions. Workers in the ecologically hazardous industries are both producers and risk bearers, and some of them react to this contradiction by attempting to restrict their awareness of ecology to their private lives and avoid applying it to their own work. But another group of workers tries to resolve the conflict. According to our findings, many highly skilled workers who have benefited from rationalization recognize environmental risks within the plants as well as outside. These employees often support, for example, production with minimal emissions and products that do not pollute the environment: privately they may support the concern for ecology which is gaining ground in German society.

POLITICS IN AN ERA OF TRANSITION

Politically, one of the most interesting questions regarding the new concepts of production is whether in the long run West German society can remain stable with its large army of unemployed workers. To be sure, those who have lost their jobs or who have never been included in the work process—the "nonclass of the postindustrial proletarians"[27]—represent a strong potential for unrest. Yet it is a mistake to expect that this group will find sufficient power and persistence to transform their critical feelings into a vigorous and effective political movement. Unlike André Gorz, we do not believe that this group holds many revolutionary hopes. If this nonclass remains isolated, it is likely to be worn out in its fight against the establishment. The establishment rules the work system, which remains the basis of economic reproduction and of the power system within society, whatever the theory of postindustrialism may claim.

Regarding the stability of West German society vis-à-vis long-term unemployment, we must shift our attention to the interests and probable behavior of the powerful group of employees in sunshine sectors. Being winners in the game of rationalization, they may be content with society as it is. Together with the traditional power groups—management, financial capitalists, and governing bureaucrats—these winners could form a new establishment whose social power is based on the joint disposition of society's production system and which suppresses the demonstrating nonclass of postindustrial proletarians. Should social conflicts result in a class struggle within the working class, the fate of the nonclass would be sealed.

On the other hand, the interests of the different factions of the

27. André Gorz, *Abschied vom Proletariat* (Reinbek: Rohwohlt, 1983), p. 61.

workers—the personnel cadres in the modern plants and the risk takers in the marketplace—could well be assimilated to form a common political ideal. Although the prerequisites for such solidarity among workers are anything but ensured, one should not underestimate the readiness of all categories of workers to assist one another. In the first place, every worker, even those who have bargaining power, is affected by the uncertainty of future conditions. The strong may be strong only temporarily. Second, if one defines workers' interests not only as job interests but in the context of all their entire lives (for example, the brother of an unemployed person or the father of a girl looking for one of the few open apprenticeships), it becomes clear that these days even the strong can suffer in a capitalist economy. So ties exist that may unite workers. It is not difficult to imagine the cadres using their key positions to fight for reducing work time, for enlarging the groups of winners, and for giving social security to the nonwinners, in short, for removing the narrowness that characterizes the capitalist version of the new concepts of production.

In the context of solidarity among workers the question of whether the new issue of ecology will establish further distinctions within the working class is becoming increasingly important. The findings of Heine and Mautz remind us to be cautious about simplifying the impact of ecology on social behavior. Although the winners in rationalization are by no means automatically apathetic toward ecological risks, the nonwinners are not predestined to be acutely aware of the ecology problem. The interpretation that best fits the changing attitudes of workers is that of an enlarged plurality of interests, opinions, and behavior. The decision to act in a particular way in a particular situation is less predetermined than sociologists often assumed and can be understood in different ways. Only one unequivocal conclusion seems to be justified. Even a typical group of winners—for example, the chemical workers—may show increased sensibility toward the general social risks that accompany modern technology, but this sensibility does not undermine their capacity to work effectively. In our sample of chemical workers, most demonstrated nearly total optimism toward technology; even those who were fully aware of the ecological risks posed by the industry believed that technology itself would provide a solution to the crisis it has caused.

Accordingly, almost all winners opt at least implicitly for continued technological progress. Therefore, the most radical criticism presented in the debate on ecology seems unacceptable to these workers. They support only those who do not condemn technology wholesale. Although these workers are probably more aware than many of technological risks, they are not open to denunciations of the technology they use or produce each workday.

Do the important political forces in West Germany realize that the conditions of politics are changing under the influence of the new concepts of production? The new constellation we described above has cast doubt on the traditional strategies of political parties and presents them with a challenge. Both the conservative and the progressive camps are currently rethinking their platforms.

To understand the revision occurring in the conservative party, one must keep in mind that modern conservative policy cannot be equated with a deliberate rejection of the social consensus and with political pressures toward a dualistic society. Taking a tough line and forcing polarization in society are not goals of German conservatives. At least since World War II they have urged pacification, not segregation, of the poor, notwithstanding the actions of a few old-fashioned plant managers who may still abide by the adage "divide and conquer." In fact, conservatives attempt to avoid activities that associate them with polarization in society and hence bring them into conflict with their own political image. Instead they must pursue a policy that promises at least to look for a solution to the problems. How do the statements of leading German conservatives address the current unemployment and environmental crisis? Not all conservatives retain faith in the healing capacity of laissez-faire technological progress or a free enterprise system in the face of the steady high rate of unemployment and the obvious destruction of nature occurring throughout Germany. Thoughtful conservatives such as Heinz Riesenhuber[28] and Kurt Biedenkopf[29] do not consider the new technologies or the deregulation of the economy to be satisfactory answers.

The most comprehensive response to the changed situation is included in Lothar Späth's attempt to redesign conservative policy.[30] A typical conservative, Späth pleads for fewer work regulations and more flexible and differentiated use of workers; he emphasizes that he does not intend to circumvent long-existing shop control by unions and thereby deny workers their traditional advantages. Like most conservatives, he expects expansion and new jobs to result from acceleration of the new technologies. Nevertheless, he does not speak of a guaranteed reduction of mass unemployment. He realizes that a combination of policies, including coordinated government support for business and workers, is necessary. Although he hopes that the market economy will prove self-regulating, he recognizes that the uncontrolled private de-

28. Heinz Riesenhuber, "Entscheidend ist die Leidenschaft für das, was wir tun. Ansprache vor der Festversammlung der Max-Planck-Gesellschaft," *MPG-Spiegel*, 1987, no. 4, pp. 35–36; Riesenhuber, "Neue Technologien: Verantwortung des Staates," *Zeitschrift für Ingenieure und Techniker* (1987), pp. 105ff.

29. Kurt H. Biedenkopf, *Die neue Sicht der Dinge* (Munich: Piper, 1985), p. 154.

30. Lothar Späth, *Wende in die Zukunft* (Reinbek: Rohwohlt, 1985), pp. 220, 222, 204, 205, 86, 87.

velopment of science and technology could be dangerous. Finally, he stakes his hopes on the "third industrial revolution," which he thinks could result in a synthesis of ecology and productivity and a regeneration of nature, but he believes the state should have the responsibility for controlling the final results of industrial change. Such ideas imply that like left-wingers, conservatives interpret modern society to be all but pacified. Therefore, they include items on their agenda which were in the past typical of the Left: the direction of the future and the role of progress.

It is possible to blame Späth, as the Social Democrats sometimes do, for implementing his plans inconsistently. His program may never be fully accepted even in his own political camp.[31] Späth's ideas, however, indicate a sensitivity to the political reality of the new social crisis. In our opinion the main defect of Späth's policy is that it neglects the difficulties of making the transition from present to future. The ideal of social reconciliation, which is the leitmotiv of Späth's program, is dubious, and to base steps toward an effective redesign of technology, work, and ecology on such a value is unrealistic. Insisting on peaceableness as a fundamental rule of conduct ignores the social conflict inherent in political intervention. In the end, Späth seems interested in masking ongoing disputes instead of solving the underlying problems.

Even more adamant than the Right that its program be adopted, the Left has responded vigorously to West Germany's changed social constellation. At one time a prominent leftist argument interpreted technological change as a prerequisite to historical progress. Yet proponents of this argument did acknowledge (and sometimes still do) that the capitalist version of technological change had a dark side as well as the sunny one.[32] According to that argument, the dark side is caused by the tendency of capitalist enterprises to increase productivity not only by developing productive forces but also by intensifying work (that is, enlarging work load) and by imposing on society the social costs generated by a private, narrow-minded organization of technology. Consequently, the historical mission of the labor movement should be to guarantee that the changes in industry will not lead to negative results but achieve instead progress in productivity as well as more humane working conditions. The creative potential of workers should be culti-

31. We should indeed not underestimate the number of conservatives who naively put their trust in new technologies or market forces. This is also the opinion of the small "liberal" party on whose support the conservatives depend. For a typical example of this neoliberalism, which in economic terms looks like traditional conservatism, see Hans-Dietrich Genscher, "Die technologische Herausforderung," *Aussenpolitik. Zeitschrift für internationale Fragen* (1984), p. 3.

32. Otto Bauer, *Rationalisierung und Fehlrationalisierung* (1931), new ed., vol. 3 (Vienna: Europaverlag, 1976).

vated, not wasted; and the resources of society should be promoted, not spoiled by unnecessary social risks. A remarkable merit of this interpretation was its integration of political aims with the social actors who were expected to carry them out. According to this approach, those who suffer the most from capitalism will most easily recognize its inhumanity. The daily stress they feel from their jobs is nearly impossible to repress. Inasmuch as the labor movement politicizes this work experience, workers become more and more motivated to fight for social reason and a humane future. The workers stand a chance of winning this battle thanks to the power their central positions in the production process gives them.

However effectively or accurately this vision may have represented past situations, it is obviously unsatisfactory. First, capitalist development has become so contradictory and its potential for causing ecological harm so huge that the very principle of technologically founded progress has been called into question. Progress becomes an absurdity in the face of technological development that threatens nature and man, regardless of its benefits for work and wealth. The emphasis on developing productive forces and fostering historical progress, that peculiarity of the traditional leftist model, has obviously been undermined by today's realities. Furthermore, the old strategy of the Left has been called into question as factors that help mobilize party support change. As we have explained, those workers who are strong thanks to their central position in the production process no longer suffer from the shortcomings of capitalism.

The Left is currently marked by a great deal of dissent and confusion. Today it is perfectly possible to encounter views that are leftist and that nonetheless sound like classic comments from conservative critics of industrial civilization. With respect to further technological development this combination of progressive and conservative ideas ends up in a defensive strategy and is often nothing more than a combination of rhetorical radicalism and practical passivity. Such a position may simply hand the political initiative to neoconservatives such as Späth. It also helps to divide the West German Left into Greens and Social Democrats. Yet although the most skeptical voters often support the Greens, skepticism is also found among the Social Democrats. Most Social Democrats admittedly uphold technological progress. In the words of Peter Glotz, "The Social Democrats have to join up with the trade unions and together both should work for a development which realizes social ideals by means of technological innovations, i.e. we must force technology into a new direction for the fulfillment of our utopia."[33] Many Social

33. Peter Glotz, "Arbeit und Technik. Zum Stand der Diskussion," *Die neue Gesellschaft/ Frankfurter Hefte* (1985), p. 213. See also "Die Malaise der Linken," *Der Spiegel* 51 (1987): 128–29.

Democrats are apparently looking for a middle course between a "euphoria toward modernization," associated with the conservatives, and a "dread of technology and progress," associated with the Greens.[34]

Trying to dissociate themselves from the others, these Social Democrats aim to give the conception of progress a sharper specific Social Democratic image. Progress is specified as "new" or "alternative."[35] It does not include developments that haphazardly explore all given technological opportunities and rigidly try to bring people into line. On the contrary, it is intended to select carefully among technological possibilities according to the criteria of suitability for social wealth and the quality of life. Following this consideration, "positive technologies" should enjoy generous government and political support insofar as they increase employment and add to social security. Support should also be given to technologies that offer alternatives to the inhumanity of industrial work. In general, Social Democrats view the new technologies as an important source of progress. But they regard some aspects of the modern technology as dangerous and best avoided (military high technology and nuclear technology) or at least strictly controlled (commercial use of communication technologies, biotechnologies). All these ideas, which appear on the Social Democratic agenda under the slogan "ecological reorientation and revival of economy," demonstrate the party's sensitivity to both the positive and negative sides of technological and economic change. On this basis there is some similarity between Social Democrats and neoconservatives like Späth. This similarity ends when Social Democrats interpret the development as it really is, namely, contradictory (and not as "positive but with some problems"). For this reason they have a better chance of designing a more realistic road to a better future. Control of the transition process, which is Späth's weakness, could be the Social Democrats' strength.

But do the Social Democrats actually have a program that will motivate all their potential supporters and win over a majority of voters in the elections? The Social Democrats today must cope with divisions that have emerged among their traditional constituents as a result of new production concepts and other changes. Their policy has to attract and bring together disparate groups with different experiences and expectations—the technician in the nuclear power plant and the young unemployed person demonstrating against this plant, the computer specialist and the older clerical worker who has been fired, the skilled chemical worker with good chances for employment and the skilled steelworker who has been made redundant, and so on. One of the

34. Willy Brandt, "Technischer Wandel und politische Verantwortung," *Die neue Gesellschaft/Frankfurter Hefte* (1986), p. 314, author's translation.

35. Oskar Lafontaine, *Der andere Fortschritt* (Hamburg: Hoffmann and Campe, 1985); Dieter Spöri, *Aussagen*, election campaign paper, 1987.

party's advantages is its history, which includes its struggle for social justice. But the party's ideas about how to handle the problem of modern technology still seem a bit provisional and patched together. They do not include a message that moves people and excites them to collective action. When it comes to practical policy, this deficiency in conception turns out to be a source of opportunism. Depending on the concrete situation and the party representative speaking, one part of the catalog is stressed and others are forgotten, some groups are appealed to and others neglected. Sometimes the party seems to tend toward leftist postindustrialism, at other times technology freaks dominate the scene. When the party addresses voters, this indecisiveness can turn into propaganda that coddles some groups and hurts others, but those who may be hurt are winked at because they are needed to gain a majority (this has happened in Lower Saxony and also in national elections).

It is, of course, very complicated for the Social Democrats to state their policy in concrete terms that articulate the hidden common denominator of the different groups and interests within the party's electorate. Yet there is the potential for solidarity among the winners in rationalization and the openness of this group to ecological considerations. By affirming a policy that appeals to the attitudes of such voters and articulates them politically, the party could attract these important constituents. But these winners could be won over only if the party agreed to abstain from all antitechnological sentiment, which could cost the Social Democrats the support of the losers. In the long term, however, even this group will not be able to claim that anti-industrialism offers them something. An efficient industrial system that can provide and distribute the necessary resources will be the cornerstone of social equality.

For reasons we have described, West Germany's current political situation is very complicated. The traditional politics of both the Right and the Left have been watered down. The Right-Left division no longer has much bearing on political and economic realities, and there is no telling yet how the final lines among voters will be drawn. One unknown quantity of future development, as we have seen, is the political behavior of personnel in the modernized plants. Will conservatives in Späth's vein succeed in winning over this group, or will the Social Democrats for "new progress" be able to keep it in the labor movement? It is important to know whether the losers in rationalization will turn away from the political system out of disappointment or wrath, or whether ultimately they can be integrated by the Social Democrats. All in all, the situation looks less precarious for the conservatives than for the Social Democrats. Because the Right has a stable core of supporters, it needs to gain the votes of only a few of the rationalization winners and to neutralize the unrest created by the losers in order to win. The Left, on the other hand, confronts extreme difficulties. The party can succeed only by integrating opposed expectations with varied intermediate positions. The political situation in West Germany thus seems a bit absurd. Those with the more stable constituency have the weaker platform; those who are perhaps more convincing have a harder time securing a majority.

Appendix. Data Material Consulted

	Researcher	Topic	Sample	Method	Time	Reference
I	Horst Kern, Michael Schumann	trends of rationalization in industry	chemical industry, car industry, machine tools industry	observations of workplaces and work processes; interviews with management, industrial engineers, workers' representatives, and workers	1981–1983	Kern/Schumann, *Das Ende der Arbeitsteilung?* 1984. Kern/Schumann, "Limits of the Division of Labour," *Economic and Industrial Democracy* 8 (1987), 151–169.
II	Uwe Neumann, Roland Springer, Michael Schumann et al.	"trend report," follow-up study to I	as I (the same plants plus others)	as I	1986–1989	nothing yet published
III	Michael Schumann, Klaus Peter Wittemann, Volker Wittke	trends of rationalization in industry	electric industry	as I	1986–1989	Wittemann/Wittke, "Rationalisierungsstrategien im Umbruch?" *Sofi-Mitteilungen* 14 (1987), 47–86, and Voskamp/Wittemann/Wittke, "Automationskonzepte der Elektroindustrie im Vergleich," *Sofi-Mitteilungen* 15 (1988), 80–94.

The provisional results of survey II do not demand a revision of our main argument. Survey III demonstrates that the electric industry operates on specific conditions that include many restrictions but also some possibilities for the new concepts of production.
  We have left the service sector out of consideration. The research done in this field by our colleagues Martin Baethge and Herbert Oberbeck (see their contribution to this volume) reveals how much the history of rationalization in the tertiary sector differs from that in industrial production. Nevertheless, the employers in the services currently also prefer complete use of their work force, i.e., put a value on the well-qualified white-collar workers.

Part III

INDUSTRY RESPONSES

CHAPTER FIVE

Successful Adjustment to Turbulent Markets: The Automobile Industry

WOLFGANG STREECK

By the mid-1970s, the future of the West German automobile industry looked extremely gloomy. For several years the domestic market had been showing signs of saturation. The first oil shock in 1973 had brought energy shortages and high fuel prices, and the ensuing general economic crisis was bound to depress further the demand for new cars. The revaluation of the deutschemark in 1969 made West German automobiles more expensive in foreign markets, and the breakdown of the Bretton Woods agreement in 1972 added further uncertainties for an industry that was heavily dependent on exports, especially to the United States. Moreover, a new concern with environmental problems had arisen and was likely to make the auto industry a target of extensive regulation. The largest West German producer, Volkswagen, had not replaced its outdated mass production model, the Beetle, with a more modern design. As if all this were not enough, the Japanese, with their superior production system and with goods of unmatched price and

In writing this essay I was helped by Winnetou Sosa, who provided essential research assistance. Unless otherwise indicated, quantitative data have been drawn from the following sources: VDA, *Tatsachen und Zahlen aus der Kraftverkehrswirtschaft,* consecutive editions; VDA, *Das Auto International in Zahlen,* consecutive editions; telephone communications from various staff members of the VDA and representatives of Daimler Benz and Porsche; Automobil-Datenbank des WZB (Lutz Atzert); Karl H. Pitz, "Beschäftigungsrisiken in der Autoindustrie: Nationale und internationale Lösungsansätze aus gewerkschaftlicher Sicht, Frankfurt," manuscript; Business Reports of VW, Audi, Daimler Benz, Opel, Ford, BMW, Porsche, consecutive editions; various reports in *Handelsblatt* and *Manager Magazin*; *Statistische Mitteilungen des Kraftfahrt-Bundesamtes,* consecutive editions; *Fachserie 4 des Statistischen Bundesamtes,* Produzierendes Gewerbe, Reihe 4.2.2., 1982; *Monats-berichte der Deutschen Bank,* various editions: VDA Pressedienst.

quality that conformed to changed consumer preferences, were entering the industry's domestic and foreign markets, and lurking over the horizon were the newly developing countries with their huge supply of cheap labor. Not least, increased militancy among workers after 1969 had added substantially to the industry's wage bill, and a new trade union strategy to overcome the Fordist organization of work in mass manufacturing had led to a successful strike in 1971 for "humanization of working life," which imposed hitherto unknown limitations on managerial perogative.

A decade later, the pessimistic predictions of inevitable decline of one of the key industries of the West German economy have become bizarre exhibits in the museum of economic history. Today, the automobile industry, together perhaps with the chemical and machine tools industries, has become the favorite example of those who continue to believe that West Germany can remain a major economic and industrial power. Many more automobiles were sold in West Germany in 1986 than in 1971, the peak year before the crisis (2.83 million as compared to 2.15 million), and more cars were produced (4.31 million in 1986 as compared to 3.70 million in 1971). In 1986 West German producers still held 67.6 percent of their domestic market, and their export share has increased steadily since 1978 (48.9 percent) to 61.6 percent in 1986. The energy problem has turned out to be far less drastic than expected, and it was considerably eased by technical innovations that cut average fuel consumption of new cars by 23 percent between 1978 and 1985. Japanese competition was countered with a wave of product and process innovations in what had been seen by many as a mature industry with little potential for technical change. Perhaps most important, after a decade of vigorous rationalization, domestic employment in the West German auto industry has actually increased, reaching 717,200 in 1985 as compared to 609,000 in 1973, the year with the highest employment before the crisis. VW, the sick giant of the early 1970s, has rebounded to become again the largest producer in Europe. The West German auto industry is clearly the winner among the old industrial countries of the restructuring period of the 1970s and 1980s, producing today 38 percent of all European automobiles as compared to 32 percent in 1973 and having become the only serious European competitor of the Japanese.

The spectacular performance of West German automobile manufacturers in the extremely competitive world markets of the 1980s was associated with a peculiar product strategy. German automobile production always had a strong specialist element. Daimler-Benz, BMW, and Porsche do not produce a full range of models but concentrate on a comparatively secure niche in the world market for expensive, high-quality, high-performance cars. Their market was largely unaffected by the crisis and remains unchallenged by the Japanese. Like the two Swedish manufacturers, Volvo and Saab—which also expanded considerably during the restructuring period—the German specialist producers kept to their traditional strategy of low-volume, high-margin production, cutting out smaller models and increasing steadily the value added per unit.

Unlike Sweden, however, specialist production alone cannot account for the industry's success because the bulk of German automobile production remains in the volume range. Yet it has been argued that the distinction between specialist and volume production was eroded in the 1970s. Although for a long time the "conventional wisdom" in the industry was "Be a GM or a BMW, but nothing in between,"[1] the Japanese manufacturers were successful in the small and medium-sized mass market largely because they introduced a level of quality and a number of features that had previously been confined to large specialist cars. West German mass manufacturers responded to the quality and price competitiveness of the Japanese by moving upmarket: improving product design and product quality; offering a broader range of options and model specifications to meet better the individual customer's preferences and thereby relieve the pressure of price competition; and generally increasing the value added per car, which largely offset the unemployment resulting from the introduction of microelectronic production equipment. Most notable in this respect was VW, which moved away from "Beetle monoculture" in 1974 and introduced a completely new model range—including the Golf GTI (1976), which combined the features of a mass-market automobile with those of a specialist car—while at the same time not only extending its separate upmarket Audi line but also using Audi technology for design of other models. In many ways, this was a Swedish product strategy, with marketing methods abroad that successfully exploited national stereotypes of German quality manufacturing and with a pricing policy of high margins especially in foreign countries.[2]

This product and process strategy of an upmarket move within the mass-market segment—with high product variety, flexible specifications, and a strong emphasis on quality engineering and manufacturing—brought commercial success in the face of increased competition and sustained high and growing employment in spite of more efficient production technologies. In effect, the West German automobile indus-

---

1. Alan Altshuler et al., *The Future of the Automobile: The Report of MIT's International Automobile Program* (Cambridge, Mass.: MIT Press, 1984).
2. A famous Audi advertisement on British television ends with the words, "*Vorsprung durch Technik,* as they say in Germany, France, Italy, Spain, etc. etc." The German words are not translated.

try in the 1970s restructured mass production in the mold of specialist production, blending important elements of both, and producing small quantities of specific model variations along with large quantities of basic models.[3] This strategy may have been inspired by the strong specialist tradition in the West German automobile industry, and it was almost symmetrically reciprocated by the two leading specialist producers, BMW and Daimler Benz, which in the same period gradually entered the family car market, applying quality manufacturing methods to mass production. The culmination of this process was the introduction in the early 1980s of the first Daimler Benz compact, the 190, which increased the company's sales of passenger cars to no less than half of total VW sales; raised its market share in West Germany above that of Ford; and resulted in a yearly output of Daimler Benz cars far in excess of, for example, the British mass manufacturer BL.[4] High-volume specialist production, based on superior product design and rigorous quality standards, is now generally regarded as the most likely success formula for automobile production in old industrial, high-wage countries. It also fits in astonishingly well with the traditional pattern of West German manufacturing, which has always drawn its strength from high quality and customized design.[5] Moreover, it seems to be of importance far beyond the automobile industry itself, providing a model of restructuring and adjustment for other old industries such as steel and textiles which need to find new profitable markets sheltered from price competition.[6]

How exactly was the restructuring of the industry in the 1970s and 1980s toward a product strategy of high-volume, diversified quality production accomplished? What were the political, historical, and institutional resources on which West German automobile manufacturers could draw in this remarkably successful industrial adjustment? This chapter will address these subjects in some detail, but it will place them in a more general and more forward-looking perspective. Its main objective is to discuss the question whether this impressive performance is likely to be continued and repeated and whether there are lessons to be learned from the past that can usefully be applied in the future, both in the automobile industry and others. To do this, the chapter will start

3. For a more general discussion see Arndt Sorge and Wolfgang Streeck, "Industrial Relations and Technical Change: The Case for an Extended Perspective," in Richard Hyman and Wolfgang Streeck, eds., *New Technology and Industrial Relations* (Oxford: Blackwell, 1988), pp. 19–47.

4. In 1985, BL built 465,100 and Daimler Benz 537,910 passenger cars.

5. Jean C. Cox and Herbert Kriegbaum, *Growth, Innovation and Employment: An Anglo-German Comparison* (London: Anglo-German Foundation for the Study of Industrial Society, 1980).

6. Michael J. Piore and Charles F. Sabel, *The Second Industrial Divide* (New York: Basic Books, 1984).

with a brief description of the structure of the West German auto industry, paying special attention to what may be typical and untypical for West German industry in general. It will then look at both emerging problems—or sources of possible change—and the potential of the industry to respond to them successfully at three separate levels: the shop floor and the individual enterprise, the national political system, and the global economy.

THE INDUSTRIAL STRUCTURE OF AUTOMOBILE MANUFACTURING IN WEST GERMANY

There are five major automobile manufacturers in West Germany: Volkswagen (VW) with Audi, Opel (the German subsidiary of General Motors), Daimler Benz, Ford, and BMW. The largest producer is VW, with a work force, at the end of 1985, of 160,000 (22 percent of the industry as a whole), an output of 1.7 million passenger cars (42 percent), and a sales of DM 48,531 million (29 percent). Daimler Benz sales of passenger cars exceed those of any other producer except VW (Table 5.1); if the company's substantial truck division is included, motor vehicle sales increase to DM 37,078.5 million. The second largest number of passenger cars is produced by Opel, the German subsidiary of General Motors, followed by Daimler Benz, Ford, and BMW.

Table 5.1. The six major West German automobile manufacturers in 1985 (passenger cars and domestic operations only)

Manufacturer	Employees	Output units	Sales million DM
VW	159,991[a]	1,734,853	48,531.4[a]
VW	123,598[a]	1,376,241	38,920.6[a]
Audi	36,393	358,612	9,610.8
Opel	57,273	903,150	14,794.7
Daimler Benz	109,000[b]	537,909	23,862.0
Ford	45,991	505,231	14,443.5
BMW	46,814	431,085	14,246.4
Porsche	7,915	54,458	3,567.9

SOURCES: VDA; business reports.
[a] Including a light truck component.
[b] Including trucks.

Concentration is lower in the West German auto industry than in any other leading producer country except Japan. Going by what up to a few years ago was received opinion in industrial economics, the industry's highly decentralized structure would appear to be in urgent need of rationalization and integration. But although the pattern of industrial

117

organization seems to correspond to an early stage of the product cycle, it has been stable for several years and there are no indications of impending change. This situation contrasts sharply with that in the United Kingdom, where a number of independent producers were merged in the 1960s and 1970s into one national car manufacturer to achieve higher economies of scale.[7] Today, it is increasingly recognized—not least in view of the Japanese case—that the presence of a large number of independent firms may be a source of strength, making the vital domestic market an exercise ground for competition abroad and preserving a variety of designs and engineering philosophies which seem to be conducive to success in turbulent and diversified world markets.[8]

Domestic competition is vigorous, both among German producers and between them and foreign manufacturers.[9] For reasons that will be discussed later, German manufacturers enjoy little protection in their home market. Nevertheless, they have together managed to hold on to a market share of 67.6 percent in 1986. Of this share, 28.6 percent was held by VW (including Audi), followed by Opel (13.3 percent), Daimler Benz (10.7 percent), Ford (9.4 percent), and BMW (5.2 percent). The fragmentation of their highly contested home market forces West German producers to expand into exports because their domestic sales potential does not normally permit sufficient economies of scale. In this sense, West German-built cars are by economic necessity "world cars" (or, better, "Europa cars"). The demanding West German market also requires producers to offer a broad range of models, and in 1986 the ten highest-selling models accounted for only 56 percent of all West German-built cars sold in West Germany.

West German producers represent a wide variety of manufacturing traditions and histories. Mass manufacturing methods were introduced by the two American multinationals, GM and Ford, that set up German subsidiaries in 1925 (Ford in Berlin) and 1929 (GM taking over Adam Opel AG in Rüsselheim). They met with sustained skepticism and resistance on the part of established, small, craft-style manufacturers. The Nazis failed in their attempt to make the industry join together for the mass production of a "people's car" (Volkswagen) and built their own automobile factory on a green-field site that was later called Wolfsburg. The company, owned by a subsidiary of Arbeitsfront (the Nazi *Ersatz* of

7. Stephen Wilks, *Industrial Policy and the Motor Industry* (Manchester: Manchester University Press, 1984).

8. Altshuler et al., *Future of the Automobile*.

9. Competition among the German manufacturers has increased in recent years as a result of the restructuring process. For example, just as Daimler Benz moved into the traditional BMW market by developing the 190 model, BMW now challenges Daimler Benz with its 7 series. Moreover, Audi—and thus VW—today operates in a market segment in which it competes with both Daimler Benz and BMW.

the trade unions), bought its production equipment from Ford. For his contribution to the modernization of German industry, Henry Ford in 1939 received the highest civilian German decoration, the *Schwarzer Adlerorden,* from a grateful Führer. When shortly thereafter the war began, the new plant was used exclusively to build vehicles for the army.

After the war and the division of the country, a north-south divide emerged between north German mass production (VW, Ford, Opel) and south German craft production (BMW, Daimler Benz, Audi, NSU, Porsche, and others), especially after the collapse in 1963 of the Bremen company, Borgward, whose production strategy resembled that of the south Germans. Regional differences correspond to differences in manufacturing philosophies although these are difficult to pin down, with the south Germans having always had a ("small and beautiful") image of technological creativity and engineering perfectionism. The regional divide was crossed only twice, by two significant events: the takeover of Audi (1964) and NSU (1969) by VW, which ultimately enabled the parent company to accomplish its critical model change in the first half of the 1970s (the new models were based on designs that had been developed at NSU); and the location in Bremen of the new Daimler Benz plant for the "mass" production of the 190 compact, which started in 1984. It is remarkable that except for these two cases, none of the south German producers has ever set up a plant in north Germany and vice versa. Moreover, Audi has managed up to the present day to resist its full integration into Volkswagen and maintains a degree of independence which is only grudgingly granted by central VW management.

Ownership patterns vary strongly among German manufacturers. Opel and Ford are owned fully by their American parent companies and are to different degrees integrated in their worldwide operations. VW was held in trust after the war by the federal government and the Land of Lower Saxony. In 1960, 60 percent of the shares were sold in small allotments to private owners ("people's shares"), with the Federal Republic and Lower Saxony each keeping 20 percent of the capital. At present, the federal government is planning to privatize its remaining shareholding. A large part of Daimler Benz capital (about 39 percent) was for a long time in the hands of the Flick industrial dynasty. After a family quarrel in 1975, they decided to sell most of their Daimler Benz shares, amounting to 29 percent of the company's total stock. Among the would-be buyers was the shah of Iran. Under pressure from the federal government, which had to be shielded from the public to avoid foreign policy complications, the shares were sold to the Deutsche Bank, which held them for several years and then placed them on the market. To prevent ownership becoming too dispersed, the bank did not sell the shares directly but set up a special holding company, which today owns 25.2 percent of the Daimler Benz capital. Shares in the holding were sold to the public, one-half to institutional investors and the rest to small shareholders. Deutsche Bank itself owns another 28.1 percent of Daimler Benz shares, and since 1974 14 percent have been owned by the state of Kuwait. In 1986 the Flick family sold its remaining 10 percent of Daimler Benz stock, again to the Deutsche Bank, which distributed it in small quantities. As a result, 32.7 percent is now held by about 160,000 small shareholders. Approximately 50 percent of BMW is still owned by the Quandt family, which also has interests in the automobile supply sector (holding in particular a majority share in Varta) and which until 1974 held the 14 percent share in Daimler Benz that was sold to the emir of Kuwait. Porsche is owned by the numerous descendants of the legendary Ferdinand Porsche who, among other things, designed the Volkswagen Beetle.

As is generally the case in West German industry, the influence of the banks on the automobile sector, especially on the four West German-owned companies, is strong. Bank representatives sit on all five supervisory boards, either as shareholders or representing the proxy votes for shares they have in deposit. Each manufacturer has a long-term standing relationship with one bank, which serves as *Hausbank*.[10] Little is known about the way the banks exercise their influence, but in the VW crisis of 1974 the Deutsche Bank was crucial in stimulating reorganization by threatening, in a supervisory board meeting, to withhold further credit and let the company go to the receiver.[11]

West Germany has a strong and technically advanced automobile supply industry, as exemplified by firms like Varta, VDO, and, in particular, the industrial giant Bosch. West German auto manufacturers buy most of their supplies domestically although suppliers are subject to the same industrial wage agreement as assemblers. Domestic sources account for 64.9 percent of total supply purchases of West German assemblers, including the two American multinationals.[12] One reason for this high use of domestic suppliers is certainly the traditional obsession of German manufacturers with product quality. It also offers opportunities for close cooperation between assemblers and suppliers not

10. In 1985, the supervisory boards of the German auto manufacturers included representatives of the following banks: VW: Deutsche Bank, Dresdner Bank; Audi: Bayerische Vereinsbank, Commerzbank; Daimler Benz: Deutsche Bank, Commerzbank; Ford: Commerzbank; BMW: Dresdner Bank; Porsche: Landesgirokasse, Landessparkasse.

11. Wolfgang Streeck, *Industrial Relations in West Germany: A Case Study of the Car Industry* (New York: St. Martin's, 1984).

12. It seems that in the late 1970s even more components were produced in West Germany. Our calculations indicate that 72.7 percent of components were produced in West Germany in 1979, but statistics are poor on this subject and further inquiry is needed.

just in quality control but also in research and development. One example is the long-standing alliance between Daimler Benz and Bosch (both located in Stuttgart), which resulted among other things in the development of a sophisticated antiblocking system (ABS) device. Domestic sourcing also makes for short supply lines, and in this respect the German manufacturers were always closer to the "Kanban" than to the "world car" philosophy. In fact, recent efforts to introduce a zero-stock purchasing policy went remarkably smoothly. Especially the south German manufacturers rely extensively on local networks of small craft (*Handwerk*) firms for specialized supplies,[13] which is one reason why in Baden-Württemberg, a regional economy largely dominated by Daimler Benz, unemployment is lower than anywhere else in the Federal Republic.

West German auto assemblers are highly vertically integrated, and this is one major difference from their Japanese competitors. In-house value added accounts on average for 40 percent of total production value, as compared to 30 percent in France, 33 percent in Italy, and 35 percent in the United Kingdom. This integration occurs in spite of the presence of the two American producers that are closely integrated into their companies' worldwide production networks. The apparent preference for making rather than buying parts seems in part to be accounted for by pressures from the works councils for high and stable employment. Also, West German manufacturers seem to be less interested than most of their international competitors in joint ventures with other companies, unless they are the dominant party and in control of the engineering element. None of the major international cooperative arrangements in the industry in recent years includes a West German manufacturer. There is also a preference for large, integrated plants; the biggest German plant, VW Wolfsburg, employs no less than sixty-five thousand people.

Furthermore, West German automobile manufacturers, like other big West German firms, have not made significant efforts at diversification, and they are certainly far from being or becoming multi-industrial conglomerates. (This is in stark contrast to the recent development of Volvo.) BMW and Porsche produce only automobiles, although Porsche has recently been branching out into general engineering services. In 1979 VW invested some of its immense profits by acquiring an ailing West German office equipment manufacturer, TA, for its potential in producing microelectronic components. The takeover, which can be interpreted as a move toward higher vertical integration, turned out to

---

13. On the concept of *Handwerk* see Wolfgang Streeck, "The Territorial Organization of Interests and the Logics of Associative Action: The Case of Handwerk in West Germany," *Discussion Paper* IIM/LMP 86-24 (Wissenschaftszenstrum Berlin, 1986).

be a commercial disaster, and the adventure was ended in 1986 with a loss of more than DM 2,000 million. Having sold TA, VW decided to invest its remaining money in a majority share in the Spanish automobile producer SEAT. Finally, until 1985 Daimler Benz was exclusively an automobile producer, diversifying only by drawing half its sales from trucks (the production of which has always been comparatively craftlike).

In 1985 and 1986, however, Daimler Benz bought, out of its giant cash flow, the high-technology engine manufacturer MTU, the aerospace company Dornier, and the reorganized electrotechnical corporation AEG, all located in south Germany. As a result, Daimler Benz became the largest private employer in West Germany, with a work force of 273,000 in 1986. It remains to be seen, however, to what extent this represents a move toward genuine diversification. As the three acquisitions become integrated in the Daimler Benz organization, it is becoming clear that AEG will serve as an in-house source of microelectronic components, accounting for an increasing share of the value added especially in large cars. The integration of AEG is bound to affect Daimler Benz's privileged relationship with its presently most important electronics supplier, Bosch. Moreover, Siemens is now rapidly moving, for commercial as well as technological reasons, into the market for microelectronic automobile components, which will result in three major German corporations competing with each other in the same field. These moves have given rise to speculations that the banks' influence on industrial strategies will decline given that the Deutsche Bank has long been the *Hausbank* of Daimler Benz, Bosch, and Siemens. Indeed it is said that the bank has tried in vain to protect Bosch from the emerging powerful competition from two other members of what used to be called the "Deutsche Bank Club."

The strong conservatism that pervades the German automobile industry is also apparent in its single-minded pursuit of engineering excellence. West German car manufacturers invest large sums in research and development so that the costs of introducing a new model are considerably higher than in all competitor countries. In addition, firms hold strong, deeply rooted opinions on what distinguishes sound from poor engineering, and such opinions often take precedence over marketing considerations. For example, buyers who expect a new model every two or three years are not likely to be accommodated by German producers, who consider serving such frivolous preferences contradictory to their "sound engineering" philosophy. West German manufacturers typically choose to undergo a long trial and testing period before marketing a technical innovation so they can be sure that the new technology is *ausgereift* (mature). Sometimes this has meant that competitors were able to come out with a similar feature earlier. But a firm like Daimler Benz is known to be content with being "the better second" if necessary to satisfy its engineers' quest for perfection. A similar attitude seems to exist in the West German high-technology sector as Gerd Junne argues in this volume. Similarly, when Japanese firms offer features like four-wheel steering, the typical response of a West German design department would be that it could of course make the same thing and better; but it is in the business of sound engineering, and if people want gimmicks, they can always buy a Japanese car. This technological snobbery can be economically viable only as long as there are enough customers who are willing to be educated by professional engineers on what technology is good for them and what is not; if more and more car buyers were to prefer a toy over a high-performance tool, the German "engineering culture" would likely be in trouble. Up to now, however, its formula has worked very well, and in the 1970s and 1980s both Ford and GM have increasingly relied for their worldwide operations on their West German design departments in Cologne and Rüsselsheim, although engineering services per hour were more expensive there than in other European countries.

In sum, the West German automobile industry offers a picture of remarkable traditionalism. Companies are highly integrated, operate giant plants, and diversify, if at all, only into closely related sectors, perhaps because of the leading role played by engineers in top management. Old-fashioned competition has not given way to sophisticated cooperative arrangements, and financial strategies are conservative, with current profits and *Hausbank* credit being much more important sources of capital than equity. There is even a degree of parochialism in the habit of "buying German," cultivating a domestic supply base of small artisanal firms, and rejecting cross-national cooperation—a tendency that is also visible in the low degree of multinationalization of the West German auto manufacturers. All this is, to different degrees, characteristic of the rest of the West German manufacturing sector, and by explaining how this apparent traditionalism could have gone together with the industry's astonishing performance in the difficult world markets of the 1980s, we may be able to draw some conclusions about the prospects of the entire West German economy.

PRESSURES FOR ADJUSTMENT AND SOURCES OF CHANGE

The Shop Floor and the Enterprise

Nowhere else has the West German industrial relations system performed better than in the automobile industry, and no industry has in the past contributed more to the evolution of the system than autos.[14] Most of the important innovations in West German industrial relations originated in this industry and then spread to other branches and sectors. Especially in the 1970s and 1980s, the industry's labor relations have been a model case for the ability of West German enterprise and shop floor institutional settings to process and absorb rapid economic and technical changes. Indeed, their flexibility and contribution to manufacturing performance enabled them to bear the brunt of an unprecedented adjustment process without requiring political intervention. This was not because of trade union weakness; if there is a stronghold of trade unionism in West Germany, it is in the big auto manufacturers. But trade union strength in the industry is organized in a highly governable pattern of institutions at the point of production,[15] which in the 1970s and 1980s revealed a remarkable "elective affinity" to the new production methods and product strategies that enabled the industry to compete so successfully—so much so that one feels tempted to speculate whether and how the industry's strategic choices may have been conditioned in part by its labor relations system.[16]

One remarkable aspect of the industry's performance is its increasingly important role as a source of employment. Employment in the automobile industry in the mid-1980s was higher than before the first oil shock. More astonishing, perhaps, much of the increase took place in the 1980s, a period of steeply rising unemployment and declining employment. In 1985, the West German automobile industry (passenger cars and trucks) employed 717,200 workers, or 3.2 percent of the total national work force and 7.8 percent of the work force in manufacturing. Of these, about 245,000 were engaged in the production of automobile components. This was well above the level of 1981, when automobile manufacturing employed 670,400 workers equivalent to 2.9 percent of total employment and 6.6 percent of manufacturing employment (220,000 of these workers produced components). Thus in the 1980s a trend continued that had already been visible in the late 1970s, when the automobile industry was found to be one of the few industrial sectors in West Germany to generate employment growth inside an overall declining manufacturing sector.[17]

14. For more detail on automobile industrial relations in West Germany, see Streeck, *Industrial Relations in West Germany.*

15. Ian Maitland, *The Causes of Industrial Disorder: A Comparison between a British and a German Factory* (London: Routledge & Kegan Paul, 1983).

16. Wolfgang Streeck, "Industrial Change and Industrial Relations in the Motor Industry: An International View," *Economic and Industrial Democracy* 8 (1987): 437–62.

17. Wolfgang Streeck and Andreas Hoff, "Manpower Management and Industrial Relations in the Restructuring of the World Automobile Industry," *Discussion Paper* IIM/ LMP 83–35 (Wissenschaftszentrum Berlin, 1983).

Absolute and relative employment gains were achieved by an industry that is, by domestic standards, highly unionized. In an economy in which union members constituted 40.5 percent of the work force in 1986, roughly 70 percent of the automobile work force (excluding the car repair shops) were members of IG Metall in 1984, the last year for which exact calculations are possible. Membership in other unions is negligible. IG Metall is an industrial union with as many as 2.7 million members in 1986, which organizes both blue- and white-collar workers in the entire metalworking sector. Union membership among workers of the big assemblers is even higher and can be estimated to range between 80 and 95 percent, even though the closed shop is illegal in West Germany. Other forms of union security do exist, however, notably check-off arrangements and participation of union representatives in the hiring of new workers, which often amounts to a de facto union shop.

The road vehicles industry is covered by industrial agreements on wages and other, "qualitative" matters that are negotiated for the entire metalworking sector between IG Metall and the employers' association, Gesamtmetall. Again, the car repair shops are excepted because they are part of the artisanal sector, which has a separate employers' association; workers in car repair shops are also represented by IG Metall although union membership is low in this area. Another special case is VW, which, because of its history of public ownership, never joined an employers' association and negotiates a special industrial agreement with IG Metall. In principle, however, VW agreements follow the general outlines of the metalworking agreement.

As a result of informal but effective intersectoral coordination of collective bargaining in West Germany, interindustry wage spread is low by international standards,[18] especially in the different branches of the metalworking industry, which are covered by the same encompassing wage agreement. Wage drift in individual plants or enterprises is limited by institutional factors. Enterprise-level work-force representatives are barred under codetermination law from negotiating on wages, and industrial unions jealously guard their wage bargaining and strike monopoly. Nevertheless, some wage drift exists, and wages at the big car assemblers are about 20 to 25 percent higher than stipulated by the metal industry agreement. About the same difference exists between the VW agreement and the industrial agreement.[19] In the national wage structure, the auto industry is doing well, with wages in road vehicle

18. David Marsden, "Collective Bargaining and Positive Adjustment Policies," Report to the OECD Working Party on Industrial Relations, MAS/WP3(81)4 (Paris: OECD, 1981).

19. But there is no wage drift at VW because wages are determined by company agreement.

building amounting to about 120 percent of average wages in the West German economy.[20] Wages in the West German automobile industry are also high by international standards; total labor costs per hour in 1986 amounted to about 87 percent of U.S. labor costs and 115 percent of labor costs in Japan.[21] Wages in the West German automobile industry are also higher than in other Western European countries, amounting to 141 percent of French, 139 percent of Italian, and 186 percent of British labor costs.[22] High and sticky labor costs are an important factor forcing West German automobile manufacturers to orient themselves toward non-price-competitive markets.

Being covered by the general agreement for the metal industry has advantages as well as disadvantages for West German auto manufacturers. Although it does not protect them from high labor costs, the legal enforceability of agreements during their currency—normally about one year—precludes short-term opportunistic wage militancy especially by sectional groups in the labor force in periods of prosperity. By preventing competitive bargaining, settlements at the sectoral level enhance predictability and provide for a stable, governable wage structure. The resulting stability of shop-floor labor relations contributes to high productivity, which may make up for high labor costs. Ford's West German plants, for example, throughout the 1970s had lower unit costs than the British plants, with identical models and technology. Coverage by the general industrial agreement also means that firms with above average performance can make high profits before wages are adjusted; to the extent that such profits are reinvested this is not necessarily in contradiction with union objectives. It means, however, that firms experiencing losses cannot expect to get short-term wage concessions. For example, VW, although not included in the metal industry agreement, had to concede a wage increase in 1974 of 11.0 percent—about the level of the metal industry in general—even though the company was operating on the brink of bankruptcy.[23]

Inside the encompassing bargaining unit of the metal sector, the auto industry performs something of a pilot role for the union. Strikes by IG Metall in pursuit of an industrial agreement are always selective, and since the 1960s they have regularly included the auto industry, espe-

20. Hans-Jürgen Krupp, "Herausforderungen des Strukturwandels für die Wirtschaftspolitik," *Schriftenreihe über Arbeit und Arbeitsbeziehungen* 5/1985 (Vienna: Bundesministerium für soziale Verwaltung, 1984), pp. 28–38.
21. Exchange rates obviously play an important part in such calculations. Applying the DM-dollar rate of February 1987, West German labor costs are equivalent to 103 percent of U.S. labor costs. Under the exchange rates of 1980, German labor costs were as high as 186 percent of Japanese labor costs.
22. These calculations are based on a communication from the VDA.
23. Streeck, *Industrial Relations in West Germany*.

cially in a prosperous area in northern Baden-Württemberg which is economically dominated by Daimler Benz. The three largest and by far most important strikes of the 1970s and 1980s were called here, resulting in regional pilot settlements that were then transferred by the parties to the entire country and later gradually diffused throughout the economy: the strike for improvements in working conditions and work organization ("humanization of working life") in 1971, the strike for "protection against rationalization" in 1978, and the strike for reduction of working hours in 1984. Each settlement represented a breakthrough for the trade union movement and a major innovation in industrial relations. Although the conflicts that preceded them were long and bitter and always involved a large number of workers being locked out, each time relations were repaired afterward, and in spite of its role as a testing ground and battlefield for trade union policy the auto industry has remained a paragon example of a style of industrial relations that has aptly been described as "cooperative conflict resolution."[24]

If industrial unionism is one cornerstone of the industry's industrial relations system, codetermination—the "peculiar institution" of West German labor relations—is the other.[25] Workers in West Germany are represented under the Works Constitution Act (last amended in 1972) by works councils elected every three years by an establishment's entire work force. Works councils have legal rights to information, consultation, and co-decision making on a wide range of subjects. They may negotiate works agreements with the employer that are an equivalent to industrial agreements at the enterprise level but must not deviate from an industrial agreement if one exists. Works councils are not permitted to call strikes; they always have to take recourse to arbitration or mediation. In large firms, there are elected work-force and trade-union representatives on the supervisory board, which outside the coal and steel industry falls short of the 50 percent of the votes demanded by the unions.

Works councils in the large auto assembly firms generally have more influence on more subjects than given to them by the law. The works council at VW Wolfsburg has sixty-five members who are released from their normal duties and serve as practically full-time union representatives. Works council influence differs between firms, the two opposite extremes probably being VW and Ford, but generally the situation is

24. E. Jacobs, S. Orwell, P. Paterson, and F. Weltz, *The Approach to Industrial Change in Britain and Germany* (London: Anglo-German Foundation for the Study of Industrial Society, 1978).
25. For a detailed account of codetermination see Wolfgang Streeck, "Co-determination: The Fourth Decade," in Bernhard· Wilpert and Arndt Sorge, eds., *International Perspectives on Organizational Democracy* (New York: Wiley, 1984), pp. 391–422.

well described by a General Motors manager who concluded about Opel Rüsselsheim: "Without the works council nothing goes; with the works council everything goes."[26]

Leading works councillors are always also elected supervisory board members in which capacity they represent the work force together with full-time union officials. The structure of influence at the supervisory board level differs markedly between West-German- and American-owned firms; whereas at Opel and Ford the shareholder representatives are all delegates from the American parent company, in the German firms the shareholder side is less monolithic. The influence of the work force on the supervisory board is clearly strongest at VW, with the president of IG Metall serving traditionally as vice-president of the VW supervisory board, much to the dismay of small shareholders. VW also as a rule reserves the personnel director's seat on the management board for a trade union nominee, following the practice in the coal and steel industry.

Codetermination and industrial unionism complement each other in a complex pattern of interaction. More than 80 percent of elected works councillors are trade unionists, and except for a few cases of factional strife and local discontent this has been the case for decades. Works councils have become the center of trade union organization at the workplace, in the auto industry even more than elsewhere. Moreover, all external work-force representatives on supervisory boards are full-time IG Metall officials, and leading works councillors hold important trade union offices; for example, the chairman of the central VW works council is routinely elected to the IG Metall national executive committee. Works councils perform vital security functions for trade unions. The legal no-strike rule under codetermination serves to protect the strike monopoly of industrial unions, and works councils are charged by law with supervising the implementation of industrial agreements. There is also the possibility for industrial agreements to delegate specific subjects to works councils and employers for regulation by works agreement, and this practice has been increasingly used in recent years in response to the growing complexity of industrial relations issues. The result was an inconspicuous but nevertheless significant decentralization of the industrial relations system which has increased its flexibility. Again, this trend was particularly strong in the automobile industry.

Codetermination, with its peculiar rules of the game, has become the institutional core of what is best described as a firmly established productivity coalition between management and labor at the point of production. Prototypically in the automobile industry, codetermination has provided the basis for a trade union policy of cooperative productivism

26. Interview with the author.

which is not adequately caught by the often-used concept of "enterprise patriotism" (*Betriebspatriotismus*) as it is generally supported by the full-time union officials sitting on the industry's supervisory boards and giving advice to works councils. The tendency of works councils in West Germany to identify with the economic fate of their firm because they are elected as representatives of an enterprise's entire work force is reinforced in the auto industry by a keen sense, shared by the external union, of exposure to a volatile and competitive world market. As a consequence, hardly anywhere is there greater willingness than among automobile trade unionists to think through and accept the consequences of labor-management cooperation. Together with the opportunities offered by the framework of industrial unionism and codetermination, this has given rise in the 1970s and 1980s to an interactive configuration of policies and institutional structures which appears to have formed a "virtuous circle" ideally matched to, and indeed almost making inevitable, an industrial strategy of upmarket restructuring.[27] This configuration includes:

(1) *The emergence of internal labor markets.* Employment in the West German auto industry has always been comparatively stable, with firms such as Daimler Benz and BMW having an informal policy, as part of their corporate culture, not to dismiss workers for economic reasons. But employment stability increased further in the critical second half of the 1970s, when in all other countries it declined.[28] This reflects the effect of industrial agreements on protection against rationalization and of works council influence as well as the codetermination legislation of 1972 and 1976. For example, VW conceded a far-reaching employment guarantee in 1976 in return for works council and union agreement to production in the United States. Works councils also generally oppose fixed-term contracts, which had in the past been given primarily to foreign workers, so management could not use hiring and firing to adjust employment. In compensation for the growing (external) rigidity of employment, works councils in the 1970s cooperated in making the internal labor market more flexible and supported the introduction of medium- and long-term manpower planning, in which they became closely involved.[29] The trend toward internal labor markets was reinforced by industrial agreements making it obligatory for employers to offer new jobs first to the existing work force. In 1978 a landmark agreement was signed at VW on a new payment system that simplified

27. For more detailed discussion, see Streeck, "Industrial Change and Industrial Relations."

28. Streeck and Hoff, "Manpower Management and Industrial Relations."

29. Andreas Hoff, "Assessing Investment-Related Medium-Term Manpower Needs: A Case Study from the German Automobile Industry," *Discussion Paper* IIM/LMP 84-3 (Wissenschaftszentrum Berlin, 1984).

the wage structure and introduced broader job descriptions, thereby facilitating internal mobility.[30] The growing fixity of employment made it necessary for managements to devise manpower, production, product, and marketing strategies capable of sustaining a constant work force. At the same time, growing sophistication of internal labor market management, with works councils serving as effective comanagers, afforded the internal flexibility required for diversified high-quality production.

(2) *A large-scale training and retraining effort.* German manufacturing industries have always employed a comparatively large proportion of skilled workers, which formed a human resource base compatible with paternalistic policies of stable employment. This tradition was reinforced in the automobile industry during the restructuring phase by a strong commitment of unions and works councils to training as a way of maintaining employment in internal labor markets and reducing unemployment among youth. In the second half of the 1970s, the number of apprentices in the West German automobile industry increased sharply while in other countries, apprenticeship programs were cut.[31] This increase is attributable to the neocorporatist West German vocational training system, which provides trade unions and employers' associations with institutionalized opportunities to influence individual employers' training decisions. Overskilling contributed to the emergence of internal labor markets in that new recruitment was often limited to apprentices, who, in the absence of vacancies for skilled workers, were temporarily assigned to production jobs. It also added to firms' stock of human capital, increasing their capacity to absorb technological change and giving them a competitive edge over foreign producers. Investment in retraining and further training was also expanded, for technological reasons as well as to facilitate redeployment. Offering displaced workers retraining is obligatory for employers under rationalization protection agreements and works agreements on new technology. This general policy of upskilling seems to explain more than any other factor the decline in the number of foreign workers, which is paralleled by an overall decline in employment of the unskilled. Both employers and works councils in the automobile industry played a leading role in the adaptation of the metal industry vocational training scheme to new technology.

(3) *A long-term investment perspective on the part of both firms and workers' representatives.* Strong worker representation under codetermination has

---

30. Eva Brumlop, *Arbeitsbewertung bei flexiblem Personaleinsatz: Das Beispiel Volkswagen AG* (Frankfurt am Main: Campus, 1986); Brumlop and Ulrich Jürgens, "Rationalization and Technical Change: A Case Study of Volkswagen," in O. Jacobi et al., eds., *Technological Change, Rationalization and Industrial Relations* (London: Croom Helm, 1986), pp. 73–94.
31. Streeck and Hoff, "Manpower Management and Industrial Relations."

several times been found to coincide with high reinvestment of profits, with professional management and works councils sometimes conspiring against shareholders.[32] It has also been shown that German firms in sectors exposed to the world market tend to have long-term profit expectations and performance standards and high intangible investment in marketing and research, which pays only over a long period.[33] This fits with a characteristic conservative attitude toward technology that places more emphasis on perfection than on being the first in the market. Moreover, the share of the total receipts of a West German automobile firm that is paid out in wages is lower than, for example, in British automobile firms although wages are much higher, both being the result of higher long-term investment that sustains a high real wage level.[34] The emphasis on production as opposed to distribution, as institutionalized in both the finance and the industrial relations systems, corresponds to a pattern of high value-added manufacturing, which in turn is conditional upon high skills and cultivation of a continuously employed work force. This constellation is obvious in the West German automobile industry where it is protected by the system of industrywide wage bargaining and by works councils, which under codetermination can afford to wait, just as prudent investors on the capital side, for long-term restructuring projects to bear fruit.

(4) *De-Taylorization of work organization.* Since the 1960s IG Metall has actively pursued programs for a "humanization of working life" aimed, among other things, at broader job contents and a reintegration of conception and execution. It was able to do this because, as an industrial union, it is not pledged to the special interests of either skilled or unskilled workers. Such initiatives were also facilitated by the large supply of broadly skilled workers generated by the apprenticeship system. In the restructuring period of the 1970s and 1980s, broad job descriptions proved a crucial asset for redeployment in internal labor markets, and the presence of young skilled workers in production jobs resulting from excess training and internalization of labor markets put further pressure on the existing division of labor. The automobile industry was found to be one of the strongholds of the new production concepts described by Kern and Schumann,[35] which combine a commitment to diversified high-quality production with more integrated job contents. Traditional trade union policies for a less Fordized organiza-

32. Werner Tegtmeier, *Wirkungen der Mitbestimmung der Arbeitnehmer* (Göttingen: Vandenhoeck und Ruprecht, 1973); E. Witte, "Die Unabhängigkeit des Vorstandes im Einflusssystem der Unternehmung," *Zeitschrift für betriebswirtschaftliche Forschung* 33 (1981): 273–96.

33. Cox and Kriegbaum, *Growth, Innovation and Employment.*

34. Ibid.

35. Horst Kern and Michael Schumann, *Das Ende der Arbeitsteilung? Rationalisierung in der industriellen Produktion* (Munich: Beck, 1984).

tion of work have thus converged with the requirements of quality-competitive, high value-added production.

(5) *Rapid absorption of technical change.* West German unions, being industrial unions, have never needed to impose restrictive job demarcations. This together with wage maintenance and retraining under protection against rationalization agreements, as well as steady employment under codetermination and internal labor market human resource management, has made for a highly flexible shop floor capable of absorbing technical change without disruption. The push to improve skills of the 1970s, the influx of highly skilled apprentices, and the gradual erosion of the distinction between direct and indirect work under humanization of working life projects have further prepared the ground for the new microelectronic technologies. Employment protection has also ensured that new technologies were not used to reduce the work force but to create diversified, high-quality production. Today, the West German auto industry is among the leaders in production technology, especially in automation of final assembly, which used to be a mainstay of unskilled labor. The automated final assembly of the Golf at Volkswagen Wolfsburg (Halle 54) was introduced with works council and union support although on paper it eliminated about a thousand jobs. In fact, employment increased because of growing production volume.[36]

This configuration, which has coped so well with the challenges of the 1970s and early 1980s, still appears to be both stable and well adapted to current industrial adjustment problems. Not that there were no pressures for change. But change has always occurred, and the capacity of the German industrial relations system to evolve gradually in response to a changing environment accounted for its successful performance in the past. One important area in which existing arrangements may by now have reached their limits, calling for a major overhaul of the institutional structure at the workplace, is quality assurance. In 1987, quality problems for the first time affected Daimler Benz, which during the year introduced more than two hundred new model variations, resulting in an unprecedented number of faulty cars reaching the customers. At Volkswagen, both the need to extend warranty periods and the high costs of rectification—with the number of faulty cars exceeding by far that in Japanese factories—caused considerable concern not just among the management but also with the works council. In both cases, it appears that product diversification had been driven to a level at which even under West German conditions it ceased to be compatible with

36. Wolfgang Streeck, "Introduction: Industrial Relations, Technical Change and Economic Restructuring," in Streeck, ed., "Industrial Relations and Technical Change in the British, Italian and German Automobile Industries: Three Case Studies," *Discussion Paper* IIM/LMP 85-5 (Wissenschaftszentrum Berlin, 1985).

product quality—the second and equally indispensable element of the diversified quality production strategy. By the mid-1980s, it thus seems to have become necessary for German auto manufacturers to update their traditional methods of quality assurance by new, special measures.

Most of these measures, however, are not likely to cause dramatic deviations from existing patterns of shop-floor cooperation and industrial relations. The most natural response in the West German manufacturing environment to such problems is intensified training and further training, combined with new, more integrated forms of work organization that make it possible to use higher and more polyvalent skills. After the reform of initial vocational training in the metal industry, which is now being gradually implemented, increased attention is presently being paid by both management and work-force representatives to further training. Although there is some disagreement over the exact terms, both sides are committed to what they tellingly call a "qualification offensive," involving considerable investment in human resources aimed at safeguarding the international competitiveness of West German manufacturers. A first, comprehensive works agreement on the subject was signed at Volkswagen in early 1987. IG Metall, in a national policy document, has even gone so far as to suggest cutting working hours to allow for training at the workplace as a way of combining redistribution of work with improving the industry's skill base.

Though it took a long time for the quality circle movement to hit the German auto industry, it now has forcefully arrived, and with it various managerial initiatives for more substantial decentralization of the organization of work ("team working" or "group work"). For some years, quality circles and group work were regarded by many in the industry as a foreign fad, useful at best for firms and countries with a history of excessively Tayloristic work organization and large skill deficits. The prevailing belief was that the traditional organization of the German shop floor, in combination with the important role played by the *Meister* (the highly skilled German equivalent of the foreman), provided for sufficient quality and flexibility. Now this view has changed, and there is growing interest among management, not just at the subsidiaries of the two American multinationals, in new, "Japanese" forms of work organization.

Whether the objectives pursued with team working and quality circles will eventually be accommodated in a modified West German pattern, or whether there will have to be more fundamental changes is difficult to say; in any case, it may not be the most important problem. That might well turn out to be the compatibility of quality circles, and team working in particular, with the present system of codetermination and the veto powers of works councils vis-à-vis management. Most works councils and IG Metall have long believed that delegation of codecision rights from management to small groups of workers primarily serves the purpose of undermining codetermination and workers' trade union loyalties. In 1986, however, the new leadership of the VW central works council signed a works agreement on the introduction of quality circles which gave the works council a measure of influence on their operation, and IG Metall, not least in response to changing works councils attitudes, is now beginning to take a much less adverse position. Uncertain as the outcome is, its tradition would lead one to expect the union to try everything possible to avoid having to choose between becoming an obstacle to improved competitiveness and resigning its industrial power and influence; and from the traditions of the employers in the sector, it appears likely that after some hesitation, they will find it advisable to help the union avoid this choice.

The National Polity

The West German state has no strong tradition of "industrial policy" or "selective intervention."[37] Nor is there much public ownership in the manufacturing sector, and where the federal government does hold shares in manufacturing companies, it does not use them as an instrument of economic or employment policy. The powerful federal Ministry of Economic Affairs has throughout its history practiced a German version of liberal supply-side policy under which the principal responsibility of the government is to safeguard the functioning of the market, in part through free international trade and promotion of domestic competition. The privatization of the majority of VW shares in 1960 was in line with this philosophy, and since its reelection the present government intends to sell its remaining VW stock.

Public (minority) ownership in VW has had much less effect on the way the company is run than is often assumed. Except for the strong position of the union and the codetermination bodies, VW was always required to operate like a private enterprise, and it has never received significant public subsidies.[38] This was true even in 1974 when the company was about to falter. At the peak of the crisis, the leadership of

37. D. Webber, "The Framework of Government-Industry Relations and Industrial Policy Making in the Federal Republic of Germany," *University of Sussex Working Papers Series on Government-Industry Relations* no. 1 (Brighton: University of Sussex, 1986).

38. Grants and tax concessions per employee in the automobile industry amounted to DM 480 in 1981, as compared to DM 37,840 in the railways, DM 23,830 in coal mining, and DM 14,660 in the aerospace industry, the three most-favored sectors. The machine tools industry received DM 1,190. An amount comparable to that received by the auto industry was received by the textile and clothing industry, which was supported at a level of DM 400 per employee. See ibid.

IG Metall and the works council asked the Social Democratic minister of finance for financial support, only to be told that the federal government had not one deutschemark to spare for automobiles that nobody was willing to buy. This attitude had the full support of the chancellor, Helmut Schmidt, who on various occasions had committed himself publicly to what he called a "private sector solution," which in the end was extremely successful. All the government did was to prepare a range of regional labor market measures to relieve possible mass unemployment.[39]

The government's lack of enthusiasm about industrial policy is clearly not shared by the union. In its "Automobile Policy Paper,"[40] IG Metall reiterated its long-standing proposal for a tripartite industry council to oversee and guide private investment in the industry to prevent overcapacity. But this demand, which of course is anathema to employers, had gone unheeded under the Social-Liberal government, and the present government has rejected a parallel proposal even to help the ailing steel industry. Since the automobile industry, with its outstanding performance, seems to provide excellent confirmation of the government's free market philosophy, the union's demand for an institutionalized sectoral policy stands no chance of acceptance.

In a sense, this lack of action may not be totally against IG Metall's interest. As a union for the entire metalworking sector, IG Metall has found it difficult enough to assume the role of "sectoral mastermind" for the steel industry, in which it plays a special role through a particular form of codetermination (see the chapter by Fach and Esser in this volume). Assuming the same responsibility for more subsectors of the industry may be too much for a trade union. There are, after all, good reasons why IG Metall is organized on a unitary basis without special divisions for individual industries (the exception again being steel): a divisional organization, as would be required to formulate specific industrial strategies, would easily set free too many centrifugal forces. In the past, IG Metall has maintained solidarity among its 2.7 million members by focusing on their common interests in the labor market and involving itself as little as possible in the much more diverse interests of their firms and industries in the product market. Interestingly, the same holds true for the employers' association, Gesamtmetall, which also represents the entire metal industry. Although there is a trade associa-

39. Streeck, *Industrial Relations in West Germany.*
40. IG Metall, "Beschäftigungsrisiken in der Autoindustrie. Vorschläge der IG Metall zur Beschäftigungssicherung und zur Strukturpolitik in diesem Industriebereich." Frankfurt am Main, November 1984; IG Metall, "Beschäftigungsrisiken in der Autoindustrie: Eine aktualisierte Berichterstattung zur Entwicklung der Beschäftigung in der Autoindustrie unter Einbeziehung der Arbeitsplatzeffekte aus der Verkürzung der Arbeitszeit. Vorgelegt vom Vorstand der IG Metall," Frankfurt am Main, September 1985.

tion for the automobile industry, the VDA, it is weak because it is not simultaneously an employers' association; because its internal politics are dominated by five large, prosperous, independent companies that fiercely believe they can take care of themselves; and because of the split among its ranks between West-German- and American-owned firms, which makes a joint strategy very difficult to formulate.

The unwillingness of the government to intervene in sectoral restructuring and the weakness of both the union and the trade association as agents of industrial policy have placed the burden of adjustment exclusively on the individual enterprise and the shop floor. Their flexible performance depends in large measure on the capacity of the industrial relations system for cooperative conflict resolution,[41] which, in turn, is enhanced by a legal and political framework that facilitates and encourages "social partnership." In many ways, then, liberal economic policy in West Germany, in the automobile industry and others, is viable and successful because it is supported, and its potential deficits are compensated, by a neocorporatist social policy—just as the government's abstention from direct intervention in industrial strategy is made possible by procedural intervention in industrial relations. It is this mixture of three elements: the government's unwillingness to fend off adjustment pressures; the trade union and the trade association's inability to act as lobbies for protective-selective intervention; and a legally based industrial relations system safeguarding governability of the workplace by imposing obligations and responsibilities on both "sides of industry" that seems to have been needed for successful performance in turbulent markets.

Not only has the West German automobile industry not had the benefit—or, if one looks at the United Kingdom, the liability[42]—of selective government intervention on its behalf, it has not even received financial support for research and development, which goes almost exclusively to sectors such as telecommunications, microelectronics, nuclear energy, and the aerospace industry.[43] Like other export-oriented manufacturing sectors, the auto industry has been one beneficiary among many of global economic, fiscal, and monetary policies that were and are attuned to the need for the West German economy to remain competitive in world markets. It has also been favored by the

41. Jacobs et al., *Approach to Industrial Change in Britain and Germany.*
42. Wilks, *Industrial Policy and the Motor Industry.*
43. Among the large firms that were given financial support for research and development projects from the federal Ministry of Research and Technology between 1972 and 1982, VW ranks sixteenth and Daimler Benz eighteenth. The two firms received 1.0 and 0.9 percent, respectively, of the ministry's total payments. The three largest recipients alone (Siemens, Brown Boveri & Cie, and MBB) accounted for 56.1 percent of total grants. See Webber, "Framework of Government-Industry Relations."

pervasive political consensus during most of West Germany's history that both public investment and regulatory policies should promote, or at least not undermine, industrial performance. The latter at least is now being forcefully challenged by the "new politics," and the automobile industry and its traditional hold over government policy have come under attack in three policy areas.[44]

(1) West Germany, like other industrialized countries, has a strong "road lobby" consisting of the automobile associations with their large membership, the construction industry, and the automobile industry. Owing at least in part to their activities, the country now has one of the most extensive and expensive road systems, with a network of 8,200 kilometers (4,970 miles) of large superhighways, or *Autobahnen*. For a long time support for road building was bipartisan. When in 1966 the Social Democrats joined the federal government, they appointed the leader of the construction workers union, IGBSE, minister of transportation. During his tenure the government committed itself to a national *Autobahn* program to provide each citizen, wherever in the country he might live, with access to an *Autobahn* in a range of no more than ten kilometers.

This ambitious project had to be revised because of lack of funds. In addition, there was increasing resistance in local communities to building new roads in a country as small and densely populated as the Federal Republic. Since the Social-Liberal government improved the rights of citizens to have public building projects reviewed in the courts, *Autobahn* construction has become difficult, and very few new projects are presently under way. Hardly any major road project, *Autobahn* or not, today proceeds without lengthy litigation, and frequently the courts uphold claims that projected roads are unnecessary and damaging to the environment. Moreover, the Green party is demanding that a significant number of existing roads be scrapped to restore the natural environment, and to some extent this became government policy in the state of Hesse when the Greens were in coalition with the Social Democrats.

44. The following discussion is limited to problems that beset the automobile industry specifically. There are other challenges by the "new politics" which affect industry as a whole and most large organizations and institutions in West Germany. For example, in a recent wave of renewed interest in the Nazi past, both Daimler Benz and VW were confronted with questions and charges relating to their employment of forced labor and concentration camp inmates during the war. Among other things, it turned out that Ferdinand Porsche, the designer of the original Volkswagen Beetle, seems to have been much more closely involved in the barbaric use of prison labor at VW than had long been believed. Large German firms, in the automobile industry and others, are only slowly realizing that anyone who scratches the surface of forty years of postwar West German accomplishment is likely to find something of this kind, and that such scratching will continue especially if attempts are made to prevent it. Both Volkswagen and Daimler have made moves to open their archives to independent historians, but it is certain that many more such steps will be demanded of them.

The industry that is hardest hit by this opposition to road building is, of course, construction, which, for this reason and others, has for years been going through a painful contraction. For the automobile industry, the expansion of the road network has in the past been helpful first because it made car ownership attractive and later because it relieved its growing disutilities for the individual user. This holds in particular for the congested inner cities, where parking prohibitions or a total ban on private car traffic were avoided, or at least postponed, by improvement of the road system and the construction of new parking facilities. (The same effect, incidentally, was caused by the replacement in several large cities of streetcars with subway systems.) Today this solution has become less politically viable, and a collective preference is developing for stricter regulation of private automobile use to prevent further depletion of the natural or urban environment.

It is hard to see, however, how the declining acceptance of public construction projects could seriously damage the industry's domestic sales prospects. The relationship between the size of the road network and the number of cars has for some time been deteriorating. In 1970, there were 13.9 million passenger cars in a road network of 408,000 kilometers, which amounts to 34 cars per kilometer. In 1985, the number of passenger cars had increased to 25.8 million whereas the road system had grown to only 472,000 kilometers, which meant 55 passenger cars per kilometer. Nevertheless, it is expected that in the year 2000, there will be between 29.5 and 30.6 million automobiles on West Germany's roads.[45] Similarly, pedestrian zones have spread in the inner cities during the 1970s without visibly affecting the automobile industry. West Germany also has, by comparative standards, extensive mass transit systems and a large and well-functioning railway, neither of which has stopped the growth of the private automobile fleet. Bicycle ownership has dramatically increased in recent years, especially among young urban people, but most of them also own cars, often more than one per family. Although in the past the expansion of private automobile ownership may have been conditional on the simultaneous expansion of the road system, today this connection seems no longer to exist.

(2) West German *Autobahnen* have no general speed limit, and this has for some time been a highly emotional and divisive issue in domestic politics. (There are, of course, frequent specific speed limits, and it is a punishable offense not to adjust one's speed to driving conditions.) A general speed limit of 100 kilometers (60 miles) per hour was first proposed by the Social Democrats after the 1972 election and later became one of the central themes of the Greens. Although the demand

---

45. Deutsche Shell-Aktiengesellschaft, *Verunsicherung hinterlässt Bremsspuren—Shell-Prognose des PKW-Bestandes bis zum Jahr 2000* (Hamburg, 1985).

remained the same, the reasons that were given for it changed over time—the high number of accidents was emphasized in the early 1970s; energy conservation figured prominently in the years immediately after 1973; and in the 1980s, the environmental hazards of fast driving as exemplified by, in particular, the *Baumsterben* (literally, the "dying of the trees") became a concern. The industry has always forcefully objected to a general speed limit, and the proposal is not popular with the majority of the electorate in a country where much of social life is subject to effectively enforced legal regulation. The present government clearly opposes a general speed limit, and to close the issue it conducted a large-scale test in 1985 which appears to have shown no significant energy savings, only a minor decline in pollution and a low level of compliance.[46]

There are complex reasons for the industry's resistance to a general *Autobahn* speed limit. Publicly, industry spokespersons argue that the high engineering standards of West German cars derive from the pressure to make cars capable of continuous high-speed performance, at 160 kilometers (100 miles) per hour and more for many successive hours. This allegation is questioned by the proponents of a speed limit, who cannot see why West German manufacturers should give up their competitive advantage just because of stricter driving regulations on the German *Autobahn*. Indeed, more important for the industry may be the image abroad of West German cars capable of relentless racing at unheard-of speeds. It may also be true that the preference of West German consumers for domestically produced cars has to do with a belief that foreign cars are not capable of the performance possible, and indeed almost required, on *Autobahnen*. If fast driving were banned, West German consumers might no longer be willing to buy the expensive upmarket models in which West German producers specialize. Thus the absence of an *Autobahn* speed limit may be a form of free advertisement in foreign markets and a nontariff trade barrier in the domestic market at the same time. This may explain why the European Community presses West Germany to introduce a speed limit as a precondition of joint action to reduce exhaust emissions. The possibility of fast driving may also be a compensation for the inevitable relative shrinking of the road network resulting from increased car ownership.

In any case, the industry has prevailed on the subject and no general speed limit is in sight barring a red-green coalition government in Bonn. In part, the successful defense of "free driving for free citizens" (the

46. Vereinigung der Technischen Überwachungsvereine im Auftrage des Bundesministers für Verkehr, ed., *Untersuchung der Auswirkungen einer Geschwindigkeitsbegrenzung auf das Abgas-Emissionsverhalten von Personenkraftwagen auf Autobahnen: Abgas-Grossversuch* (Cologne, 1986).

road lobby's slogan in the early 1970s) was possible because the industry invalidated some of the arguments of its opponents. The number of road accidents in relation to driving performance has been declining sharply since the early 1970s, partly because of improved safety features and despite the increased average speed. *Autobahn* accidents in particular are infrequent.[47] Moreover, fuel consumption per car strongly declined after the two oil shocks because of improved engine and body design. When the proponents of the speed limit shifted their argument to the *Baumsterben* in the 1980s, the industry was once again able, after some fumbling, to take the momentum out of their attack through technical improvements that offered, at least for a time, an alternative to restrictive behavioral regulation.

(3) Environmental protection has always been a problem for the German automobile industry since it became a political issue, and the industry and its association, the VDA, have proven remarkably inept in dealing with it. When in the early 1970s the Social-Liberal government took measures to reduce the lead content of gasoline, the industry began an aggressive publicity campaign to convince the voters that less lead would result in lasting damage to their beloved automobile engines. After a law was passed in 1971 setting the maximum lead content at 0.4 grams per liter of gasoline, the government in 1975 proposed to lower the lead content further to 0.15 grams. Why the industry fought this bill so violently is far from clear, even with hindsight; a benevolent interpretation would be that the campaign was intended to deter once and for all any attempt at environmental regulation such as American producers faced in the 1970s. In any case, the law was passed and took force in 1976. No engine breakdowns were reported, West German automobile production continued to soar, and the industry had lost much of its credibility with both the public and the government.

The situation repeated itself in the 1980s on a larger scale. When the

47. The number of people killed in road accidents has steadily declined in recent years, from 14,614 in 1974 to 8,400 in 1985. In 1985, 669 (8.0 percent) deaths resulted from accidents on *Autobahnen*. In 1985, 69 percent of all registered traffic accidents occurred in inner cities; only 4.4 percent of accidents happened on *Autobahnen* (*Statistisches Jahrbuch der Bundesrepublik Deutschland*). Although the *Autobahn* network in West Germany takes about 27 percent of total traffic volume (France 15, UK 12 percent), *Autobahn* traffic accounts for only 5.2 percent of all casualties (France 2.5, UK 2.2 percent; European Conference of Ministers of Transport 1987, p. 42). Austria, Belgium, Switzerland, and France in 1984 led Germany in deaths per million population, per million cars, and per million motor vehicles. Spain and Ireland ranked higher in two of these areas; and Denmark and the United States ranked higher in one. Fewer deaths in all three measures were recorded in Finland, Italy, Norway, the Netherlands, Sweden, and the United Kingdom (European Conference of Ministers of Transport 1987, 28). Countries with low values on the three indicators seem to have little or no transit traffic. Unfortunately, there are no cross-nationally comparable data on traffic performance, making it impossible to relate accidents, casualties, and deaths to the total volume of vehicle or passenger kilometers.

new conservative government took over, it felt it had to do something about the *Baumsterben*. The problem was perceived as a national catastrophe even by many voters in the conservative camp, and visible and dramatic action was felt to be required, preferably of the "blood, sweat and tears" type involving some opportunity for sacrifice by citizens who were feeling guilty about what their prosperity was doing to the trees. Since a speed limit was seen as too much of a sacrifice, however, the government in the summer of 1984 came up with the idea of making catalytic converters meeting U.S. pollution standards obligatory for all new cars, allowing only for a very short transition period until the end of 1985.

Initially, this proposal was violently opposed by the industry, which seems to have been afraid the measure would further increase the Japanese price advantage, especially with smaller cars (the Japanese had longer experience with converter technology and better economies of scale in their large domestic and American markets). Later the technological problems of gearing catalytic converters to high-speed *Autobahn* driving took front stage. Mutual accusations of bad faith between the minister of the interior, one of the most conservative government members, and the industry made almost daily copy, and the theme of the impending decline of profits and employment in one of the core sectors of West German industry was repeated again and again. When it became clear that the government would not back down—and, one supposes, after the engineers had finally been able to communicate to their superiors that the technical problems were after all solvable—the industry in late 1985 made a turnaround, which hardly restored its credibility, and came out in favor of the catalytic converter provided the requirement would apply also to imported cars.

At this stage, opposition arose from West Germany's partners in the European Community, which regarded the intended measures as a nontariff trade barrier and announced legal action in the European Court. Other European producers may have felt less confident than the West Germans that they could master the converter technology, or they may have preferred to put their scarcer research and development money to other, more potentially profitable purposes. As the discussions in the Council of Ministers proceeded, it became clear in early 1985, to the government's considerable embarrassment, that unilateral West German action was not only legally impossible but, more important, might impair the willingness of West Germany's partners in the European Community to continue to absorb the giant trade surplus of the West German automobile industry.

The issue was resolved in a typically European way. Agreement was reached in June 1985 on a complicated set of common European pollution standards, which are to come into force during the 1980s and 1990s, as well as on additional national action by the West German government to provide tax relief for the purchase of new cars that meet the European standards. At this point the West German automobile industry began to discover that it had never really opposed the catalytic converter. Meanwhile, it has learned to live exceedingly well with the new law, which not only gives it technological edge on catalytic converters but also provides it with a new way of selling more expensive cars by making catalytic converters, and the tax relief that goes with them, available only for models with many other extras. Moreover, since diesel engines get the same tax break, the European regulation also favors those German producers who are leaders in diesel technology, especially Daimler Benz and VW.[48]

The automobile, and the automotive system as a whole, is one of the favorite targets of the "green" postindustrial Left. But it is also a favorite toy of people in the mainstream of West German society, who are still the vast majority. In the war of faith between its opponents and supporters—which is fought with the usual German rudeness and *Gründlichkeit*—the latter have clearly prevailed, and the automobile industry has weathered the storm undamaged. Compared to the chemical and nuclear energy industries, its problems with the new politics are minor, although the industry still has to learn to respond to political intervention by other means than predictions of impending doom and decline, which have too often been disproved. The cultural challenge to the habits of the automotive society has been successfully met by technical improvements—high fuel economy, more effective safety features, and better pollution control—which have, if anything, further reinforced those habits. As a side effect, technical progress in response to domestic political threats has increased the industry's international competitiveness.

The Global Economy

The critical changes in the global economy of the 1980s can be described, in a nutshell, as an increase in the number of competitors in international trade, coinciding with a decline in institutional stability

48. Rising concern about the environment affects the automobile industry in other ways as well, but it shares this experience with all of manufacturing industry. For example, in 1987 the Federal Constitutional Court struck down plans by Daimler Benz to build a new, large test track in a rural area in Baden-Württemberg. Opposition to the track had been widespread, and local farmers successfully resisted expropriation of their land by the state government on behalf of the company. Where the test track will now be built has not yet been determined; one possibility is across the border in France, another in Bremen, where the local government is more concerned about unemployment than the environment.

and the willingness to comply with free trade rules. These developments may affect manufacturing industries in old industrial countries in essentially three ways. First, increased competition from newly industrializing countries may cut into their domestic market shares and restrict their export opportunities. Second, exports from industrialized countries may further suffer from unpredictable exchange rates, protectionist policies in receiving countries, and restrictions by leading nations on the international transfer of technology. Finally, workers in old industrial countries may have to fear that their employers increase the foreign content of their products or even relocate production abroad. In all these respects, the West German automobile industry has suffered remarkably little. As a result, however, it has run up an enormous trade surplus, which, to the extent that it adds to the endemic surplus of the West German economy and thereby to the general imbalance in international trade, may in itself begin to constitute a political and economic problem.

As has been said, the domestic market of West German automobile manufacturers receives little to no protection, certainly much less than in France, Italy, or the United States. This holds in particular with regard to Japanese imports. Japanese penetration of the West German automobile market has grown steadily since the mid-1970s. When in the early 1980s the United States began to impose voluntary restraint agreements on the Japanese, there was concern in West Germany that Japanese producers would redirect their exports to the last major free market, West Germany. At this time, the Japanese market share in West Germany was about 10 percent. There were rumors that on a trip to Japan in early 1982, on the occasion of a meeting of the Trilateral Commission, the minister of economic affairs had reached an informal understanding with the Japanese that this market share would not be expanded as a result of American protectionism; the existence of such an agreement was, however, never publicly admitted. If there was indeed such an understanding, it was the only political intervention that came close to protecting the domestic market. In any case, by 1986 the Japanese market share in West Germany had risen to about 15 percent.

In spite of the still growing strength of the Japanese, government, industry, and even the trade union remain strongly committed to the principle of free international trade, and they have good reasons to do so. West Germany is more vulnerable than any other major country except Japan to protectionist retaliation. Since it exports a broad range of products, protectionism in favor of one industry might damage the interests of many other industries, which would therefore oppose it, for example in the Bundesverband der Deutschen Industrie (BDI, Federation of German Industry). The same constellation exists within the trade union movement, and even inside an individual union like IG Metall, which organizes thirteen other industries in addition to automobiles. Demands from IG Metall for protection for the German automobile manufacturers from foreign competition would meet with opposition not only from unions like the Chemical Workers Union but also from its own members in, for example, the machine tools industry, who would fear for their employment.

It has been indicated that there are certain functional equivalents to formal market protection in West Germany which explain why German producers have still been able to hold on to such a large market share. One example that has been mentioned is the absence of an *Autobahn* speed limit. More generally, one might point to the high quality consciousness of German consumers, which is matched, again, only by that of their Japanese counterparts. The high market share of the extremely expensive Daimler Benz passenger cars is only one characteristic of an automobile culture for which quality engineering counts more than low prices, and whose members are willing to wait for up to one year for delivery of their custom-made Mercedes or BMW. The diverse and sophisticated model range of the German manufacturers is well adapted to these preferences, and it is above all this match that accounts for the apparent consumer nationalism that has up to now kept the West German automobile market largely in the hands of West German manufacturers.

Nevertheless, Japanese penetration is strong and has recently been growing. For a long time, however, this growth was limited to the market segment of smaller cars in which American and European producers, perhaps with the exception of Fiat, have found it increasingly difficult to make profits. Japanese competition has not hit Daimler Benz or BMW, and VW and Opel, which were initially affected, have responded by vacating the lower market segment, leaving it to the Japanese and moving their own model ranges upmarket. The manufacturer that has suffered most from the Japanese advance was Ford, whose low West German market share may explain why Ford more than any other company is calling for European-level protectionist measures against Japanese competition. There is now consensus between the VW company, the works council, and the union that small cars can no longer be profitably built in West Germany. To remain able to offer a full model range, VW in 1986 bought a majority share in the Spanish automobile manufacturer SEAT, to which it will gradually transfer the production of the Polo, the smallest VW, which, though it is generally considered a well-designed car, today sells poorly because of its high price. Union and works council participated in the SEAT decision under codetermination and have not objected to a relocation of production, which may reduce employment opportunities in Germany.

Everything else being equal, it is unlikely that the emerging new producers, South Korea in particular, will be able to catch a significant share of the domestic or foreign markets of West German manufacturers in spite of their enormous cost advantages even over the Japanese. Unless there is a sudden increase in West German consumers' price consciousness, Korean cars in West Germany will primarily compete with the Japanese (or perhaps the downmarket Ford models). Nevertheless, the new Korean scare seems to feed certain protectionist temptations to which the automobile group in IG Metall was sometimes subject. Under the prevailing legal and political situation and trade patterns, such protection would be available only at the European Community level. Here indeed, if the West German automobile industry came out in favor of import restrictions, it might find potential allies in France, Italy, and perhaps even the United Kingdom. Although West German cars are the best-selling foreign cars in Japan, the Japanese market absorbs a minuscule number of exports,[49] and neither Japanese nor Korean retaliation would hurt directly. Similarly, restrictions on automobile imports would not affect trade relations with the United States because it does not export cars to Western Europe. Japanese firms, however, seem to be preparing for a large buildup of production capacity in Britain, probably in anticipation of future European import limitations. Since automobiles manufactured in Britain would have to be considered domestic production in the entire European Community, trade restrictions may at most boost employment in the United Kingdom.

The temptation to protect the West German auto industry may grow further when the Japanese, as they are already doing, continue to move upmarket, not least in response to Korean and perhaps, in the future, Taiwanese competition. Although Daimler Benz and BMW in particular profess optimism, arguing that it takes a long time to learn to compete successfully in their markets, nobody doubts that at some point the Japanese will be able to do so. It is possible that such a development will change the rules of the international trade game at the European level. In this context, Daimler Benz's takeover in 1985 and 1986 of a majority shareholding in AEG and the establishment of a strong national base in West Germany for microelectronic automobile components may be interpreted as a move in preparation for anticipated Japanese competition in upper market segments. As a side effect, it also offers some insurance

49. In 1985, 3.1 million new passenger cars were registered in Japan, 50,172 (1.6 percent) of them imported, and 80 percent of the imported cars (40,157) came from West Germany (almost exclusively from VW/Audi, BMW, and Daimler Benz). Exports to Japan in 1985 accounted for 0.9 percent of all West German car exports (calculations based on data from Japan Automobile Manufacturers Association, 1986).

against American restrictions on trade in microelectronic technology on national security grounds.

German automobile exports have grown in spite of floating exchange rates and successive revaluations of the deutschemark. The European currency system devised in 1978 has considerably eased the uncertainties of the post–Bretton Woods trade regime, and the West German government has done its best to keep the system alive. West German firms have also for a long time been able to live with the strong fluctuations of the dollar. When the dollar was overvalued in the mid-1980s, West German exporters such as Daimler Benz and VW/Audi kept their prices in the American market high and collected extra profits, rather than dramatically expanding the volume of trade.[50] Up to October 1987, the latest decline of the dollar did not significantly affect their share in the U.S. market, especially since they have never tried to be price competitive. An exception is Porsche, by far the smallest German producer, which in 1986 sold 57.6 percent (in 1980, 37.0 percent) of its production in the United States and which seems to have become dependent on its windfall dollar profits. Also, Porsche suffered more than other automobile manufacturers from the changed spending habits of American "Yuppie" consumers after the 1987 stock market crash. As a result, by the end of the year the company was about to become the first West German automobile producer since the mid-1970s to introduce short-time work. The West German press put the blame for Porsche's predicaments on the firm itself, arguing that in the "fat years" of the high dollar, it had failed to renew its dated model range and diversify its markets. This was why it was now vulnerable not just to the volatility of the U.S. economy but also to Japanese competition (Toyota and its "Porsche killer").

Protectionism in receiving countries poses more difficult problems, but a changing pattern of exports has done much to relieve the threat. Trade barriers to the United States and to other countries have always existed for the two American subsidiaries, Opel and Ford, which have to follow the general corporate strategies of their parent companies. This has contributed to the concentration of West German automobile exports on countries other than the United States, in particular Western Europe. The West German Ford and General Motors plants have in the 1970s exported even to the United Kingdom, resulting in a transfer of production volume inside multinational enterprises from Britain to

50. In 1980, VW and Audi sold 8.9 percent of their production in the United States; this percentage had increased in 1986 to 11.4 percent. The respective values for Daimler Benz were 13.2 and 16.8 percent. BMW has expanded more aggressively in the United States, increasing the share of its production going to this country from 11.2 percent in 1980 to 22.4 percent in 1986.

West Germany in spite of the much higher West German wages.[51] "Europeanization" was also advanced, although involuntarily, by VW's failure to compete successfully with the Japanese in the American market (except for the special case of Audi). Whereas in 1971 30.5 percent of all VW cars went to the United States, in 1985 this percentage had fallen to 9.7. This progressive withdrawal from the United States may increase the incentives and opportunities to seek European-level trade protection.

As long as the European currency system and, indeed, the European Community hold together, the European strategy of West German auto manufacturers is likely to remain a workable response to changes in the global economic environment. In fact, given the West German producers' specific model range, there is hardly any other area in the world that could absorb their production. How keenly aware both industry and government are of the importance of the European market became obvious when unilateral West German action on pollution control was rescinded following accusations by the other European Community countries that it amounted to the creation of intra-European trade barriers.

One way of avoiding protectionist trade restrictions and the uncertainties of floating exchange rates is production abroad. Again leaving aside Ford and Opel, in this respect the West German automobile industry has clearly been lagging behind or is altogether disinterested. Whereas the Japanese are forcefully setting up production plants all over the world, in particular in the United States and the United Kingdom, Daimler Benz and BMW have no foreign production plants, and VW's two plants in the United States were a spectacular commercial, technical, and industrial relations failure. VW, which began production in the United States in 1978, reached its highest output there in 1980 with 197,106 units; from 1982 on, output per year was below 100,000, and in 1986 it dropped to 84,397, the third lowest level since production was started. In November 1987, VW announced that it would gradually shut down its United States manufacturing plants, serving what was left of its American markets from Mexico, Brazil, and West Germany. At this time the U.S. dollar was at an all-time low, when there should have been an overwhelming economic incentive to produce in the United States. It is tempting to compare this with the confidence with which Japanese firms have successfully transferred their management and production methods, including their work organization, to Western societies, which undoubtedly differ much more from theirs than they differ from the West

51. Whereas in 1975 the European Community absorbed 42.4 percent of West German car exports, ten years later this ratio had risen to 55.0 percent.

German. Remarkably, it has been argued by the business press that one of the reasons why the two VW plants in the United States perform so poorly is that VW took great care to Americanize not only its product, the Golf-turned-Rabbit, but also management methods and industrial relations.

Multinationalization of German automobile companies is also undeveloped with respect to other countries than the United States. In Europe VW has a small plant in Brussels, and when the company recently entered Spain, it followed Ford and General Motors by a long period. No other West German plants exist in European countries, not even in Britain, where low wages have attracted the Japanese. Outside Europe, in the developing countries, there is only VW, which is a major producer in Brazil, Mexico, and South Africa. Again, however, its presence is not the result of an aggressive strategy of multinationalization. Although such a strategy may have existed in the mass production era of the 1960s, today it seems to have stopped dead. The number of workers VW employs in the Third World has for more than ten years remained essentially unchanged, at a level of about 33 percent of the domestic work force. The number of automobiles produced abroad was a little lower, at about 31 or 32 percent. VW exports from West Germany still exceed foreign production by far; in 1985, the relationship between the two, in production value, was 1.63 to 1. Moreover, the models VW produces in Latin America and Africa differ considerably from those produced at home; there is no reimport of cars and very little of components; and there apparently are no plans for expansion. The Latin American operations kept the company afloat during the transition period of the early 1970s, but today they are loss makers, just as the U.S. plants always were, and a merger is imminent of the Brazilian VW subsidiary with the local Ford operation. The importance of VW's Third World plants seems to lie primarily in the access they give to potentially large markets with strict local content regulations, not in their contribution to a world car-manufacturing policy.

The low degree of multinationalization of German automobile manufacturers is not necessarily caused by trade union resistance to relocation of production. On the contrary, when VW in 1975 set up a plant in the United States, it had the full support of union and works council, which agreed that delivering components to an American assembly plant was preferable to losing the American market altogether.[52] On the whole, it seems that West German manufacturers are more comfortable producing at home, regardless of the high wage level to which they have grown

52. Streeck, *Industrial Relations in West Germany*.

accustomed. It is also possible, although difficult to prove, that building the automobiles in which West German producers specialize requires a social, organizational, and institutional infrastructure, or "manufacturing culture," which firms find hard or not worthwhile to create in foreign countries. For example, there are no foreign BMW plants.

The same seems to apply to foreign sourcing of components. The high domestic content of West German automobiles has already been mentioned. During the 1970s, Ford and Opel increased the production volume of their German operations, not least with respect to engineering and design, although they did have European low-wage alternatives in Britain and Spain. While the two American firms do rely on their parent companies' worldwide network and have frequently threatened their works councils that they might relocate, they seem to have little intention of increasing foreign production dramatically in coming years. Daimler Benz and BMW rely on their regional West German supply networks and this tendency toward local autarky is reinforced by the new Kanban logistics, which emphasize not only zero stocks but also spatial closeness between supplier and assembler to facilitate cooperation in engineering and quality control.

The greatest liability of the West German automobile industry is its success, as expressed in its gigantic trade surplus. In 1985, West Germany exported DM 80.2 billion worth of passenger cars and components, generating a surplus of about DM 58 billion, which was equivalent to roughly 80 percent of the country's total trade surplus. Auto industry exports as a share of total German exports rose steadily from 12 percent in 1980 to 15 percent in 1985. The big uncertainty that confronts the West German economy as a whole thus confronts its automobile industry as well: the question of how long West Germany's trading partners will be willing to accept this enormous trade imbalance. For some time, the issue has been overshadowed by the even larger trade surplus of the Japanese, which is politically more sensitive because of the low international openness of the Japanese economy—a charge that cannot be leveled against West Germany. But this may not help forever. Should trade restrictions become common international practice, West Germany, and especially its automobile industry, seems to place their hope on something like European autarky, and to keep the European Community together they may increasingly be willing to compromise their free trade principles and agree to common European trade protection. To what extent this may in the end help a small country like West Germany with an oversized and overcompetitive manufacturing sector—in which the automobile industry plays a leading part—remains an open question.

CONCLUSIONS: PROSPECTS FOR THE FUTURE

The West German automobile industry was competitively successful in the period of worldwide restructuring in the 1970s and 1980s. The industry's strong position today, after more than a decade of social, political, technological, and economic turbulence, lends support to a number of generalizations on industrial adjustment in high-wage countries, of which the following six appear of particular interest: (1) Upward restructuring toward diversified quality production can be a superior adjustment path, not least in stabilizing employment. (2) A traditional industrial structure (low concentration, low dispersion of ownership of individual companies, high vertical integration, high self-sufficiency of individual firms, low internationalization and diversification, dominance of conservative engineering over marketing and finance, a strong craft tradition) may well have competitive advantages over more modern structures. (3) In a context of unmitigated world market pressure and institutionalized responsibility through codetermination and legally regulated collective bargaining (*Tarifautonomie*), strong trade unions and the rigidities they impose upon management not only do not hurt but may indeed help in that they press firms to embark on more demanding and, in the long run, more successful adjustment strategies. (4) At least over the short and medium term, the negative impact of the new social movements on core sectors of manufacturing industry may be overestimated, in part because large firms may develop a capacity to respond flexibly to political opposition; as a result, political turbulence may sometimes be another source of competitive strength. (5) The specific West German success formula of high-quality production and high-skill work can be remarkably robust in the face of strong fluctuations in the exchange rate. (6) A country may not have to aspire to be a world power for its industries to be economically successful. In particular, the West Germans' European strategy—concentrating on the European market, hiding their own size and responsibility behind Europe, and refusing to accept a major role in world economic politics—has carried them farther than many would have predicted.

Is the success of the German automobile industry—and, more generally, of German manufacturing industries and the German economy as a whole—likely to continue under the auspices of what the authors of this volume have agreed to call the Third Republic? In a rapidly changing world, there can be no guarantee that something that has worked yesterday will work tomorrow. Moreover, in a world that has grown increasingly interdependent, it is hard to imagine how there could be islands of prosperity and high performance that could remain unaffected by an eventual breakdown of what is left of international economic coordination. It is easy to conceive a catastrophic scenario that will undo all individual accomplishments, and no such scenario can be easily dismissed as exotic. Even short of this, unpredictable change is the very essence of a competitive market economy; economic life is therefore by definition full of surprises; and if one draws the time horizon wide enough, it is always safe to predict that nothing will last forever.

A pessimistic prediction, then, would certainly be far from counter-intuitive, and indeed for the industry and its trade union a moderate degree of pessimism serves a useful function by preventing complacency. Obviously, the competitive game in today's world automobile industry differs from the 1970s in at least one important respect: then Germany was one among a number of more or less coequal rivals; now it has in many respects become a leader under attack. This position can be extremely uncomfortable and may require entirely new competitive strategies. With the usual tendency to overstate the weaknesses of the leader and the strengths of the pursuers, one might easily arrive at rather dire prospects. On the other hand, if one looks in detail at the risks the industry today faces, it appears that none of them threatens its traditional sources of strength in its political economy and that present and future challenges are not so categorically new as to render the industry's existing, proven strengths useless. Assuming this to be the case, it might not be unrealistic to expect that the next ten years will not be fundamentally different from the last decade for the West German auto industry. It is this optimistic position that the present essay has adopted.

When considering present and future performance risks, it might be useful to distinguish between risks that emanate from general changes in the industry's economic and political context and those that originate in the sector itself. Beginning with the first, even though economic sectors seem to be growing increasingly "special"—for example, in their business cycles—contextual changes may weaken or preempt the capacity of sectoral actors to continue on a previously successful course. In particular, three contextual risks can be identified that may have a negative impact on the institutional stability and economic performance of the West German automobile sector.

First, at the level of the political economy of the workplace, continuing and growing structural unemployment may affect the relations between union and management in automobiles, even if the industry itself were to continue its good employment performance. This is because the auto industry in West Germany is integrated in the bargaining system of the metalworking industry, which is the most visible and leading element of the national industrial relations system. General unemployment may affect West German industrial relations in two ways. It represents a

151

temptation for employers and their political allies to impose, in the name of fighting unemployment, more flexibility on the external labor market without, of course, accepting internal rigidities in exchange. The result would be an undermining of trade unions, which would feel permanently threatened by a populist alliance between their political enemies and the unemployed. Also, trade union hard-liners may use unemployment to press for a more redistributive policy of reducing working hours, and they would try to revive theories of "technological unemployment" calling for "social control of new technology." The ensuing heightened distributional conflict would not leave the auto industry unaffected, even though here the advantages of technological leadership are more visible than almost everywhere else. The negative economic consequences would make themselves felt only after some time, and by then the damage might already be done. On the other hand, both trade unions and employers' associations have in the past been able to contain disruptive elements in their respective member-ships, and short of a major economic downturn they may continue to do so. To fight unemployment, both sides have embarked on a national "qualification offensive" designed to upgrade human resources so as to attract more quality-competitive production. Although the hoped-for expansion effect is unlikely to do away with unemployment altogether, it may mitigate its political impact.

Second, at the level of the national polity, the successful German configuration of liberal economic policy and neocorporatist joint regula-tion of the workplace is inherently vulnerable to ideological politics. Destabilization may come from radicalization of trade unions and the resulting intensified distributional conflict, which would produce costly rigidities in the absorption of technical change. But at least during the conflict over the government's Section 116 bill and the collapse of the Neue Heimat,[53] the more likely possibility seemed to be that destabiliza-tion might originate from pressures inside the government camp for the final consummation of the "*Wende.*" Indeed, if the Third Republic came to be identified with a political project of completing the building of liberal *Ordnungspolitik* and extending the liberalism of national eco-nomic policy to the shop floor, the subsequent disruptions might entail high economic costs for a sector like automobiles—which is why ideolog-ical motivation would be needed to bring this about. If the leadership of the conservative government and the employers' associations fail to keep their hard-liners in check and prevent them from settling old bills with a labor movement weakened by high unemployment, the main domestic threat to the prosperity of West German core manufacturing

53. Streeck, "Industrial Relations in West Germany: Agenda for Change," *Discussion Paper* IIM/LMP 87-5 (Wissenschaftszentrum Berlin, 1987).

sectors would not be the new social movement of green environmentalism but the old social movement of liberal capitalism. At the same time,
though in early 1987 it seemed possible that after the government's
reelection, more along the line of Section 116 was in store, the victory
was much less decisive than expected, and since then the government
has been busy surviving a series of disappointing *Länder* elections, fighting a succession of scandals, and trying to cope with the crisis of the
international economy. All this points to a continuation of centrist, more
or less consensual policies that, from the perspective of the ideological
right, may justifiably appear as betraying a lack of vision and determina-
tion on the part of the leadership.

Third, at the international level, the fluctuations of the U.S. dollar
have for a long time left the West German automobile industry un-
impaired. In the fall of 1987, however, there was no doubt that if the
dollar were to continue its apparently bottomless decline, this would at
some stage begin to hurt, even if accompanied by a revaluation of the
yen. Two developments might converge: growing pressure on West
German firms to relocate production abroad—with the accompanying
inevitable conflicts with works councils and union—and declining sales
in foreign markets as the prices of West German cars finally crossed a
"sensitivity threshold" and purchasing power of consumers would collapse in a world recession. There is nothing the West German auto
industry can do to prevent such events. It is, however, remarkable that in
November 1987, the first West German business leader to speak up
publicly against what he called the incompetence and shortsightedness
of international economic policy makers was Edzard Reuter, the chief
executive of Daimler Benz. (Reuter, by the way, is the only card-carrying
Social Democrat to lead a major German firm.) In a widely publicized
speech in New York City, he called for more effective international
coordination and a serious effort by the West German government to
stimulate domestic growth, even at the expense of cherished fiscal and
monetary stability targets.

Turning now to industry-specific sources of potential crisis, the following stand out as important. First, up to now, the number of workers in
the West German automobile industry has increased because of expanding sales and world market shares—by far the most desirable source of
stable employment. In the few years in which employment declined,
forced dismissals could be avoided. But this need not always remain so.
Whatever the reasons—the low dollar, technical change, increased foreign sources of components, protectionism in receiving countries—
nobody can preclude that at some future point, employment may have to
decline in spite of institutional safeguards like reduction of working time
and short-time work. That declining employment would exacerbate

whatever conflicts of interest there may be between the winners and the (mostly unskilled) losers of industrial modernization is obvious,[54] and there certainly are limits to the extent to which IG Metall could accept employment cuts without taking to some form of overt conflict. Although the union emphasizes the risks of worldwide overcapacity in the industry to support its call for tripartite sectoral investment planning, more optimistic voices stress that it was possible to increase employment in the past against severe odds, and in practice both management and labor continue to place their hopes on further improvements in design, performance, and quality together with intensive training and retraining and, perhaps, further moderate cuts in working hours.

Second, both works councils and the industrial union have found their positions in certain respects threatened by economic and institutional change, which has created temptations to behave in a way that may be detrimental to the industry's performance. Works councils, as explained above, may find it difficult to accept decentralization of decision rights to the shop floor even if this may be economically productive because it may undermine their codetermination rights. The industrial union may find enterprise-level negotiating systems becoming too autonomous and diversified; in response it may seek confrontation at the industrial level to regain control over works councils. Neither of these developments seems, however, inevitable. Works councils are beginning to get used to quality circles, the 1984 strike over working hours was not repeated in 1987, and the union has signed a long-term plan for hours reduction which both provides for stability at the industry level and leaves room for negotiated flexibility in the individual enterprise. Nevertheless, the compatibility of the present industrial relations system with new forms of work organization and new needs for joint regulation may well remain a problem, and institutional changes may be required to prevent a process of decay with negative economic side effects.

Third, West German labor costs have always been high, but this was well compensated in the past by high skills, high organizational flexibility, and the resulting high productivity. Nevertheless, though the latter conditions are unlikely to change, expensive social policies and high levels of paid absenteeism may cease to be viable under heightened competitive pressures. Labor costs in West German automobile manufacturing will never be competitive with, say, those in Italy or Britain, and the system of paid sick leave will not disappear. But some cost control at the margins may become necessary. Here the cooperative tradition of works councils can probably be counted on to manage inevitable cutbacks. Reductions in working hours, which seem to have

54. Kern and Schumann, *Das Ende der Arbeitsteilung?*

resulted in a new kind of rather rigid work rules, however, are a different matter. This does not so much apply to production departments for which works councils will more or less grudgingly accept working on Saturdays and other means of extending production. It appears, however, that design and engineering departments in particular may find it difficult to operate under the strict thirty-five-hour regime that union and works councils are about to impose on them, which would require, among other things, a vastly expanded division of labor between engineers. Given both the crucial importance of creative engineering to the industry's competitive success in the future and the already high engineering costs in the West German auto industry, union intervention in these areas may well have much less "virtuous" consequences than on the shop floor.

Finally, during the restructuring period, the West German automobile industry has largely escaped direct Japanese competition by moving into market segments where Japanese firms were not present. This movement cannot continue forever, and indeed the strong yen has been pushing Japanese producers to follow the West Germans and increase the size and value of their cars. Indications are that in this market segment, Japanese producers might have cost advantages of a magnitude that would count even in what are basically non-price-competitive markets. To the extent that Japanese manufacturers are about to move production to European low-wage countries like Britain, even a Fortress Europe strategy would not protect West German producers. Moreover, consumer preferences may turn away from the German design philosophy to the benefit of producers like Honda and Toyota, which, because of lower engineering costs and perhaps a different engineering culture, are able to offer more frequent model changes with more technical gimmicks.

Taking everything together, it appears that probably the single most important challenge the industry will face in future years will be in the area of engineering. This challenge will come not just from the Japanese but, albeit perhaps to a lesser extent, from European competitors like Fiat or Peugeot as well. A successful response on the part of German manufacturers would seem to require no less than a repetition of their main accomplishment of the 1970s: taking the lead in product development and thereby changing the balance of consumer tastes and preferences in favor of what West German producers have to offer. This implies that the main burden of adjustment in coming years will probably not rest on the shop floor and the system of labor relations but on the design departments. Very little research has been done on national differences in design philosophies and on what could be called the social-institutional design of design processes in automobile manufacturing; so we know little to nothing about the comparative strength of West German producers on this crucial point, except that under the conditions of the past decade it has obviously, for some reason, helped the industry to come out ahead of most of its competitors.

There is nothing to indicate that the prosperity of the West German core industrial sectors is about to end. But neither can one dismiss entirely the possibility that an accumulation of small, normal crises—not to mention the one "big crash"—could at some point overtax the capacity of the West German political economy to accomplish successful adjustment. We know that for the automobile industry this capacity has been vastly underestimated by knowledgeable observers in the 1970s. We also know that whatever the challenges of the coming decade may be, the West German auto industry, and the country's manufacturing sector in general, is poised as in the past to cope with them through incremental changes of existing patterns. What we do not know is if this will be enough; however, the industrial history of the past one and a half decades tells us that it may well be even under the most demanding circumstances.

CHAPTER SIX

Political Consequences of Change: The Chemical Industry

CHRISTOPHER S. ALLEN

Change is not difficult to discern in the West German chemical industry. From the creation of dyestuffs in the mid-nineteenth century to the contemporary development of multiple varieties of exotic synthetic compounds, the industry has relied on a heavy use of basic and applied research as a foundation for its evolution and growth.[1] In a fundamental sense, the sector has almost defined the concept of change among the key sectors in advanced capitalist countries. Unlike the automobile industry, which has essentially refined the same product for a hundred years,[2] the chemical industry has depended for its success on the rapid creation of numerous products each of which possesses a relatively short shelf life.

Yet because of such constraining international factors as the need to import raw materials and export finished goods, and such domestic factors as the necessity of integrating many of its products with the needs of other German sectors, the key actors in the chemicals sector have not been entirely able to shape their own destiny.[3] These constraints are not

For comments on earlier drafts, I thank my colleagues on this project, especially Peter Katzenstein. I also acknowledge the comments and advice of Angelika Christ, Gerard Braunthal, Wyn Grant, Martin Hillenbrand, Hans Maier, and Wolfgang Weber. Preparation of this chapter was aided by the diligent research assistance of Deirdre Walker and Nikos Zahariardis of the University of Georgia. Finally, I thank the staff of Johns Hopkins University's American Institute for Contemporary German Studies in Washington, D.C., for help in preparing the final version of this chapter.

1. See Ralf Schaumann, *Technik und technischer Fortschritt im Industrialisierungsprozess* (Bonn: Ludwig Röhrscheid Verlag, 1977).

2. See the chapter by Wolfgang Streeck in this volume.

3. In this sense, the chemical sector as "industry's industry" is similar to the machine tool sector, which also must coordinate its production with the capital equipment needs of other industries. See the chapter by Gary Herrigel in this volume.

a new phenomenon. Throughout its history, the German chemicals industry has been strong and dynamic, but it has often depended on factors beyond its direct control. The sector's leaders have had to take a long view of the industry's requirements and the direction its development would take. But because of this "fragile strength,"[4] the sector's institutional actors have developed a strong capacity to manage change. Some analysts have suggested that the "organized capitalism" of the chemical industry is a metaphor for the adaptive institutional capacities of the entire German political economy.[5] The larger question of the adaptive capacities of the West German political economy underlie the specific analysis of the chemical industry presented in this chapter.

The industry's ability to manage change has been evident in its rebuilding following the devastation of World War II, as well as after the two OPEC oil price increases that directly affected a primary raw material for the industry. Yet the challenges posed in the 1980s by such issues as overcapacity and the need for new product technologies, a sharpened ecological debate, and the emergence of chemical producers in the newly industrializing countries (NICs) and in the Eastern bloc have all recently called into question the adaptive capacities of the sector's major actors.

This chapter will examine the issue of change in the West German chemical industry by first offering an overview of the industry and then looking at the industry at three levels: plant, national politics, and international economy. In so doing, it will assess how the industry's response to these challenges affects the political system at each of these three levels. Despite the challenges posed by new product technologies at the plant level, environmental conflict at the national political level, and uncertainties of trade and currency fluctuations at the international

---

4. For an elaboration of this concept, see Christopher S. Allen, "Structural and Technological Change in West Germany: Employer and Trade Union Responses in the Chemical and Automobile Industries," diss., Brandeis University, 1983. The term was an original formulation in the above work, referring to Germany's historical shortage of abundant raw materials (with the notable exception of iron and coal deposits), its dependence on exports as a major component of its growth, and the need for a comprehensive social spending plan to buffer the social instability that late and rapid industrialization—as well as post–World War II reindustrialization—tended to produce. The two most obvious examples of such social spending programs were Bismarck's initiation of welfare measures in the 1880s and the "social" portion of the Social Market Economy of the 1950s. In short, what has made German economic strength "fragile" has been the potential resource and export market constraints, combined with the expense of maintaining public welfare measures. Inspiration for this formulation of the term *fragile strength* was drawn from the works of Alexander Gerschenkron, Gordon Craig, Geoffrey Barraclough, Andrew Shonfield, and Karl Schorske.

5. For the foundations of this assessment, see Rudolf Hilferding, *Finance Capital* (London: Routledge & Kegan Paul, 1981), esp. pts. 3 and 5; Gerard Braunthal, *The Federation of German Industry in Politics* (Ithaca: Cornell University Press, 1965); and Heinz Josef Varain, *Interessenverbände in Deutschland* (Cologne: Kiepenhauer & Witsch, 1977).

level, the chemical industry has developed a successful pattern of managed change.

The central argument will show that many small changes within institutions that are both stable and flexible have replicated similar developments in other core West German sectors. Wolfgang Streeck's chapter on the automobile industry has shown how the auto manufacturers have overcome high wage costs and strong international competition and produced the skilled workers necessary to use sophisticated process technology to maintain the industry's profitable world market niche. Gary Herrigel's chapter in this volume articulates how the machine tool industry has created and nurtured a supportive institutional structure that has enabled an industry dominated by small and medium-sized firms to retain its leading share of world markets. Gerd Junne's chapter on high technology has identified an institutional pattern whereby this sector's strength has come from its strong links with other sectors. And Martin Bäthge and Herbert Oberbeck have shown how large financial institutions such as banks and insurance companies have developed a surprising degree of internal flexibility that has been underestimated by the United States and Japan. The pattern of managed change in the chemical industry is part of a generalized institutional response in the core sectors that defines the Third West German Republic.

BACKGROUND OF THE CHEMICAL INDUSTRY

Since its inception, the West German chemical industry has been dominated by its major firms, BASF, Bayer, and Hoechst. All have had a century of experience in constructing an elaborate industrial framework to develop and commercialize thousands of new and different products.[6] The chemical industry sprang to life in the mid-nineteenth century by both creating and taking advantage of a complex and integrated series of events. It drew on an innovative technology (deriving aniline from coal tar), access to a key raw material (Ruhr coal), an advanced educational system (supportive of scientific pursuits), a growing world demand for chemical products (the dyes were used in the expanding textile industry and exported throughout the industrializing world), an elaborate financial and legal system (which favored large units of pro-

6. For an overview of the industry's remarkable growth in the late nineteenth and early twentieth centuries, see Hans Schall, *Die Chemische Industrie Deutschlands* (Nuremburg: Wirtschafts- und sozialgeographische Arbeiten, 1959); L. F. Haber, *The Chemical Industry in the Nineteenth Century* (London: Oxford University Press, 1958); Haber, *The Chemical Industry, 1900–1930* (London: Oxford University Press, 1971); and William O. Henderson, *The Rise of German Industrial Power, 1834–1914* (Berkeley and Los Angeles: University of California Press, 1975).

duction), a centralized banking system (for the rapid amassing of vast amounts of needed capital), comprehensive training programs, and the general assimilation of its work force (supported both by Bismarck's creation of the welfare state and the general paternalism of the large firms). For an overview of the West German chemical industry over the past two decades, see Table 6.1.

During the course of the twentieth century, this industrial structure was created to produce such products as dyes, synthetic fibers, fertilizers, pesticides, synthetic rubber, plastics, pharmaceuticals, paints, food additives, and petrochemicals. Over the century, the industry's firms often have had to make dramatic shifts in product lines because of wars, economic depression, lack of access to raw materials, decartelization after World War II, the need to change the industry's feedstock base from coal to oil within a generation, and competitive pressures from producers in other countries.[7] Yet despite—or perhaps because of—these competitive pressures, the leading firms in the industry have developed areas of product specialization that prevent direct competition among them. Bayer has emphasized synthetic rubber and, later, specialty chemicals, polyurethane, and pharmaceuticals. BASF has stressed basic petrochemicals, fertilizers, and video and audiotape, and Hoechst has been the leader in dyestuffs and synthetic fibers. For the big three chemical firms, competition has been defined in international terms far more than in domestic ones, as the three have used this diversification to achieve their rank among the top five chemical firms in the world.[8] The big three also avoid direct competition in another sense. Unlike the coal and steel industries, which have been concentrated in the Ruhr,[9] the chemical industry has been more geographically diversified. Each firm has established autonomous centers of strength in three different federal *Länder*. Bayer's large plants (Leverkusen and Urdingen) are located in North Rhine Westphalia, BASF's complex (Ludwigshafen) in Rhineland-Palatinate, and Hoechst (Frankfurt) in Hesse. Each of these three firms has established strong working relationships with their respective regional governments.[10] During the brief SPD-Green coalition

7. For an analysis of the postwar rebuilding of individual firms after their fusion into IG Farben during the 1925–45 period, see Raymond George Stokes, "Recovery and Resurgence in the West German Chemical Industry: Allied Policy and the I.G. Farben Successor Companies, 1945–1951," diss., Ohio State University, 1986.

8. For an overview of the strategic choices the industry has faced, see Sandra Elizabeth Peterson, "Structural Continuity and Industrial Strategies: The Case of the German Chemical Industry," Honors thesis, Cornell University, May 1980; and for analysis of diversification, see Giovanni Rufo, *Technical Change and Economic Policy: Sector Report—The Fertilizer and Pesticides Industry* (Paris: OECD, 1980).

9. See the chapter by Josef Esser and Wolfgang Fach on steel in this volume.

10. Wyn Grant, William Paterson, and Colin Whitson, "Government-Industry Relations in the Chemical Industry: An Anglo-German Comparison," manuscript, 1986. For

Table 6.1. Statistical Summary of the Chemical Industry

	1972	1986
Number of firms	59	60
Employees	577,000	543,000
Percent employees unionized	47.4 (1975)	46.0 (est)
Total sales	DM 56.0 billion	DM 140.0 billion
Sales as percent of FRG mining and manufacturing sales	9.4	10.8
Exports as percent of sales	38.0	51.4
Exports as percent of FRG exports	14.3	13.7
Imports as percent of FRG imports	9.1	9.9

SOURCES: *Chemiewirtschaft in Zahlen,* 1980 and 1987; Andrei S. Markovits, *The Politics of the West German Trade Unions: Strategies of Class and Interest Representation in Growth and Crisis* (Cambridge: Cambridge University Press, 1986); and *Jahrbuch: Bergbau, öl und Gas, Elektrizität, Chemie* (1972 and 1986/87).

(1985–86) in Hesse, Hoechst worked very closely with the Land Economics Ministry to overcome any potentially adverse action by the Environment Ministry that was headed by a member of the Greens. But the presence of the Greens in the Hesse government proved not to be a serious threat to Hoechst. After attaining office, Joschka Fischer, the environment minister, offered strong criticism of Hoechst's discharging effluents into river water, but the challenge proved more symbolic than real as the chemical firm quickly announced that its standards for allowable levels of pollution were already below the level Fischer had demanded.[11]

As important as they are, the big three are not the entire chemical industry. Total employment in the sector during 1986 was 543,000, but BASF, Bayer, and Hoechst accounted for only 181,396 of this figure. In annual sales figures, the big three occupy a similar position. During 1986, BASF had sales of DM 18.7 billion, Bayer had DM 16.7 billion, and Hoechst had DM 14.1 billion. Total industry sales for 1986 were DM 140.0 billion, which meant that the three large firms generated only 35.4 percent of the sector's turnover.[12] Two of the industry's more important smaller firms are Hüls AG with 15,013 employees and sales of DM 4.5 billion in 1986, and Schering AG with 10,881 employees and sales of DM

---

an overview of the politics of regional industrial policies in West Germany, see Christopher S. Allen, "Corporatism and Regional Economic Policies in the Federal Republic of Germany: The 'Meso' Politics of Industrial Adjustment," *Publius* (forthcoming).

11. "Fischer's First 100 Days," *German Tribune,* 13 April 1986, p. 3.

12. Verband der Chemischen Industrie, *Chemiewirtschaft in Zahlen* (Frankfurt: VCI, 1987); *Annual Reports,* Bayer, BASF, and Hoechst, 1986; and Wyn Grant and William Patterson, "Large Firms as Political Actors: The Case of the Chemical Industry in Britain and West Germany," paper presented at the Annual Conference of the Political Studies Association, Aberdeen, April 1987.

2.2 billion in 1986.[13] Thus despite their generally dominant position, the three large firms must remain sensitive to the needs and concerns of the smaller firms, many of which are either suppliers or customers. In fact, the presidency of the Verband der Chemischen Industrie (VCI)— the chemical industry association—alternates between a representative of one of the big three and a representative of one of the smaller companies. Not only does the coordination between small and large firms enhance the solidarity of the VCI, it also is politically important in resonating with the *Mittelständische Politik* of the F.D.P. and the small business faction of the CDU/CSU.[14] The representation in the VCI of all member firms, however, does not diminish the big three's leading position in the sector.

The industry enjoyed spectacular postwar growth as one of the leading forces in the *Wirtschaftswunder,* but by the early and mid-1970s, the industry's strategies of product diversification and new product creation ran into several obstacles. One was the dramatic quadrupling of oil prices just after the industry had turned from coal to petroleum as a basic raw material. Another was the growing overcapacity for chemical products in the industrialized world.[15] Both factors challenged the industry's ability successfully to produce and market its sophisticated products. The oil price rise increased the cost of the industry's increasingly exotic output, and the overcapacity meant that the potential market for these products—not a long-lasting one to begin with because of the rapid technological advances in the industry—faced dramatic constraints. Moreover, because petroleum-based products were such a major portion of the industry, its ability to produce new products might face certain technical limits to growth.

By the end of the second OPEC price shock in the early 1980s, the industry was faced with the need to expand the range of products even more rapidly than before.[16] Products that seemed to offer little future promise included inorganic chemicals, synthetic rubber, "simple" chemical fibers, and soaps. Traditional products that still seemed to offer profitable opportunities were herbicides, agrichemicals, portions of pharmaceuticals, and specialized office supply products. Product lines that the industry continued to develop were organic industrial chemicals, photo chemicals, advanced textile fibers, and solvents used by other industries in the manufacture of specialized products. But the

13. *Annual Reports,* Schering AG and Hüls AG, 1986.
14. Grant and Patterson, "Large Firms as Political Actors," pp. 16–17.
15. For an analysis of the new problems facing the industry during this period, see Wolf Rüdiger Streck, *Chemische Industrie: Strukturwandlungen und Entwicklungsperspektiven* (Berlin: Dunckner and Humbolt, 1984).
16. Ibid.

areas that seemed to offer the greatest potential for a technological leap forward were advanced pharmaceuticals and biotechnology.[17] Whether biotechnology will become absorbed by the chemical industry or "spin off" on its own is still an open question. Despite the uncertainty of these challenges, the industry bounced back and enjoyed large growth during the mid-1980s. In 1983 sales rose 7.6 percent; in 1984, 11.1 percent; and in 1985, 5.6 percent. But sales declined in 1986 by 5.9 percent as a result of the fall of the dollar vis-à-vis the deutschemark. But because oil—the sector's primary raw material—is priced in dollars, costs dropped by a greater percentage than did sales.[18] This issue remains a two-edged sword because the price of oil is denominated in dollars, whereas the deutschemark and the European currencies have all appreciated vis-à-vis the dollar. Continued strengthening of the deutschemark relative to the dollar could represent an opportunity for American firms to gain a greater market share in Europe.

Another reason why these changes would not confront the chemical industry with a major challenge is that the sector never fully adopted the Fordist mass production model—completely standardized products with simple and repetitive work processes—of such other leading sectors as automobiles.[19] Because of the nature of the industry's products and plant-level work organization, such a model never penetrated the sector. The constant product innovation in the industry prevented the long production runs that defined traditional mass production industries. This rapid pace of innovation frustrated those who tried to apply product cycle theory to the industry. Chemicals has been a special industry because it has been able to use technological change in such a way that it could run through many product cycles and never be victimized by any single one of them.[20]

Yet this should not suggest that the chemical industry in the early twentieth century was a craft-based sector that was dislodged by mass production in the Piore/Sabel model. Because the industry was science-based, capital-intensive, and technology-driven, it had no handicraft background and thus relied on unskilled workers as the largest segment

17. See Gerd Junne's chapter in this volume; and Sheila Jasanoff, "Technological Innovation in a Corporatist State: The Case of Biotechnology in the Federal Republic of Germany," *Research Policy* 14 (1985): 23–38.

18. VCI, *Chemiewirtschaft in Zahlen.*

19. For the now standard works on the change away from mass production in the major industrialized countries, see Charles Sabel, *Work and Politics* (Cambridge: Cambridge University Press, 1982); and Michael Piore and Charles Sabel, *The Second Industrial Divide* (New York: Basic Books, 1984).

20. For a discussion of the relationship between the chemical industry and the product cycle literature, see Thomas Ilgen, "'Better Living through Chemistry': The Chemical Industry in the World Economy," *International Organization* 37 (Autumn 1983): 647–80; and Allen, "Structural and Technological Change," p. 146.

of the work force during all of the nineteenth century and most of the twentieth. It was only during the postwar period that the increasingly sophisticated production techniques of these capital-intensive processes required workers with greater skills to monitor complex procedures.[21] Although the industry did rely on unskilled workers before World War II, the rapid changes in product lines did not allow development of a classic mass production sector. Craig Patton argues that the industry was able to circumvent the militance of the small number of skilled workers in the chemical industry during the early portion of this century. He suggests that it was the skilled, not the unskilled, workers who were the most militant because they resented the high-handed authority relations in the factory during this period. By the early 1920s the large firms were able to beat back this challenge. Patton implies that the paternalism of the large firms characteristic of the industry through all but the Third Reich was further refined in handling this challenge from a militant segment of its work force. This generally nonmilitant tradition may help account for the generally cooperative, if not docile, posture of chemical workers in Germany.[22]

In short, from its inception the chemical industry in Germany has been characterized by a mix of capital-intensive mass production and only in the postwar period did flexible specialization among skilled workers become important. This mix of production processes depending on product line has enabled the chemical industry to avoid some of the upheavals characteristic of other industries that had to make the transition to flexible specialization from a much heavier reliance on mass production. In essence, large firms emerged because of both the large capital requirements and the flexibility resulting from rapid product innovation.

NEW PRODUCT TECHNOLOGIES AT THE PLANT LEVEL

At first glance, the plant-level changes accompanying the introduction of new product technologies should be the easiest of the three challenges facing the West German chemical industry. The most significant and comprehensive analysis of the effects in the workplace of new product technology in West German industry has been done by Horst Kern and Michael Schumann.[23] They discovered that in the machine

21. Horst Kern and Michael Schumann, *Das Ende der Arbeitsteilung? Rationalisierung in der industriellen Produktion* (Munich: Beck, 1984).
22. Craig Dean Patton, "Labor Protest in the German Inflation, 1914–1923: The Case of the Chemical Industry," diss., University of California, Berkeley, 1985.
23. Kern and Schumann, *Das Ende der Arbeitsteilung?*

tool, automobile, and chemical industries the work process may be even more segmented than much of the contemporary literature on flexible specialization would suggest. For the chemical industry they note the increased growth of both capital intensity and specialized, professional work of many—but not all—jobs, depending on the firm and the particular product line. This 1984 study was a follow-up to one done in 1970, so this growth is a continuation of a postwar trend.[24] The 1984 study pointed out the importance of skilled professional workers for the adaptive capacity of the chemical industry during this period. The significance of both studies is to show that the dominant pattern in the late nineteenth and the first half of the twentieth century of capital intensity and unskilled workers changed to one of a technology-driven regime of continued capital intensity and a much higher qualification of the work force.

Kern and Schumann have correctly noted that the mix of chemical industry employees has shifted dramatically from low-skilled toward professional workers. But though professional workers have been crucial for the development of new product technologies, the capital intensity of the industry has not created a net increase in jobs. As a result of the fallout from the first oil crisis in the mid-1970s, employment in the industry declined from 553,000 in 1977 to 543,000 in 1986. To be sure, the 1986 figure is an improvement from the industry low of 524,000 in both 1983 and 1984,[25] but the important distinction here is that the industry is not likely to make a substantial contribution to alleviating West German unemployment, which ranged between 8 and 9 percent during the mid-1980s. Even with the industry's rapid growth during 1984 and 1985—enhanced by the then weak deutschemark and falling petroleum feedstock prices—employment did not reach 1977 levels. Moreover, the nature of the professional jobs that were created in the industry differed from those in other flexibly specialized work. The primary characteristic of these jobs has been the monitoring of sophisticated equipment rather than working with chemicals in the laboratory. This has called into question the issue of whether a chemical worker should be educated in traditional chemical skills or with advanced computer training.[26] It has also caused Kern and Schumann to characterize a work in such a job as a *Fahrer* rather than a *Führer*.[27] The literal English translations, *driver* and *leader*, only partially convey the subtle difference

24. See Kern and Schumann, *Industriearbeit und Arbeiterbewusstsein*, 2 vols. (Frankfurt: Studienausgabe, Frankfurt, 1977).

25. VCI, *Chemiewirtschaft in Zahlen.*

26. Jürgen Walter and Kurt Meier, "Soziale Qualifikationen in der Berufsausbildung," *Gewerkschaftliche Umschau*, no. 4 (August–October 1987), pp. 10–11.

27. Kern and Schumann, *Das Ende der Arbeitsteilung?* p. 265.

between skilled, professional work in the chemical industry and its counterpart in the machine tool or automobile industries. Although chemical workers are clearly professionals, they have less control over the production process than do comparable workers in other core sectors. More seriously, in the 1980s skilled workers in the industry have become substantially overqualified. In essence, the work process has changed but the production system has not. Kern and Schumann ultimately conclude that the chemical firms possess the upper hand over their workers in defining the nature of the work process in the industry. But because these professional workers are so important for the industry, and because the works councils (*Betriebsräte*) are so institutionally well placed in these firms, there is potentially enough space for workers in the chemical industry to attempt to create different political configurations that might produce more jobs in the industry.[28]

The management of the industry's large firms will decide how it is to change.[29] Along with the VCI as an industry organization, the sector has a very strong and influential employers' organization, the Bundesarbeitgeberverband Chemie (BVAC). The function of the VCI is to deal with a wide range of issues of direct concern to the industry, government policy on environmental issues being the most obvious. The function of the BVAC is to aggregate the interests of individual firms, particularly in such areas as collective bargaining, because the employers wish to maintain a united front in their dealings with IG Chemie, the chemical workers' union. Together the VCI and the BVAC provide a stable institutional framework within which the individual firms achieve adaptive patterns of flexibility. Yet these two important institutions do not play a large role in micro-level change. Considerably reinforced by their long history of success in industrial adaptation, the management of these firms relies on a strong sense of paternalism in deciding how best to organize the work process.

Because the chemical workers' union (IG Chemie) organizes workers throughout the industry, the firms prefer to work with the works councils (*Betriebsräte*), which are specific to individual firms. BASF, Bayer, and Hoechst have had a long history of successfully dealing with the

28. Michael Piore, in extending the distinction between mass production and flexible specialization articulated with Sabel in *The Second Industrial Divide*, suggests a richer typology of possible configurations: classic mass production, mass production with cosmetic variation, flexible mass production, closed flexible specialization, open flexible specialization with marginal adjustment, and open flexible specialization with discontinuous adjustment. See Piore, "Corporate Reform in American Manufacturing and the Challenge to Economic Theory," paper presented at the Workshop on Production Reorganization and Skills, Berkeley Roundtable on the International Economy, University of California, 10–12 September 1987.

29. "Chemie: Grenzen des Wachstums?" *Wirtschaftswoche* 34 (17 August 1984): 28–38; and Grant and Paterson, "Large Firms as Political Actors."

worker organization over which they have the most control—the works council—rather than the one that represents chemical workers across the entire industry—IG Chemie. Its subordinate position represented a thorn in the side of IG Chemie and in the late 1970s and early 1980s produced both internal divisions in the union and frustration over its inability to have more influence in controlling change in the workplace.[30] By the mid-1980s, however, IG Chemie realized that it would remain a junior partner to the *Betriebsräte* on these issues. Thus under the moderate leadership of Hermann Rappe, IG Chemie entered into an agreement with the *Betriebsräte* and the management of industry firms on the regulation of part-time work. Though this agreement was seen as an important victory for IG Chemie, a similar proposal by IG Metall for the metalworking industries obtained greater concessions by management in these sectors than IG Chemie had settled for with the chemical industry.[31] One interpretation of IG Chemie's moderation holds that Rappe has taken these steps from a position of strength. Yet if agreement on the issue of part-time work depended more on the economic strength of the industry and the institutional power of the *Betriebsräte,* then this settlement might not have been the victory the union thought it had achieved.

The introduction of new product technologies in the chemical industry in the 1980s has produced two important changes: a more insistent need for the creation of more advanced product lines and the growing professionalization of a stable work force. Together these factors have enabled the industry to move into specialized areas that have been called "fine chem" or "high chem" and begin to push in the direction of biotechnology.[32] This process has been greatly aided by massive amounts of research and development spending, reaching DM 8.5 billion in 1986. But rather than relying heavily on the Federal Ministry for Research and Technology (BMFT), the industry controls 96 percent of its research and development spending. Under the provisions of the BMFT, allocation of any public funds to firms must also be determined by representatives of the workers plus ministry officials, thus creating an inducement for chemical firms to use their strong cash position to self-finance these

30. For extensive elaboration of this pattern, see D. R. Ebsworth, "Industrial Relations in the West German and British Chemical Industries," diss., University of Surrey, 1981; Andrei S. Markovits, *The Politics of the West German Trade Unions: Strategies of Class and Interest Representation in Growth and Crisis* (Cambridge: Cambridge University Press, 1986); and Allen, "Structural and Technological Change," chap. 4.

31. See Werner Vitt, "Mitbestimmung ausbauen—Arbeitnehmerrechte sichern!" *Der Betriebsrat,* April 1985, pp. 100–105; and "Chemicals Union Gets Deal on Part Time Work," *German Tribune,* 14 April 1987.

32. See Junne's chapter in this volume. See also J. C. Cox and H. Kriegbaum, *Growth, Innovation and Employment: An Anglo-German Comparison* (London: Anglo-German Foundation for the Study of Industrial Society, 1980).

innovations.[33] The reason that the share of government support is so small is that the industry receives its funds in the form of indirect support through tax breaks. The VCI prefers this method to direct state support because it wishes to "circumvent attempts by the state to influence the structure of research as well as avoid the distortion of competition." This mode of financing contrasts sharply with that for German industry as a whole, which receives 39.7 percent of its research and development support from the public sector.[34] In addition to this basic support, the VCI's Fund of the Chemical Industry (to which all chemical firms contribute) spent an additional DM 3.7 million for the promotion of junior scientists and DM 2.1 million for promotional literature to help ensure the supply of future expertise for the industry. Precisely because the industry has been able to combine rapid product innovation with high skills within its work force, it has been able to turn many of the "Eurosclerosis" arguments on their head.[35] To the extent that this replicates the flexibility within large firms and institutions of other industries, it has become part of the definitive pattern of plant-level change in West German industry.

Yet, as favorable as these plant-level changes appear for the chemical industry, a number of important reservations remain. The first major political question is whether this model of the rapid creation of ever more sophisticated products with a stable, professionalized work force represents either a generalizable, effective strategy for the challenges confronting the entire chemical industry or a potential model for other German sectors. Since change at this level has been so firm-specific, how is it possible to extend these successful patterns beyond the big three firms or even to other sectors? Also, since this advanced product technology and reliance on skilled workers requires such heavy financial commitment, how easy will it be for smaller firms, or suppliers to the large firms, to emulate this pattern?

Moreover, since each of the big three firms has had a different area of product specialization, how effective a model is this if one of the firms proves less successful with its strategic area of choice? For example, BASF has been more heavily involved in petrochemicals, an area that has suffered greater competitive pressures than other segments of the industry.[36] BASF has had to expend a great deal of effort in contracting this segment of the business and has been less aggressive in pushing forward with the pattern outlined in the previous portion of this chap-

33. VCI, *Annual Report, 1987*, p. 25; Grant, Paterson, and Whitson, "Government-Industry Relations in the Chemical Industry," pp. 28–32.

34. VCI, *Annual Report, 1987*, pp. 25, 27.

35. Bruce Nussbaum, *The World after Oil* (New York: Simon & Schuster, 1983).

36. See Benjamin Gomes-Casseres, "Restructuring European Petrochemicals: BASF AG," Harvard Business School Case 4-385-201, March 1985 (rev.).

ter. In short, the first political consequence of this plant-level change is whether it is confined to a small portion of the industry or, more important, whether it can ever go beyond a few highly visible examples.

Second, the firm-specific nature of these changes in the industry also highlights the surprising absence of either the VCI or the BVAC as major actors in this process. Though historically very important in helping firms manage change,[37] these two institutions have been much less active in this area and at the plant level in general. For example, the VCI helps raise research and development funds, but the major decisions about spending are controlled by the firms. The point is that, if this pattern of innovation is to diffuse beyond a few firms, some outside institution such as the VCI or the BVAC will have to take greater responsibility. The BVAC has recently worked with the firms to change the collective bargaining distinction between white- and blue-collar workers.[38] In this way the BVAC is trying to help the firms make the adjustment to a more flexible arrangement since professional workers represent a growing proportion of the industry's work force.

The only other active institution to play such a role would be the banks, which hold large blocks of stock in all of the major chemical firms (some 25 percent of all firms in the industry).[39] Yet if either the VCI or the banks played such a direct role at the firm level, it might cause antitrust difficulties with the Cartel Office. Both the VCI and the banks have been able to avoid direct confrontation with this agency by finding the many loopholes which this 1957 law allows.[40] It is doubtful that they would still be able to do so with a more active role at the microeconomic level. Wyn Grant, William Paterson, and Colin Whitson have recently argued that the dominant *Hausbank* pattern in which the three large firms work closely with the three large German banks (Deutsche Bank, Dresdner Bank, and Commerzbank) has given way to a more international pattern with the firms increasingly relying on foreign banks.[41] Although this certainly is to the advantage of individual firms, it may be less helpful in diffusing successful patterns throughout the entire industry.

Third, the failure of these changes to create a substantial number of jobs in the industry may represent a potential political problem. From

37. See Felix Ehrmann, *Hundert Jahre Verband der Chemischen Industrie* (Frankfurt: Verband der Chemische Industrie, 1980).
38. Frank Bünte, "Chemicals Industry Deal Blurs Distinction between Wage and Salary Earners," *German Tribune*, 29 June 1986, p. 6.
39. See Paterson, "Structural Continuity and Industrial Strategies"; also Hans T. Thanheiser, "Strategy and Structure of German Industrial Enterprise," diss., Harvard University, 1972.
40. See Braunthal, *Federation of German Industry*, passim.
41. Grant, Paterson, and Whitson, "Government-Industry Relations in the Chemical Industry."

1961 until the first oil crisis in 1973–74, unemployment in the Federal Republic averaged between 1 and 2 percent. Even during the mid- and late 1970s, the figure was only between 4 and 5 percent. During the 1980s, however, the nation's unemployment has averaged between 8 and 9 percent. Any industrial strategy that not only does not offer the possibility of creating new jobs but shows a net loss of jobs would seem to provoke considerable questioning. To expand the argument of Kern and Schumann, such a strategy of increasing professionalization of a minority of jobs in the industry combined with a net loss of overall jobs may represent a "new aristocracy of the working class." Already in the mid-1980s, the persistent unemployment in the Federal Republic has given rise to debates about a "two-thirds society" in which a permanent underclass is never able to achieve the benefits of a full-employment, advanced capitalist welfare state.

The junior partner role of IG Chemie in new product technology compared to the plant-specific works councils has the potential of making a greater impact on the industry.[42] In trying to confine these changes within an institutional structure that they can contain, the chemical firms may run the risk of failing fully to use an institution—IG Chemie—that could help diffuse this innovation process more widely. If future successes depend on the ability of skilled workers in the industry to adapt to change, then an industrywide not a firm-specific institution will prove more important. Thus the minor role of IG Chemie in the process of shaping new technology could represent a major missed opportunity for the industry and its workers.[43]

In conclusion, although the key firms in the industry seem to be well in control of the changes in new product technology in the late 1980s, there are several important unanswered questions that could represent potential difficulties for the industry's pattern of many small changes within an adaptive institutional framework.

NEW SOCIAL MOVEMENTS IN NATIONAL POLITICS

The postwar successes of the West German chemical industry have not come without costs at the national level.[44] Despite the industry's rapid growth and strategic positioning as a major supplier to the other core sectors of the German economy,[45] the West German chemicals sector bore increased scrutiny beginning in the late 1960s and early

42. IG Chemie, *Technologie und Beschäftigung* (Hannover: IG Chemie, 1984).
43. See Allen, "Structural and Technological Change," chap. 4.
44. Grant, Patterson, and Whitson, "Government-Industry Relations in the Chemical Industry."
45. See Ilgen, "'Better Living through Chemistry,'" p. 650, and Allen, "Structural and Technological Change," chap. 4.

1970s. Chief among the issues that continue to challenge the chemical industry in the 1980s have been health and safety in the workplace and in society, the general questioning of growth and technology, and especially the growing impact of an organized environmental movement.

The chemical industry produces a large number of highly toxic products, and in an age when environmental concerns came to the forefront, the industry's activities merited increased concern. Moreover, the dominance of the three large firms in West German society occasionally caused many alternatively inclined West Germans to resent and challenge these great pillars of the postwar economic establishment. In the early 1970s, revelations about the links between certain chemicals and cancer prompted great concern and criticism of the chemical industry and the government regulatory processes that were supposed to safeguard the public and chemical workers from danger. These concerns surfaced in many industrialized countries, and West Germany was not immune to them.[46] Far from dissipating, these concerns intensified during the 1980s and produced additional studies detailing the potential hazards to society of chemical products.[47]

The most active groups in placing pressure on the West German chemical industry were the citizen action groups (*Bürgerinitiativen*) in the late 1970s and the Green party, which formed in 1979. These "alternative" new social movements found in the powerful—if not imperial—chemical industry a comparatively easy target for criticism.[48] The Greens were heavily criticized by the industry, but they were also castigated by the leader of IG Chemie, Hermann Rappe. Although Rappe wished that the union could have more influence on the works council–dominated plant floor, he was not prepared to support a movement that took such anti-industry positions.[49]

Despite these defenses of the chemical sector by both industry and

46. See Joseph L. Badaracco, Jr., *Loading the Dice: A Five-Country Study of Vinyl Chloride Regulation* (Boston: Harvard Business School Press, 1985); Ronald Brickman, Sheila Jasanoff, and Thomas Ilgen, "Chemical Regulation and Cancer: A Cross-National Study of Policy and Politics," Program on Science, Technology, Society, Cornell University, November 1982.

47. See Walter Ballew III, "Chemicals Regulation—Recent Developments," *Georgia Journal of International and Comparative Law* 12 (1982): 95–105; Organization for Economic Cooperation and Development, *Economic Aspects of International Chemicals Control* (Paris: OECD, 1983); Francis J. C. Roe, ed., *The Chemical Industry and the Health of the Community* (London: Royal Society of Medicine, 1985); and Joanne K. Nichols and Peter J. Crawford, *Managing Chemicals in the 1980s* (Paris: OECD, 1983).

48. Karl-Werner Brand, Detlev Busser, and Dieter Rucht, *Aufbruch in einandere Gesellschaft: Neue Soziale Bewegungen in der Bundesrepublik* (Frankfurt: Campus, 1983); and Herbert Kitschelt, *Reinventing the Party: Ecological Politics in Belgium and West Germany* (Ithaca: Cornell University Press, 1989).

49. See "Schwankerei ist nicht am Platz" (interview with Hermann Rappe), *Der Spiegel* 37 (27 June 1983), pp. 23–28; see also Markovits, *West German Trade Unions*, for a more detailed account of Rappe's aversion to any individuals or forces that might criticize the growth potential of the chemical industry.

CHRISTOPHER S. ALLEN

union spokesmen during the late 1970s and early 1980s, the environmental problems continued to raise troublesome questions for the industry. Although the major chemical firms seemed to bounce back from the second oil shock in 1979–80 and the 1981–82 recession to achieve growth levels above those of their major competitors,[50] environmental issues seemed to be the primary image on which the industry was judged at the national level during this period. The ecological disaster in Seveso, Italy, where lethal dioxin was released in 1976, continued to be at the forefront of criticism of the industry in West Germany well into the early and mid-1980s. The tragedies at Bhopal and Chernobyl—far beyond the Federal Republic's borders—still had a profound effect in increasing environmental anxieties inside West Germany.[51] Perhaps second only to the nuclear power industry, the chemical industry has been vulnerable on such issues because of the potentially high adverse public impact of any major accident, even when such accidents take place outside the country.

Consequently, the industry has been very active in publicizing its concern for the environment. The VCI has been aggressive in promoting its safety and stressing how effective the firms in the sector have been at self-regulation.[52] Similar to Herrigel's argument for the machine tool industry in his chapter in this volume, the industry association acted collectively to protect its member firms on a core issue for the sector. In 1978, the VCI established a special fund, Initiative geschützes Leben, financed by member firms, for coordinating its spending on the environment. From the mid-1970s to the mid-1980s, the industry reportedly spent DM 30 billion on environmental protection, a figure twice as high as the American chemical industry spent and three times as high as the French when measured as a ratio to annual sales.[53]

In November 1986, another major environmental disaster struck, the twin spills of chemicals into the Rhine near Basel, Switzerland. The plants were owned by two Swiss firms, Sandoz and Ciba-Geigy, but since the Rhine runs to the sea through the entire length of the Federal Republic, the spills have had a greater effect on West Germans than on the Swiss. The initial press reports were harshly critical of the chemical industry in general, not just the two offending Swiss firms.[54] Not only

50. See Joseph Bower, *When Markets Quake* (Boston: Harvard Business School Press, 1986).

51. See Heinz Verfürth, "Chernobyl Gives Greens' 'fundi' Wing a Boost," *German Tribune*, 1 June 1986, p. 4.

52. See VCI, *Chemie und Umwelt* (Frankfurt: Verband der Chemischen Industrie, 1985).

53. Grant, Paterson, and Whitson, "Government-Industry Relations in the Chemical Industry," p. 19.

54. See "Counting the Cost as the Rhine Runs Red with Chemicals," *German Tribune*, 30 November 1986, p. 12; "Chernobyl, the Rhine and the Price of the Future," ibid., 7 December 1986, p. 9; "Suddenly, a Deathwatch on the Rhine," *Business Week*, 24 Novem-

did the German portion of the Rhine bear the greatest effects of the spills, but subsequent investigations found that German chemical firms had been dumping small amounts of chemical waste into the river for some time without notifying environmental authorities as prescribed by West German law. Moreover, West German public and private authorities were accused of not notifying the public quickly enough after the first disaster at Sandoz was discovered.[55]

In short, the major change at the national level for the chemical industry during the 1980s was that health, ecological, and technology-related problems—always a potential hazard for the firms in the sector—have placed the industry in a particularly vulnerable position. Just as the firms were trying to use their usual low-key methods to adapt themselves to new patterns of production and international competitiveness, these issues seemed to threaten the industry-specific institutional process by which the industry has historically transformed itself.

The major national political consequence of these changes, particularly after the Rhine spills, has been that the industry has begun to face increasing regulatory scrutiny. This has particular significance in that for one hundred years the industry has jealously guarded its ability to self-regulate.[56] In the 1970s, the industry's firms and the VCI worked together to deal with the vinyl chloride issue[57] and the industry has hoped that the same cooperation could work to deal with the effects of the Rhine spills.

These self-regulatory policies in the chemical industry came under considerable threat after the Rhine spills. But after a momentary setback, the VCI mobilized its considerable lobbying forces and published a hitherto closely held "comprehensive catalog of measures" (*Massnahmenkatalog*) in its 1986–87 annual report published in March 1987.[58] Among these measures were a series of safety concepts developed by the industry to deal with fire prevention in chemical plants, water polluting substances, water circulation systems, and rules of procedure for production and analytical characterization of combustion gases. In addi-

---

ber 1987, p. 52; and John Tagliabue, "The Rhine Struggles to Survive," *New York Times*, 15 February 1987, p. 4.

55. See "An Industry in Disgrace: Door Slams on Failed Voluntary Alarm System," *German Tribune*, 21 December 1986, p. 9.

56. The chemical industry (and the VCI) have long preferred *Ordnungspolitik*—loosely translated, the "politics of industrial order"—to *Strukturpolitik* (industrial policy in which the government is more actively involved). The chemical industry—and German industry in general—have jealously tried to guard this key management or sectoral prerogative. For a recent exposition of the distinction between *Ordnungspolitik* and *Strukturpolitik*, see Ernst Dürr, "Alternativen der Strukturpolitik," *Jahrbuch für Sozialwissenschaft* 35 (1984): 402–12.

57. See Badaracco, *Loading the Dice*.

58. VCI, *Jahresbericht 1986/87* (Frankfurt: VCI, 1987).

tion, the VCI published an extensive list of measures that the individual firms were to take themselves. The VCI also took the highly unusual step of establishing a regular series of meetings with an environmental group—the Bund für Umwelt- und Naturschutz (BUND)—to indicate that it intended to work aggressively to protect the environment.[59] The big three firms have begun to move away from choosing chief executive officers whose primary academic training was only in chemicals. By the mid-1980s, the leadership of BASF, Bayer, and Hoechst was increasingly being drawn from people with broader backgrounds. These firms wanted to take a more aggressive public relations posture on environmental issues themselves and not just as members of the VCI. The belief was that generalists rather than specialists might be more politically sensitive to adverse developments in the chemical industry.[60]

Yet despite these steps by the VCI, the challenge to the industry raises a more theoretical issue. These regulatory pressures threaten to undermine the capacity of a key institutional system that has been crucial for the industry to make adaptations and changes at the national and international levels.[61] Unlike in the United States, relations between the government and the chemical industry in the Federal Republic on regulatory issues have depended on trust. Environmental laws are not spelled out in detail as they are in the United States; rather, the West German pattern has been to give broad power to the VCI and the government with an "early coordination system" to work out the framework of a bill before it is passed. The industry expects that the state will not wield a particularly heavy hand and the state expects that the industry will act out of a sense of "collective self-responsibility." To do so, the VCI must speak for the entire chemical industry. But to the extent that the political opposition—particularly the Greens—has targeted the industry for criticism in the wake of the Rhine spills, the Kohl government (and perhaps also international agencies) may be under increasing pressure to take a more heavy hand with the industry.[62] Since these challenges to self-regulation could spill over to other sectors, they have the potential to undermine the contemporary West German version of "organized capitalism"—"para-public institutions" and "private interest government"—that has merited such extensive recent attention.[63]

59. "Chemie will besser informieren," *Süddeutsche Zeitung*, 16–17 May 1987, p. 35.

60. Grant and Paterson, "Large Firms as Political Actors," pp. 18–19.

61. See Volker Schneider, "Corporatist and Pluralist Patterns of Policy-making for Chemicals Control: A Comparison between West Germany and the USA," in Alan Cawson, ed., *Organized Interests and the State: Studies in Meso Corporatism* (Los Angeles: Sage, 1985), 174–91; and Manfred Groser, "Die Organisation von Wirtschaftsinteressen in der pharmazeutischen Industrie der BRD," 1984.

62. Volker Schneider, *Politiknetzwerke der Chemikalienkontrolle* (Berlin: deGruyter, 1988).

63. See Peter Katzenstein, *Policy and Politics in West Germany: The Growth of a Semi-Sovereign State* (Philadelphia: Temple University Press, 1987), and Wolfgang Streeck and Philippe Schmitter, *Private Interest Government* (Los Angeles: Sage, 1985).

Beyond their active political opposition, the Greens, specifically, and the new social movements, generally, pose a structural problem for the West German political economy that the postwar political system has studiously tried to avoid. The elaborate quasi-corporatist institutionalization has been an effort to create a framework for political debate in which there are "no outlyers." That is, the goal has been to have this "parapublic" system incorporate the demands of parties and interest groups in which dissent and criticism can be addressed and managed. As Katzenstein suggests, industrial adjustment has been one of the areas in which these efforts have been the most successful.[64] The participation of the Greens in the Hesse Landtag ended in 1987, after two turbulent years.[65] The opposition the party's presence provoked from Hoechst, the VCI, the BDI, and especially IG Chemie, however, could be repeated in other *Länder,* if not at the national level, should the Greens take part in other regional governments. Precisely because their members claim that they are not a "party like the others," the Greens will likely continue to resist the dominant institutional pattern. Moreover, the political problems the Greens pose for the industry are only a part of a larger institutional division that all of West German industry faces, one between the environmental movement and the trade unions.[66] Michael Baun has argued that there are three positions taken by unions on the Greens and environmental issues: hostile, neutral, and friendly. IG Chemie has traditionally fallen into the first camp, along with IG Bergbau (mining) and IG Bau-Steine-Erden (construction). Yet the political fallout from the Rhine spills has caused IG Chemie to become more sensitive to environmental issues, if not to the Greens as a party. The union has tried to emphasize that environmental protection could stimulate "qualitative" job growth.[67]

These problems suggest that dissent among the major actors in the industry and in the political system at large may not be so easily managed as in the past. As they have faced the growing ecological concern, those actors who hold dominant positions in the industry's elaborate institutional structure have tried to freeze out forces that seem to present the most potential threat to the institutional coherence of the sector while simultaneously attempting to incorporate their demands. It appears that the dominant actors in the industry have concluded that

64. Katzenstein, *Policy and Politics in West Germany.*
65. "End of SPD-Greens Coalition Forces Early Poll in Hesse," *German Tribune,* 22 February 1987; and "A Smooth Start for the New Hesse Premier," ibid., 3 May 1987.
66. Michael J. Baun, "The Trade Unions and the Green Movement in West Germany," paper presented at the 1987 Annual Meetings of the Southern Political Science Association, Charlotte, N.C., 5–7 November 1987.
67. Wolfgang Schultze, "Gerwerkschaften und Umweltschutz," *Gewerkschaftliche Umschau,* nos. 2–3 (April–July 1987), pp. 2–6; and Schultze, "Bessere Information—Mehr Mitwirkung," *Gewerkschaftliche Umschau,* no. 4 (August–October 1987), pp. 12–15.

either the external challenges are too formidable, their own resources are too weak, or the opposition forces are too difficult to incorporate. Whatever the reason, the key point is that they have departed from past patterns in dealing with challenges. In other words, the large firms and the VCI have tried to challenge and circumvent increased government regulations that have been demanded by the Greens and the SPD, just as they have used the works councils to circumscribe IG Chemie's plant-level presence. Yet the unintended consequence of such a "stonewalling" position by the firms and the VCI would likely adversely affect the capacity of other institutions within the industry to manage change. That is, the current formula in which the dominant actors in the industry are dealing with these environmental changes at the national level threatens to undermine the basic ways the industry has historically dealt with change. If self-regulation is threatened at the national level, it might indicate major uncertainties as the industry tries to deal with increased pressures in the international arena.

CHANGE IN THE INTERNATIONAL ECONOMY

In the late 1970s and early 1980s a series of international-level changes threatened the West German chemical industry. One was the complex of issues around international competitiveness, which encompassed such themes as market saturation, threats of reduced trade, comparatively high labor costs, direct foreign investment, and fluctuations in the deutschemark exchange rate. A second was the issue of raw materials, both the availability of oil as a primary feedstock source and development of product lines that would rely less heavily on oil, such as bio-technology. A third was the increasing interpenetration of the German chemicals industry with those in other Western European countries, principally via the EC and the CEFIC (the European chemical industry association). As important as these international developments were, they were not as great a challenge to the sector as the environmental issue at the national political level.

International competitiveness was one reason why the chemical industry was so concerned to develop new product technologies in the 1980s (as outlined in the first portion of the chapter). The large West German firms were facing increased competitive pressure from producers in other advanced capitalist countries, from the state-supported firms in the Eastern bloc, and from several of the NICs.[68] Many of the comparatively simple technology products which the firms in the indus-

68. For details of the problems of overcapacity in the world chemical industry, see Ilgen, "'Better Living through Chemistry'"; and Bower, *When Markets Quake*.

try formerly could rely on for several years of profitable production were being produced at lower costs in other countries. One area the industry continued to stress in the mid- and late 1980s was pharmaceuticals, which Japan had also targeted as an important sector. Yet, though the Japanese were emphasizing the importance of pharmaceuticals for international competition, a substantial portion of the development of pharmaceuticals by the West German chemical firms was informed by concern for reform of the welfare and health system.[69] Pharmaceuticals were also stressed in conjunction with growth of biotechnology, but the attention they received as a domestic issue when the Japanese saw the sector in international terms represented a cause for concern.

Stepping up their new product development strategy was obviously one way to deal with these competitive challenges, but the West German chemical industry also tried to manage the threat posed by the Eastern bloc nations by increasing trade with them during the late 1970s and early 1980s.[70] During the post–1973–74 period of generally stagnating growth in many countries, the reduced trade among advanced capitalist nations (as well as between the first and third worlds in general) induced the West German producers to turn to the East as a potential solution to their problems. The West German firms reasoned that because they were in a relatively stronger position than their Eastern bloc partners, they would derive a greater share of the benefits from such an exchange than would their trading partners. The general issue of trade was of great concern to the West German firms because roughly 50 percent of their production was geared for export.

International competitiveness was also affected by the relatively high labor costs in the industry.[71] The high degree of capital intensity, however, made this problem less severe in chemicals than in other sectors. Yet the issue of labor costs contained several additional dimensions. If the chemical industry were to develop its strategy of producing ever more technologically sophisticated products, it would need highly skilled professional workers, and they would not come cheaply. In addition, the firms' strategy of preferring to deal primarily with the works councils rather than with IG Chemie meant that freezing the union out of the process of change would require some quid pro quo that the union leadership could justify to its membership. The "quid" was the maintenance of a generous wage package for IG Chemie during the 1980s, even

69. Bundesverband der Pharmazeutischen Industrie, "Positionpapier zur gesetzlichen-Krankenversicherung-Strukturreform," 24 September 1987.

70. See Organization for Economic Cooperation and Development, *East-West Trade in Chemicals* (Paris: OECD, 1980).

71. For details see Peterson, "Structural Continuity and Industrial Strategies"; Markovits, *Politics of West German Trade Unions*; and Kern and Schumann, *Das Ende der Arbeitsteilung?*

177

during the troughs of the two post–1973–74 recessions. Unlike the "givebacks" and other direct attacks on the union movement in the United States, the West German chemical producers preferred to live with the comparatively high wage structure so they could manage change in the industry with as little interruption as possible. Nonetheless, by the mid-1980s the industry's cost position merited concern among industry leaders.

The industry's competitive position was also affected by the chemical firms' increased direct foreign investment.[72] The West German firms took increased interest in the United States as a major locus of foreign investment beginning in the late 1970s for four main reasons: American market size and growth potential, the desire to secure U.S. markets, American stability, and risk diversification.[73] The industry was aided in this process by the termination of the American Selling Price (ASP) system during the Tokyo Round of the GATT negotiations in 1978 and 1979. Ever since World War I, the then comparatively "infant" United States chemical industry had been protected by the ASP system, which decreed that imports could not be sold for less than 8 percent above the average American selling price.[74] Although the splashy billion-deutschemark investment by Hoechst in Massachusetts General Hospital's biotechnology program was the most obvious example, it was only part of a much larger—if less spectacular—presence by the large West German firms in America. As part of this process, the large chemical firms deepened their relationship with American banks and continued to rely less heavily on the traditional *Hausbank* system of the past.[75] These developments gave the West German firms a greater sense of international stability as they have increasingly seen themselves as world companies and not just German ones. An indication of this world profile can be seen in the relationship between their domestic sales and their total world sales. For the five leading companies, the figures for 1986 are as follows: Bayer (domestic, DM 16.8 billion; world, DM 40.8 billion); BASF (domestic, DM 18.7 billion; world, DM 40.4 billion); Hoechst (domestic, DM 14.1 billion; world, DM 38.0 billion); Hüls (domestic, DM 4.5 billion; world, DM 5.5 billion); and Schering (domestic, DM 2.2 billion; world, DM 5.1 billion). World sales derive not only from strong exports but also from direct foreign investment, which has been en-

72. See Enzio von Pfeil, *German Direct Investments in the United States* (Greenwich, Conn.: JAI Press, 1985); "Hoechst to Acquire Celanese," *New York Times,* 4 November 1986, p. 33; and "Hoechst Heads List of Euro Takeover Raids in USA," *German Tribune,* 23 November 1986, p. 8.

73. Pfeil, *German Direct Investments in the United States,* p. 40.

74. Bower, *When Markets Quake,* p. 118.

75. Grant, Paterson, and Whitson, "Government-Industry Relations in the Chemical Industry," pp. 24–27.

hanced in the United States by the weak dollar after 1986. These firms have strongly emphasized that their international posture has strengthened their domestic position. The trade unions (among others), however, have maintained that the investment abroad diminished to some degree the amount of capital that would otherwise be invested inside the Federal Republic.

International competitiveness was also affected by the fluctuation in the deutschemark exchange rate with respect to the major currencies (principally the dollar). At first glance, the roughly 50 percent appreciation of the deutschemark versus the dollar from 1985 until late 1987 represented a formidable problem for the chemical industry. In a sector heavily geared toward exports, any such change in the value of a major trading partner's currency would seem to be near catastrophic.[76] But the industry had a similar experience during the late 1970s (during the second oil crisis), when the deutschemark appreciated to 1.70 to the dollar, and the industry weathered that crisis comparatively easily. One reason why the rapid fluctuation in the exchange rate has not been a serious threat to the West German chemical industry is that its primary raw materials feedstock—oil—is priced in dollars. This means that although the exchange rate hurts the export markets at one level, the lower price of oil means that the industry's production costs have been substantially reduced.[77] This pattern during late 1985 and all of 1986 produced high profits for the industry, but it also induced the firms to step up their direct investment in the United States as well as their domestic investment in advanced research and development.

The first and most significant political consequence of this heightened international competition is that it may threaten the world trading system—and hence the exports—so crucial to the health of the chemical industry in West Germany.[78] A key measure of the fragile strength of this industry has been its exposure to the world economy. As the above account would suggest, the issues of market saturation, threats of reduced trade, high labor costs, diversification of investment, and currency fluctuation have all been debated within the industry. These challenges have instilled in the major actors of the chemical industry a sense of a long-term mission to safeguard its international position upon which it so heavily relies. Yet what will be the effects on the uncertainties that this fragile strength produces as the industry continues to struggle with questions of international competitiveness remain to be seen. The

76. See M. D. Hibbs, P. M. Black, and T. Marinelli, "West German Chemicals: Regrouping Global Assets," *Chemical Week,* 18 May 1986, p. 24.
77. See "Chemieindustrie: Gewinne aus der Retorte," *Wirtschaftswoche* 40 (16 May 1986): 120.
78. See Streck, *Chemische Industrie.*

issue of trade with the Eastern bloc may become another political problem for the industry. Since the mid-1970s, the chemical industry has stressed the need to increase its trade with the USSR and its allies. Since the early 1980s, the Reagan administration has tried to discourage Western European firms from increasing trade with the East. Yet for the West Germans, questions of national security have as much to do with economics and trade as they do with missiles and defense issues. In short, the importance of trade with the East for the chemical industry could spill over into certain strategic foreign policy debates.

The second major international issue affecting the industry was raw materials. As mentioned in the first section of the chapter, the West German chemical industry had transformed its raw materials base from coal to oil from the late 1940s to the early 1970s. Just when this transition was completed, the industry faced the uncertainty of access to oil when the OPEC oil embargo hit in the fall of 1973. The industry was able to make adjustments so that this change would not prove debilitating. Still, the uncertainties over both the price and availability of oil caused the industry to question how secure its future would be if this key component of present and future growth was not under its direct control.[79]

This uncertainty over raw materials is related to a third issue, maintaining the skillful synthesis of different products and technologies. For example, the stress on biotechnology and the most advanced pharmaceutical research seemed to offer a "high chem" or "fine chem" approach as a way out of the chemical industry's oil-based dilemma.[80] Yet this potential path raised the issue of whether the big three chemical firms would be the leading players in the emerging biotechnology industry. The relationship between chemicals and biotechnology has prompted the question of where to draw the boundary lines between sectors. It is clearly a long way from dyestuffs to plastics and videotape, yet all three are still considered within the domain of the chemical industry.[81] If Bayer, BASF, and Hoechst were not involved in all of these products, would the industry still be called the chemical industry? Will biotechnol-

79. See Herbert Grunewald, "The European Chemicals Industry in the 1980s," in D. H. Sharp and T. F. West, eds., *The Chemical Industry* (West Sussex: Elliot Howard, 1982), pp. 89–98.

80. See Junne's chapter in this volume. See also Ernst Truscheit, "Die Bedeutung der Biotechnologie für die pharmazeutische Industrie," *Die Pharmazeutische Industrie* 48 (1986): 741–49; and Jürgen Drews, "Biotechnologie," paper presented at the Symposium Chemie, Basel, Switzerland, 16 January 1987.

81. For an argument on the political criteria for determining what constitutes an industry, see Philippe C. Schmitter, "Democratic Theory and Neo-Corporatist Practice," *Social Research* 50 (1983): 885–928. See also Christian Deubner, "Change and Internationalization in Industry: Toward a Sectoral Interpretation of West German Politics," *International Organization* 38 (Summer 1984): 501–36.

ogy continue to be viewed as a sector in its own right, or will it too be subsumed under chemicals? Will the large chemical firms make the full leap into this technology? If so, what does this mean for the smaller firms that are already involved?[82] Given the technological sophistication and the huge, yet highly adaptive, institutionalized power of the chemical industry—especially its three large firms—it seems likely to embrace biotechnology in the long term. Moreover, the industry's ability to manage sophisticated changes while simultaneously self-regulating and thereby avoiding significant government regulation also seems likely.

The larger political consequences of these developments point to a complex series of questions regarding oil-based raw materials and the possible transition out of chemicals per se into biotechnology. Will what is now known as the chemical industry undergo major contraction? More important for the traditional chemicals sector, would such a departure by the large firms toward biotechnology accelerate the contraction of other portions of the sector, producing increased job loss and regional and industrial dislocation? Will the extremely high research and development needs for this new technology make the firms more reliant on government funding? If so, what does this mean for the firms' attempts to prevent IG Chemie from being involved in the process?[83] And what will such changes mean for the institutional structure of the industry, relying as it does on the banks and the VCI for major coordinating actions in lieu of the heavy hand of the central state? In short, the complex of issues that include raw materials, biotechnology, and pharmaceuticals will continue to be major themes in the industry for the foreseeable future. If Junne is correct, the institutional capacity of the chemical industry will enable it to adapt the technological innovations generated by new breakthroughs in high chem and fine chem in ways that replicate past patterns in which the chemical firms have made leaps into new technological areas without fundamentally disturbing the power they wield.

The fourth major international issue facing the industry in the 1980s was its increased interpenetration with other European producers.[84] The West German chemical industry has been the strongest in Western Europe, during the postwar boom years and especially during the past fourteen years of uneven growth. Yet with the development of the EEC and the CEFIC, the ability of the West German firms to set their own

82. See Junne's chapter in this volume; and Jasanoff, "Technological Innovation in a Corporatist State."
83. See Jürgen Walter, "Für eine sozialverträgliche Entwicklung der Biotechnologie," *Gewerkschaftliche Monatschefte* 10 (1984): 655–60.
84. See CEFIC, *Annual Report* (Brussels: CEFIC, various years); Bower, *When Markets Quake*; Ilgen, "'Better Living through Chemistry'"; and Nichols and Crawford, *Managing Chemicals in the 1980s.*

agenda and control their own industry has increasingly been encroached upon. The creation in 1992 of a Western European market of 350 million gives the large chemical producers a certain advantage, but it also will mean that the chemical industries in other European countries could force West German firms to avoid certain product lines or marketing strategies. In other words, participation in such cross-national institutions is seen by some industry actors as potentially more of a drawback than an advantage. Because the big three firms are ranked among the world's top five firms, they view themselves primarily as world players and not just as Europeans.

An important political consequence of the European question has to do with the role of other actors in shaping change in the world chemical industry. The West German industry certainly believes that its pattern of self-reliance—firms, VCI, and banks—to "shape the framework for industrial order" may be superior to the more activist role of the state in other countries. It also believes that it can best identify its own needs and that reliance on international agencies such as the CEFIC may not be to the sector's benefit. Yet in both of these cases, forces outside West Germany may influence the West German industry's preferred pattern. Other trading partners often prefer to set up "crisis cartels" to find mutual ways to shrink capacity in unprofitable chemical lines.[85] The West German firms have preferred not to participate in such ventures, arguing that they weaken the industry rather than strengthening it. Moreover, since the West German firms are generally among the top performers in any such crisis cartel, they tend to have more to lose. They also resent the EEC's challenging their attempts to resolve their own overcapacity problems without relying on such an international agency.[86] Yet one by-product of the environmental fallout has been the individual firms' more active role on the European level rather than relying on the actions of the VCI. The big three West German firms feared purely national regulations on environmental issues and reasoned that, if stronger regulations were in the offing, a European-wide pattern would be easier for them to deal with as major world actors.[87]

A more general political consequence of change at the international level relates to a potential by-product of the earlier exclusion of IG Chemie from plant-level adaptive strategies. Throughout the postwar period, IG Chemie—and West German unions in general—have been very supportive of the export-led growth strategies of the major firms in

85. See Bower, *When Markets Quake*; and Ilgen, "'Better Living through Chemistry.'"
86. See "Probe into Chemicals Industry Price Rings Runs into Closed Doors," *German Tribune,* 1 March 1987, p. 7.
87. Grant and Paterson, "Large Firms as Political Actors," pp. 19–20.

the Federal Republic. A major reason for this support has been that because so many West German jobs depend on exports, any protectionist response on the part of organized labor would be suicidal. This part of the equation still holds; the industry's jobs are still highly export-dependent. But continued attempts to exclude the union from the process of industrial adaptation might adversely affect this beneficial pattern for the industry. Although there is no evidence of any immediate likelihood of this developing, it does point up the importance of finding some more institutionally solid form of accommodation with IG Chemie—rather than just with the individual works councils—at a time when employment levels are contracting in the industry.[88]

The chemical industry faces challenges similar to those that face the other core sectors in the West German political economy. At the plant level, the industry has been able to combine a high chem–fine chem pattern of high value-added new product innovation and a reliance on highly skilled professional workers with the dominance of large firms. On these issues, the chemical industry replicates the adaptive patterns in the automobile and machine tool industries, as Kern and Schumann have also suggested. Both of these other sectors have placed a very strong emphasis on upgrading the skill levels of their work forces through vocational education. The chemical sector also must rely on a core of skilled professional workers. Yet the firms and the VCI, together with the universities, have recruited the most advanced chemists to the industry. This is not a new development; it has held true for years. At the national level, the environmental issue seems to be more politically relevant after the Rhine spills in late 1986. But here, too, both the VCI and the firms have tried to show that they are responsible citizens and that they can help find the solution to environmental problems. As Jost Halfmann suggests, it is not yet clear whether this industry—identified as a potential environmental problem by the new social movements—will be able to meet and overcome future environmental challenges. Yet the industry's response in the wake of the Rhine spills in 1986 hints that its capabilities should not be underestimated. At the international level, the industry has used its diversification as a world, a European, and a German player to adapt to the difficulties that have beset the world chemical industry since the mid-1970s. As Gowa suggests, the leading German industries during all three republics have developed a sophisticated ability to overcome what, at first glance, seem to be fundamental challenges. Compared with the chemical sector in other countries, the

88. See Allen, "Structural and Technological Change"; Ebsworth, "Industrial Relations"; and Markovits, *Politics of West German Trade Unions*.

West German chemical industry has retained its dominant world position through the mid- and late 1980s.[89]

This investigation has shown that the problems facing the industry—at plant, national, and international levels—are not insignificant, although none of the various challenges—by themselves—seem to present the industry with insurmountable problems. But since these three levels of challenges have overlapping effects on other levels, one possible danger could be simultaneous festering of problems at all three levels. If such overlapping problems were to escape solution by the industry, the total of the problems could be greater than the sum of the parts, thereby undermining institutional legitimacy. But the concluding assessment is that such a worst-case scenario is remote and that the industry is likely to maintain its traditional institutional flexibility.

89. "Big Three Are Doing Well Worldwide: Ability to Adapt Pays Dividends," *German Tribune*, 20 December 1987.

CHAPTER SEVEN

Industrial Order and the Politics of Industrial Change: Mechanical Engineering

GARY B. HERRIGEL

During the last decade, new technologies and global changes in the character of competition combined to produce highly volatile markets for machinery products. This development elicited a general—and successful—response from West German machinery builders. They emphasized the flexibility, specialization, and production of relatively highly valued products. The traditional craft production–based industry transformed itself into a high-tech craft production–based industry. In so doing, West Germany retained its dominant position among the world's leading machinery-producing nations.

Considering the difficulties that machinery firms in the United States, Britain, and France have faced in overcoming the market changes of the last decade, the West German success is remarkable. But I argue that an equally interesting feature of the West German adjustment is that producers in different institutional and regional contexts have organized their strategic response to market changes in different ways. Indeed, two distinct patterns of organization and adjustment exist in the industry: an autarkic-firm-based pattern and a decentralized-region-based pattern, which represents alternative ways to organize flexible industrial practice and have deep institutional and political roots in the history of German industrialization. Neither pattern is currently hegemonic, nor is the coexistence of both impossible to imagine. Yet current developments in both of these patterns of industrial organization represent and forecast

I thank, in addition to the many participants in the conferences associated with this volume, Charles Sabel, Caren Addis, Joshua Cohen, Carl Kaysen, Thomas Koebler, Richard Locke, Janice McCormick, Annalee Saxenian, Nicholas Ziegler, and the members of the SOFI Institute in Goettingen for comments on earlier drafts.

changes in the public and private institutional order that governs industrial practice at all levels of West German society.

This chapter looks at the same phenomena from two points of view. First, it explains how the successful response to market change—the shift to higher-quality, flexible production—developed out of two distinct patterns of industrial organization. The term *industrial organization,* however, typically presupposes a sharp distinction between the role of firms and that of social and political institutions in the organization of production and its adminstration. Since the argument here is that, despite their differences, both of the patterns of productive organization are deeply embedded in society, I refer to them as forms of *industrial order.* By focusing on the differences in flexible organization in this way, the chapter is meant to contribute to contemporary debates about its institutional and political preconditions.

Second, the chapter argues that if industrial change is viewed as being embedded in the social and political system, problems concerning the changing relationship between industry and politics at the national level can be cast in a new light. The boundaries between state and industry are constituted differently in each of the forms of industrial order to be described. Current processes of change in both have begun to blur the boundaries of the political both within each of the forms of industrial order and between them. The consequence has been to reopen basic questions concerning the proper role of the state and of private interest associations in the maintenance of economic order in the Federal Republic. Indeed, the national-level political problem in the Federal Republic has become how to reconcile the demands generated by different, and changing, forms of capitalist organization within a single political and economic unit.

The chapter contains four parts. The first describes the machinery industry in West Germany and its significance within both the domestic and the world economies. The second characterizes the current adjustment and the two patterns of industrial order that made it possible. The third shows the relation between these two forms of industrial order and the larger West German polity. The concluding section discusses the problem of change and the possibilities of long-term coexistence between these two patterns of industrial order in the context of the politics of industry in the Federal Republic.

THE WEST GERMAN MACHINERY INDUSTRY

There were 4,657 machinery-producing establishments in West Germany in 1985.[1] The trade association for the machinery industry, the

1. With more than twenty employees.

Verein Deutscher Maschinen- und Anlagenbau, e.V. (VDMA), estimates that its members produce more than seventeen thousand different types of machines, ranging from miniature ball bearings for electrical motors through machine tools to complete industrial plants such as cement works, petrochemical refineries, and steelmaking facilities.

The VDMA divides the industry into thirty-seven different branches. The top six branches by employment and sales in 1984, as defined by the VDMA, were office and information technology, machine tools, power transmission engineering, agricultural equipment, mechanical handling machinery, and food and beverage making and packaging equipment. These branches accounted for 41.5 percent of employment and 43.7 percent of output by value in the industry. But there is no reason to privilege these six because the next ten branches employ and sell only small gradations less than the top six.

By most measures, the machinery industry is the largest in the Federal Republic. It is consistently at the top of West German industry in annual sales and exports. In 1986, the industry accounted for 13.1 percent of all sales of manufacturing products and 18.4 percent of all merchandise exports in West Germany. Automobiles accounted for a slightly greater percentage of total sales (13.2 percent) but a smaller percentage of total exports (18.0 percent) in that year. The other two major sectors in the Federal Republic, chemicals and electrotechnical producers, were considerably smaller than the machinery industry. Chemicals accounted for 11.1 percent of total manufacturing sales and 13.3 percent of exports, while electrotechnical producers accounted for 11.0 percent of sales and 10.8 percent of production. The machinery industry has held this leading position within German industry for much of the twentieth century.[2]

In 1986, West German machinery builders employed 1,072,715 workers; no other West German industry has ever employed more than 900,000. Since 1975, there has been a net loss in the industry of approximately 76,000 jobs. Two major factors account for the decline in employment levels: planned attrition with old workers retiring without being replaced and closures and movements of firms out of the industry. Over two hundred fewer firms are active in the machinery industry today than in 1973. The low point in the adjustment was in 1984, when the level of total employment fell to 999,831. Nevertheless, the employment situation in the industry has been consistently better than for West German manufacturing as a whole. The overall percentage of manufacturing employment accounted for by the machinery industry increased from 14.5 percent in 1974 to 15.9 percent in 1986.

2. Unless otherwise noted, all statistics are from VDMA, *Statistisches Handbuch für den Maschinenbau* (*SHfdM*), various years.

GARY B. HERRIGEL

The average wage for a male production worker in the industry in January 1987 was DM 18.43 per hour, which was slightly above the average for male workers in industry as a whole (DM 18.24 per hour). Thirty-six percent of all those employed in the industry in 1985 were skilled workers; 39 percent were white-collar employees and 25 percent were semi- and unskilled workers. A look at the same figures at the beginning of the period of adjustment reveals a growth in the percentage of white-collar workers relative to skilled workers. In 1972, semi- and unskilled workers accounted for 26.9 percent of machinery employees, skilled workers 39.2 percent, and white-collar workers 33.6 percent.[3]

Large producers in the industry include some of the most renowned firms in West German industry such as Krupp, Mannesmann, Klöckner-Humboldt-Deutz (KHD), and Gutehoffnungshütte (GHH). But a very significant portion of the machinery industry is composed of small and medium-sized producers. Of total sales in 1985, about 58 percent was accounted for by firms with fewer than a thousand workers. The percentage share of such firms in total production has actually increased over the last fifteen years. In 1972, the share in total production of producers with under a thousand employees was only 45.5 percent. In 1984, the top one hundred firms in the industry accounted for 44.3 percent of total sales and 36.4 percent of total employment in the sector.[4] This deconcentration is even more interesting when one recalls that the industry lost more than two hundred firms during the same period.

Historically, the German machinery industry has been among the two or three largest industries of its kind in the world. Up to the end of World War II, the United States, Britain, and Germany dominated world machinery production and export trade. In 1913, they produced over 90 percent of the world's machines. In the post–World War II period, the world machinery market has opened up, mostly at the expense first of Great Britain and then of the United States. The most important gainer in the postwar period has been Japan, but Italy, France, Switzerland, and Sweden as well as many of the Comecon countries (especially the East Germans) have developed into important machinery producers. Despite these inroads, the West Germans have consistently maintained their position among the world's leading machinery producers. By 1960, West Germany had passed Britain to take second place among market economies in machinery production. It then ceded second place to Japan in 1969. Since the mid-1960s, Japanese machinery producers have grown

3. VDMA, *Mechanical Engineering: Partner for Industrial Development* (Frankfurt am Main: Maschinenbau-Verlag, 1982), p. 8.
4. Monopolkommission, *Forstschreitende Konzentration bei Grossunternehmen, Hauptgutachten, 1976/77* (Baden-Baden: Nomos, 1978); see also *SHfdM*, 1975 and 1985.

steadily at a rate 1.5 times as fast as the West Germans. In 1986, they had a sales volume 1.8 times greater than the Germans. Both have gained on the United States, though that country continues to be the world's largest single producer of nonelectrical machinery.

World trade in machinery products has traditionally been dominated by the Western industrialized countries, and the West Germans have always been among the leading exporters in that group. In 1955, 76.7 percent of world trade in metal and engineering products was supplied by developed European market economies and North America (over 47 percent of world trade was accounted for by the United States alone). By 1970, that figure had fallen to 51 percent (and the U.S. total to less than 25 percent). The West Germans passed the British to become the world's second leading exporter (behind the United States) in 1956 and have exchanged the lead with the United States many times since 1971. In 1985, not counting trade in office equipment and information technology, the Germans captured 22.4 percent of world exports in machinery products, the United States 18.3 percent, and Japan 16 percent.[5]

Here again, since the mid-1960s the Japanese have made the most significant gains. In 1964, the Japanese accounted for only 3.1 percent of Western market economy machinery exports. Yet Japan's gains have been mostly at the expense of the United States. In that same year, 1964, the United States accounted for 30.8 percent of Western machinery exports and Britain 14.9 percent. West Germany's 1964 share in world machinery trade was almost identical to its 1968 share, 23.1 percent.

Consistent specialization on markets in industrialized countries largely explains how the growth of Japanese machinery production left the West Germans relatively undisturbed, despite the significant differences in the size and rate of growth of the two industries. In 1981, Western advanced industrialized countries took 68.8 percent of all West German machinery exports. Japan, however, traditionally has focused its machinery export trade on developing countries.[6] As late as 1980, in the middle of the adjustment period under review, 61.1 percent of Japanese machinery exports went to developing countries. In that same year, the West Germans sent just 25.0 percent of their exports to those markets. More revealing, in 1980, 45 percent of total Japanese machinery exports went to Asian markets while only 11.7 percent of West German exports went to those markets. That same year the Japanese sent only 14 percent of their output to Western Europe, while the Germans sent 53.3 percent there. To a large extent, then, Japanese growth has taken place in markets in which the West Germans have had very little presence.[7]

5. United Nations Economic Commission for Europe, *Role and Place of Engineering Industries in National and World Economies*, vol. 1 (New York: United Nations, 1974), p. 10.
6. Non-OECD and non-Comecon countries.
7. See Rolf Dick, *Die Arbeitsteilung zwischen Industrie- und Entwicklungsländer in Maschinenbau* (Tübingen: J. C. B. Mohr, 1981), p. 3; figures for 1980 came from *SHfdM*, 1982.

As we shall see, West Germany's strengths on the world market lie in specialization. It excels in branches of machinery production that have long been abandoned by the oldest machinery-producing nations. For example, in 1983, the West Germans held over 40 percent of the world market in drying plants and surface treatment machinery (45.8 percent), coal-mining equipment (43.3 percent), and printing presses (40.5 percent). Eleven additional branches gained over 30 percent of world trade.[8]

Because it is so dependent upon its export trade (over 60 percent of the industry's output has gone abroad since 1974), the industry and its association have been consistently among the most vocal and strongest advocates of free trade in West Germany. This is true even though imports have risen consistently. In 1978, the value of machinery imports accounted for 30.2 percent of the value of exports. By 1986, imports accounted for 40.2 percent of exports.

THE GENERAL RESPONSE

It has become a truism in the industry's trade literature that world markets for machinery products have become highly volatile in the 1980s.[9] Three factors seem to have contributed to the present situation. First, the emergence of new competitors in the 1970s from Europe (especially Italy), the developing world, Japan, and the Comecon bloc began to compete seriously on a world market once dominated by a handful of developed countries.[10] Second, there have been dramatic advances in technology. Not only has the pace of technological change accelerated, but the nature of some of the changes—especially in micro-electronics—has so completely revolutionized the uses to which old products, such as a conventional cutting lathe, can be put that traditional strategies for producing them no longer work.[11] Third, and perhaps most important, investment demand for capital goods in Europe throughout the 1970s was extremely flat, leading to considerable over-

8. Machine tools, 30.9 percent; steel ovens and rolling mills, 35.8 percent; testing equipment, 33.7 percent; woodworking machinery, 34.9 percent; precision tools, 35.9 percent; building materials machinery, 39.0 percent; plastic and rubber-making machinery, 36.0 percent; food and packaging machinery, 37.1 percent; textile machinery, 31.3 percent; power transmission technology (gears and gear units), 34.6 percent (*SHfdM*, 1985).

9. For a sampling see *Industrie Magazine*, May 1976, April 1979, November 1980, April 1982, June 1982; *Wirschaftswoche*, 39, no. 38 (13 April 1985): 182–85.

10. Sanjaya Lall, *Developing Countries in the International Economy* (London: Macmillan, 1981), pp. 173–257.

11. M. E. Merchant, "Welttrends moderner Werkzeugmaschinenentwicklung und Fertigungstechnik," in *Zeitschrift für Wirtschaftliches Fertigung* 76 (1981): 1–7.

capacity in many sectors. Firms found that if they were to survive, they had to improve the technological sophistication of their product continuously.[12]

Under these volatile conditions, one strategy for success was to produce machines using microelectronics in a way that made them as universally applicable as possible. The producer could thus satisfy a broad variety of continually changing needs on the market with a single product, and the principles of volume production could be applied to the traditionally craft production–based methods of capital goods production. This was a strategy that many Japanese machine tool producers took. By relying on computer numerical controllers to provide flexibility, Japanese firms have radically standardized their products and gained tremendous economies of scale in production.[13]

Only in special cases, however, has this strategy been adopted by West German producers. The reason is straightforward. In the middle of the 1970s, well over two-thirds of all West German machinery output was in one of a kind or small series batches.[14] Highly specialized craft production dominated the industry. Its overwhelmingly skilled work force was the backbone of the metalworkers union, IG Metall. Hourly wage rates were nearly twice those in Japan in 1975 and still one and a half times as great in 1983.[15] Even if the Japanese had not been already competing in markets for standardized flexible machinery, a standardization strategy would have been next to impossible. Firms would have had to go to war with one another and with their highly organized craft workers.[16]

Forced to come up with an alternative strategy, the West Germans opted for the flexible production of higher-quality products, often made to customers' specifications.[17] The traditional craft industry converted

12. Peter Steinmüller, *Lage und Entwicklungschancen der deutschen Maschinen Industrie* (Frankfurt: Gewiplan, 1977).

13. For arguments that contradict West German perceptions of the Japanese machine tool producers see David Friedman, *The Misunderstood Miracle* (Ithaca: Cornell University Press, 1988).

14. Steinmüller, *Lage und Entwicklungschancen der deutschen Maschinen Industrie*, pp. 40–56.

15. VDMA, *Daten zur internationalen Wettbewerbsfaehigkeit des deutschen Maschinen- und Anlagenbaus. Längerfristiger Vergleich zu den Hauptkonkurrenten* (Frankfurt am Main: VDMA/Maschinebau-Verlag, 1984), p. 9.

16. Most of the literature that claimed that the Japanese would overrun German machinery producers in the early 1980s assumed that the constraints imposed by standards of efficiency in the world economy allowed only one best solution. Had that been true, the Germans might have been in trouble. Examples of this large literature are Boston Consulting Group/VDW, "Japan Studie: Zusammenfassung und Ergebnisse" manuscript, Frankfurt, VDW, September 1981; Jao O. Rendeiro, "How the Japanese Came to Dominate the Machine Tool Business," *Long Range Planning* 18, no. 3 (1985): 62–67; *Der Gewerkschafter*, December 1985, June 1984, February 1984, May 1983.

17. A good summary of the strategy is in Hans-Jürgen Warnecke and Thomas Zipse, "Perspectiven der Werkzeugmaschinenproduktion in der EG und Japan," in *VDI-Z*, 127 (May 1985): 351–56.

itself into a high-technology craft industry by incorporating the new forms of technology into its products and production processes and cutting the cost of its customized goods in relation to standard products. Two pairs of examples illustrate the general trend.

The Traub Maschinenfabrik A.G. of Reichenbach/Fils and the Index-Werke of Esslingen, two former producers of conventional cutting lathes, found it impossible to compete directly with Japanese producers in standardized CNC lathes. Both responded by producing highly flexible CNC lathes that contained special characteristics lacking in Japanese machines: greater precision and greater durability at higher cutting speeds. Unable to mass-produce the higher-quality machines, the companies developed sophisticated modular-design systems that allowed them to tailor their machines to their customers' special needs. Similar responses can be observed in Krupp's Kautex-Werke and SMS's Battenfeld subsidiary, both producers of injection molding and plastic extrusion equipment.

A variant of this strategy is to emphasize the ability to combine high-technology engineering prowess with handicraft skill in the production of special-purpose machinery. Thus Mannesmann Demag regularly competes with Orenstein & Koppel for the distinction of having constructed the world's largest heavy-duty hydraulic excavator—one of the latest from Demag had a service weight of five hundred tons. The medium-sized firm PM Putzmeister-Werk, a cement pump maker in Filderstadt near Stuttgart, is another good example. It constructed four lead enshrouded cement pump trucks, each with a remote-controlled delivery pipe over one hundred meters long, for use in the Soviet Union at the Chernobyl nuclear power plant disaster site—within four months of the disaster.

None of these firms is producing standard products or competing in markets in which price is the determining factor. Instead, the emphasis is on quality of production, quality of product, and the use of technology to solve particular problems. The strength of West German producers, large and small, lies in their ability to provide machinery with precisely the qualities standard machinery lacks, at higher but still competitive prices.

This successful adjustment is embedded in West German society within two different forms of industrial order: an autarkic-firm-based order and a decentralized-region-based order. In the former, production and its administration are governed within the institutional boundaries of firms; in the latter, the institutional framework that governs production and its administration encompasses entire regions. Both forms of industrial order were favorably situated to adopt the high-tech craft production strategies just described because they had traditionally pursued a craft production strategy. But neither passed unchanged through the period of adjustment. The principles of organization governing production and its administration in both forms of order were redefined in extremely important ways.

Autarkic-Firm-Based Industrial Order

Producers within the autarkic-firm-based form of industrial order are located in the Ruhr Valley, Westfalen more generally, and in many of the old court and trading cities such as Hanover, Kassel, Nuremberg, Augsburg, and Munich. It was in these poor agricultural regions, relatively free of preindustrial handicraft infrastructure, that the classic large-concern form of German industrialization took place. Firms grew very large very rapidly because the lack of surrounding infrastructure forced them to incorporate most of the stages of manufacture under their control.[18] And because the capital requirements of such a strategy were so high, large German firms grew up with very close relationships to major universal banks.[19] The traditional large German machinery firms—Demag in Duisburg, Krupp's machinery division in Essen, Henschel in Kassel, the MAN in Augsburg and Nuremberg, and others—all grew up this way. They started out manufacturing very large machinery such as locomotives or steelmaking equipment and then diversified into other areas of machinery to maintain continuous revenues and to provide stable employment.[20]

Unlike their American counterparts, large German machinery producers were never able to apply mass production techniques to the production of machines. The presence of strong British and later American producers in most export markets and the tremendous political and regional heterogeneity throughout Europe made it difficult for firms to gain a position in the market that would allow them to control the evolution of technology; or, if they could, they were not able to impose standard designs on customers.[21]

18. Alexander Gerschenkron, "Economic Backwardness in Historical Perspective," in Gerschenkron, *Economic Backwardness in Historical Perspective* (Cambridge, Mass.: Harvard University Press, 1962); Jürgen Kocka, "The Rise of Modern Industrial Enterprise in Germany," in Alfred Chandler and Herman Daems, eds., *Managerial Hierarchies* (Cambridge, Mass.: Harvard University Press, 1980), pp. 77–117.

19. Andrew Schonfield, *Modern Capitalism* (New York: Oxford University Press, 1964). The historical dimensions of this relationship are developed in the work of Richard Tilly, *Kapital, Staat und Sozialer Protest in der deutschen Industrialisierung* (Göttingen: Vandenhoeck & Ruprecht, 1980), esp. pp. 15–94.

20. Jürgen Kocka and Hannes Siegrist, "Die hundert grossten deutschen Industrie Unternehmen im spaeten 19 und 20 Jahrhundert," in Norbert Horn and Kocka, eds., *Recht und Entwicklung der Grossunternehmen im 19 Jh und fruehen 20 Jh.* (Göttingen: Vandenhoeck & Ruprecht, 1979).

21. This is a truism in the historical literature. See, for example, Friedrich Frölich, *Stellung der deutsche Maschinenindustrie im deutschen Wirtschaft und auf dem Weltmarkt* (Charlottenberg: VDMA, 1914); J. J. Pastor, "Die Ausfuhr der deutschen Maschinenindustrie

The upshot was an alternative market strategy. Throughout the twentieth century firms consistently sought to adapt new techniques to occupy specialized niches safe from the competition of British and American standardized products. This meant producing higher-quality products, in small or single series, which were frequently customized. This system prevailed well into the 1970s. In 1977 at the MAN Augsburg diesel engine and printing machinery works, for example, the average series size of products was five.

This market orientation led production and its administration, over time, to be organized in a unique way. Three levels are important: the production process, administration, and relations with the surrounding regional political economy. Two features of the production processes in these craft production–based firms are important. First, firms depended upon workers being skilled enough to work on a continuously changing variety of jobs and products.[22] Second, because work was so specialized and the series so small, plant organization evolved into a collection of specialized workshops. Each workshop received orders for and produced parts as varied and uneven in shape and volume as there were products in the firm's total output. The logic behind production organization was the opposite of that in large series and mass production processes: instead of building rigidity into process organization in the plant to produce a large series standard product efficiently, these firms sought to create structures—workshops—that enhanced the firm's ability to reorganize production quickly.

Administering such a production process was complicated. Typically, problems concerning the way order in the system would be maintained and resources distributed found institutional solutions in central, functionally organized management and in paternalistic labor practices. Centralization and functional organization facilitated both control and close communication between the components of the works. Functional organization grouped responsibility for the design, production, and sale of all goods the firm produced into discrete departments within the central office. Because everything passed through that office, ideas and experiences concerning new technologies could enter the structure from all parts of the firm. Managers could mix and match technical problems with the specialties of workshops and engineering departments. The continual recombination of these resources from and through the center

---

und ihre Volkswirtschaftliche Bedeutung," diss., Cologne, 1937; Kurt H. Biedenkopf, "Massenproduktion, Wettbewerb und Europaische Vereinigung," *Europa Archiv* 5 (June 1956): 8915–18.

22. Joachim Bergmann et al., *Rationalisierung, Technisierung und Kontrolle des Arbeitsprozesses* (Frankfurt: Campus, 1986).

helped create a reservoir of technological memory within the firm which facilitated both customization and the development of new products.[23]

Paternalism created the environment the firms needed at the workplace. Management willingly communicated not only with the representative bodies in the plants (*Betriebsräte*) but also directly with the workshops on matters relating to both production decisions and workers' grievances. Firms also went to great lengths to avoid layoffs. For example, when demand for deep boring machinery for use in nuclear power plant construction dried up in the early 1980s, Krupp Industrietechnik in Essen converted those workshops into job shops that subcontracted for the entire concern rather than lay people off. This attention to the welfare of its workers along with management's willingness to communicate fostered trust among workers.

In most machinery companies during the nineteenth century, paternalism was traditional in that it depended on the personal concern and charisma of the factory owner.[24] But in the post–World War II Federal Republic the precondition for successful paternalism in firms has been a delicate balance between labor's power in the workplace and managerial interest. Union representation of workers in the autarkic machinery firms is extremely strong, and West German labor law makes it difficult to lay off workers, especially skilled workers. In this sense, the institutional strength of unions is just as important a precondition for maintaining the strategy of flexibility and specialization in the machinery industry as Streeck has shown it to be in the automobile industry. But to understand the way craft production and its administration fit together in this industrial order, one should not lose sight of the benefit management derives from the arrangement. In return for formal and informal recognition of the autonomy of the skilled, the firms receive these workers' acceptance of the lines of hierarchy and control that are indispensable for management continually to reorganize production and adopt new technologies.

The autarkic-firm-based character of this form of industrial order had three related external consequences for the regional political economies in which they grew up. First, autarkic beginnings tended to perpetuate autarkic growth. The organizational challenge of coordinating multiple workshops simultaneously working on a wide variety of customized

23. On functional organization in Germany see Gareth P. Dyas and Heinz T. Thanheiser, *The Emerging European Enterprise: Strategy and Structure in French and German Industry* (Boulder: Westview, 1976); Otto Poensgen, *Geschaeftsbereichsorganisation* (Opladen: Westdeutscher Verlag, 1973).

24. J. J. Lee, "Labor in German Industrialization," and Jürgen Kocka, "Entrepreneurs and Managers in German Industrialization," in M. M. Postan, D. C. Coleman, and Peter Mathias, eds., *The Cambridge Economic History of Europe* (New York: Cambridge University Press, 1983), pp. 442–90, esp. 453–71, and 492–589, esp. 546–49.

products discouraged firms from contracting work outside the factory. Subcontracting increased the logistic complexity of production while diffusing the control of the center. Consequently, autarkic-firm-based regions such as the Ruhr Valley did not develop an infrastructure of small and medium-sized firms that could supply parts and specialty products.[25] If they needed specialty parts, the large firms looked outside the region.[26]

Second, large, diversified, vertically integrated firms dominated the market for skilled labor in autarkic regions. In many cases, they were not only responsible for training the work force of entire regions, they ultimately offered the main sources of machinery employment in those regions as well. Thus layoffs resulting from restructuring or, worse, the collapse of firms in crisis could be accommodated only with great difficulty by the surrounding economy.

Finally, the consequences of both of these factors on the development of infrastructure in these regions was profound. It not only shaped relations between the state and industry, it also shaped conceptions of what was possible and permissible between state and economy. Because of their dominant place in the regional economy, infrastructural and political bodies such as municipal and regional governments, universities (*Technische Universitäten* and *Fachhochschulen*), and vocational training facilities tended to orient themselves to the needs of larger firms rather than smaller ones. As a result, the few small and medium-sized producers that have been able to succeed in the autarkic regions of Nordrhein Westfalen or Bavaria, for example, have done so with minimal support from public institutions and without any expectation of public support.[27] As I will show below, conceptions of the relationship between industry and the state evolved very differently in the decentralized region-based form of industrial order.

In summary, the principles of organization governing production and its administration within this form of industrial order were very distinct from other important institutions in society and the polity such as banks, trade unions, technical universities, and business associations. All of these background institutions helped supplement activities that the au-

25. This is a common argument made about the Ruhr. See Theo Beckmann, "Das Handwerk im Ruhrgebiet," *Mitteilungen des RWI*, 2 (1968): 169–79; Paul Wiel, *Agglomerations- und dezentralizationstendenzen der Nordrhein Westfailischen Wirtschaft seit der Vorkriegszeit* (Opladen: Westdeutscher Verlag, 1962).

26. See Wolfram Hasselmann and Jürgen Scheinholz, *Interregionale Interdependenzen: Das Ruhrgebiet als Absatzmarkt für die Wirtschaft der Randzonen dargestellt am Beispiel Westmuensterland und Remscheid* (Münster: Institute für Siedlungs und Wohnungswesen, 1971).

27. The head of a medium-sized family firm Westfalia Separator in Oelde in Westfalen demonstrated this attitude when he remarked in an interview that outside research institutes and universities were for large companies, not medium-sized firms like his (interview, November 1985).

tarkic firms already conducted extensively on their own. But all were a step removed from the actual process of coordinating and directing the production of machinery products. The point here is not that there was no connection between industry and society. The autarkic firms were ultimately embedded in society. The point is that flexible production and its administration were embedded entirely within the institutional boundaries of a firm.

This form of order went through two sets of changes in the 1970s. First, many autarkic machinery firms were bought out by larger companies. Rapid change forced internal reorganization and new technology placed development costs on the firms that they were not able to handle alone. This financial dilemma meshed well in the realm of West German big business with the crisis in the steel industry and many of the steel companies. Mannesmann, Krupp, Thyssen, and Hoesch purchased large machinery firms as a move toward diversification.

The second set of changes was far more profound with respect to the character of the industrial order. Markets in the 1970s became so unstable and changed so rapidly that firms found that they were forced to reorganize their internal workshop networks in a radical way. The end result of this internal reorganization forced a complete redefinition of the organizational principles governing production and its administration within the industrial order as a whole.

The logistical problem for these firms is that when their workshops become too generalized or the number of products made in an operating unit too vast or, as was the case in the 1970s, market change occurs very rapidly, coordination grows unwieldy. Managers start routing projects across more and more departments, work gets lost or misdirected, mistakes are made, lead times increase, and so on. The result is that the firm loses orders.

To make the process of customization more efficient, autarkic firms started to collect particular product lines together, place them in a discrete number of plants, and then localize control. Rather than trying to manage a massive array of products in a vast series of workshops all over a region, production and its administration became more localized and focused. In effect, large companies turned themselves into several smaller ones. Rather than coordinate production directly, the larger parent company became a holding that provided services to the local units. The best example is the case of the Gutehoffnungshütte (GHH) and its relationship to the MAN holding.

MAN was thoroughly reorganized twice in seventeen years.[28] Up to

---

28. Kurt A. Detzer and Klaus Petit, "Die Organization der M.A.N.-Gruppe," *Zeitschrift für Organization* 8 (May 1979): 191–201.

1970, the company was a very large, centralized, functionally organized multiproduct firm of the kind described above. In 1970, it was reorganized into four divisions.[29] Each division was organized in a functional manner. Divisional leadership was shared between representatives of the central MAN group and the management of the division. In turn, the central group took responsibility for managing all financing, basic research, relations with major suppliers, and labor relations. Two major benefits resulted from this reorganization. First, a dual structure of division-level applied research and development and group-level basic research was created which helped extend the technological horizons of the concern. Second, the density of interworkshop linkages was reduced by confining the coordination problem to the construction of intradivisional networks.

But by the end of the decade, as the market environment became more volatile and two major product lines[30] fell into crisis, pressure for still greater decentralization intensified. After a long and acrimonious struggle between the MAN holding and its parent company, the GHH holding, the MAN group was dissolved. Its divisions were reconstituted as legally independent companies, 100 percent owned by the GHH holding.[31] Whereas in the earlier reorganization, plants were simply organized into divisions of a single company, in the latest decentralization move, those original plants have been turned into legally autonomous companies, fully independent of the holding.[32] The reason for this breakup of the corporation is to enhance its ability to respond rapidly to market change. Making the operating unit an independent company naturally increases its vulnerability. But the holding provides certain essential resources designed to help: a research institute for long-term research and development, export financing, general marketing, and information. If the MAN example can be seen as a logical outcome of the pressures encountered in this adjustment period by firms within this autarkic-firm-based form of industrial order, then it is possible that the order could turn into confederations of specialized, independent companies linked by loose ties to a central holding structure.

29. Trucks and buses (one main plant, three branch plants), diesel motors and printing presses (two plants), machinery and structural steel division (two plants), and machinery and plant building (one plant, one dock, and one shipyard).
30. Trucks and buses and large diesel engines for ships.
31. The name of GHH was changed to MAN AG but continues to have GHH in its insignia. There are now eight independent companies part of the MAN/GHH group: Utility Vehicles, Machinery and Plant Building, MAN new technology, MAN Roland Printing Machines, MAN/B&W Diesel, Ferrostal, Renk, and Deggendorfer Werft und Eisenbau.
32. See the particularly good press accounts of the restructuring in *Manager Magazine*, April 1983, September 1985.

Decentralized-Region-Based Industrial Order

Firms within this form of industrial order are located in Württemberg, Baden, the Rhineland west and south of the Ruhr, the Allgäu, Siegerland, and parts of northern Germany. Industry in these regions developed out of a preindustrial infrastructure of craft skills. Many areas such as Württemberg were dominated by the putting-out system; other areas such as Remscheid and Solingen had been traditional centers of handicraft metalworking for centuries.[33] Regardless of the specific roots, the existence of an infrastructure of skill and handicraft meant that the pressure on firms to grow large and vertically integrated was not as intense as it was in regions that produced the alternative order.

Most firms remained small and medium-sized. Usually they were family owned. The handicraft infrastructure meant that firms did not have to incorporate all phases of the production process under their control so their capital costs were correspondingly lower. In general, they developed outside the purview of the universal banks which Alexander Gerschenkron saw as crucial for Germany's economic growth in the nineteenth century.[34] To a large extent, they created their own cooperative banks, pooling capital from among the many family-owned craft establishments in the community.[35] It was only when they began actively exporting their products that they used the large banks. The decentralized industrial order is the breeding ground of the German *Mittelstand*.

Like the firms within the autarkic-firm-based industrial order, the inability of firms in decentralized regions to apply mass production techniques to machinery production was a defining feature of their development. Firms found they could prosper in world markets by producing specialized machinery which they would adapt to the particular requirements of their customers.

On one level, the organization of production and its administration in this industrial order did not differ greatly from that in the previous order. Skilled labor was no less and perhaps more important in these firms than it was in the larger centralized concerns. Plants were organized into workshops. The production process was controlled through a

33. See Klaus Megerle, *Württemberg im Industrialisierungsprozess* (Stuttgart: Klett-Cotta, 1982); Horst Jordan and Heinz Wolf, eds., *Werden und Wachsen in der Wuppertaller Wirtschaft* (Wuppertal: Peter Hammer, 1977); Otto Albert Borman, "Zur Enstehung und Entwicklung der Metalverarbeitenden Industrie im Monchengladbacher Industriebezirk," diss., Cologne, 1924.

34. Gerschenkron, "Economic Backwardness in Historical Perspective"; Arthur Löwenstein, *Geschichte des wuerttembergischen Kreditbankwesens und seiner Beziehungen zu Handel und Industrie* (Tübingen: Mohr, 1912).

35. A good book that summarizes the development of these banks in Württemberg is Alfred Gemming, *Das Handwerkgenossenschaftswesen in Württemberg* (Stuttgart: Enke, 1911).

balance between central authority and respect for the skilled worker's autonomy similar to that in the other order.

On another level, however, there were important differences between the two forms of industrial order, especially at the level of administration. Unlike the autarkic order, the institution of the firm was not the central unit of administration in the decentralized order. Instead, the maintenance of order and the distribution of technical and material resources among independent producers became embedded in a host of relationships and institutions within the community and political structure of a region. This was true both for the relationship between firms and the relationship between workers and the firms that employed them.

Specialized craft production encounters unique administrative problems when it occurs within a regional agglomeration of producers rather than in the framework of an autarkic firm. The problem is simple. Independent small and medium-sized craft-production-based machinery firms are extremely flexible. Skilled workers with general purpose equipment can construct an infinite variety of machinery if given the chance. This creates a constant threat of market breakdown. Potentially, all firms can compete in all markets all at once.

Indeed, after repeated experiences of murderous competition during industrialization, producers realized that if they were going to profit from their flexibility, they would have to control it in some way. Institutions among firms and in society were created that channeled flexibility into specialization and socialized risk. An important part of the administration of machinery production was thereby elevated above the individual firm to a more decentralized-region-based set of institutions.[36]

The core logic of the system of order is as follows. Firms agree to specialize on particular lines of product and coordinate their choice of specialties with other firms in the same branch. The aim is to make sure that nobody produces machines that overlap with another firm's product market.[37] Furthermore, institutions that serve all in the industry are constructed to help compensate for the added risk each individual producer incurs from specialization.

Though the logic is simple, the process is complex. Because there is much specialization and customization, drawing the boundary lines between one firm's area of expertise and that of another is not always easy.

36. For a more detailed historical discussion and references, see my dissertation "Industry and Politics: The German Case" (MIT).

37. For a discussion of this phenomenon in textile machinery production in Baden-Württemberg, see Charles Sabel, Gary Herrigel, Richard Kazis, and Richard Deeg, "Regional Prosperities Compared: Massachusetts and Baden Württemberg in the 1980s," *Discussion Paper* IIM/LMP 87-10b (Wissenschaftszentrum Berlin, 1987).

Strategy is never clear. Firms must continuously negotiate with one another about what their markets are and what they are becoming. In the end, the process combines the individual interest of the firm with the long-term interest of the industry as a whole. Firms must remain innovative to stay in the process of negotiation, and the continuous exchange of technical information and strategy with other firms helps them do so.

Many institutions have come to be involved directly and indirectly in this form of coordinated specialization. The relationship between public institutions and industrial production evolved in a way that was profoundly different than the one described in the autarkic-firm-based order. Most directly, trade associations such as the VDMA and the local Chambers of Commerce and Industry (IHKs) provide a forum in which negotiation can take place. They also provide many public goods to the producers. The VDMA and its numerous subassociations, for example, help to coordinate joint research projects in the industry and ensure that local universities are outfitted with the appropriate facilities for industrial research.[38] In a different way, the IHKs help firms by organizing contact with local authorities and with other firms in other branches.[39]

Second, whereas in the autarkic-firm-dominated regions small and medium-sized producers do not consider public research and development to be accessible, in the decentralized regions public research institutes, Technische Hochschulen (TH) and especially Fachhochschulen (FH) play an important role in enabling small and medium-sized firms to sustain a strategy of specialization. They pool the separate resources of many independent firms to provide all with continuous access to technological information that each would not be able to obtain alone. Some FH institutes, such as those for textile technology in Reutlingen, Krefeld, and Monchengladbach or the Precision Tool Institute in Remscheid were originally formed by firms in the region to help them collectively acquire technical and market information. Gradually the responsibility for funding these institutes was taken over by the state, but their central role in conducting applied research for local firms and in training the technicians and engineers they need remains the same.[40]

The dual system of vocational training in Germany also plays an important role in the decentered structure of administration. The system, which combines practical training in actual workshops with public vocational training in *Berufschulen*, originally emerged as a victory of an

38. Hajo Weber, "Intermediäre Organization: Zur Organization von Wirtschaftsinteressen zwischen Markt, Staat und Gewerkschaften," diss., Bielefeld, 1984; Manfred Borst, "Kooperation im Maschinenbau," *Werkstatt und Betrieb* 12 (1984) and 2 (1985).

39. Ernst Neuffer, "Zwischenbetriebliche Kooperation und Kooperationsvermittlung in Baden Württemberg," *Mittlerer Neckar*, September 1973.

40. For example, see *Hundert Jahre Technicum für Textilindustrie* (Reutlingen, 1955).

alliance of industrial craft producers and artisans over the forces of liberalism in Germany. Artisan organizations were entrusted by the state with the authority to oversee and organize the education of skilled workers. This system provided the artisante and their guild organizations with political legitimacy and a material and functional basis for survival in the emerging industrial world. But it also ensured that the costs of training highly skilled workers would not have to be borne by individual firms in the industrial sector. Small and medium-sized producers committed to strategies of customization, therefore, resolved the problem of training costs in a political and public way.[41]

Regional governments such as the Land of Baden-Württemberg and many municipal governments in Nordrhein-Westfalen (NRW) such as Remscheid have also played an important supportive role for the specialized producers in the decentralized order. They offer consulting services, solve locational and space problems, and service infrastructural needs. Many governments also have traditionally provided small subsidies for the development of certain technologies.[42]

All of these institutions were external to the firms that composed this form of industrial order, yet they were all indispensable for the production of specialized machinery products in these regions. The final component of this decentered form of administration concerns the way firms within the order came to relate to one another. Because coordinated specialization meant that firms could not reduce losses by diversifying into new areas, they had to survive by improving or customizing existing product lines. To do that, they had to be open to new sources of know-how and willing to accept that they would not always be able to produce all of a given product themselves. This created a market for specialized supplier firms that could provide a particular technology or simply solid technological advice.[43] But it also encouraged firms to turn for advice to old customers and other local machine makers in related but noncompeting fields. They in turn were forthcoming with advice themselves. A key part of the system of decentered administration within the regional economies in Württemberg, the Bergisches Land or the Rhineland's Left Bank, was thus a semipublic sphere of honorable and reciprocal ties of trust and dependence between independent firms.

41. Jürgen Schriewer, "Intermediare Instanzen, Selbstverwaltung und berufliche Ausbildungsstrukturen im Historischen Vergleich," *Zeitschrift für Pädegogik* 32 (1986).

42. On Baden-Württemberg, see Sabel et al., "Regional Prosperities Compared," and Hans E. Maier, "Das Model Baden Württemberg—Eine Skizze," *Discussion Paper* IIM/LMP 87-10a (Wissenschaftszentrum Berlin, 1987).

43. Jürgen W. Hutzel, *Interdependenzen zwischen Klein-und Grossfirmen: Eine Empirische Untersuchung am Beispiel der Metallindustrie Baden Württembergs* (Tübingen: Institut für Angewandte Wirtschaftsforschung, 1981).

All of these regional relations of administration between firms depend on and are supported by a particular form of labor relations. The modern forms of paternalism characteristic of the autarkic firms are equally important in the decentralized-region-based order. The difference is that union power in many cases is felt indirectly. Moreover, community solidarity often compensates for the absence of union power in creating the background conditions for the maintenance of trust in the workplace.

To the extent that firms are located in important regional agglomerations, such as the greater Neckar region around Stuttgart, or the Bergisches Land around Remscheid-Solingen-Wuppertal, most firms are highly unionized. Consequently, flexibility and order are maintained by the direct balance between union power and producer interest similar to that in the other order.[44]

But it is distinctive of the decentralized-region-based order that many of the small specialized firms that participate in it are located in less thickly industrialized regions such as the Black Forest, southern Württemberg, or the Allgäu, where the union movement has more localized rather than pervasive representation among firms. Here, the existence of important workplace power needed for the maintenance of shop-floor trust is produced in two, in most cases mutually reinforcing, ways.

The first is a dynamic set in motion by the character of vocational training and the way skill is disseminated in West German society. All West German workers who have skills, regardless of where they ultimately work, must participate in the vocational education system in which the unions play a central role. Skilled workers in nonunionized shops have contact with the union because the union in many respects controls their access to qualified occupations. The education each worker receives instills a sense of pride in the product of his or her labor and, more important, a sense of the integrity and indispensability of skilled trades. Skilled workers in nonunionized plants share this self-conception with those in unionized plants. If a nonunion machinery firm neglects or

44. Often it is argued that the union role in small and medium-sized machinery shops is more passive than in the larger firms. But this view ignores the dependence of the entire system on worker power, that is, a delicate balance between the interests of management and labor. The recent investigation by Hildebrandt et al. of thirteen machine tool companies in Baden-Württemberg found that the companies were high-trust organizations that depended on the existence of a mostly implicit yet very effective social pact between management and labor concerning mutual obligations and rights in the shop. See Eckart Hildebrandt, "Work, Participation and Co-Determination in Computer-Based Manufacturing," paper presented at the Fourth Annual Conference on Organization and Control of the Labor Process, January 1986; and especially Rudiger Seltz and Eckart Hildebrandt, "Produktion, Politik und Kontrolle—arbeitspolitische Varianten am Beispiel der Einfuehrung von Produktionsplanungs- und Steuerungssystemen im Maschinenbau," in Frieder Naschold, ed., *Arbeit und Politik: Gesellschaftliche Regulierung der Arbeit und der sozialen Sicherung* (Frankfurt: Campus, 1986), pp. 91–125.

disrespects the values of its workers this can lead to discontent or demoralization, especially if conditions differ significantly from those known to exist in unionized plants. In this way, the lines between unionized and nonunionized regions in the Federal Republic are blurred.

This dynamic in the relationship between workers and employers is reinforced by a second set of factors relating to the character of community life in those regions. Unlike the large industrial city, small and medium-sized industrial towns in Württemberg, Baden, the Allgäu, or the Siegerland have traditionally been environments in which the potential divisiveness of economic stratification has been tempered by the mutual tendency of employers and employed to identify themselves as members of the same local community. Local identity comes from tradition and shared experience. Many of the employers, especially in small shops, have the same craft or agricultural backgrounds as their employees. Children attend the same schools. More significantly, in these regions most workers, like their employers, tend to own property and live in their own houses. In 1968, 80 percent of all worker families that owned houses (about a third of the German working class) lived in communities with fewer than twenty thousand inhabitants.[45]

This community identity contains within it a social code of right practice and mutual obligation. A provincial employer who offends that code runs the risk of encountering resistance not only from his work force but from the broader community as well. In this way, the power of community in many outlying regions in the decentralized order compensated for the absence of direct union power. Employer excesses that could destroy the balance between control and autonomy necessary for successful industrial craft production were checked by the force of community morality.[46]

So in contrast to the autarkic-firm-based industrial order, flexible production and its administration in this decentralized-region-based order grew in almost every respect to be deeply embedded in the regional society around it. The ability of specialized firms to remain innovative and react flexibly on a market depended on an entire exoskeleton of public and private institutions that socialized risk and pooled technological experience. Whereas in the autarkic-firm-based order the boundaries between the industry and society were identical with those of the firm, in the decentralized order the boundaries between firm, industry, and society were completely blurred.

---

45. Josef Mooser, *Arbeiterleben in Deutschland 1900–1970* (Frankfurt: Suhrkamp, 1984), pp. 160–78.

46. A good general discussion of the role of social relations in shaping economic action can be found in Mark Granovetter, "Economic Action and Social Structure: The Problem of Embeddedness," *American Journal of Sociology* 91 (November 1985): 481–510.

The main change in this form of decentralized industrial order during the crisis of the 1970s and 1980s was a shift toward even more intensive subcontracting. There were two reasons for this shift. First, as product markets became more volatile, firms converted their fixed costs to variable costs by shifting work onto suppliers. This enabled them to shift production profitably from one job and kind of product to the next. Second, because of the high costs of developing microelectronic technologies in-house, firms sought to spread the process of product development onto a supplier base of specialist firms.

Typically the machinery producer tried to cultivate a broad circle of suppliers with which it could work intimately, providing manufacturing know-how and collaborating on production engineering of single parts and subassemblies. Many firms even helped their suppliers purchase the equipment they needed to produce a given part. Usually this was done by guaranteeing a certain quantity of orders so that the supplier firm could get the capital it needed from its local bank. The machinery firm essentially tied its own existence to a network of suppliers.

At the same time, as intimate as many of these relations have become, firms generally refrain from becoming too dependent upon any one supplier. Most cultivate at least two sources for a part and confine their purchases from single suppliers to 10 to 20 percent of that supplier's output. Suppliers are thus forced to develop similar relationships with a variety of—not necessarily machinery—manufacturers in the regional economy. This arrangement allows original equipment manufacturers (OEM) to reduce orders to any single subcontractor when they need to, without endangering the supplier's existence. At the same time, the OEM firms continuously learn from what their suppliers are doing for other customers.[47]

The decentralized-region-based industrial order in this way produces a pool of common know-how embodied in a multitude of cooperating and differently specialized firms. What before the crisis was a thick network of highly specialized machinery manufacturers sharing know-how and coordinating products among themselves now emerges as a far more expansive and diverse network of producers. Boundaries between supplier and customer as well as those between industries are becoming increasingly blurred and redefined.

Changes in the social organization of production and the conjunctural developments that provoked them gave rise to change in the superordinate institutions that govern the decentralized industrial order as well.

47. The way this system works in Baden-Württemberg is described in Sabel et al., "Regional Prosperities Compared"; see also Charles F. Sabel, "The Re-emergence of Regional Economies," in Paul Hirst and Jonathan Zeitlin, eds., *Reversing Industrial Decline* (Oxford: Berg, 1988).

The thrust of institutional adjustment aimed at the provision of financial support and technological information in a decentralized way.

The VDMA, for example, lobbied intensively and successfully for the creation of a special program to offer indirect financial support to small and medium-sized firms in the development of microelectronic applications to their machinery.[48] The modest program, *Sonderprogramm Anwendung der Mikroelektronik*, sponsored by the federal Ministry for Research and Technology from 1982 to 1985, made DM 450 million available over a three-year period to producers in all manufacturing industries. Nineteen percent of the funds (DM 85.5 million) were used by machinery firms.[49] There has also been a dramatic expansion of services provided to small and medium-sized industrial firms by both private and public organizations.[50]

Despite these successful examples of institutional adaptation, there are other cases in which adaptation has been less smooth. Politics plays a crucial role in the reorganization of the decentralized-region-based industry, most noticeably in education. Because the extension of subcontracting has taken computer numerically controlled machinery to the shop floors of even the smallest of job shops, demands for the improvement of vocational and technical education have become intense. But changes have been uneven. In Baden-Württemberg, for example, technical demands on FHs have resulted in an expansion of services and courses that at the upper levels overlap with those provided at THs. The same is increasingly true of the relationship between FHs and the vocational training schools (*Berufschulen*). In Länder such as NRW and Bavaria, however, where both forms of industrial order are present in the same regional political unit, the educational system has been slower to respond.

The case of Gesamthochschulen (GHS) or integrated universities in NRW is a good example. The NRW Social Democratic party, traditionally focused on the autarkic heavy industries in the state, created GHSs as part of the educational reform of the early 1970s. The aim was to eliminate the two-track system of education such as exists in Baden-

48. Indirect funding refers to the lack of specifically targeted firms or industries. In effect, the government makes available to any firm below a certain size a partial subsidy for that part of development costs concerned with microelectronic technologies in any product.

49. See Hajo Weber, "Technokorporatismus. Die Steuerung des Technologischen Wandels durch Staat, Wirtschaftsverbaende und Gewerkschaften," manuscript, Bielefeld, 1986. Figures in the text are from VDI/VDE Technologiezentrum, *Wirkungsanalyse zum Sonderprogramm Anwendung der Mikroelektronik: Forschungsbericht* (Berlin: Markt & Technik Verlag, 1986), pp. 18–20, my calculations.

50. See Sabel et al., "Regional Prosperities Compared"; and Meier, "Das Model Baden Württemberg—Eine Skizze." For the more halting developments in Nordrhein Westfalen, see *Die Zeit*, 10 May and 18 October 1985.

Württemberg, by assimilating vocational training schools into the college preparatory program. The effect, however, has not been assimilation but the gradual atrophy of the middle-level, applied research orientation of the typical FH. So whereas in Baden-Württemberg, FHs have enjoyed a technological renaissance, in NRW decentralization has forced a re-evaluation of the GHS system.[51]

This regional difference in institutional adaptation to industrial change points to the problems that confront producers in the decentralized-region-based order. Where flexible production is embedded in society, industrial adjustment necessarily involves adjustment in social and political institutions. Where the shape of institutions, or their capacity to change, is limited by political alignments that exclude producers within the decentralized order, the changes necessary for stable adjustment can become blocked or occur only incompletely. The decentralized industrial order was so hegemonic in Baden-Württemberg that the notion of a GHS was unable to gain a foothold in the region.[52] In NRW, decentralized machinery producers in the Bergisches Land, the Siegerland, and on the left bank of the Rhine were not able to block the SPD's reform goals. The autarkic producers in the Ruhr and Westfalen, less reliant on FHs, were not interested in doing so. Politics, then, plays a central role in the process of reorganizing flexible production within the decentralized-region-based order.

INDUSTRY AND POLITICS

This section will look at both forms of industrial order from a different perspective: How do they relate to the institutions of West German politics? How have changes in the institutional structure and orientation of the different forms of industrial order affected political institutions and policies?

Three cases of contemporary importance in West German politics will be considered: institutional and strategic dilemmas in the metalworkers union, IG Metall; debates about industrial policy; and discussions of trade policy. The first case focuses on the way a major institution within the West German political economy at the national level is responding to the decentralization tendencies outlined in each of the industrial orders. The second and third cases illuminate in different ways how the changes

51. Jürgen Kluver, Wolfdietrich Jost, and Karl-Ludwig Hesse, *Gesamthochschule—Versaeumte Chancen? Zehn Jahre Gesamthochschulen in Nordrhein Westfalen* (Opladen: Leske & Budrich, 1983).

52. Peter Neumann-Mahlkan, "Die Grundungsphase der Gesamthochschule: Zielvorstellung und Perspektiven," in ibid., pp. 23–30.

in each of the forms of industrial order have reopened fundamental questions concerning the proper role for the state and for private interest associations in the maintenance of industrial order.

None of the cases points to the emergence of a single clear solution. The traditional institutional boundaries of political economic order in the Federal Republic are in the process of being redefined. Different forms of industrial order that embody different conceptions of the proper boundaries between industry and the state are given expression and contend with one another in the national debate. This process has created a climate of great political openness.

Trade Unions

The contemporary process of transformation in industry has confronted the metalworkers union, IG Metall, with a considerable dilemma. Although most of the strategic thinking within the union is shaped by the dominant place of the automobile industry with its very large concentrations of union members in a handful of companies, it is interesting to look at developments in the more decentralized machinery industry for two reasons. First, as Streeck's chapter in this volume shows, there is considerable evidence of decentralized production in the automobile industry itself so the dynamics in both industries are, at least tendentially, converging. Second, the character of the machinery industry resembles the forms of organization that predominate in many other sectors of the metal industry (for example, the optical and fine mechanical branches, metalwares, noniron metals, and extensive parts of the electronics industry) so it is interesting to consider what the possible consequences of current reform thinking within the union could be on the rest of the (very large) nonautomobile contingent within IG Metall.

The union's dilemma is clear: different processes of decentralization in both forms of industrial order create conflicts at plant and regional levels to which the central union must respond. Increasingly, the union is being pressured to devolve decision-making authority away from the central headquarters down to the local level of the plant council and regional administrative offices (*Verwaltungstellen*). Potentially, such a decentralization of authority could undermine the larger role that the union plays in West German political life: upholding and protecting the general economic and ultimately political interests of its membership. Failure to decentralize, on the other hand, could have the same results.

There are two opinions within the union about what to do. First, there are those who fear decentralization and view the union's moves in that direction as certain to undermine its ability to act as an opposing force against the power of capital in the Federal Republic. Decentralization, which they view as being encouraged by the employers, threatens to result in a myriad of company unions clustered around an impotent central headquarters.[53] Second, there are those who advocate union decentralization as the only way to protect the interests of the membership in the face of technological change and hence to preserve the representational role of the union at work and in society. By devolving decision-making power down to the local level and limiting the central union's role to the provision of services and information to local representatives, the union as a whole can foster the solidarity it needs to represent the interests of all those employed in the metal industry.[54] One side views union decentralization as capitulation to capital; the other views it as an opportunity to empower the working class both in the workplace and in society.

The two forms of industrial order present very different difficulties for the different union strategies. In this regard, the decisive difference between the two forms of industrial order concerns the different way that each structures the regional labor market.

Workers in machinery factories in the autarkic-firm-based order, we saw, tend to have fewer alternative sources of employment: no infrastructure of small and medium-sized firms exists into which skilled workers could go if reorganization forced layoffs. Workers are bound to the large firm in a way that compromises their strategic bargaining ability. For much of the postwar period, this structural vulnerability within the autarkic-firm-based industrial order was invisible. Prospering steel and coal industries in the Ruhr or consumer electronics manufacturers in Nuremberg created tight labor markets that worked to the advantage of the union. But as each of those neighboring industries went into structural decline near the end of the 1970s, the labor market disadvantages for remaining machinery workers have become apparent. Workers are very dependent on the firm they work for.

In such a situation, a union strategy that gave greater bargaining autonomy to the local level with the hope that broader solidarity would result would be vulnerable to failure. Insecure in its position and with no alternative in the regional economy, the union would face intense pressure to forsake solidarity for a separate peace with the large firm.[55]

53. See the discussion of H. Jansen and K. Lang's position in Josef Esser, "State, Business and Trade Unions in West Germany after the Political Wende," *West European Politics* 9 (April 1986): 198–214, esp. p. 213.

54. See the IG Metall pamphlet *Aktionsprogramm: Arbeit und Technik* (Frankfurt: IG Metall, 1985).

55. Wolfgang Streeck, "Neo-Corporatist Industrial Relations and the Economic Crisis in West Germany," in J. H. Goldthorpe, ed., *Order and Conflict in Contemporary Capitalism* (New York: Oxford University Press, 1984). See also Gerd Lobadda and Gerhard Richter, eds., *Antworten auf den Spaethkapitalismus: Ausgewaehlte Konzepte, Aktionen, modelle in Betrieb, Branche und Region* (Munich: IMU-Institute, 1985).

Within the decentralized form of industrial order, the union's chances with this strategy are much better. Networks of small and medium-sized firms and job shops are dense so workers have many alternative opportunities for employment. These structural factors are reinforced because the regions where this form of order predominates currently enjoy the lowest rates of unemployment in the Federal Republic.

Workers in individual plants within the decentralized-region-based order thus have considerable bargaining power. But they also have an interest in maintaining bonds of solidarity with other workers in other plants—especially with those in supplier plants. The prosperity of all skilled workers in these regions depends on competition in machinery markets remaining based on the quality of the product. The central way of ensuring that employers do not seek to shift their competitive strategy away from quality to price is to ensure that workers in subcontracting houses receive wages in line with those in the OEM firms.[56] Without such intraindustry solidarity on wages, cooperative specialization could easily degenerate into the competitive sweating of labor.

Workers in the decentralized-region-based order thus possess both market power and the incentive to forge bonds of intraindustry solidarity. Not surprisingly, there are signs that they are forging these bonds. An example is the strike at Gerstetten in Baden-Württemberg in the fall of 1985. A small automobile supplier of electronic radios was lured to the Schwabische Alb by the government of Baden-Württemberg's program to foster firm start-ups in areas of electronics technology. The owners of the firm hired seventy workers and paid them wages well below the general collectively bargained minimum wage. Workers were also working longer hours. The Heidenheim *Verwaltungstelle* of the IG Metall struck the plant, finding support from the community and from workers all over the region. Several other *Verwaltungsstellen* sent people to the picket lines during the sixty-day strike. Ultimately, the dispute was resolved and the firm was forced to pay the workers wages in accord with the minimum set down in the general wage agreement bargained by the union that year.[57]

In this context, it is possible to argue that a union strategy that ceded more autonomy to the local level would help strengthen intrafirm solidarity and hence the role of the union as the representative of the interests of all workers. In the context of regionally embedded decentralized production, a decentralization strategy could conceivably

56. This has been historically the central focus of many of the major union struggles in areas of decentralized industrial production. See the excellent accounts by Rudolf Boch, *Handwerkersozialisten gegen Fabrikgesellschaft* (Göttingen: Vandenhoeck & Ruprecht, 1985), on Solingen, and Erhard Lucas, *Zwei Formen von Radikalismus in der deutschen Arbeiterbewegung* (Frankfurt: Roter Stern, 1976), on Remscheid.

57. *Wirtschaftswoche*, 15 November 1985; *Financial Times*, 11 December 1985.

enhance workers' and the union's role in shaping the process of change in industry in ways that a more centralized strategy could not.[58]

Differences between the strategic position of the union within each industrial order show that divisions within IG Metall around questions of internal reform and strategy correspond to actual cleavages in the institutional structure of the West German metalworking industry. Problems arise, then, when a strategy appropriate to one order is applied to conditions in the other. IG Metall tried, for example, to offer suggestions on alternative product ideas to Mannesmann Demag's Sack division in the Ruhr Valley in an effort to stave off Demag's plans to close the plant. The alternative strategy was formulated in an experimental local "decentralized" union institution, an innovation and consulting office, which worked in conjunction with the *Vertrauensleute* at Demag-Sack. After the project was given widespread attention in the regional press, Demag closed the plant anyway, without ever responding to the proposals of the decentralized union organ.[59]

Industrial Policy

The current discussion of industrial policy shows how debate about the redefinition of the boundaries of industry has provoked broader political and ideological disagreements about what the proper relationship between industry and the state should be in the Federal Republic. Although these debates are not conducted in industry-specific terms, their character is interesting when seen in light of the current changes in industrial order in the machinery industry just outlined. As in the discussion of the union, the assumption here will be that the institutional characteristics described in this chapter with reference to the machinery industry have far wider applicability within German manufacturing.

There is no uniform official industrial policy or even policy position in the Kohl government. Instead there are contending positions within the government or within the CDU/CSU/F.D.P. public discussion more generally. The following, then, will attempt to clarify the conflicts that arise among the different positions and point to possible lines of stress. It will be a catalog of possibilities and limits. Since the conservative government came to power in 1983, three major ideological and policy currents have been contending with one another.

58. See Charles F. Sabel, "Struktureller Wandel der Produktion und neue Gewerkschaftsstrategien," *Prokla* 62 (March 1986): 41–60, for a discussion of analogous union strategies in decentralized production environments in Italy.
59. Max Angemeier and Ulrich Weber, "Technologieberatung in NRW: Erfahrungen und Perspektive eines Modells fuer eine qualitative Strukturpolitik," in Siegfried Bleicher, *Ausstieg? Gewerkschaftliche Reformpolitik in der Industriegesellschaft* (Hamburg: VSA-Verlag, 1985), pp. 45–76, esp. pp. 63–73.

The first, associated most prominently with Lothar Späth, the minister president of Baden-Württemberg, argues that the state should play an active role in facilitating the adjustment of small and medium-sized firms to the production of new technologies. To do this, the government must reinterpret its traditional responsibility for the maintenance of infrastructure to include all those institutions and services, such as universities, research institutes, and marketing agencies, concerned with the production and flow of information about new technologies and markets. Concretely this means, among other things, providing money and state consulting services to help small and medium-sized firms find out about and move into new areas of technology. Universities and research institutes should be directed to make contact with and counsel small and medium-sized producers about new technologies.[60]

The second is taken by trade associations or Verbände, such as the VDMA, the Federation of German Industry (BDI), the Association of German Engineers (VDI), and the Diet of German Industry and Commerce (DIHT). They also recognize a need to shape market mechanisms to facilitate the adjustment of small and medium-sized firms into new areas of technology. But, against Späth, they are concerned that state power be limited by the already existing responsibilities of the private organizations that represent the interests of actors in the economy. Concretely this means that state efforts to encourage the adoption of new technologies should be indirect and that responsibility for administering state programs should be shared with the relevant private interest organizations.[61]

The third position is the traditional liberal position. This is really more of a critical position in the debate than it is a set of policies. Its proponents, Graf Lambsdorff, Kurt Biedenkopf, and many at the Institute for the World Economy at Kiel, argue that the proper role for the state in a market economy is to maintain a stable order of competitive markets. Concretely, this means strengthening the power of the state to protect market order from the incursions of organized interests such as cartels or unions in society. With proper attention to the institutional outlines of market order (Rahmenbedingungen), industrial adjustment will be driven by individual creativity, courage, and autonomous choice.[62]

60. Lothar Späth, Wende in die Zukunft (Hamburg: Rowohlt, 1985), esp. the chapter "Ein altes Problem in neuem Gewand: Markt und Staat."

61. For example, VDMA, Taetigkeitsbericht von 1980–1983 (Frankfurt: Maschinenbau-Verlag, 1984), p. 23; Berthold Leibinger, "Begrussungsrede von Berthold Leibinger, Praesident der IHK Mittlerer Neckar, anlässlich der Vortragsveranstaltung der ICC am 6. November 1985 in der IHK," manuscript, Trumpf AG, Ditzingen 1986; Leibinger, "Die Bedeutung der staatlichen Forschungsförderung für die Wirtschaft," speech before the Landesvertretung Baden-Württemberg in Bonn, 19 February 1981.

62. See Graf Lambsdorff's critique of Späth and Franz Josef Strauss's industrial policies in Handlesblatt, 2 December 1985, pp. 1–2; Der Spiegel 39, no. 52 (1985), pp. 34–46; K. H.

The different valuations that each of these views places on the role of the market and the state imply different things for development within each form of industrial order. But the ways in which the policies conflict with one another show how changes in the boundaries of industrial order have reopened questions about what the proper relationship between the state and industry should be in late twentieth-century West Germany.

The first and second positions, for example, more or less explicitly respond to the needs of producers in the decentralized order. When they come together in policy, as they did in the Ministry of Research and Technology's *Sonderprogramm Anwendung der Mikroelektronik,* the policies can be effective. The program was coadministered by the participating *Verbände,* including the VDMA, VDI, and ZVEI, the electrical producers association. State subsidies for the application of microelectronic technologies were ultimately disseminated by the associations, not the state.

Yet there are clear points of conflict between the first and second positions. They show how intimately considerations of political reorganization are intertwined with those of industrial order. Späth's aggressive advocacy of the use of state power conflicts with the traditional German political idea of *Selbstverwaltung,* or the self-government of society by organized groups within it. Traditionally this position has been central to the concerns of those within the decentralized-region-based order. The intrusion of the state in the technological decisions of an independent producer is resented because it disrupts the intricate processes of exchange and negotiation that are institutionalized in the industrial order. The fear is that dirigism will be substituted for a public process of self-definition among autonomous actors.

The political conflicts that have arisen between the Späth government and the *Verbände* in Baden-Württemberg have all revolved around this issue. For example, in 1984–85, Späth attempted to reorganize the structure of the Land government policy machinery to enable the government to circumvent the traditional corporatist channels of industrial policy making and intervene more directly in the economy. This proposal for reform, set forth by a Späth-selected commission of experts known as the Bulling Kommission, was passionately opposed by the industrial *Verbände* in Baden-Württemberg, especially the IHK.[63] Ultimately, Späth was forced to withdraw the proposals.

In a less concrete though perhaps more fundamental way, there are

Biedenkopf, *Die Neue Sicht Der Dinge* (Munich: Piper, 1985). The Kiel view is most articulately and globally formulated by the institute's director, Heribert Giersch, who coined the term *Eurosclerosis.*

63. Manfred Bulling, A. P. Bäumer, E. Vetter, and L. Sparberg, *Neue Führungsstruktur Baden-Württemberg. Bericht der Kommission Neue Führungsstrukture Baden-Württemberg ,* Vol. 1: *Leitbilder und Vorschläge* (Stuttgart: Staatsministerium Baden-Württemberg, 1985).

also differences between the position of the *Verbände* and that of the liberal critics in the Federal Republic today. There is an important difference between the antipathy for the state on the part of those concerned with *Selbstverwaltung* and the idea of the state in the liberal position. They represent very different conceptions of how to maintain order (and fight monopoly power) in industry. The two political traditions have come into conflict throughout the history of the Federal Republic because the liberal position's emphasis on the sovereignty of the market has traditionally led its proponents to oppose the institutional arrangements that control market competition that the proponents of *Selbstverwaltung* defend.[64]

This traditional conflict in German political economic debate can easily be traced to differences between the forms of industrial order in the way they relate to the state. During the postwar period, there has been an affinity between autarkic producers and the liberal free market position. In large autarkic firms, where many processes once regulated by the market are now regulated by internal hierarchies, transactions that are still conducted through contracts depend on the efficient functioning of the market. Hence these large firms have tended traditionally to support—at least in the postwar period—the liberal position on the role of the state in the market economy. Current changes in the autarkic-firm-based order can in many ways only reinforce the affinity that firms within it have with the ideology of the liberal critics.

The interests of the decentralized-region-based producers, not surprisingly, run in the other direction. A turn toward more liberal domestic economic policy, which sought to dismantle the formal and informal collusion and cooperation between firms, would be disastrous for producers within the decentralized industrial order.

All of these considerations are implicit in the contemporary industrial policy discussion. But because none of the positions outlined above are dominant, and because the process of industrial reorganization in both forms of industrial order is so complex, the full implications of any of the positions are seldom clearly articulated. Confusion is common.

For example, many municipal and Länder government policies directed toward autarkic regions, such as Bavarian policies regarding technology transfer to small and medium-sized firms[65] or the many municipal programs for the formation of technology parks in the Ruhr Val-

---

64. An important example of this conflict in the early years of the republic was the decade-long debate on the Cartel Law. See the excellent article by Peter Huettenberger, "Wirtschaftsordnung und Interessenpolitik in der Kartellgesetzgebung der BRD 1949–1957," *Vierteljahresheft für Zeitgeschichte* 24 (July 1976): 3.
65. *Handelsblatt*, 10 April 1985, p. 20.

ley,[66] have attempted to encourage adjustment by fostering the growth of small innovative firms. The policy makers believe they are imitating the prospering industrial structure in decentralized regions such as Baden-Württemberg or, more popularly, Silicon Valley in the United States. The problem—and the reason why these programs have proven so unsuccessful—is that they apply liberal ideas about the state and autarkic ideas about the role of the firm in the organization of production and its administration which are incompatible with what they want to achieve. Their ideas encourage them to exalt the virtues of independence and market competition when, in fact, the successes they imitate stem from forms of cooperation and order that control the market and enhance individual autonomy by acknowledging its dependence on extrafirm institutions and practices.

Trade Policy

Conflicting external interests of firms within different industrial orders come together with differing political positions very clearly in the area of trade policy. The political dilemmas posed in the industrial policy debate are expressed here in a concrete way.

West German machinery producers consider Asia to be an important growth market. Many within the industry have argued that it was their failure to gain a foothold in that region that was largely responsible for the decline, relative to the Japanese, of the West German share in world machinery production during the 1970s.[67] One of the reasons for and an important consequence of this decline is that very little infrastructure for the representation of West German export interests in Asian markets exists. There are few foreign branches of the DIHT in the region; West German banks have only recently begun to position themselves for financing trade in the region, and the West German government traditionally has been reluctant to intervene on behalf of particular firms or industries on international trade deals.

To overcome the lack of existing infrastructure for small and medium-sized firms in non-European export markets, in 1978 the government of Baden-Württemberg set up an export promotion agency that sponsored shows of Baden-Württemberg industrial products abroad. In the early 1980s, the government began sending trade delegations to the Soviet Union, China, and other Asian countries, particularly among the ASEAN nations, to market Baden-Württemberg industries. Invitations

66. See the articles on the technology policy debates in NRW in *Die Zeit*, 3 May 1985, p. 22; 10 May 1985, p. 30; 18 October 1985, p. 41.

67. Arno Mock (president of the External Trade Committee of the VDMA), "Germany Looks East," *Journal of Japanese Trade and Industry*, no. 6 (1985), pp. 36–38.

215

were also extended to foreign governments to send trade delegations to Baden-Württemberg. That Land's success prompted imitators. The Bavarian government has also led numerous trade expeditions to Asia and the Soviet Union, as has NRW.

Critiques of these regional government trade policies came from two directions. First, liberal economists and politicians criticized the use of state power for mercantilist ends.[68] The argument was that if the small and medium-sized producers were meant to enter foreign markets, the market would allow them to. Second, the *Verbände*, such as the DIHT and the BDI, criticized the regional governments for working for particular regional interests and not the general interests of industry in the West German economy and for working outside the existing structure of institutions supporting West German external trade.

The *Verbände*'s first argument maintained that regional mercantilism undermined the bargaining position of West German producers abroad; foreign states could force regional governments into competitive bargaining on financing, credits, and other terms of delivery just as they did to major states. A unified policy, on the other hand, would strengthen the position of German producers. The second argument is a political one. The business associations fear that extensive Länder activity in trade for small and medium-sized businesses will undermine their own role and hence threaten the principle of self-government in the economy.[69]

This controversy has important implications for producers in both forms of industrial order. Many autarkic firms, such as Demag, Krupp, and others, have extensive plant-building operations that depend on strong support from the central government. Along with the universal banks to which they are tied, their support for regional mercantilism is low. Small and medium-sized producers in Baden-Württemberg, on the other hand, favor the efforts of their governor Lothar Späth but only because there is no adequate federal trade support infrastructure in non-European markets. The political problem facing both sets of producers, the state and the business associations, is to arrive at a workable set of federal policies favorable to both autarkic and decentralized producers. Solutions advantageous to the one are potentially damaging to the position of the other.

IS THERE A SOLUTION?

This is not the first time in German history that the adjustment pressures felt by industrial producers within different institutional con-

---

68. See Lambsdorff's critique of Späth and Strauss.
69. Siegfried Mann, "Die Förderung neuer Märkte koordinieren," *Wirtschaftswoche* 39

texts have resulted in political conflict. During the 1920s, cleavages within German industry were even deeper than they are today and required political resolution. Then, in the face of a dramatically changed world market, new competition, and domestic stagnation, large autarkic machinery firms sought alliances with larger, richer companies to secure their supplies of raw materials and stabilize their access to export markets.[70] These moves directly disadvantaged small and medium-sized producers in decentralized regions by forcing them to pay higher rates for coal and steel. A political agreement over the definition of order in raw materials markets was reached between the large autarkic steel concerns and the *Verbände* representing the small and medium-sized manufacturers in the form of a system of negotiated rebates for exporters.[71]

This national-level intraindustrial corporatist bargain was congenial to the political sensibilities of producers within each of the forms of industrial order. By both excluding the state and replacing the market with a system of negotiation it respected the principles of industrial self-government held by both kinds of producers.

The dramatic economic crisis of the world depression destroyed the political balance that had been created between the autarkic and decentralized orders in the 1920s. On one hand, autarkic combines such as GHH-MAN reneged on their commitment to negotiation and sought to consolidate their market power, not simply against the decentralized producers but against the political institutions of democracy in German society as well. On the other hand, with their export markets collapsing and prices for raw materials rising, small and medium-sized producers in Württemberg appealed to their regional government for political support against the perceived irresponsibility of big industrial and financial capital. The decentralized industrial *Mittelstand* in Remscheid and Solingen in the Rhineland, even then outside the regional power structure, turned to the National Socialists for the same reasons.[72] In

---

(29 November 1985): 44; Otto Wolf von Amerongen's criticisms of the mercantilism of the *Bundesländer* are well known.

70. Gerald D. Feldman, "The Large Firm in the German Industrial System: The MAN, 1900–1925," in Dirk Stegmann, Bernd-Juergen Wendt, and Peter-Christian Witt, eds., *Industrielle Gesellschaft und politisches System* (Bonn: Verlag Neue Gesellschaft GmbH, 1978), pp. 241–59; Harald James, *The German Slump: Politics and Economics, 1924–1936* (New York: Oxford University Press, 1986), esp. pp. 110–62.

71. Ulrich Nocken, "Interindustrial Conflicts and Alliances as Exemplified in the AVI-Agreement," in H. Mommsen et al., eds., *Industrielles System und politische Entwicklung in der Weimarer Republik* (Kronberg/Ts: Athenäum, 1974), pp. 693–704.

72. See the account in Ulrich Nocken, "Interindustrial Conflicts and Alliances in the Weimar Republic: Experiments in Societal Corporatism," diss., University of California, Berkeley, 1979), esp. pp. 540ff.; also Volker Wuenderlich, *Arbeiterbewegung und Selbstverwaltung: KPD und Kommunalpolitik in der Weimarer Republik mit dem Beispiel Solingen* (Wuppertal: Peter Hammer, 1980).

different ways but under the singular strain of a crisis situation that threatened to undermine the foundations of their industrial order, all the producers abandoned the national-level institutions they had created out of compromise and reached for alternative political means to defend and reconstitute their own systems of order.

Although the current political conflicts that arise as a result of the existence of two forms of industrial order in the same economy cannot be said to be heading in the same direction as those that occurred over fifty years ago, the historical conflicts cast the current problem of the relationship between industry and politics in late twentieth-century West Germany into interesting relief. Now as then, the primary political problem is how to reconcile the demands generated by two different forms of capitalist organization in German society.

The national-level institutions that were created during the Weimar Republic to govern the relationship between the two orders could not withstand the centrifugal pressures generated by the international depression. Current political debates about the proper role for the state in the process of industrial adjustment indicate that the central or national-level institutions that have governed West German politics in the postwar period have been destabilized by current processes of change within the different forms of industrial order in West German industry. The aggressiveness of regional authorities, for example, can be understood as a response to the paralysis of central ones. The trade unions have been compelled to consider significant institutional reforms and strategic reorientation to preserve their role in society. National *Verbände* have had to defend their place in society from political challenges that would have been unthinkable in the 1960s.

The fortunate absence of interminable international and domestic economic chaos should not be allowed to distract from the profound political transformation that is taking place. Political reorganization at the national level of politics cannot be understood without paying attention to the processes of redefinition going on within and between the different forms of capitalist industrial organization in the economy.

Theoretically, there are three alternative ways in which the current conflicts between the two systems of industrial order can develop. In a general sense, these alternatives resemble those emerging in many other contemporary European advanced industrial nations.

The first possible alternative is that there will be a decline of decentralized production. But as we have seen, producers in both orders have large incentives to unburden themselves of financial and technological risk by devolving it onto operating units or dispersing it onto networks of suppliers. The resolution of political conflicts arising from the decentralization of production through the disappearance of the problems that give rise to them is, therefore, not likely.

The second alternative, the decentralization of the autarkic order, is already happening. Operating units of large groups are having difficulty maintaining high degrees of vertical integration. They are forced to bear relatively higher costs in wages and inventory than those producers who can disperse such costs onto suppliers. As a result, major concerns in the industry such as Krupp, Mannesmann, and GHH have moved, through merger, into regions where decentralized production predominates. The difference, of course, is that beyond a heavy use of suppliers, these operating units are oriented to the resources of the holding, not to the network of public and private institutions provided by the alternative order.

A radical expansion of these holding firms into decentralized production could ultimately make redundant many of the integral services performed by the *Verbände* and other public institutions in the governance of decentralized industrial production in West German society. Theoretically, at least, if the logic of the argument is extended, it could undermine the foundations of the decentralized-region-based order. Coordinated specialization would be maintained through relations of property and market within vast holdings, rather than through the fundamentally political process of negotiation that is involved when flexible production and its administration are embedded in society.

This scenario underscores the highly political stakes implicit in the current processes of reorganization within the different forms of industrial order in the West German economy. The third scenario turns the last one on its head. It is equally plausible to argue that current developments within the autarkic and decentralized forms of industrial order will lead to the mutual convergence of the systems that govern large and small firms.[73] Large holding companies can rely on the infrastructure of the decentralized order to support their increasingly decentralized operations. Doing so would eliminate organizational complexity in their operations and reduce costs. But it would also require the firms to relinquish more control over the organization of production than they are accustomed to. Most important, the mutual convergence of autarky and decentralization would require the abandonment of the liberal ideas of the state and market that have been a foundation stone of corporate ideology in postwar West Germany. The state plays a crucial role in the decentralized industrial order's ability to reproduce itself.

Indeterminacy, if unsettling to the social scientist, is certainly not

73. As Charles Sabel has recently argued; see "The Re-emergence of Regional Economies."

unusual in processes of political and economic reorganization. Machiavelli, it is always helpful to remember, stressed the importance of *Fortuna* as well as *Virtue* in political conflict. It is difficult, if not impossible, to say which of the scenarios outlined above will prevail. What is certain, however, is something that most studies of industrial change often fail to appreciate. Industrial adjustment will be guided by and completely inseparable from political negotiation at all levels of economy and society.

CHAPTER EIGHT

Crisis Management "Made in Germany": The Steel Industry

JOSEF ESSER AND
WOLFGANG FACH

Economic depressions produce miracles as well as tragedies. When a world economic crisis occurred in the 1970s, some nations dealt with it markedly better than others. Their success prompted an international search for the secret of their survival in the midst of general decline and for lessons that less fortunate nations could apply.

The Federal Republic of Germany has played a varied role in this international discussion. At first, the Federal Republic was considered— and considered itself—a model for other nations. Then it fell into disrepute, but recently its reputation has recovered. This latest change in fortune has been imputed above all to the preeminence of high-tech industries in several regions.[1] But it is easy to forget that the worldwide reputation of the West German model also depends on its older economic sectors with their "rusty" industries.

At issue here is the institutional sclerosis[2] of a society. The decisive question is whether a nation is flexible enough to modernize its economy or whether it clings desperately to antiquated conditions regardless of the opportunity costs associated with the futile attempt to preserve the

1. Bruce Nussbaum, *The World after Oil: The Shifting Axis of Power and Wealth* (New York: Simon & Schuster, 1983); John Zysman, *Governments, Markets, and Growth* (Ithaca: Cornell University Press, 1983); Peter Drucker, "Deutsche als Lehrmeister," *Wirtschaftswoche* 40 (1986): 25–31 (first published in the *Wall Street Journal*, 11 March 1986); Charles F. Sabel et al., *Regional Prosperities Compared: Massachusetts and Baden-Württemberg in the 1980s* (Berlin: Wissenschaftszentrum, 1987); Herbert Giersch, *Gegen Europessimismus* (Stuttgart: Deutsche Verlagsanstalt, 1986).
2. Mancur Olsen, *The Rise and Decline of Nations* (New Haven: Yale University Press, 1982).

status quo. In this context the protracted decline of the steel industry is a special burden for all Western industrial nations and an ideal measure for the quality of national crisis management.[3]

In the Federal Republic, steel is an important economic sector because of its size (about 210,000 workers) and its relevance for other, related sectors. The steel industry's decline is especially revealing about crisis management because the industry is politicized to a high degree. First, it has traditionally had an almost symbiotic relationship with the government. The political role of the early "steel barons" is legendary, and the top-level managers of the steel industry today maintain a close and profitable contact with the government. Second, industrial relations in the steel industry are usually more democratic than elsewhere. Since the beginning of the 1950s the industry has operated under a legal system of almost parity codetermination (the "Montan model" affecting the steel, iron, and coal industries), under which the privileged union (IG Metall) can influence decisions in the plants. Third, this industry has a long tradition of forming international cartels, which protect European steel from ruinous competition on the world market and thus enable Europeans to preserve parts of their home markets for domestic producers.

Normally, this threefold politicization would present a serious barrier to modernization. The powers inherent in each aspect could be employed, either singly or together, to block economic reforms and to displace the resulting costs onto the national or international community. In fact, in the critical years since 1975 Europe's steel industry has reacted in just this way, except for the West German firms. They too have been guilty of delays, but overall they have succeeded in modernizing efficiently. This "deviant" behavior makes it necessary (and interesting) to investigate the nature of West German crisis management, that is, its special motives and mechanisms.

THE NATURE OF CRISIS MANAGEMENT

Even when pessimism was in vogue, some commentators predicted a rosy future for the "Model Germany." One member of this minority noted that West Germany, together with several small European nations, would "develop and lead the way in the flexible adaptation of social policy to economic necessity."[4] This untimely optimism was surpris-

3. Yves Mény and Vincent Wright, eds., *The Politics of Steel: Western Europe and the Steel Industry in the Crisis Years, 1974–1984* (Berlin: deGruyter, 1987).

4. Harold Wilensky, "Democratic Corporatism, Consensus, and Social Policy: Reflections on Changing Values and the 'Crisis' of the Welfare State," in Organization for Economic Cooperation and Development, ed., *The Welfare State in Crisis* (Paris: OECD, 1981), p. 194. See also Peter J. Katzenstein, *Small States in World Markets: Industrial Policy in Europe* (Ithaca: Cornell University Press, 1985).

ing because it was based on precisely the same conditions as the predominant pessimism. The optimists believed that consensus and corporatism, which the pessimists saw as inhibiting economic progress, were the ideal preconditions for smooth modernization of the economy.[5] These optimists still propagate the equation that ideological consensus plus political corporatism equals economic competence—an equation that, on first impression, largely describes the management of restructuring the West German steel industry.

Consensus

Since the mid-1970s, the number of workers in the steel industry has been reduced from 340,000 to approximately 210,000.[6] The elimination of 130,000 jobs, which is impressive enough in itself, becomes even more impressive when these losses are distributed regionally. Thyssen, Krupp, and Hoesch, three of the five largest West German steelmakers, have their factories in the Ruhr, the traditional center of steel production. Because this region is also the center of the coal-mining industry, it has suffered doubly during the recent crisis. A fourth steelmaker, Klöckner, is based in the state of Bremen, which was hard hit by the decline of the shipbuilding industry. Salzgitter, the fifth large steelmaker, is located not far from the East German border in a region with a hopelessly undiversified economic base. Finally, the Saarland's economy was devastated when Arbed, a Luxembourg concern and the largest employer in the state, cut employment from 30,000 to 14,000. Hence the shrinkage of the West German steel industry has already imposed double-digit unemployment and the concomitant high social costs on several regions. Furthermore, the outlook is bleak: it is projected that employment will fall by at least an additional 40,000 jobs in the coming years.

All the Western European steel-producing nations have undergone this process of contraction. But only the West Germans have managed to reduce production capacity and eliminate jobs peaceably. In Great Britain, by contrast, labor unions consistently sought to thwart timely accommodation. In 1979 their opposition culminated in a thirteen-week strike, one of the longest in Britain's history. The ultraconservative Thatcher government ultimately broke the unions' resistance but had to take harsh measures to do so. France also encountered similar difficulties during this period. In Lorraine the steelworkers rioted against factory closings. The workers engaged the police in pitched battle, streets were blocked off, cars set on fire, radio stations occupied, all to no avail. Across

5. Volker Hauff and Fritz W. Scharpf, *Modernisierung der Volkswirtschaft* (Frankfurt: Europaische Verlagsanstalt, 1975).
6. Arbeitgeberverband Eisen und Stahl, *Jahresbericht 1984–1986* (Düsseldorf, 1987), p. 41.

the border in the Saarland, meanwhile, the shrinking of the steel industry was accomplished without any major disorders.

Thus the West German model differs from other patterns of response to industrial decline in that it is characterized by a general consensus that it makes no sense to fight modernization. This consensus includes even those who are directly affected by the reduction of production capacity and the elimination of jobs. As the head of Hoesch reported about his experiences during the cutbacks: "When I came to Hoesch in 1979, our factories employed 28,000 people. We started 1987 with 14,800. Last fall the factory councils agreed to a further cutback of 4,000 jobs over the next two years."[7] Similarly, a leading officer of the Association of Steel Industrialists announced that although they wished to see the transition to a more flexible pay scale oriented toward world markets (one that can move down as well as up), he recognized that this could be accomplished only "in consensus with the labor unions," that they could not undo "gains made in the area of the minimum pay scale, but could only freeze the status quo in place," and that the transition to a more flexible pay scale, although economically urgent, would take about ten years because of social and policy concerns.[8] The emphasis given to mutual consideration in this process has a pragmatic aspect as well. Modernization can probably be achieved most easily if the victims are justly treated and adequately compensated.[9] For that reason the German federal government will contribute DM 600 million over the period 1987–91 to aid economic adjustment. The general agreement as to the level of these compensatory payments indicates that they are based on common sense. Politicians, industrialists, workers, and the public behave as if modernization of the economy were an economic law that must be observed by all, but that the rate of modernization cannot be based solely on an economic calculus. Social concerns must also be considered. Collective assumptions of this nature are not produced by the concrete experience of a crisis; they are merely actualized by it.[10]

Corporatism

This latent common sense did not mobilize itself on its own. Those affected by the crisis, or their representatives, must update it from time

7. *Der Spiegel*, 41, no. 9 (1987): 81–82.

8. *Südkurier*, 27 January 1988, p. 5.

9. Wilensky, "Democratic Corporatism"; Robert Reich, *The Next American Frontier* (New York: Times Books, 1983).

10. Kenneth Dyson, "The Cultural, Ideological, and Structural Context," in Dyson and Stephen Wilks, eds., *Industrial Crisis* (New York: St. Martin's, 1983), pp. 26–66; Josef Esser and Wolfgang Fach with Kenneth Dyson, "Social Market and Modernization Policy: West Germany," in ibid., pp. 102–27; Peter J. Katzenstein, *The Growth of a Semisovereign State: Policy and Politics in West Germany* (Philadelphia: Temple University Press, 1987).

to time by negotiating to determine which strategy of adjustment to adopt and how to allocate the resulting costs. The participants in each case of corporate decision making discussed here are largely the same. They include representatives of the state, the banks, the firms, and the labor unions concerned. At least one aspect of their pattern of response repeats itself regularly: the solutions are limited as to time and place. Long-range national solutions (which would ultimately mean nationalization), although demanded by the unions, would not be politically feasible under either a socialist-liberal or a conservative-liberal government. Thus the federal government has been willing to mitigate the effects of decline in certain localities by providing funds for investment and social purposes but has sought to avoid raising the issue to a national level, which would politicize the situation and, perhaps, threaten economic "rationality." Moreover, to insulate the economy from politics, the federal government has repeatedly premised its cooperation in managing the steel crisis on two conditions. First, each of the other participants in the corporate cartel must also make a substantial contribution. State governments, the banks, the firms, and the unions will not be permitted to evade this responsibility. Second, the core of the corporatist "covenant," restructuring the industry to restore it to health, must be designed in an economically sound way.

The corporatist crisis management functioned in an exemplary way in the Saarland, at least initially, before some of the turbulences that occurred later on.[11] The federal government was so heavily involved financially that critics spoke of a "fall from grace." It issued DM 900 million in bank guarantees, one-third of the sum the state government was later to contribute; DM 244 million, conditionally repayable, for new investments, as part of an investment total of DM 1.3 billion; and DM 480 million in cash for immediate social measures. In return the state government had to pay DM 120 million for construction of a new foundry. The banks were pressured to write off DM 60 million of outstanding interest and principal. At the same time, the crisis managers restructured the industry's ownership. Arbed, just established as a regional monopoly, made plans to rationalize the Saarland's steel industry and agreed to contribute DM 120 million in new capital. Arbed's plans for modernization were carefully scrutinized for soundness and feasibility by a government consulting agency, Treuarbeit. Last but not least the unions accepted responsibility for identifying the employment slots to be eliminated. Their task was made easier because the negotiated settlement relied on early retirement rather than forced terminations.

Although the federal government's role in managing this crisis may

---

11. Josef Esser and Werner Väth, "Overcoming the Steel Crisis in the Federal Republic of Germany, 1975–83," in Mény and Wright, eds., *Politics of Steel*, pp. 623–97.

seem interventionist, it is based on a sound economic calculus. Consequently, the West Germans have succeeded in cutting by half the number of steel jobs in the Saarland. This is not to say that all the goals of the Saarland plan have been realized—its steel industry has been scaled down, for example, but is still not healthy. Nor is it to say that the Saarland model could automatically be reproduced elsewhere or under other conditions. Even in the Saarland new circumstances have brought, as we note below, modifications of the plan. Nevertheless, the corporatist mode of decision making has been established as the norm, and its success in the Ruhr, the heart of the industry, proves that this mode of decision making is effective.

Competence

It may seem paradoxical to speak of the success of a declining industry that has eliminated about 130,000 jobs in a decade. A few statistics will show what management of the decline of the West German steel industry has accomplished in addition to the peaceful elimination of jobs (see Table 8.1). There are no comparable figures for the fifth large firm, Hoesch, because it merged with the Dutch steel producer Estel for a couple of years. But this omission does not greatly affect the results shown in the table; Hoesch made a profit of DM 4 million in 1986 and it employs more than thirty-three thousand people. A consideration of Mannesmann will complete the picture of the Montan firms in the Ruhr. Mannesmann produces steel only for its own use. With its more than one hundred thousand employees and its 1985 profit of over DM 250 million, it contributes substantially to an optimistic evaluation of this branch of industry.

Not every part of the West German steel industry has weathered the crisis of the past ten years equally well, but one basic tendency emerges clearly from the numbers: social costs have been transformed into economic competence. The maxims governing this transformation are rationalization of production (since the mid-1970s the number of blast furnaces dropped from eighty-four to forty); modernization of technology (90 percent of raw steel is processed using the advanced continuous casting technique; worldwide only 55 percent of raw steel is so processed); and product diversification (fabrication and production of high-grade steel and related high-tech products). The "steel" companies are once again flourishing. Steel plants, steel regions, and steelworkers, however, are still suffering; they have received few blessings from the transformation of this industry. Investments have flowed into other divisions of these firms, often benefiting other regions and creating jobs in other lines of work. As the union periodical *Metall* noted: "It has been

Table 8.1. Performance of the largest West German steelmaking firms, 1969–1986

Category	Thyssen		Krupp		Salzgitter		Klöckner	
	1969–70	1985–86	1970	1985	1969–70	1985–86	1969–70	1985–86
Sales (billions of DM)	15.33	39.99	7.20	20.66	3.90	11.10	2.34	7.46
Profits (millions of DM)	219.00	320.00	110.00	125.00	-1.30	61.00	69.00	00.00
Employees (thousands)	97.60	127.70	80.30	68.00	28.60	38.90	31.40	35.20
Percentage of sales by market								
Domestic	78.50	48.60	76.30	59.10	82.74	66.00	71.64	54.55
Foreign	21.50	51.40	23.70	40.90	17.26	34.00	28.36	45.45
Percentage of sales by product								
Processing	4.20	23.70	34.00	47.00	12.11	—	39.04	50.49
Commerce	35.50	40.40	34.10	25.40	41.66	32.31	—	—
High-grade steel	8.60	9.40	—	—	—	—	—	—
Steel	51.70	26.50	31.90	25.30	47.95	26.73	60.96	49.51

SOURCE: *Wirtschaftswoche* 14, no. 41 (1987): 76–77.

and is fatal for the steel regions that the billions in profits earned by the steelworkers have been invested almost exclusively in the southern part of Germany or abroad. The steel concerns have invested their funds to buy into the industries of the future, rather than here where jobs are desperately needed."[12]

The industry leader, Thyssen, exemplifies this entrepreneurial activism. Thyssen has confidently renamed itself Thyssen Neu (New), because it has "overcome" its steel-producing past. Raw steel, the industry's classic product, now accounts for little more than a quarter of Thyssen's sales and further reduction seems inevitable despite Thyssen's comparative advantage in modernization over its European competitors. In contrast, high-grade steel now accounts for a growing share of Thyssen's business because new markets are opening up (autocatalysts, railed vehicles, environmental technology). Mechanical engineering (switching devices, assembly mechanisms, and the like) offers good growth opportunities, as do transportation and environmental technology (locomotives, railroad cars, elevators, general engineering). The situation with respect to industrial components is also favorable (technologies for casting, processing, and synthesizing material) as it is in commerce (sales of DM 16 billion are envisioned for steel and related products) and in large-scale plant construction (including financing and marketing). The prospects are especially promising for Thyssen's American subsidiary, the Budd Company (auto bodies and robotics).

The situations of the other German steel companies are roughly comparable. Their economic performance is amazing, especially when compared with that of their European competitors (see Table 8.2).

The performance of the West German steel industry is all the more impressive when we compare the government subsidies to the steel industries of the European Economic Community (EEC). All steel firms in the EEC receive government aid, but the amounts received by West Germany's competitors are startling. The Federal Republic provided a subsidy averaging DM 656 million per annum during the last ten years of the crisis, France provided DM 2,134 million, Great Britain, 2,466, and Italy, 2,968.[13]

To sum up, with few exceptions, most notably Arbed in the Saarland, the West German steel industry's success in crisis has resulted from the formula mentioned: consensus plus corporatism indeed equals competence. That is, general acquiescence in an industrial policy open to a world market and a skilled management of acute cases smooth the way for venturesome modernization plans. This equation presupposes a

12. *Metall*, no. 1, 1988, p. 15.
13. *Wirtschaftswoche* 41, no. 39 (1987): 167.

Table 8.2. Value of production of West German and other EEC steel firms, 1982–1986 (in millions of DM)

Firms	1982	1983	1984	1985	1986
German firms	+564	−1,294	+82	+641	+204
Other EEC firms	−10,103	−9,598	−8,750	−4,389	−5,510

SOURCE: *Wirtschaftswoche* 41, no. 39 (1987): 168.

vital "spirit of enterprise"[14]—an essential, irreplaceable characteristic of the West German model.

THE INSTABILITY OF CRISIS MANAGEMENT

The prominent role assigned to entrepreneurship is one of the risky aspects of the West German model, especially in the steel industry, because in West Germany as elsewhere the political significance and regional importance of that industry gave it the opportunity to hide its own failures with government aid. The debacle in the Saarland, for instance, came about largely because the regional power elite, the steel barons, not only failed to modernize their industry but also impeded modernization of their region.[15] This is sufficient indication that the West German model might conceal problems. That the neighboring countries have done less well than West Germany is not dispositive either for what might have been possible or for what is to come. Another look at the steel industry thus seems appropriate.

Stressed Consensus

In the Saarland, the workers at the time of the crisis were outraged that the steel industrialists were irresponsibly blocking progress. This public outrage was the result of a labor union campaign to "enlighten" the workers, deploying calculated and controlled aggression to influence the basis for the allocation of power in the corporatist process of bargaining. Thus functionalized, the "pressure from the people" does not imply a fissure in the consensus about modernization. Throughout the long crisis, in fact, the regional policy management has never been in danger of losing control of the situation. Even in the few confrontational demonstrations, the union (IG Metall) stressed that the demonstrators

14. George Gilder, *The Spirit of Enterprise* (New York: Simon & Schuster, 1984).
15. Josef Esser, Wolfgang Fach, and Werner Väth, *Krisenregulierung* (Frankfurt: Suhrkamp, 1983).

behaved in a "disciplined and orderly" way so that the protest ran its course "without incident."[16] And according to a poll taken recently, about three-fourths of the population thought the minister president of the state was performing satisfactorily and regarded his objective lack of success with equanimity or even (as was true of over half) with praise.[17]

The labor situation is more precarious in the Ruhr region, especially since rationalization has advanced into the core of the steel district, where Thyssen and Krupp, as well as the steel pipe producer Mannesmann, are located. The very "un-German" militance that has been apparent since 1987 has burdened conflict management in novel ways and placed the union in an especially difficult position. Headlines like the following give an idea of how explosive the situation has become: "The Workers Mobilize" (*Der Spiegel*); "The Ruhr is Burning" (*Die Zeit*). An agitated report from the scene illustrates the explosive, sensational atmosphere:

> Yesterday was "Steel Action Day." In the freezing hours from 3 A.M. on, several hundred thousand demonstrators—steelworkers, miners, farmers, garbage collectors, and ordinary citizens—united to form a fist that strangled traffic and prevented daily work in large parts of the district and other industrial cities of Nordrhein-Westfalen. Duisburg [the central location] looked like a ghost town until the evening. No vehicles moved. Conditions were like those under a general strike. The workers and their unions, like a military general staff, ignited a fire storm from the Rhine to deep in Westphalia. Masses of people blocked crossings and traffic junctions in many cities. The men and women, concerned about work and bread for their families, borne up by a strong wave of solidarity from the populace, sealed off many highways. . . . Children collected money for the solidarity fund with the Krupp steel workers. Butchers, bakers, and housewives provided the demonstrators with coffee, tea, soup, Christmas baked goods, and waffles in the bitter cold. Everywhere little coal stoves were glowing, surrounded by shivering demonstrators, on the streets and squares in the sea of heads, banners, and posters.[18]

This "Steel Action Day" was initiated by the union and was meant to protest the secret plans of the directors of Krupp for closing the Krupp factory in Rheinhausen, a suburb of Duisburg. Nonetheless, it is clear, especially in comparison with the protests in the Saarland, that in the Ruhr the masses were committed to the strike, which was led, by the way, by the church. A leading union official on the scene expressed the

16. Josef Esser and Wolfgang Fach, "Korporatistische Krisenregulierung im 'Modell Deutschland,'" in Ulrich von Alemann, ed., *Neokorporatismus* (Frankfurt: Campus, 1981), pp. 158–79.
17. *Frankfurter Allgemeine Zeitung*, 28 January 1988, p. 5.
18. *Südkurier*, 11 December 1987, p. 3.

justified fear that "events could spiral out of control" if the protest were to continue.[19] For some time it seemed possible that events might get out of hand. The spontaneous occupation of the Krupp villa, the legendary temple of the grandeur of the German steel industry, symbolized the new radicalism. The disruption of a Krupp board of directors meeting was hardly less shocking; the protesters ate the bosses' cold buffet and smoked their cigars. And a "warning vigil" in front of the house of a Krupp manager attracted much attention. In short, the precursors of West German radicalism have equaled their counterparts in the French district of Lorraine, up to now the opposite pole to German discipline. Consensus has been renounced, at least for the moment and in a single place.

Limited Corporatism

A shift of mass loyalty such as occurred in the Ruhr affects the corporatist elite consensus. Crisis management has been brought to a halt and must confront a new challenge. In this situation two opposing strategies have been developed. Both are practiced simultaneously, which indicates how charged the political atmosphere is.

On one hand there is the "cooperative" camp, led by the union (IG Metall), Social Democratic politicians, enlightened steel industry managers, and the populist wing of the conservatives. Its strategy is to end the "moment of madness"[20] as quickly as possible. Direct action, with its unpredictable dynamics, is to be tamed and channeled into the corporatist bargaining system, where it could pressure "unenlightened" industrialists to negotiate concessions. The imperatives of modernization are not at issue in this process; instead, actual radicalization is preempted by verbal radicalism.[21] The success of this precarious game depends on cooperation from the conservative power bloc; otherwise the cooperative camp runs the risk of embarrassing failure. The risk is all the greater because the Montan codetermination makes union officials complicit and arouses the suspicion that the cooperative camp is playing a false game. "He wants to get rid of us," a union member, speaking for the membership, said recently about his president.[22]

This basic dilemma was intensified when that other side, the "conflict-oriented" camp, swerved from the corporatist path toward confrontation. Part of the prehistory of this open confrontation is an agreement

19. *Der Spiegel* 41, no. 50 (1987): 17–19.
20. Aristide Zolberg, "Moments of Madness," *Politics and Society* 2 (1972): 183–207.
21. "Heisses Herz und kühler Kopf": Spiegel-Redakteur H. J. Noack über Franz Steinkühler im Revier, *Der Spiegel*, 41, no. 51 (1987): 25–26.
22. *Die Zeit*, 22 January 1988, pp. 19–20.

of September 1987, reached in the traditional way among "all participants," which provided for a government-subsidized modernization without mass firings. In exchange for these terms and for the "political and moral" promise that it would be consulted in the future, the union agreed to the gradual elimination of 35,000 jobs. Nonetheless, three firms (Thyssen, Krupp, and Mannesmann) secretly developed cooperative plans that were to culminate in the closing of the Rheinhausen plant with its 5,300 jobs. The riots broke out when this agreement became known to the public.

This first offense against the corporatist approach to decision making was exacerbated by the commission of a second. Some steel industry managers and representatives of the conservative-liberal government parties wanted, at least initially, to turn this social conflict into a test of political power. Thus Thyssen's spokesman issued the slogan: "Stop up your ears and plunge ahead!" The head of Klöckner compared the crisis with a disease that must be treated quickly, sometimes by radical means, and recommended the English method of treatment. Leading politicians characterized the riots as the work of outside agitators, who would destroy the "good image of the 'diligent German.' "[23] And finally, the demand that government force be used to end threats to "public safety and order" and to prevent them in the future was especially inflammatory.[24]

There is no question that this uncompromising therapy would have resulted in a civil war imposed from above. According to the state minister for internal affairs, responding to the demands of the advocates of law and order, "It would have led to unforeseeable consequences if I had followed your wishes and called the police out against the striking workers."[25] This is all the more true because unaffiliated groups, those with communist, syndicalist, or populist roots, not controlled by the union, can seek to profit from an extreme situation.[26] Whatever the rightist battle slogans were meant to accomplish, they document the unwillingness of some circles to continue the corporatist tradition. In keeping with this analysis, the president of IG Metall complained that he was unable to meet with the appropriate minister in Bonn.[27] Thus at this critical moment even the minimal preconditions for corporatism were lacking. And this further intensified the crisis. Union leadership, abandoned by political leaders, is squeezed between discontented workers and aggressive industrialists. In this bind it has lost its flexibility and will

23. *Der Spiegel* 41, no. 52 (1987): 79; *Der Spiegel*, 42, no. 1 (1988): 44; *Wirtschaftswoche* 42, no. 5 (1988): 29.
24. *Der Spiegel* 41, no. 51 (1987): 19; *Frankfurter Allgemeine Zeitung*, 11 December 1987, p. 1.
25. *Handelsblatt*, 28 January 1988, p. 3.
26. *Express* 26, no. 1 (1988): 4ff.; *Express* 26, no. 2 (1988): 4ff.
27. *Wirtschaftswoche* 42, no. 5 (1988): 24.

not easily be able to return to the bargaining table if and when employers signal their readiness to compromise. "At Krupp," it had been reported after the first heat of conflict had cooled, "people complain that it is difficult to find a bargaining power to talk to."[28] This situation protracts and complicates negotiations about economic adaptation, a departure from the path of corporatist virtue which lowers the standard of economic rationality.

Reduced Competence

The debacle in the Ruhr eventually took the expected form. The outbreak of conflict and the breakdown of crisis decision making have retarded modernization of the steel industry. It is not improbable that this short-term effect will be accompanied by negative long-term consequences such as the destruction of mutual trust and an increased inclination to confrontation.

There are, to be sure, cases in which reduced competence is triggered by other mechanisms. Roles in crisis management can, after all, be reversed. In that case the firm is no longer the dynamic center of the decision-making process, its decisions supported by government and legitimized by union cooperation. Instead, the industry's managers must be driven to take action. This variant of crisis management—economic competence through ersatz industrialists—was to play a role in the West German steel industry in 1981–82, when the "real" industrialists had completely muddled the situation.

Then, according to the head of Thyssen, the industry had "consumed its substance in the long years of confrontation with EEC competitors."[29] The banks demanded drastic reforms because they had to cope with the steel industry's burden of debt, which had grown to DM 10 billion, and anticipated further demands for credit. A radical cure was called for and had in principle already been accepted: coordination, concentration, consolidation. While the heads of the firms conjured up the "community of need" in public, they were actually more removed from such a community than ever. Attempts at consolidation either foundered on the negotiating partner's lack of seriousness or were torpedoed by strategic offers from competitors. This happened in 1982, for example, when Thyssen intentionally interfered in Krupp's negotiations with Hoesch. At the same time each firm sought to enhance its own competitive position, counting on massive government aid. Thus in summer of 1982 the federal government was unexpectedly confronted with demands for over DM 14 billion in investment aid. Clearly, the

28. *Frankfurter Allgemeine Zeitung*, 29 January 1988, p. 3.
29. Dietrich Spethman, "Die Bundesregierung soll am deutschen Stahlmarkt endlich die Notbremse ziehen," *Handelsblatt* (13 November 1982): 6.

government had to intervene to bring a halt to this wasteful rivalry, to the counterproductive carousel of honest and strategic offers, real and false negotiations, serious and fictional plans for reform. The government did not want to rely on the union (whose mediation had played an important role in the Saarland crisis). Instead, the conservative-liberal coalition that had just come to power established a kind of semicorporatism (without the union), relying on the sources of financial capital, the banks that issued loans and the insurance firms, to straighten things out. Three "steel moderators" from the financial industry were to confer with the firms in adjusting the structure of the German steel industry to its market. The moderators' report, issued in 1983, envisioned a comprehensive reorganization of the steel sector. The report's key component was a plan for consolidation that would have organized the industry into two competitive groups: a "Rhine group," consisting of Thyssen and Krupp, and a "Ruhr group," consisting of Hoesch, Klöckner, and Salzgitter. To finance this consolidation, the government was to provide a total of DM 3 billion.[30]

This plan was politically flawed. The Ruhr cartel, with the giant firm Thyssen at its center, promised to become an integrated combine that could compete successfully in world markets, but the second group had no long-term chance of survival—nor was this piecemeal conglomerate designed to survive. Furthermore, the plan ignored the Saarland firm of Arbed. Consequently, the liberal-conservative government's semicorporatism quickly proved ineffective. However economically sound its proposals might have been, the federal government's alliance with the banks was not a sufficient condition for their success. The disadvantaged concerns, together with their state governments (independent of their party composition) and the marginalized union, successfully united against the government's consolidation plan. Moreover, the government failed to use its financial resources to bring pressure to bear so its grand plan went up in smoke. Under these conditions only a complete corporatism, with an activist state applying pressure and actively integrated unions, might have overcome the supercapacity and redundancy in the steel area. In hindsight, however, a radical cure was unnecessary. The West German steel producers have survived on their own and are even relatively comfortable despite their handicaps.

THE STABILITY OF CRISIS MANAGEMENT

The economic competence of crisis management in the West German steel industry is characterized by its concern with second-best solutions.

30. Esser and Väth, "Overcoming the Steel Crisis," pp. 623–91.

This emphasis on pragmatism manifests itself in other areas as well. The ideological consensus has wavered from time to time, but even in the Ruhr, scene of the riots, forces were not released that could not be tamed. Although corporatist decision making has been severely tested, it has shown itself to be remarkably resilient. Even the highly explosive Ruhr confrontation was defused in the usual style: through concerted action. Regional and national steel conferences, initially characterized as "gab feasts" by a good number of steel managers, have taken place; the most important results of the process of political negotiation—DM 1 billion in government aid for high-tech industries in the Ruhr region and a slightly modified schedule for the shutdown of Krupp's Rhein-hausen plant—has guided the most sensational labor struggle in the history of the Federal Republic back onto the course of consensual modernization:

> Satisfaction on all sides, but bitter disappointment for those who instigated the whole thing. That is the sum of the reactions on the day following the Ruhr conference held by Chancellor Kohl. Thousands of Krupp workers were waiting for news on Wednesday evening in their factory assembly hall. It was their uprising against the closing of the Duisburg foundry at Rhein-hausen that caused all this political activity, yet the chairman of their factory works committee was unable to bring them a single word of comfort about the survival of the foundry from Bonn. Just the opposite, in fact: The reason for the uprising, the death of Krupp's Rheinhausen foundry, has now been accepted by all sides. Anyone who is still fighting against that fact is fighting at an abandoned outpost.[31]

That is, the tense situation relaxed because the regressive protest was isolated and a progressive consensus purchased. This stability, understood as the tendency of the system to stay within bounds, gives West German crisis management its special character. Deviations appear, but they are corrected to preserve the essential nature of the model. This certainty of response is not miraculous; it is produced by specific mechanisms.

Consensus by Diffusion

At the height of the Ruhr riots workers from all over West Germany journeyed to the scene of confrontation to show solidarity by demonstrating alongside the strikers against the "arbitrariness of the industrialists." A short time later this movement reversed itself: the affected workers visited the personnel of other steel works to explain their con-

31. *Die Welt*, 26 February 1988, p. 2.

cerns and to recruit for future actions showing solidarity. Their success was limited. For instance, the two thousand workers who traveled to the Krupp plant in Bochum found only a few colleagues there; the rest were "in hiding."[32] It was obvious that the protest was beginning to disintegrate. The increased militance of the Ruhr action did not translate into longer duration; resistance trickled off regardless of its intensity.

It looks as though this protest will repeat the history of the protest in the Saarland steel crisis.[33] In the Saarland the protest was doomed from the beginning owing to the divided interests and loyalties of the workers. The "common interest" failed because its costs and benefits were distributed unequally. Many workers were fired outright; others retained the hope of secure jobs. Whole plants were not always closed; sometimes only part of a facility was shut down, such as the blast furnaces or a rolling mill. The result was the destruction of unity among the workers. Decline at one facility benefited others, which could then expand their production. "In this situation it is hard to keep the workers from marching against each other," a union member complained at the time. The frightened workers naturally sought to take care of their own interests first, even at the expense of a colleague. The factory works committees were inundated with complaints from people who wanted to avoid being pensioned off or transferred, naming colleagues for whom these fates would be more appropriate. The labor courts were burdened with similar complaints. Actions to show solidarity became very difficult to stage once it became apparent how much the fates of the steelworkers differed. And collective protests meant to demonstrate the workers' readiness to fight risked embarrassment. Many were attended by a mere handful of the faithful and the directly interested: the mayor, a few union officials (especially the older ones), several dozen interested inhabitants, and a frustratingly small number of steelworkers. The prospects for resistance on a broader front were even dimmer. Eyewitnesses reported that at the height of the protest, the Saarland union failed to fill even one of the buses it chartered to bring workers from other locations to the site of its demonstration. The motto that explains this lack of solidarity is "Nothing else matters if *we* have work." Egotism obscures the common concern. After the experience of the steel crisis, it seems likely that "moments of madness" will be limited to short periods of spontaneous outrage.

The pattern taken by the steel crisis as it diffused through the industry was not caused solely by real differences between workers such as age or qualifications or between factories in their products or costs. In addition to these objective factors, the response was influenced by certain strate-

32. *Die Zeit*, 22 January 1988, pp. 19–20.
33. Esser, Fach, and Väth, *Krisenregulierung*, pp. 188–267.

gic considerations: the crisis was managed so that the losers neither fully recognized its costs nor experienced them all at once. Such was the case in the Saarland, and the Ruhr is repeating that pattern. With the wisdom of hindsight, the managers of the Ruhr crisis now regret their tactical error in giving the masses too little hope. It is unlikely that "that 5,000 Krupp workers would have taken to the streets, had they known in advance that only a few of them would be affected. As it was, they all had to live with uncertainty and fear, ideal soil for radical action."[34] Now even the Ruhr industrialists appear to have recovered their appreciation of incremental rationalization and piecemeal dismissal. In effect, they have transformed a large crisis into a series of small crises, dealing with them at one location at a time: "Thyssen has managed its two conflicts, Hattingen and Oberhausen, and Krupp has kept peace at its Rheinhausen location without involving Bochum [the next endangered location]. Once the Rheinhausen situation is cleared up, by 1989 at the latest, Hoesch will be confronted with the choice of continuing or giving up steel production. Then Thyssen will have to address the situation in Duisburg. 'Everyone dies alone'—the steel industry's timing has been guided by this motto."[35]

Only an equally systematic defense by labor would limit the concerted campaign of divide and conquer waged by capital. The only force that could mount such a defense is the union. Nearly 80 percent of the steelworkers are unionized, and union representatives vote on the board of directors of the steel firms, which gives them access to information about the rationalization plans of the industrialists. In other words, if preserving the consensus about the need for modernization depends on diffusing workers' hostility, then the corporatistically involved union leadership must share much of the credit for this outcome.

Corporatism by "Implication"

The high level of cooperation among unions, industrialists, and the government is a characteristic of industrial relations in West Germany. This pattern of cooperation is especially marked in the steel industry, where corporatistic decision making seems to function almost automatically, although not without friction.

Union participation in the corporatist coalition evolved in part from an institution—the Montan codetermination[36]—that dates to the origins of the Federal Republic. After World War II, the steel bosses were

34. *Die Zeit*, 12 February 1988, p. 22.
35. Gerhard Sailer, "High noon im Stahlbereich," *Revier* 10, no. 9 (1987): 4–7.
36. Andrei S. Markovits, *The Politics of West German Trade Unions* (Cambridge: Cambridge University Press, 1986).

willing to make concessions to the union to avoid even more threatening outcomes of the political realignment. First, they needed the union to help them defeat plans by certain of Germany's conquerors to dismantle the steel industry. This threat arose as a result of the steel industry's political, economic, and military contributions to the Nazis. The steel bosses needed the union because it was not similarly tainted by collaboration. Second, some groups of workers had seized upon the Nazi past as an opportunity to demand the implementation of socialism, and the industrialists wanted to nip this movement in the bud.

The unions generally favored economic democracy and entered into the Montan bargain because it advanced their own ideas. The concept of economic democracy was elaborated during the Weimar Republic and aimed to combine government economic planning with industrial codetermination. Parliament, which the unions hoped would be dominated by the Social Democrats, could thereby guarantee "prosperity for all" and find a "peaceful path to socialism."[37] The cornerstone of economic democracy, a majority in parliament committed to socialism, has proven illusory. Nonetheless, the union movement has kept its part of the bargain and has sought to make codetermination work. Union representatives now occupy about half the seats on most boards of directors and often behave as if they could best provide for the well-being of their members by promoting the well-being of the firm. The so-called labor directors are generally responsible for their firms' personnel and social policies and are supposed to balance the concerns of both labor and management. They cannot be elected over a contrary union vote, and in times of crisis they cooperate especially closely with management committees and employees' representatives on boards of directors. According to prevailing opinion, the Montan codetermination agreement has proven successful. Although the steel industrialists later regretted the concessions they made under duress to the union and to an extent still regret them, they have not yet resolutely sought to revise them. More important, there has been no political majority to support such revisions.

The West German steel industry and the government have shared a long and intimate relationship.[38] The current form of this relationship reflects the constellation of economic and political forces that emerged during the years of reconstruction following World War II. The Marshall Plan gave the highest priority to the redevelopment of the strate-

37. Ulrich Nocken, "Korporatistische Theorien und Strukturen in der deutschen Geschichte des 19. und frühen 20. Jahrhunderts," in Alemann, ed., *Neokorporatismus*, pp. 17–39.

38. Berndt Weisbrod, *Schwerindustrie in der Weimarer Republik* (Wuppertal: Hammer, 1978).

gically important sectors of the economy: steelmaking, coal mining, shipbuilding, and electrical power generating.[39] The West German government also promoted the reconstruction of the steel industry through indirect subsidies: special tax credits and approval of accelerated depreciation for tax reporting purposes, relaxation of regulatory standards and deadlines, and access to credit on favorable terms. The culmination of these policies came with the "investment aid law" of 1952, which obligated all the industries in West Germany to put aside DM 1 billion to complete the rebuilding of the economy. This governmentally mandated "private" effort was administered by the Kreditanstalt für Wiederaufbau, a federally owned bank that specialized in allocating credit for pressing investment needs in coal, steel, and energy.[40] These loans ensured that the West German steel industry would be reborn in the postwar era when, because of its poor economic condition, it could not rely on private investors.[41] Thus the West German steel industry owes both its survival and its capital structure to public intervention.

Unlike their American counterparts, West German banks play a direct governance role in industry.[42] Their influence in the steel industry is largely exercised silently, but the more than DM 10 billion they have lent the industry is a measure of their interest in its fate. The major banks have taken pains to assure themselves of a voice in the industry's future. Representatives of the Deutsche Bank, the Dresdner Bank, and the Commerzbank sit on the boards of each of the steel firms.[43] Thus it is no accident that the major banks have been instrumental in shaping every aspect of the industry's strategy and its structure. The salvage action carried out by the large banks in the Krupp case was especially noteworthy. Under their guidance Krupp was saved from bankruptcy in 1967 and reorganized into a modern firm.[44]

Hence it appears that corporatist decision making in the steel industry is based on long-standing practices and well-established institutions. In a serious crisis, the industry can call upon the knowledge and resources of all the participants in the corporatist coalition to translate the consensus on modernization into a coherent response. The actions ultimately

---

39. Henry C. Wallich, *Triebkräfte des deutschen Wiederaufstiegs* (Frankfurt: Knapp, 1955), p. 345.

40. Andrew Shonfield, *Modern Capitalism* (Oxford: Oxford University Press, 1965); Marianne Welteke, *Theorie und Praxis der sozialen Marktwirtschaft* (Frankfurt: Campus, 1976).

41. Welteke, *Theorie und Praxis der sozialen Marktwirtschaft*, p. 25.

42. Shonfield, *Modern Capitalism*; Zysman, *Governments, Markets, and Growth*; Peter Hall, *Governing the Economy* (Oxford: Polity Press, 1986), pp. 235–36.

43. Monopolkommission, *Fortschreitende Konzentration bei Grossunternehmen* (Baden-Baden: Nomos, 1978).

44. Projektgruppe Ruhrgebietsanalyse, *Ruhrstahl und Imperialismus*, 2 vols. (Gaiganz: Gegendruck 1975), 1:129–31; Esser and Fach with Dyson, "Social Market," p. 114.

taken by the diverse participants may not be perfectly harmonized, but they will almost certainly be coherent enough to avert damage to the industry's structure.

Competence by Protectionism

The West German steel industry weathered the collapse of the 1970s better than its competitors in the EEC and then modernized more rapidly. Since the German steel industry possessed a comparative advantage vis-à-vis its potential competitors, it initially rejected protectionist measures and international cartel arrangements. Instead it sought to exploit the difficulties of its European competitors in the crisis.[45] Thus when the EEC was considering protectionist measures, both the federal government and the steel producers opposed them. When the EEC finally protected steel in 1977, the West Germans were the harshest critics of the measures. One steel producer, Klöckner, even risked an open break with the cartel managers of the EEC and the West German steel community in 1980 because it was dissatisfied with its production quota and tried to evade it secretly.

Arbed's needs, however, undermined the West German position. It soon became abundantly clear that they could be addressed only within the context of a supranational agreement on prices and production quotas. Moreover, lacking such a supranational agreement, even the healthy West German steel firms could well have been drawn into ruinous price competition by their more highly subsidized Common Market rivals. Finally, many doubted that the West German steel industry could cope with the Japanese. In technology and organization Japan's steel industry was its superior, and the Japanese advantage held with respect to product quality as well as production technology (see Table 8.3). The picture is similar for firm size. In 1977 there were thirteen large steel companies in Japan, compared with five in Germany, three in the United States, one in France, and one in England. Figures on labor productivity indicate similar standings: in 1975 a Japanese worker required 6.2 hours to produce a ton of raw steel, a German worker required 8.9, an American worker 10.5, a French worker 12.1, and a British worker 17.4.[46]

In sum, the official justification given by the EEC for protecting itself from Japanese competition, to "give the industry a breathing space to restructure itself,"[47] also reflected the needs of the West German steel

45. Thomas Grunert, "Decision-Making Processes in the Steel Crisis Policy of the EEC," in Mény and Wright, eds., *Politics of Steel*, pp. 222–307; Loukas Tsoukalis and Robert Strauss, "Community Policies on Steel, 1974–1982," in ibid., pp. 186–221.

46. *Die Zeit*, 21 April 1978, p. 22.

47. Tsoukalis and Strauss, "Community Policies on Steel," p. 201.

Table 8.3. Comparison of quality and technology of the world's leading steel-producing nations

Country	Quality: Percentage of oxygen steel, 1977 (1985)	Technology: Percentage of continuous casting, 1975 (1985)
United States	60 (59)	9 (44)
Japan	83 (71)	31 (91)
Federal Republic	69 (82)	24 (80)
France	63 (81)	13 (81)
Great Britain	50 (71)	8 (55)

SOURCE: Willy Dzielak et al., *Arbeitskampf um Arbeitsplätze* (Frankfurt am Main: Campus, 1980), p. 52; *Statistisches Jahrbüch der Eisen- und Stahlindustrie* (Düsseldorf: Stahleisen, 1986), pp. 89, 193, 279, 302.

producers. In 1978 Japan agreed to "voluntary" quotas on its steel exports to the EEC. Subsequently, Japanese exports to the EEC fell from about 1.7 million tons in 1977 to about 160,000 tons in 1981.[48] Protected from the Japanese, the West German steel industry was given the room it needed to modernize on its own terms, that is, on the basis of the social consensus created by the corporatist bargaining system.

THE FLEXIBILITY OF CRISIS MANAGEMENT

West German crisis management has a coherent identity—it is built on consensus, corporatism, and competence. Although it has experienced occasional periods of unstability, it has been able just as regularly to restabilize itself. West German crisis management appears to be highly adaptable and remarkably flexible. This raises the question of which forces have inserted "slack" in the West German model and whether crisis management in the steel industry is typical of the West German way of coping with industrial decline. Three factors are especially important to a better understanding of these issues. They are political change, economic hierarchy, and social impact.

Change

The Federal Republic has undergone several changes in political direction. Although the corporatist strategy is more deeply entrenched in the steel industry than elsewhere, these political fluctuations have not failed to leave their traces on it. A few years ago, for instance, following the political turn to the right, the firm of Mannesmann tried to topple the Montan codetermination agreement with the help of some organiza-

48. Ibid., p. 197.

tional sleight of hand. This attempt was thwarted after vigorous confrontations.

The effects of changes in the political climate can also be seen in the details of the corporatist consensus. The Saarland serves as an example. Before 1982–83, when the conservative-liberal coalition came to power in Bonn, a corporatist consensus was firmly established, according to which the workers' sacrifices for modernization would consist of conceding the necessary decrease in number of jobs. This commitment was guaranteed by the union, which negotiated relief measures or compensation for the workers affected.

After the turn, the relative weights given the participants in the bargaining system shifted noticeably, to the disadvantage of the union and its members.[49] The new federal government insisted that the Arbed workers accept a "contract of solidarity" as a precondition for financial aid. Under the terms of this agreement the Arbed workers were to forego part of their Christmas bonus for two years. These bonuses amounted to only DM 60 million, a ridiculously small amount compared to the DM 2.4 billion Arbed had already received in state subsidies. Furthermore, they were to be reimbursed at a later date. Given the size of the pecuniary stakes involved, it is unlikely that the bonus issue was seriously intended to reduce the burden on the public fisc but was instead a political power play on the part of the new government. Surrounding events bear out this suspicion. In the first place, the concessions required from steelworkers were not negotiated as usual. The federal government simply issued an ultimatum that threatened to let the firm go bankrupt if the union did not immediately capitulate to its demands. Second, these demands violated existing wage agreements. Capitulation to them would have undermined the power of the union's leaders both within the union and externally and would have established a far-reaching precedent. Third, uncompromising opposition to the government's ultimatum could have split the workers' camp because "the sanctity of wage agreements was understandably not the central issue to workers whose existence was hanging in the balance."[50] In a futile attempt to forestall the disaffection of any of its members, the union adopted a double line: it continued to defend the wage agreement in principle but capitulated in practice. Fourth, when this capitulation became evident, the union was weakened because its members, the ultimate source of union power, saw that they could no longer fully trust the union's officials.

In the Saarland steel crisis the conservative-liberal government ap-

49. Wolfgang Gruber and Peter Sörgel, eds., *Stahl ohne Zukunft? Der Überlebenskampf in den Revieren* (Hamburg: Verlag fur das Studium der Arbeiterbewegung, 1984).
50. *Metall* no. 1 (1983).

peared willing to stress corporatist consensus to exploit a change in the general political climate and to translate that change into concrete gains. The Ruhr case, however, shows that the presumption that conservative power is inimical to corporatist practice is by no means entirely correct. Indeed, it is possible that the conservatives are better situated to deal with industrial decline than are the Social Democrats. It is not unlikely that the Social Democratic party, the political home of West Germany's "social conscience," would have found it painful to reconcile its social concerns and its popular support with the need for modernization and efficiency. Hence the Social Democrats governing in the Ruhr have sought to evade the dilemma posed by the decline of the steel industry by demonstrating their impotence in the face of the political shift to the right at the federal level. The states, according to them, "cannot compensate for the failures of the federal government. Not only because of the difficult budget situation, but also for political reasons: the federal government must be held accountable for its decisions. Wrong decisions by the federal government are the responsibility of the federal government."[51] Thus the leftists in charge of the state policy ascribe both the capacity and the responsibility for dealing with industrial decline to their political opponents running the federal government: "The protests must be directed to Bonn."[52] Of course, Bonn can more easily deal with protest because of its distance from the situation. The ruling conservative-liberal coalition in Bonn can also seek to shift responsibility for the costs of modernization to a higher, more distant level—to Brussels, headquarters of the EEC.

Hierarchy and Impact

The steel industry's complaints about "unfair" competition from its European rivals are notorious. That these complaints have produced no results in the ten years they have been heard suggests that the steel industry has lost some of its political influence. If so, it is likely that this loss reflects the decline in the industry's importance to the West German economy.

Until the 1960s, the steel industry was an engine of growth for the entire West German economy. This role has been taken over by other industries. Meanwhile mechanical engineering, construction, vehicle manufacture, chemical and pharmaceutical products, electrotechnology, and consumer durables all rank higher in the economic hierarchy. The West German model now depends on these industries. The steel

51. Klaus-Dieter Leister, "Dieses Land kann nicht das soziale Gewissen der Republik sein," *Frankfurter Rundschau*, 30 May 1987, p. 12.
52. *Das Parlament* 45 (1987): 4.

industry's share of total manufacturing output was only 3.6 percent in 1985.[53] Therefore, the economy as a whole has not been seriously disrupted by the steel crisis. On the contrary; the Federal Republic has continued to compete successfully in world markets and exports have climbed from 23 to over 27 percent of GNP. The Federal Republic closed 1986 with a record balance of trade surplus of DM 112.6 billion. More than half of these exports were to other Common Market countries; thus it is not surprising that the steel industry failed to persuade any West German government to risk a trade war on its behalf. To be sure, among the declining industries steel still retains a privileged position, even economically. There is no question that the industry has a robust core whose products are highly valued as inputs by the high-tech sectors of the economy (sometimes in the same firms). Consequently, one might say that steel is going through a process of "shrinking to a healthy size," while many other declining industries are being "cured to death."

The shipbuilding industry is an example. Its share of the world market was nearly 20 percent in 1950; it is now barely 6 percent. There are two reasons for its decline: first, worldwide overcapacity of about 100 percent, and second, a faulty product-market strategy. Most German shipbuilders bet on the wrong horse: technologically simple, largely standardized giant tankers. Thus they entered a hopeless competition with the East Asian suppliers, not only Japan but also South Korea, Taiwan, and India.[54] In 1975 there were about eighty thousand workers in the shipbuilding industry; by 1984 the number had declined to about forty-six thousand. The core of the industry, commercial shipbuilding, is slowly but surely dying. Today it employs fewer than twenty-two thousand people. Only those parts of the industry that serve specific market niches such as the military and refitting are likely to survive. The industry's fate will ultimately be decided in the headquarters of Thyssen, Krupp, and Salzgitter, the coowners of the most important German shipyards. Thus the shipbuilding industry's present misery reflects its low present value in the hierarchies of the big steel firms.[55]

The decline of the shipbuilding industry provoked loud protests, reflecting the tremendous social impact of this industry's economic decline. The shipbuilding industry consists of a handful of large docks concentrated along a narrow coastal strip. The crisis in the shipbuilding

53. *Statistisches Jahrbuch der Eisen- und Stahlindustrie 1986* (Düsseldorf: Stahleisen, 1986), p. 5.
54. Dieter Rother, "Strukturwandel im Weltschiffbau: Auswirkungen auf die westeuropäische Schiffbauindustrie," *Beihefte zur Konjunkturpolitik* 31 (1985): 131–50.
55. Stefan Ryll and Werner Väth, "Industrielle Strategien und politische Konfliktstrukturen," in Heidrun Abromeit and Bernhard Blanke, eds., *Arbeitsmarkt, Arbeitsbeziehungen und Politik in den 8oer Jahren* (Opladen: Westdeutscher Verlag, 1987), pp. 270–92.

industry thus entailed concentrated costs and local mass unemployment, which in turn stimulated the union (IG Metall), the shipbuilding industrialists, and the governments of the affected states to form an alliance to appeal to Bonn for money to deal with the acute crisis, as in the Saarland.[56] Their coalition was not an unqualified success. The fate of a key industry like steel was not hanging in the balance, and the workers soon found themselves abandoned. When they shifted from talk to action and occupied plants in protest, even their own union distanced itself from them. Nonetheless, they did succeed in winning substantial assistance from the federal government for dislocated workers and areas directly affected by the crisis (although here, too, a cooler wind is blowing since the conservative shift). Moreover, the shipbuilding industry has never been left entirely to its own resources. The federal and state governments have subsidized it for more than two decades.

This is the overall picture of what has happened in the shipbuilding industry. A closer look will reveal a broad range of different strategies of adjustment, reaching from corporatism like that in the steel industry to a free-market approach toward modernization typical of other West German industries in decline.

Closest to the Saarland model was the crisis management of the Vulkan shipyard in Bremen. Its largest shareholder (29 percent) during the decisive years was the state government, which acted through its own consulting agency. The Social Democratic government stepped in when the economic difficulties became evident and withdrew soon after the situation seemed to be stabilized. Part of this rescue operation was the fusion of Vulkan with three smaller shipyards with different production lines so that now the corporation offers a diversified range of products and services. An important element in this unparalleled success story is that Vulkan, as the only major shipbuilding firm, is not (co)owned by one of the big steel producers with their broader scope of profit calculation; thus it could, with the political backing of the state, act according to its own needs, the most important of which was, of course, survival.

At the same time Bremen was also the scene of the worst-case scenario when in 1983 the Krupp-owned AG Weser shut down its shipyard there. Two thousand workers were laid off and thrown into a hopelessly overcrowded local labor market. Their misery was barely cushioned by a modest set of routine social measures, and nobody really cared when in desperation they occupied the plant—after all, it was doomed to be closed anyway. With AG Weser everything went wrong. First, its closing came to play an important role in the economic consolidation of

56. Bo Stråht, "Redundancy and Solidarity: Tripartite Politics and the Concentration of the West European Shipbuilding Industry," *Cambridge Journal of Economics* 10 (1986): 147–63.

Vulkan—a constellation that created a deep cleavage within the work force, barring from the very beginning of the political struggle any possibility of common resistance. Furthermore, the state government was neither able financially nor forced to help—after all, it had demonstrated its concern by intervening in the Vulkan affair, and it was generally understood that the region's overall shipbuilding capacity could not be kept at former levels. Finally, there was no other example of a corporation headquarters, together with the local management, acting so poorly in response to the global decline of shipbuilding. Not only did Krupp continue to construct giant tankers even when orders came to an end, it also dismantled (as early as 1979) the research and development department of this shipyard, thus cutting off the path to more promising high-tech products (albeit this decision was rational if the policy was to get out of the shipbuilding business).

At this end of the spectrum, shipbuilding shares the political and social destiny of industries elsewhere in Germany that are neither important to the economy as a whole nor critical to the stability of a specific region and in a crisis cannot hope for substantial support from any source. The textile and clothing and the clockmaking industries offer striking examples. Since the 1970s both have undergone an extensive and thoroughly successful process of rationalization, in the course of which scores of factories were shut down and thousands of jobs eliminated. Since 1970 the number of employees has sunk from 880,000 to 410,000 in the textile and clothing industry and from 28,000 to 16,000 in clockmaking. In both cases the adjustment provoked neither serious social disruption nor government aid programs. The reason was that the sacrifices of the victims of rationalization could not be politicized, primarily because both industries consist of small firms. Thus the 16,000 employees in the clockmaking industry are distributed over about 250 factories (only 140 of which employ more than 20 workers). There are 15,000 shops in the clothing industry with fewer than 20 workers, and about two-thirds of the employees in the industry work for firms with fewer than 200 workers.[57]

In sum, every sector of West German industry is undergoing modernization, in some cases actively, through innovation, in others passively, through "destruction." They differ, however, in how this process is organized. The management of the steel crisis shows corporatist decision making at its best. In that case, active corporatism spreads the costs

57. Commerzbank, Brancheninformation P 22, 12 July 1984, *Textilindustrie—Hoffnung auf weitere Erholung*; Commerzbank, Brancheninformation R 13, 23 December 1986, *Bekleidungsindustrie—wieder optimistischer*; Commerzbank, Branchenbericht L 7, 24 September 1986, *Deutsche Uhrenindustrie*; *Wirtschaftswoche* 40, no. 7 (1986): 106–8; *Die Zeit*, 28 March 1986, p. 13.

of adjustment to the crisis so that they are relatively bearable and generally acceptable (under certain conditions that change with the political climate). Shipbuilding represents the case of a reactive corporatism defending antiquated interests in a ritual way, channeling the impotent rage of the affected workers without hindering or seriously meaning to impede the decline of the industry. Textiles and clothing manufacturing as well as clockmaking represent a model that might be described as active liberalism. These industries were largely unprotected, they were exposed to ruinous competition, and they modernized in an economically successful way, although the transition incurred high social costs. The West German model thus contains a second-order flexibility, a spectrum of approaches to crisis management distinguished by the efficiency and humanity with which their common goal of progress is achieved.

It is obvious that the enthusiasm about the West German model does not mean that a miraculous way of avoiding industrial crises has been found. Rather, it reflects a widespread belief that the West Germans are unusually adept in their management of industrial crisis.[58] The success of the West German model is usually attributed to its basic elements: consensus (all the relevant actors—the government, the industry, and the union—accept the principle that a national industrial policy must be oriented to success in international competition); corporatism (the steps taken in adjusting to the world market must reflect agreement between the relevant actors); and competence (economic growth enables, stimulates, and sometimes even requires the process that Joseph Schumpeter once called "creative destruction"). The West German approach to the steel crisis closely approximated this model. The other instances of industrial decline reviewed here—shipbuilding, textile and clothing manufacturing, and clockmaking—demonstrate that the West German model also comprehends "deviant cases" and that, even in West Germany, there are no guarantees that modernization will be harmonious or humane.

An industry's capacity for adjustment is in part a function of its economic relevance and its social significance. But these factors rather determine the misery of "destruction" than explain the glory of "creation." It turns out that more than anything else, the successful management of the West German steel crisis depends on that complex network of political relationships mentioned at the beginning of the chapter. The harmonious rationalization of the West German steel industry requires a series of bargains. On the national level, the steel lobby negotiates the

---

58. Reich, *Next American Frontier*; Katzenstein, *Small States in World Markets*; Wilensky, "Democratic Corporatism."

subvention of its business and its jobs, but the government demands in return peaceful adjustment to the economic environment. This pressure for modernization is translated down to the level of the factories, where participation (codetermination) does not incur counterproductive frictions but leads to a negotiated support for corporate progress. Finally, international coordination (on the EEC level) facilitates industrial adjustment by extending the time available for the transition; but it does not eliminate the pressure for modernization. Hence a complex of institutions is needed to prepare the ground for the development of corporatist decision-making arrangements in the steel arena and to allow them to function effectively to mediate consensus and competence.

Enthusiasts should therefore realize that it may not be possible to import the West German model of corporatism. They should also be aware that West Germany's experience with the industrial decline and the rationalization of industries other than steel shows that for coping with economic progress corporatism is neither absolutely necessary nor is it sufficient in every case.

CHAPTER NINE

Competitiveness and the Impact of Change: Applications of "High Technologies"

GERD JUNNE

Hardly anybody would contest West Germany's strong international position in machine tools and traditional engineering, but doubts do arise about its future competitiveness in "high-tech" industries. West Germany "continues to make the best nineteenth-century products on earth," according to Bruce Nussbaum, "but it cannot compete when it comes to high technology—robots, telecommunications, 'bug' factories, computers, semiconductors, consumer electronics."[1]

If West Germany were to lag behind in the field of high technology, the overall competitiveness of the West German economy would be significantly affected. The development and application of the new technologies is probably decisive for West Germany's future position in world markets, not only because of the economic growth they represent but because their application informs innovations in *all* sectors of the economy and thus determines the range, price, and quality of practically all products that will come to the market in the future.

To evaluate international competitiveness in the field of high technology, a suitable yardstick is necessary. Many international comparisons of competitiveness in this field are biased because they use measures derived from a specific trajectory of industrial development. Henry Ergas recently distinguished three groups of countries that are characterized either by a different emphasis on the *development* or by the *diffusion* of new technologies.[2] Measures that adequately evaluate the performance

1. Bruce Nussbaum, *The World after Oil: The Shifting Axis of Power and Wealth* (New York: Simon & Schuster, 1983), pp. 83–84.
2. Henry Ergas, *Does Technology Policy Matter?* CEPS Papers no. 29 (Brussels: Centre for European Policy Studies, 1986).

of one group of countries are not necessarily suitable to judge the performance of another. Analyses based on criteria that apply to "mission-oriented" countries such as the United States systematically underestimate the competitiveness of "diffusion-oriented" countries such as West Germany.

DIFFERENT CONCEPTS OF INTERNATIONAL COMPETITIVENESS

The product-life-cycle theory still underlies much of industrial policy thinking in OECD countries. According to this theory, new products originate in the most developed societies and regions and diffuse to other regions as they approach maturity. To retain their lead over other countries (especially the newly industrializing countries), the developed countries have to invest increasing amounts in the creation of new products and new technologies. From this theory, as Charles Sabel et al. observe, "it is an easy step . . . to the assertion that whole industries or even sectors of the economy rise and fall according to an analogous logic."[3] International competitiveness, from this perspective, is defined by a country's participation in a large share of activities in the new industries and sectors. It may be achieved by mission-oriented strategies in conjunction with public policy that encourages development of technological capabilities in technical fields considered of primary national importance.[4]

An alternative view rejects division of an economy into rising and declining sectors in favor of understanding economic development as a sequence of core technologies that get transmitted across sectors.[5] More important for the international competitiveness of a country than its share of new sectors in production and exports would, from this perspective, be its ability continually to generate new technologies and to diffuse and apply them in virtually all sectors of the economy.

Different strategies of adaptation to technological change correspond to the two approaches outlined above: *shifting* and *deepening*. Shifting "involves the transfer of resources from old to new uses—e.g., from mature industries to emerging ones"; deepening "involves increasing the productivity of resources in their existing uses."[6] The two strategies are aptly illustrated by Sabel et al., who compare industrial development

3. Charles F. Sabel et al., *Regional Prosperities Compared: Massachusetts and Baden-Württemberg in the 1980s, Discussion Paper* IIM/LMP 87-10b (Berlin: Wissenschaftszentrum, 1987), p. 5.

4. Ergas, *Does Technology Policy Matter?* p. 4.

5. See Rob van Tulder and Gerd Junne, *European Multinationals in Core Technologies* (Chichester: Wiley, 1988).

6. Ergas, *Does Technology Policy Matter?* p. 7.

and policies in two prosperous areas that command much attention in their respective countries: Massachusetts in the United States and Baden-Württemberg in West Germany:

> Massachusetts makes its fortune today primarily in sophisticated financial services—insurance, investment banking, brokerage—and what is loosely called high tech—principally minicomputers as well as semi-conductors, test equipment and the myriad products which complement or incorporate them. Industries such as machine and cutting tools, textile machines, shoes and textiles—the traditional sources of the state's wealth, and in which Massachusetts was long a world leader—are rapidly declining or already extinct. In Baden-Württemberg the situation is reversed. . . . The state's prosperity depends instead on its flourishing machine-tool, special machine, automobile and automotive-parts industries.[7]

These prosaic industries in Baden-Württemberg have become high-tech industries by applying the latest electronic components to traditional products and new production processes. Ergas points out that "the key problem for technology policies . . . is not that of generating new ideas, but rather of facilitating their widespread use. . . . In this sense, it is less important whether a country's firms operate in activities classed as 'high-tech,' 'mid-tech' or 'low-tech' than how effective they are in applying technological skills across the full range of their activities."[8]

Whereas Massachusetts (and the United States in general) can be considered a paradigmatic case of shifting, Baden-Württemberg (and West Germany in general) is "a paradigmatic case of deepening." In the United States, the factors of production are highly mobile, and "competition between firms on the open market for mobile technical and managerial skills and financial assets" is intense. "The ease with which these resources can be bid out of existing uses is such as to discourage those productivity-enhancing investments in skills and capabilities which, being specific to a particular firm or activity, can only be justified through longer-term commitments."[9] Because new firms are set up to explore new fields of activity, new sectors can easily be identified. The share of new sectors, the number of new firms, and the strength of venture

---

7. Sabel et al., *Regional Prosperities Compared*, p. 2. The analysis "illuminates the rise— but also the vulnerability—of high-tech and financial firms in Massachusetts, as well as the more robust, though almost invisible, growth of these sectors in Baden-Württemberg." In spite of this slow growth of the specific high-tech sectors, the authors conclude that "although Baden-Württemberg is currently imitating Massachusetts in matters of economic policy, both would be better off if they pursued the clues to success provided by the extraordinary vitality of the West German state's apparently prosaic industries" (ibid., p. 4).

8. Ergas, *Does Technology Policy Matter?* p. 4.

9. Ibid., p. 7.

capital to finance these new firms can be valid indicators of a shift to new areas.

The same measures, however, would underestimate the competitive strength of diffusion-oriented countries that "have put less emphasis on developing entirely new, cutting-edge technologies, than on promoting the widespread dissemination of technological capabilities throughout industry."[10] Innovation in such countries mainly takes place within existing firms, and the size of identifiable new sectors is therefore less important. Since comparatively few new firms are set up, the need for (and role of) venture capital is much less significant.

West German companies, on the average, do not spend less on research and development than American companies. But since they are often more diversified (especially in the chemical and electronics industries), they have to spread their funds over larger areas. Progress is made in many fields, implying that resources are not concentrated on a few high-tech fields. Therefore, spectacular new inventions occur less often, although the general rate of innovation is high: the per capita number of patents registered abroad of German firms is twice as high as in Japan and three times as high as in the United States.[11] West Germany still holds second place (behind the United States) in the absolute number of patents registered abroad, but the country's share in international key patents (registered at least fifteen times internationally) is somewhat lower than its share in all patents.[12] Though not usually forerunners in new (and consequently risky) fields, West German companies in general are fast to make use of foreign inventions and to incorporate new features into their own systems.

More important to the overall competitiveness of the West German economy than its actual trade position in microelectronics, telecommunications, or biotechnology is the ability of West German firms to apply and diffuse these technologies throughout the economy. It is the cross-cutting nature of these new technologies that makes them core technologies for most sectors of the economy.[13]

Many studies of West Germany's international competitiveness in

10. Ibid., p. 5. "Relations between firms, between firms and their employees, and between firms and the financial system have traditionally involved long-term commitments which favour investments in activity-specific capabilities. At the same time, high levels of education, industrial standardization, and cooperative research provide powerful mechanisms for diffusing capabilities throughout the industry, so that progress is made across a broad front" (p. 7).

11. W. Gerstenberger, "Entwicklung der Wettbewerbsfähigkeit der deutschen Industrie," *ifo-Schnelldienst* 41 (7 March 1988): 3–16.

12. Bernhard Gahlen, Fritz Rahmeyer, and Manfred Stadler, *Zur internationalen Wettbewerbsfähigkeit der deutschen Wirtschaft, Discussion Paper* IIM/IP 85-19 (Berlin: Wissenschaftszentrum, 1985), p. 32.

13. See Tulder and Junne, *European Multinationals in Core Technologies.*

high-technology sectors appear somewhat misleading because they fail to view the development and application of new technologies within the context of the total social and industrial fabric of society. A number of studies by international organizations and by national West German research institutes in the early 1980s have shown an alarming decline in West Germany's international trade position in high-tech industries.[14] All identified specific products or sectors as high-tech sectors and then analyzed recent changes in international market shares with regard to these products.[15]

These studies tend to overlook the important fact that the application of new technologies characteristically pervades almost all sectors of the economy.[16] The international position of a society in which this diffusion is well organized would be underestimated by any selection of specific high-tech sectors. A comparison of different studies of international competitiveness in high-technology fields reveals that studies with a broader definition of high technology usually show a better result for West Germany.[17]

In an unpublished study from 1983, the OECD analyzed the development of market shares between 1963 and 1980 for product groups for which research and development expenditures in the United States had been above average. Insofar as other countries show a different pattern of expenditures, such an analysis can only lead to biased results.[18]

A study of sectors and large product groups also lumps together products with very different technological levels. To define advances and backlogs in international technological and commercial competitiveness for product groups would require a level of disaggregation which existing product classifications do not reach. In specific types of laser equipment, for example, West Germany is very advanced, but not in other types.[19] Even undisputed high-tech industries like the com-

14. See survey in "Hochtechnologien und internationale Wettbewerbsfähigkeit der deutschen Wirtschaft," *BMWi Dokumentation*, no. 263 (Bonn: Bundesministerium für Wirtschaft, 1984).

15. See the critical comments on the use of such an indicator in Gahlen, Rahmeyer, and Stadler, *Zur internationalen Wettbewerbsfähigkeit der deutschen Wirtschaft*, pp. 30–32.

16. Helmar Krupp of the Fraunhofer-Institut für Systemtechnik und Innovationsforschung speaks in this context of "Querdiffusion"; see the summary of the contributions to the working group on "Strukturwandel, Forschung und Innovation" during the BDI workshop, *Perspektiven der industriellen Entwicklung in der Bundesrepublik Deutschland*, BDI-Drucksache no. 206 (Cologne: Bundesverband der Deutschen Industrie e.V., 1987), p. 101.

17. See the summaries of the studies of the OECD, the HWWA, and the Bundesbank on one hand and of the study of the Institut für Weltwirtschaft, Kiel, on the other in *BMWi Dokumentation*, no. 263, pp. 10–19, and Gahlen, Rahmeyer, and Stadler, *Zur internationalen Wettbewerbsfähigkeit der deutschen Wirtschaft*.

18. *BMWi Dokumentation*, no. 263, p. 18.

19. Thomas F. O'Boyle, "German Technology Gains on U.S., Japan. Laser Maker's Success Exemplifies the Progress," *Wall Street Journal*, 15 December 1986, p. 32; Bundes-

puter industry contain many standardized products with little high-tech content (for example, disk drives). It is not without reason that the electronics industry has transferred a large part of production to low-wage newly industrializing countries. The Ifo-Institut consequently defined as high tech those items in whose production newly industrializing and developing countries still have a low market share. The results of the Ifo-Institut's study are much more positive for West Germany than are those of the OECD study. The indicator used, however, is also somewhat biased because the market shares taken as an indicator are probably highly influenced by intracompany trade that tells little about "revealed comparative advantage."[20]

A study concentrating on sectors would disregard other product groups that may contain a large share of (sometimes imported) high-tech intermediate inputs. Such a category is especially important for West Germany, where tailor-made systems rather than standardized components account for a large share of exports. A comparison of market shares for a selection of high-tech components would underestimate the impact of the know-how needed to incorporate these elements into industrial systems on a country's international competitiveness.

Such an argument could be countered by pointing out that West Germany, even as a user of high-tech components, has fallen considerably behind the United States and Japan in its per capita consumption of semiconductors. It is questionable, however, how revealing such a trend is. Different consumer preferences for gadgetry do not say very much about international competitiveness. But the different consumption levels do not stem only from consumer electronics. Even for professional applications, however, they may not necessarily indicate differences in competitiveness. Overinvestment in competing telecommunications systems (responsible for a large share of U.S. consumption of semiconductors), rather than providing the United States with an important competitive advantage, may have siphoned away scarce investment capital in a period when that country's share of investment in GNP is already lagging behind in comparison not only to Japan but also to the Federal Republic.

Several studies suggest a decline of West German competitiveness by comparing figures for the early 1960s or 1970s with figures for the early 1980s. A more detailed year-to-year analysis, however, would reveal that the drop in West German market shares is a result of changes in 1981–

---

verband der Deutschen Industrie e.V., *Perspektiven der industriellen Entwicklung in der Bundesrepublik Deutschland*, pp. 95–97; *highTech* 1 (March–April 1987): 23–27; "Laserontwikkelingen in de Bondsrepubliek," *Technieuws/Bonn* (Den Haag: Ministerie van Economische Zaken, 1985).

20. *BMWi Dokumentation*, no. 263, pp. 14, 18.

82 and did not occur in previous years. A large part of the decline in market shares in these years can be explained by the 20 percent devaluation of the deutschemark against the U.S. dollar, in which market shares were measured.[21] These changes in market shares thus do not reflect any real changes in international trade flows.

Looking only at the most recent statistics or at the latest generation of products is as bad for the analyst of international competitiveness as the overfascination with last quarter's profits or losses is for the financial analyst. The example of Siemens's position in international telecommunications illustrates the fallacies of such a myopic approach. When Siemens brought its sophisticated electromechanical public exchange system to the market in the late 1970s, at a time when many competitors were already developing fully digital exchange equipment, many observers of the telecommunications industry agreed that Siemens would cease to be a serious competitor in that field. A few years later, however, Siemens marketed its own fully digital switching equipment, and today nobody doubts that it is one of the three strongest European firms in the field. This example should warn us not to look only at the latest generation of products when assessing international competitiveness. The factors underlying the capability of a company (or country) to produce and market highly sophisticated equipment at competitive speeds and prices are most important.

THE POWER STRUGGLE OVER FLEXIBLE SPECIALIZATION

The new technologies provide us with a myriad of new products, but they are first and foremost process technologies. Their application ensures the competitiveness of practically all branches of the economy. Their introduction into the production process, however, is the result of power struggles inside the factories because it alters relations between capital and labor and between different groups of employees. Existing structures may either ease or hinder the introduction of new process technologies and are thus of great importance for international competitiveness.

The qualification of the German work force and its impact on the introduction of new production processes is one such structure. Mass production has never been the norm in West Germany to the degree that it has been in the United States[22] (and Japan). This is true not only

21. Ibid., pp. 15, 17.
22. Even in the United States, mass production is not as widespread as one might think. About 90 percent, or one hundred thousand, of the companies in the United States that make parts for other companies are batch producers (*New Scientist,* 4 September 1986,

for the machine tools industry (see Herrigel's chapter in this volume) but also for other industries. As a consequence, Germany's factory work force shows a much stronger element of craftsmanship (see the chapter by Kern and Schumann). This is also a result of the basic education that apprentices get in addition to their on-the-job training. Recent research has shown that areas in which pre-Fordist forms of production (with a less developed division of labor among workers) continue to exist to some degree are better able to adapt to and profit from the present trend toward flexible specialization and automation.[23] Baden-Württemberg seems to be a case in point.

The high qualifications of the West German core work force implies that its workers can derive more benefits from the introduction of new technologies than can workers in other countries. For example, in West Germany workers normally program numerically controlled machinery, whereas in Great Britain such a task is normally done by extra departments and away from the work floor.[24] The result is that the introduction of new technologies does not meet the resistance from the work floor in German factories that it does in many factories elsewhere because the core work force is able (and willing) to run any new machines.

The impact of the struggle for shorter workweeks on automation is another factor that affects the introduction of new process technologies. To some degree, the large number of unemployed in West Germany, despite resumed economic growth, is a reflection of successful automation. Though not opposed to the introduction of new technologies per se, the trade unions reject this implication of increasing automation, even though they are dominated by a highly qualified core work force that is not, by and large, threatened by such a development. A reduction of the workweek, therefore, to spread the remaining work more evenly over more workers, has become a top priority for the unions. With their demand for a thirty-five-hour workweek, West Germany's trade unions are the front-runners in the struggle to shorten working time in industrial countries.

Employers have argued that a shorter workweek, especially without a concomitant wage reduction, would threaten the international competitiveness of West German industry. Because investment in automation

cited in Annemieke Roobeek and Michiel Roscam Abbing, "The International Implications of Computer Integrated Manufacturing," *International Journal of Computer Integrated Manufacturing* 1, no. 1 [1987]: 10).

23. Michael J. Piore and Charles F. Sabel, *The Second Industrial Divide: Possibilities for Prosperity* (New York: Basic Books, 1984); Michael Schumann and Horst Kern, *Das Ende der Arbeitsteilung: Rationalisierung in der industriellen Produktion* (Munich: Beck, 1984).

24. See Arndt Sorge and Malcolm Warner, *Comparative Factory Organisation: An Anglo-German Comparison of Manufacturing, Management and Manpower* (Aldershot: Gower, 1986).

devices is very expensive, companies need to use the equipment as intensively as possible to earn their investment back. Shorter working hours, therefore, seem to contradict the economics of introducing new technologies.

One can also argue that the reduction of working hours could be the precondition for full use of the new automation equipment: the shorter the working hours, the more important multishift work becomes and the more willing and flexible workers become to work at irregular times. Many companies, BASF and Siemens, for example, have concluded special arrangements with trade unions to reduce the workweek in exchange for their consent to multishift work. At Siemens alone, new work schedules have been tried in 114 different factories, including work on Saturday. Already every fifth worker in Germany, or almost five million workers (twice as many as in the mid-1960s), works more or less regularly on Saturday and Sunday.[25] Shorter working hours and more continuous machine use may complement rather than contradict each other.

The impact of new technologies on codetermination (*Mitbestimmung*) is a third factor influencing power relations between capital and labor, and hence their success. Although the qualified worker's individual job situation (and job satisfaction) may not deteriorate as a result of the introduction of flexible automation, the collective right to codetermination may be undermined by the new production processes and the organizational forms connected to them. The undermining of codetermination rights can take many forms, for example, increasing use of formally independent subcontractors for parts of production (undermining codetermination in both the supplying and the receiving firms); increasing part-time work (which can reduce the interest of workers in exercising their rights); a reduction of personal contacts and interaction on the work floor; increasing use of "home workers"; shift of plants and administrative centers to new sites outside centers with a high degree of union organization; centralization of control and on-line monitoring of increasingly dispersed activities; and concentration of responsibility for the introduction of new process technologies in specialized departments with limited access for trade unions.

Many of these practices do not (yet) play a significant role in West Germany, but further reduction of the content of codetermination would make trade unions less attractive and could lead to a lower degree of organization, which in turn might weaken codetermination. Because the

25. See *Fortune*, 14 May 1984, p. 136; *Der Spiegel* 41, no. 20 (11 May 1987): 76, 87. Some groups and even total departments work six days a week for three weeks but are free during the fourth week.

relatively cooperative attitude of West German trade unions is linked to codetermination,[26] any (further) undermining of this basis might lead to more confrontation between workers and employers.

Finally, because the new technologies pose a limited threat to middle management in West German companies, this group creates fewer obstacles to their introduction than in other countries. New concepts of logistics, coordination, and control connected to the new production technologies have a profound effect on the power relations inside firms. Both the worker at the shop floor and all ranks of middle management are profoundly affected by these changes. Next to unskilled workers, middle managers in most countries are the category of employees most likely to be seriously hit by the introduction of new technologies. But management structures differ from country to country. The peculiar characteristics of its intracompany hierarchies may provide West German industry with a considerable advantage vis-à-vis the introduction of new technologies.

Many middle managers see their jobs or their status symbols as threatened by the new technologies.[27] They can therefore be an important source of opposition to the switch to new technologies and procedures.[28] Although much less vocal and visible, the "silent opposition" (read: lack of enthusiasm) of middle management in many cases is a more important obstacle to the automation of production and services than outright resistance from the work floor. But while an average French (or American) company has about six or seven layers of middle management between the shop floor and top management, an average German company has only three or four. There are thus not so many people in a position to slow down the process of automation.

At the intracompany level, therefore, the introduction of new production technology in West Germany meets specific conditions—a highly qualified work force, a relatively short workweek as a precondition for flexible working hours, a less threatened middle management—that do not stand in the way of the diffusion of new production technology but, rather, may be conducive to it.

26. See Udo Rehfeldt, "Stratégies syndicales et négociations collectives sur les nouvelles technologies en RFA 1967–1987," paper presented at the concluding forum discussion of the international seminar "Automatisation Programmable et Conditions d'Usage du Travail," Paris, Groupement d'Intéret Public "Mutations Industrielles," 15 May 1987.

27. See Tulder and Junne, *European Multinationals in Core Technologies*, pp. 152, 153; Harley Shaiken, *Work Transformed: Automation and Labor in the Computer Age* (New York: Holt, Rinehart & Winston, 1985), pp. 231–34, 293.

28. For example, the difficulties that General Motors faces in its restructuring strategies because of the "frozen middle," the "tens of thousands of managers, made complacent by GM's past glories, [that] have not been able to see the need for scrapping old ways and responding to new challenges" (*Fortune*, 10 November 1986, p. 40).

THE ATTITUDES OF NEW SOCIAL MOVEMENTS
TOWARD THE NEW TECHNOLOGIES

The trade unions appear weakened by the application of new technologies, but technological developments have contributed to the growth of new social movements, which are particularly strong in West Germany and are known to be highly critical of the new technologies. They are often described as being hostile toward technology in general.[29] Their increasing political influence could undermine the international competitiveness of West Germany's high-tech industries.

To what extent is that loss of competitiveness a likely possibility? The influence of social movements on policy making is not necessarily direct; often it is mitigated through the absorption of their demands by the ruling parties. These parties want to neutralize opposition by accommodating at least in their rhetoric some of the highly popular demands. The Green movement unequivocally opposes nuclear energy and traditional chemical large-scale (and waste) production. The attitude of the Greens toward microelectronics and biotechnology is much more ambivalent. Their strong opposition to nuclear energy and the traditional chemical industry, however, could eventually lead to support for certain developments in the fields of microelectronics and biotechnology not so much because such support would become part of the Greens' political program but because their opposition forces the other parties to come up with programs that favor technologies which economize on energy (microelectronics, biotechnology), help to monitor pollution (microelectronics), and contribute to alternative energy sources (biotechnology).

Public attitudes toward what used to be considered the new technologies (nuclear energy, petrochemistry) have strongly influenced the acceptance of the "new" new technologies like microelectronics and biotechnology[30] and may have helped ease the antagonism that, until Chernobyl and several accidents in chemical factories in Germany and Switzerland, has characterized relations between old and new social movements. But there is still a wide gap between the position of the trade unions, which favor the rapid introduction of new technologies to increase West Germany's international competitiveness as long as negative side effects for employment and security at work are avoided,[31] and

29. See Nussbaum, *The World after Oil*; see also Dieter Jaufmann and Ernst Kistler, *Sind die Deutschen technikfeindlich? Erkenntnis oder Vorurteil* (Leverkusen: Leske & Budrich, 1987).

30. See Dieter Fuchs, "Die Akzeptanz moderner Technik in der Bevölkerung. Eine Sekundäranalyse von Umfragedaten," in Klaus Lompe, ed., *Techniktheorie—Technikforschung—Technikgestaltung* (Opladen: Westdeutscher Verlag, 1987), pp. 183–232.

31. A good survey of trade union positions with regard to new technologies is given in the documentation on the technology policy conference organized by the DGB in 1985:

the various positions in the new social movements, which are critical of the new technologies, although they would accept their application for specific purposes.

Some fundamentalists oppose almost all new (and many existing) technologies because they expect them to contribute to an exaggerated division of labor and thus to increasing alienation. Others show reservations more directly linked to *specific* new technologies. They protest the "digitalization of life" and the restrictions on human thinking (and feeling) as humans become attached to a computer and become almost an extension of it. Or they oppose genetic engineering because they equate biotechnology with a lack of respect for nature, or because they fear the manipulation of human genes and environmental pollution by an uncontrolled release of microorganisms.[32]

Microelectronics and biotechnology, however, open up possibilities for more decentralized and less polluting forms of production and are thus very attractive to at least some of the movements. The political constituency of the new social movements comes from the middle classes and professionals[33] who also make up a large group of consumers of the new microelectronic gadgets. This group views a word processor more as an extension of creative potential than as a threat of alienation. Although they fear the misuse of the new technologies, they would not resist the further development of microelectronics.

The new social movements are, of course, broader than the Green party. But a party has to come up with a coherent program, something that social movements almost by definition lack. The Green party opposes all applications of genetic engineering and demands that industrial and industry-financed use of genetic engineering methods in research and production be forbidden and that the public support of such research be stopped immediately.[34] The party's position on information technology is somewhat less harsh. The Greens support resistance to the

Siegfried Bleicher, ed., *Technik für den Menschen. Soziale Gestaltung des technischen Wandels. Eine Dokumentation* (Cologne: Bund Verlag, 1987).

32. The position of the Greens with regard to biotechnology has been put down in the "Erklärung zur Gentechnologie und zur Fortpflanzungs- und Gentechnik am Menschen," accepted at the Eighth Federal Assembly of the Greens on 15–16 February 1986. It is also explained in the dissenting vote to the report of the special enquete commission of the German parliament; see "Sondervotum von Abg. Frau Heidemarie Dann (DIE GRÜNEN) und der Fraktion Die GRÜNEN zum Bericht der Enquete-Kommission 'Chancen und Risiken der Gentechnologie,'" in Wolf-Michael Catenhusen and Hanna Neumeister, eds., *Chancen und Risiken der Gentechnologie*, Dokumentation des Berichts an den Deutschen Bundestag (Munich: J. Schweitzer Verlag, 1987), pp. 315–57. In addition, the parliamentary group of the Greens has issued numerous press releases on different aspects of the issue.

33. See Hanspeter Kriesi, "Neue soziale Bewegungen: Auf der Suche nach ihrem gemeinsamen Nenner," *Politische Vierteljahresschrift* 28, no. 3 (1987): 315–34.

34. *Farbe bekennen. Programm der Grünen für die Bundestagswahl 1987* (Bonn, 1986), p. 41.

application of new information and communication technologies, especially to control employees. They oppose the digitalization of the telephone network and the introduction of an integrated services data network, broadband communication, and cable and satellite television. They do not see many alternative uses for new information and communication technologies but favor their use to monitor and reduce pollution.[35]

This mixed attitude toward high technology may have an unintended effect. The opposition of the new movements to specific applications of new technologies ironically strengthens public acceptance of the principle that the state should intervene in the development of new technologies in a selective way (and not just with generic measures).[36] Currently only this principle out of the Greens' entire agenda receives broad-based support. In this way, the opposition of the Greens to specific applications of new technologies may be transformed in the political process into ideological support for programs to develop specific technologies.

This process of the transformation of demands can also be observed in the protests against nuclear power installations and the pollution caused by the chemical industry. The widely backed demands to find alternatives for nuclear energy[37] and to stop pollution from large-scale chemical production has to some degree been taken over by the established political parties.[38] It has become official policy that to reduce energy consumption and thus eventually to make nuclear power unnecessary, microelectronics has to be pushed (in other words, subsidized) to make production processes more efficient, avoid energy losses, and substitute the transport of information for the transport of persons and goods. Biotechnology will have to be developed to substitute increased production of fine chemicals by biotechnological fermentation processes for large-scale energy-intensive chemical production at high temperatures and under high pressure. Although the nuclear energy industry suffers

35. Ibid., p. 42.
36. About two-thirds of the respondents to representative polls in West Germany want the state to do more to monitor and control technology; see Fritz Gloede, "Vom Technikfeind zum gespaltenen Ich. Thesen zur Technikakzeptanz," in Lompe, ed., *Techniktheorie—Technikforschung—Technikgestaltung*, p. 237.
37. See Fuchs, "Die Akzeptanz moderner Technik in der Bevölkerung," pp. 194, 198; Thomas Peter, Peter Mann, and Georg Thurn, "Public Acceptance of New Technologies in the Federal Republic of Germany," in Roger Williams and Stephen Mills, eds., *Public Acceptance of New Technologies: An International Review* (London: Croom Helm, 1986), pp. 107–13.
38. Even Christian Democrats such as the prime minister of Baden-Württemberg, Lothar Späth, want to back out of nuclear energy; see "'Ich will raus aus der Kernenergie. . . .' Baden-Württembergs Ministerpräsident Lothar Späth sieht für die Atomenergie keine grosse Zukunft mehr," interview in *highTech* 2 (May 1988): 94–95.

from this trend, West German competitiveness in other high-tech areas has been boosted.[39]

Protests by the Greens against the pollution caused by large-scale production of chemicals has contributed (together with the rising competition from energy-rich countries in the Middle East) to a switch by these companies to "high-chem" products, a catchword introduced by Hoechst to describe its newest development strategy. The Bayer AG, which alternates with Dupont de Nemours as the world's largest chemical corporation (depending on the exchange rate between the U.S. dollar and the deutschemark), has followed a similar strategy in moving "away from traditional chemical markets into higher technology sectors," including biotechnology.[40] Protests against nuclear energy and chemical pollution have speeded up this switch and therefore may be said to have had a positive rather than a negative effect on West Germany's competitiveness in high-tech industries.

Although attitudes in the new social movements toward microelectronics and biotechnology are somewhat ambivalent, opposition to applications of these technologies that may be used to manipulate and control the population is clear-cut. The Greens are against the introduction of broadband telecommunciations that would make it possible to integrate every workplace and household into two-way telecommunication networks that transmit moving images, voices, and data at the same time.[41] And they strictly oppose manipulation of human genes, the use of gene analysis for control of workers, and such other applications of biotechnology as animal growth hormones to increase productivity or the deliberate release of bacteria under uncontrolled circumstances. Broadband telecommunications is much more important for the competitiveness of German industry than biotechnology because most interesting (and profitable) applications lie in fields (agriculture) other than those mentioned.

Siemens played an important role in formulating the standards for the Integrated Services Digital Network (ISDN), which will make it

---

39. The Deutsche Babcock AG, for example, has been an important power installation producer but now gets most of its sales from antipollution equipment. In an advertising campaign, the company explicitly refers to the "no future" pessimism in part of the new social movements and contrasts it with its own "pro future" program; see, for example, *VDI Nachrichten* 50 (11 December 1987): 17.

40. *Financial Times*, 13 March 1987, p. 15.

41. The arguments underlying the opposition are best elaborated in Barbara Mettler-Meibom, *Breitbandtechnologie. Über die Chancen sozialer Vernunft in technologiepolitischen Entscheidungsprozessen* (Opladen: Westdeutscher Verlag, 1986); Mettler-Meibom, *Soziale Kosten der Informationsgesellschaft. Überlegungen zu einer Kommunikationsökologie* (Frankfurt: Fischer, 1987); and in the "Optek"-report prepared by a group of scholars directed by Mettler-Meibom, see Peter Berger et al., *Optionen der Telekommunikation. Materialien für einen technologiepolitischen Bürgerdialog* (Hamburg, 1987).

possible to use the telephone network for the fast transmission of voices, texts, fixed images, and data. With the installation of optical fibers, the transmission of moving images will become possible as well. While many of its American competitors concentrated on more business-oriented Local Area Networks (LANs) and Value Added Networks (VANs), Siemens pushed ISDN with the idea that it would allow integration of private households into so-called management, information, and entertainment systems, thus creating a much larger demand for a variety of digital equipment and giving European industry a boost not only in professional but also in consumer electronics.[42]

Because the three established parties in West Germany support ISDN, the Greens can do little politically to block the introduction of the new telecommunications infrastructure.[43] But social movements can have an effect without directly influencing the political decision-making process. They can, for example, influence the behavior of consumers. The questions raised by the Greens may slow down the demand for new terminals and new services, thus reducing the relatively secure home market from which Siemens operates. The West German public has always been relatively conservative in adopting fancy new electronics equipment (perhaps because the spectrum of choices offered by the Bundespost and the equipment suppliers has always been somewhat limited).

The skepticism of West German consumers (to which the attitudes advocated by the Greens may contribute) toward the new electronics equipment has forced Siemens from the beginning to launch its ISDN systems internationally. Rather than hampering international competitiveness in this field, critical attitudes in West Germany toward broadband networks may contribute to Siemens's international orientation.

One of the main thrusts of the new social movements is their call for decentralization. They favor small, alternative enterprises that concentrate on socially useful products and practice new internal forms of organization and decision making. Thus they may support government programs whose aim is to develop innovative small enterprises. When open support for these programs does not exist, the activity of the new social movements contributes at least indirectly to establishing an atmosphere in which it becomes easier for government to favor small and

42. See Eli M. Noam, "The Political Economy of ISDN: European Network Integration vs. American System Fragmentation," paper presented at the Fourteenth Annual Telecommunications Policy Research Conference, Airlie, Virginia, April 1986; Frieder Schlupp and Gerd Junne, "Politiche statali e competizione internazionale," *Rivista Trimestrale di Scienza dell'Amministazione* 35 (1988): 91–111.

43. Frieder Schlupp, "Telekommunikationssektor und Telekommunikation: Die Bundesrepublik Deutschland in der internationalen 'Innovations'-Konkurrenz," in *Staatliche Modernisierungspolitik gegenüber dem industriellen Wirtschaftssektor*, Dossier für das Programm FAST II der EG-Kommission, erstellt von der AG Industriepolitik der Deutschen Vereinigung für Politische Wissenschaft (Göttingen, 1986).

medium-sized enterprises. The Greens' support for "alternative corporations" (*Alternativbetriebe*) and their opposition to large multinational companies contributes to the general acceptance of public programs that aim at a different category of companies. Small and medium-sized enterprises, according to German industrial statistics, can be rather large enterprises with up to 1,000 employees. (The same label in Dutch statistics, by comparison, is reserved for companies with up to 250 employees.) The Greens' belief that "small is beautiful" thus helps to create a political environment in which a category of companies which has always been crucial for Germany's strong world market position gets special attention. The very sector for which German industry is best known internationally—machine building—still consists largely of small and medium-sized companies (see Herrigel's chapter in this volume).

West Germany is one of the few countries in which subsidies to small and medium-sized companies have been relatively effective. The social and political structure of West Germany makes it possible to channel a much larger share of public funds to small and medium-sized enterprises than can be done by other countries (with the exception of Sweden and Switzerland).[44] This implies that the gap between the development of large and small companies is smaller in Germany than elsewhere. Out of the many programs for small and medium-sized companies, one deserves special attention because it may have a tremendous impact on the international competitiveness of West German machine-building companies. This is the Computer Aided Design (CAD) program of the Ministry for Research and Technology (BMFT). The BMFT expects that the percentage of machine-building companies that use CAD technology will rise during the program period from about 4 percent to 63 percent.[45] Because the introduction of CAD opens the way to "intersphere" automation,[46] it may have a far-reaching effect on the automation of these companies and their ability to keep up with their larger competitors.

THE POLITICIZATION OF INTERNATIONAL ECONOMIC RELATIONS AND COMPETITIVENESS IN HIGH-TECH SECTORS

West Germany's economy is much more export-oriented than the economies of the United States or Japan, leading one to expect that the

44. Tulder and Junne, *European Multinationals in Core Technologies*, pp. 183–84.

45. Lecture at the BMFT on BMFT-activities for foreign participants in the DGB technology congress, 12–14 September 1985; see also *Bundesbericht Forschung 1988* (Bonn: Bundesministerium für Forschung und Technologie, 1988), pp. 45, 155–58.

46. "Intersphere automation" (computer-integrated manufacturing, CIM) will link the different spheres of design, manufacturing, and coordination and control (inventories,

politicization of international economic relations would hit West Germany harder than her main competitors. Yet a number of factors seem to buffer West Germany against at least some of the political turmoil in international economic relations. First, compared to its competitors, West Germany exports many more tailor-made products and thus can escape the creeping protectionism that hits more standardized products. Second, to a large extent (84 percent) German exports go to the developed countries and are therefore less affected by the foreign exchange problems that have caused many developing countries to reduce their imports. Third, West German exports are much more evenly distributed over a large number of product categories than are the exports of either Japan or the United States. It may, therefore, even be an advantage not to have a strong position such as the Japanese electronics industry has, which makes its overwhelming presence very visible and vulnerable. Finally, in international trade conflicts, West Germany can to some extent hide behind the EEC, which is responsible for trade policy and again makes West Germany less visible. Since there are member states in the EEC that take a more interventionist attitude than does West Germany, other countries (such as the United States) tend to single out product categories for their countermeasures which would affect these more recalcitrant members rather than West Germany.

To evaluate the effect of the politicization of international economic relations, I shall examine West Germany's competitiveness in three areas.

Changing Oil Prices and Biotechnology

The Federal Republic was one of the first countries to target biotechnology as a technology of central importance for the future. Already in 1971, the science ministry had begun funding biotechnology projects— even before the breakthrough in DNA recombination in 1973. This was at a time when the newly formed SPD/F.D.P. coalition was trying to demonstrate how technological development could be guided by public subsidies. At that time one of the issues commanding public attention was the threat of a worldwide food shortage, especially the lack of protein in food consumed in developing countries. One of the first biotechnology projects funded by the federal government, consequently, was the collaboration between Hoechst and two smaller companies to develop a process for producing single-cell protein (SCP) based on petroleum

---

marketing, financial control, wage payment, production schedules, and so on) into one single system with a common data base which is built up already in the design phase if CAD equipment is used. See Raphael Kaplinsky, *Automation: The Technology and Society* (Harlow: Longman, 1984).

GERD JUNNE

derivatives. "In level of support the SCP Project remains one of the largest public-private undertakings in German biotechnology. Ten million DM were committed to the project in the first two years alone."[47]

When oil prices began to rise in late 1973, however, the process developed by Hoechst and its subsidiary Uhde became unprofitable. Large-scale commercial production of SCP would be viable only "in areas where low-cost energy sources and waste-substrates are available and conventional feedstuff proteins, such as soybean or fish meal, are in short supply."[48] This had a double negative impact on the attitude of major West German firms with regard to biotechnology: first, biotechnology became associated with a clear-cut failure, and second, companies were forced to take a close look at the commercial side of potential endeavors and were safeguarded against becoming overly fascinated with the technological feasibility of biotechnology projects. Both aspects may have contributed to the somewhat hesitant attitude among West German firms toward modern biotechnology shown in the late 1970s.[49]

Rising oil prices did stimulate the activities of some companies. The German chemical companies have been able to capitalize on the development of large-scale fermentation technology during periods when the country was cut off from major sources of petroleum imports. Along with a highly developed fermentation technology, chemical machine-building companies founded DECHEMA (the German Chemical Plant Trade Association), an organization that played a crucial role in the early identification of biotechnology as a priority area for industrial policy. Rising oil prices gave chemical companies the chance to make use of know-how acquired in the past and to look for solutions in a direction well known from past experience.

High oil prices gave a boost to fermentation technology because this was a field in which West German companies were strong and because historical development had given rise to institutions such as DECHEMA inclined to meet the energy crisis with instruments at their own disposal, namely machine building (rather than genetic engineering). The rise of oil prices, which coincided with the breakthrough in DNA recombination, thus led West Germany to answer the challenge with second-generation biotechnology (fermentation and enzyme technology) in-

47. Sheila Jasanoff, "Technological Innovation in a Corporatist State: The Case of Biotechnology in the Federal Republic of Germany," *Research Policy* 14 (1985): 30.
48. Ibid.
49. The attitude of the large West German companies in question was not more reluctant than that of the large American companies (direct communication by Klaus Weissermel, member of the board of Hoechst, 27 August 1984). The large American companies, too, according to David Jackson, Du Pont's chief of biotechnology research, "are probably three to five years behind, because they didn't get started as soon, and they go slower" than the small start-up firms (*Fortune*, 6 July 1987, p. 49).

stead of third-generation biotechnology (genetic engineering). A very large share of public support went (and still goes) to bioprocess technology (bioreactors and enzyme technology). This share is certainly underrepresented in the statistics of the BMFT because large expenditures under headings with more political appeal such as "food supply" and "reduction of pollution" go into bioprocess engineering as well.

Margaret Sharp comes to the conclusion that the crucial role which DECHEMA has played in the development of West German biotechnology ("it provided the initial stimulus to interest in biotechnology, wrote the first major report on the subject for the BMFT . . . and has since remained the focal point for the German 'biotechnology lobby'") finally has had a negative impact: "While the role of DECHEMA has been crucial, it could be argued that its prime interests (in enzyme technology and bioreactors—it is after all a chemical plant association), combined with the political pressure of the environmentalists, led biotechnology in Germany into something of a blind alley. Like the Japanese, in the 1970s West Germany was bypassed by developments in genetic engineering."[50]

As a result of research efforts begun in the 1970s, in the early 1980s, when oil prices began to fall again, West Germany had a well-developed fermentation technology for large-scale applications. This is certainly a valuable asset in the long run. But with oil prices down again, there has been little incentive to apply the fermentation production methods to large-scale chemicals production. The usefulness of biotechnology remains more or less confined to low-volume, high value-added products (pharmaceuticals), those for which the availability of a specific substance is more important than are differences in production costs. In this area West German companies seem to lag behind their American competitors.

The volatility of oil prices thus has had a negative effect on West German competitiveness in biotechnology. In the long run, however, West German companies may reap benefits from their earlier emphasis on production technology rather than fancy new products. They may not be the first to bring the new substances to the market, but they will be able to produce these substances at a cheaper price than many of their competitors.[51] This will give them considerable leverage in the future,

50. Margaret Sharp, *The New Biotechnology: European Governments in Search of a Strategy,* Sussex European Paper no. 15 (Brighton: University of Sussex, Science Policy Research Unit, 1985), p. 64.

51. Hoechst, for example, will be later than Eli Lilly to bring a human insulin to the market that has been produced making use of genetic engineering, and its production capacity will be less than that of Novo Industries (Denmark). But Hoechst expects that its productivity advantages (and the development of new sorts of insulin) will compensate for that; see Ursula Ammon et al., "Auswirkungen gentechnischer Verfahren und Pro-

especially as the new production technologies are applied more and more to the large-scale production of less costly substances and if the technologies developed earlier keep their value. But the shelf life of technologies is not unlimited, and many new technologies may have become available elsewhere at the moment that cost advantages in production will become an important determinant of international competitiveness in biotechnology industries.

Barriers against Technology Transfers

An important dimension of the politicization of international economic relations includes barriers against technology transfers, especially against transfers from the United States to Western Europe. The conflict with the United States over the gas pipeline from Siberia to Western Europe brought the continuing dependency of Europe on American technology into the limelight. A considerable number of products or components in products for the pipeline fell under the American embargo.[52] Since the strength of West German companies on the world market often lies in their ability to deliver complete systems (rather than individual components), they depend to a considerable extent on American technology embodied in some of the components.

This dependency, however, should not be exaggerated. In some respects the American embargo has been a blessing to West German competitiveness. The argument that barriers to technology transfers from the United States to Western Europe would hamper West Germany's international competitiveness assumes that West Germany is lagging behind the United States. This is true only in selected areas. In many areas, West German technology is as advanced as that of American competitors, not only in more traditional fields (like steel and automobiles; see the chapters by Esser and Fach and Streeck), but also in high-tech areas like optical electronics. When the possibility of West German participation in the American "Star Wars" (SDI) project was discussed, a study by the federal Ministry of Defense revealed that West German industry has a good to very good position in five of the eleven technology fields that SDI requires and that it holds a top position in two fields (optical sensors and subsystems of space technology).[53]

American components are used in European (and West German)

---

dukte auf Produktionsstruktur, Arbeitsplätze und Qualifikationserfordernisse," Studie im Auftrag der Enquete-Kommission "Chancen und Risiken der Gentechnologie" des 10. Deutschen Bundestages, Sozialforschungsstelle Dortmund, Dortmund, April 1986, p. 25.

52. Claus Bockslaff, in *German Yearbook of International Law*, forthcoming.

53. *Die Strategische Verteidigungsinitiative* (Bonn: Presse- und Informationsamt der Bundesregierung, 26 June 1985), p. 14.

systems not necessarily because American producers have a specific technological advantage but often because their large numbers allow American producers to offer many standard devices at a relatively cheap price. Alternative components, which do exist in the world market, are more expensive. An export embargo in the United States thus could make West German products more expensive and cause some delay in delivery, but it would not prevent delivery altogether in most cases. West German competitiveness would not be undermined as long as competing firms have to struggle with similar problems as a result of having incorporated components that fall under the American embargo.

Another way the American embargo has indirectly benefited West German industry is that it has convinced many West German managers that they must not remain or become dependent on strategically crucial technology from outside suppliers.[54] Perhaps the most prominent example of a move taken primarily to guarantee future independence is the common project of Siemens with Philips to develop and produce megabit chips.

In the "biggest cooperative R&D effort on the Continent so far by two semiconductor firms," Siemens and Philips have embarked on a $1-billion-plus project. While Philips concentrates on one-Mbit static random-access memories for low-power consumer applications, Siemens will produce four-Mbit dynamic random-access memory chips for data-processing equipment. The project will lay the groundwork for the submicron, complex logic chips the two firms plan to produce in the 1990s.[55] Siemens delivered the first megachips in December 1987.[56]

Siemens and Philips acknowledge that they will not be the first to produce these chips. But they regard the ability to master the technology involved as absolutely essential for their future. It is less relevant to them that they will continue to lag behind the most advanced Japanese producers and probably also several American producers. To avoid becoming dependent on crucial components for the core of their business, they are insisting on undertaking this project despite its very high cost.

According to the plan of an expert working group initiated by the BMFT and chaired by a Siemens representative which recently presented a study called "Mikroelektronik 2000," West German firms will do more and more to reduce their dependency on imports of electronic components from the United States and Japan. By the year 2000, do-

---

54. See, for example, " 'Chip-Defizite sind wie Aids'. Chip-Broker Erich J. Lejeune über die deutsche Abhängigkeit von amerikanischen und japanischen Chipherstellern," *high-Tech* 2 (March 1988): 86–88.

55. *Electronics*, 29 October 1984, p. 28, and 2 April 1987, p. 76.

56. *Der Spiegel* 42, no. 12 (21 March 1988), p. 126.

mestic production should correspond to domestic demand. To reach this goal, additional research and development expenditures of about DM 21 billion and additional investments of about DM 14 billion are estimated to be necessary.[57] It is an open question whether this objective can be attained; Japanese and American companies are not standing still either, of course.

A way of hedging against eventual barriers to technology transfers from the United States is to establish closer cooperation with Japanese companies. The cooperation between Siemens and Fujitsu as well as Toshiba is a case in point. But cooperation with Japanese companies is not unaffected by American trade policy measures. To escape punitive American action against the alleged dumping of semiconductors on the world market, Japanese firms had to raise prices for exports to third countries, including West Germany.[58]

The West German high-tech industry may even profit directly from American barriers to technology transfer. Many European and other companies have concluded that it is better not to use American components and technology so as to avoid the impact that haphazard changes in American foreign economic policy might have on their business.[59] When companies look for alternative sources of components and technology, they often turn to a West German company that offers similar parts though at relatively higher prices.

That many companies have started to look for alternative sources of supplies to avoid complications with U.S. export controls has increased the opposition of American companies to these controls. Recently a panel on the impact of national security controls on international technology transfer, created by a joint committee of the National Academy of Sciences, the National Academy of Engineering, and the Institute of Medicine, concluded that present export controls probably harm the U.S. economy more than they hamper the access of the Soviet Union and other socialist countries to high-tech products.[60] There is therefore

---

57. *Süddeutsche Zeitung*, 23 July 1987, p. 33; *Handelsblatt*, 23 July 1987, p. 11. This strategy is expected to have some success. According to an estimate by Integrated Circuit Engineering Corporation, Siemens will be the only European company among the top ten Merchant IC makers in 1996, which will be dominated by six Japanese companies (Per Ohlckers, "State of the Art in New Applications of Microelectronics," paper presented at the European Association of Development Research and Training Institutes Technology workshop, Institute of Development Studies, Brighton 1987, p. 14).

58. See *highTech* 2 (March 1988), pp. 84, 86. Siemens does not feel too much affected, however, because Japanese deliveries have been secured in long-term contracts; see *Handelsblatt*, 30 April 1987, p. 21.

59. *highTech* 1 (1987), p. 247; *Balancing the National Interest: U.S. National Security Export Controls and Global Economic Competition* (Washington, D.C.: National Academy Press, 1987), pp. 200, 201, 247.

60. See *Balancing the National Interest*, pp. 16–21, 150–60.

a good chance that export controls will become less tight. Any negative effect of American barriers to technology transfers on the competitiveness of West German industry will not continue for long.[61] The positive effect, however, will be more durable. Since companies cannot be sure (even after security controls are lifted or relaxed) that another political change will not lead to another backlash, they may stick to a non-American supplier even if American companies are allowed to compete on an equal basis.

West Germany's Telecommunications Industry

Another aspect of the politicization of international economic relations is the pressure on European governments to liberalize the telecommunications industry. Telecommunications is one of the most regulated sectors in almost every country, with the carrier normally a public monopoly that has close ties to a small number of preferred equipment suppliers. In the aftermath of the split-up of AT&T, the U.S. government put increasing pressure on other governments to follow suit and abolish or at least restrict their public monopolies and liberalize procurement practices.[62]

The Federal Republic of Germany scores rather low in all comparisons of the degree of liberalization of the telecommunications market.[63] Although Siemens is the third largest supplier of telecommunications equipment in the world, with a world market share of 11 percent,[64] and deliveries of its new digital exchange equipment to twenty-five countries, half of its sales in this field still go to the domestic market.[65] Because of its dominant interest in the domestic market, Siemens has been reluctant to deregulate. It has been able to resist pressure to deregulate and liberalize public procurement during the past few years

61. Despite the Reagan administration's moves toward liberalizing export controls on high-technology goods, the Pentagon is seeking power to veto export licenses for "dual-use" high-performance chips and the equipment to produce them (Policy statement of 14 May 1987), see *Financial Times*, 1 June 1987. If realized, such a move could imply a temporary setback for Siemens but would at the same time improve Siemens's market position in Europe and speed up the company's development efforts.

62. See Gerd Junne, "Technologiepolitische Perspektiven einer Deregulierung des Fernmeldewesens." Erfahrungen aus den USA, Japan und Grossbritannien," Studie im Auftrag der Hans-Böckler-Stiftung, Amsterdam, October 1987.

63. See Jürgen Müller, "Zur Neuordnung der Fernmeldemärkte," *DIW-Wochenbericht* 54, no. 37 (10 September 1987): 493; and the "Deregulation Scorecard" in "The Worldwide Information Industry" (advertisement) in *Fortune*, 21 December 1987. The recent recommendations of the Regierungskommission Fernmeldewesen for a further liberalization do not go very far either; see *Neuordnung der Telekommunikation. Bericht der Regierungskommission Fernmeldewesen* (Heidelberg: R.v. Decker's Verlag, G. Schenk, 1987).

64. Behind AT&T with 31 percent and CGE Alcatel/ITT with 14 percent (*Bulletin der Schweizerischen Kreditanstalt*, 1987, nos. 1–2, p. 42).

65. Siemens AG, *Annual Report, 1985*, p. 28, and *Annual Report, 1986*, p. 28.

for several reasons. First, the employees of the Deutsche Bundespost, the higher echelons included, are well organized in one trade union, the Deutsche Postgewerkschaft, which opposes deregulation out of fear that it would cost jobs.[66] Moreover, not only Social Democrats but also Christian Democrats are hesitant to support deregulation because a large number of suppliers and subcontractors belong to that party's constituency.[67] Even more opposed to deregulation is the Bavarian CSU (Bavarian Christian Democrats) because Siemens headquarters (and the West German electronics industry in general) are located in Bavaria. It was Siemens's decision to relocate its headquarters from Berlin to Munich after World War II that contributed more than anything else to making the Bavarian capital the electronics capital of Germany. Finally, the pressure from domestic users (large industrial companies and banks) has been less strong in Germany than elsewhere because of the close direct or indirect links of many other large companies with Siemens.[68]

This situation, however, may change quickly. To expand its telecommunications business, Siemens makes every effort to penetrate the American market and has had some success. It could be more successful if four regional Bell operation companies in the United States go ahead with plans to order Siemens EWSD exchanges. Two of these companies have confirmed Siemens as their third supplier.[69] There are strong interest groups in the United States, however, that try to restrict purchases from companies that have not opened up their own markets to American suppliers in a comparable way. The struggle between Philips AT and Siemens over the former ITT subsidiary CGCT after the takeover of ITT's telecommunication business by the French CGE has made Siemens's position in the United States problematic. It remains to be seen how much the takeover of GTE's transmission business can help Siemens overcome this obstacle by implanting itself more strongly in the United States. Because its telecommunications market share in West Germany would be affected only in the long run, the chance to get a toehold on the American market could make Siemens change its traditional protectionist attitude.

At a technology forum during the Cebit Trade Fair in Hannover in

---

66. *Computerwoche*, 12 July 1987, p. 4.

67. Douglas Webber, "Die ausbleibende Wende bei der Deutschen Bundespost. Zur Regulierung des Telekommunikationswesens in der Bundesrepublik Deutschland," *Politische Vierteljahresschrift* 27 (December 1986): 397–414; Webber, "Government-Industry Relations in the Telecommunications Sector in the Federal Republic of Germany" (Cologne, December 1986).

68. Boy Lüthje, "Telekommunikationsindustrie und Strukturwandel," MA thesis, Frankfurt, 1985.

69. Siemens AG, *Annual Report, 1986*, p. 28.

early 1987, Siemens's vice-president responsible for telecommunications, Haus Baur, expressed his approval of greater liberalization of the Bundespost.[70] Siemens has obviously agreed to a document which telecommunication equipment producers and users have recently submitted to the European Commission on how the EEC should influence telecommunications. The document called for increased consistency of technical standards and more open competition in the EEC's fragmented telecommunications industry.[71] Until now, only between 2 and 5 percent of public sector contracts are placed with other EEC member states. Siemens obviously favors increasing liberalization within Europe. As Siemens is one of the strongest telecommunications companies on the Continent, this would probably mean more business for that company instead of less.

The pressure on European governments to liberalize telecommunication equipment purchasing, therefore, may work to Siemens's advantage. Siemens was reluctant to accept deregulation as long as the company had to catch up in the field of digital exchange systems. Now that it has developed a highly competitive system (EWSD), Siemens is ready to accept deregulation if the markets of other European countries open up at the same speed.

The impact of the politicization of international economic relations on West German competitiveness thus is mixed. The rise of oil prices may in the short run have affected the development of biotechnology in Germany more than in most other countries, but export barriers erected by the United States had more positive than negative effects for West German industry. The international pressure to open up the telecommunications equipment market will not undermine Siemens's strong position as long as other European markets become available to compensate for eventual losses in the domestic market.

Doubts about West Germany's future competitiveness on world markets based on its alleged skepticism toward new technologies have little basis. Specific labor relations and high levels of qualification and continuous education among workers ensure West Germany's strong position in high-tech fields that require high-quality craftsmanship (see the chapter by Schumann and Kern in this volume) and at the same time make it possible to introduce new, highly automated production processes rather quickly without causing too much upheaval.

The "Greening of West German politics" has had little effect on West Germany's competitive position, notwithstanding the considerable hos-

70. *Wirtschaftswoche*, 13 March 1987, p. 116.
71. *Financial Times*, 23 January 1987.

tility in many of the new social movements to new technologies. The political system may transform many of the demands of these movements into indirect support for selective technology programs that improve West Germany's competitiveness in high technologies rather than reduce it.

Finally, despite its very high export orientation, West Germany may actually benefit from the politicization of international economic relations.

CHAPTER TEN

Computer and Pinstripes: Financial Institutions

HERBERT OBERBECK AND
MARTIN BAETHGE

Stagnation and economic setbacks have done little to hamper the postwar growth of German banks, savings banks, and insurance companies. On the contrary, the financial sector has recorded more prosperity and higher profits than nearly any other sector. Since 1949 the volume of its business has grown at a higher annual rate than that of the gross national product.[1]

The financial sector has been a model for all those who, for many years, have advocated a transition from an industrial to a service society. While more and more industrial sectors faced shrinking markets, decreasing employment, and a bleak future, the employment curve for the banking industry has indicated a clear upward movement over a long period of time (see Tables 10.1 and 10.2). During the 1960s and 1970s

---

1. Since the mid-1970s, the business volume of banks and savings banks has been growing by approximately 10 percent annually (according to Federal Bank figures). In the private insurance industry, the increase rate since the mid-1970s has been around 8 percent (see Martin Baethge and Herbert Oberbeck, *Changes in Work Patterns and Their Educational Implications—Adjustments in the Work Organization; Training and Technology in the Service Sector*, Research Report for the OECD [Göttingen: SOFI and Paris: OECD, 1987]). The GNP grew less quickly during this time (see K. P. Hasenkamp, "Die Zukunft des Bankensektors in qualitativer und quantitativer Hinsicht," in Congena, ed., *Bank-Entwicklung, Strategien für die Bank der Zukunft* [Wiesbaden: Gabler, 1986]).

Table 10.1. Total work force in West German credit institutions, 1970–1985

Year[a]	Private banking	Installment credit institutions	Private building societies	Public building societies	Savings banks	Central clearinghouses	Public mortgage and special credit institutions	Industrial agricultural credit cooperatives	Savings and credit banks[b]	Trade union banks	All sectors
1970	134,000	6,000	12,350	5,400	148,400	18,550	6,100	91,000	1,100	6,100	429,000
1971	143,500	5,800	13,500	6,000	156,350	19,550	5,950	99,400	1,200	6,350	457,600
1972	144,900	5,650	14,800	6,400	160,700	20,700	5,350	99,400	1,200	6,500	465,600
1973	147,800	5,400	16,300	6,950	163,350	21,200	5,350	99,900	1,200	6,700	474,150
1974	146,800	4,600	16,250	6,850	163,900	21,250	5,250	99,850	1,200	6,600	472,550
1975	146,800	4,900	16,400	6,750	165,500	21,150	6,450	99,100	1,150	6,500	474,700
1976	149,600	5,000	16,550	6,750	166,800	21,150	6,800	99,800	1,150	6,550	480,150
1977	150,650	4,850	16,550	6,800	172,100	20,850	6,950	100,450	1,200	6,700	487,100
1978	153,600	4,800	16,850	6,800	180,900	21,400	7,150	101,950	1,200	7,100	501,750
1979	160,100	4,950	17,250	6,750	187,800	21,800	7,300	109,400	1,250	7,500	524,100
1980	163,350	5,300	17,250	6,800	194,200	21,900	7,600	118,350	1,450	7,650	543,850
1981	163,150	5,200	16,950	6,650	198,600	21,700	7,700	123,500	1,600	7,650	552,700
1982	164,750	4,550	16,450	6,400	202,200	21,350	7,650	131,150	1,600	7,750	563,900
1983	166,300	3,950	16,300	6,250	205,800	21,950	8,500	136,150	1,750	7,850	574,800
1984	168,700	3,750	16,450	6,200	208,600	22,100	8,800	138,750	2,000	8,200	583,550
1985	172,500	3,250	16,550	6,050	213,650	22,850	9,100	144,400	2,150	8,400	598,900

[a]At end of calendar year.
[b]Spardabanken.
SOURCE: Employer's Association of Private Banking. Compared with tables published earlier, the employment figures have been corrected considerably in parts in this publication. Corrections have been made for savings and installment credit banks.

Table 10.2. Change of employment figures in credit institutions (Federal Republic of Germany including West Berlin), compared to previous date, 1972–1985 (in percent)

Year[a]	Private banking	Private building societies	Public building societies	Savings banks	Central clearinghouses	Industrial and agricultural credit cooperatives	All sectors
1972	+8.1	+19.8	+18.5	+8.3	+11.6	+9.2	+8.5
1974	+1.3	+9.8	+7.0	+2.0	+2.7	+0.4	+1.5
1976	+1.9	+1.8	−1.5	+1.8	−0.5	−0.1	+1.6
1978	+2.7	+1.8	+0.7	+8.5	+1.2	+2.2	+4.5
1979	+4.2	+2.4	−0.7	+3.8	+1.9	+7.3	+4.5
1980	+2.0	±0.0	+0.7	+3.4	+0.5	+8.3	+3.8
1981	−0.1	−1.7	−2.2	+2.3	−0.9	+4.4	+1.6
1982	+1.0	−2.9	−3.8	+1.8	−1.6	+6.2	+2.0
1983	+0.9	−0.9	−2.3	+1.8	+2.8	+3.8	+1.9
1984	+1.4	+0.9	−0.8	+1.4	+0.7	+1.9	+1.5
1985	+2.3	+0.6	−2.4	+2.4	+3.4	+4.1	+2.6

[a] At end of calendar year.

double-digit annual growth rates of employment were often recorded. Only within the last few years have growth rates declined for banks and savings institutions, and private insurance companies have experienced stagnation and decline in number of employees (see Table 10.3).

Nevertheless, the banking industry, which currently employs about a million people,[2] must be considered one of the core sectors of the West German economy. Employment in this sector is currently at least as high as in the chemical and electrical industries, let alone as in such crisis-ridden sectors as the steel or construction industries. Furthermore, most positions available require relatively high formal qualifications.[3]

Admittedly the veneer of the banking industry has suffered some deep scratches. Following the collapse of some financial institutions[4] and some bad decisions by prominent banks such as the Commerzbank,[5] it became clear in the 1970s and early 1980s that not all companies in this sector could count on high profits and continued expansion. The

2. There are 600,000 bank and saving bank employees, 200,000 employees in private insurance companies, 150,000 employees in the social insurance sphere, and approximately 50,000 self-employed and employees in brokering and external services.

3. More than 80 percent of all current bank and savings bank employees have had three to three and a half years of occupational training, access to which is nearly always reserved for secondary school graduates or graduates of above average modern technical secondary schools.

4. The longest-lasting effect was caused by the collapse of the Herstatt-Bank in Cologne (1974) and the Schröder-Münchmeyer-Hengst-Bank (SMH-Bank) in Frankfurt/Hamburg (1984). Both were large private banks steeped in tradition.

5. In the 1970s, the regional bank of Hessen (Helaba) and the regional bank of Nordrhein Westfalen (West LB) were saved from bankruptcy by supportive action on the part of the guaranty authorities (state government and savings banks).

Table 10.3. Employment in insurance companies, 1950–1985

Year	Employed persons	Percent change from previous year
1950	54,200	—
1967	179,300	+7.3[a]
1968	b	—
1973	b	+2.8[a]
1974	209,300	+0.6
1975	203,400	−2.8
1976	199,900	−1.7
1977	198,700	−0.6
1978	200,300	+0.8
1979	202,300	+1.0
1980	202,300	±0
1981	202,900	+0.3
1982	203,100	+0.1
1983	200,100	−1.5
1984	198,100	−1.0
1985	197,300	−0.4

[a] Annual average rate of change compared to previous year.
[b] Unaccounted for.
SOURCE: Arbeitgeberverband der Versicherungsunternehmen in Deutschland, ed., *Tätigkeitsbericht 1975 bis 1980 und Tätigkeitsbericht 1980 bis 1985 sowie Gesamtverband der Deutschen Versicherungswirtschaft, Jahrbuch 1986,* our calculations.

upheaval these cases caused did not lead to a general crisis in the banking industry, but the general public, with memories of past inflationary times, began to fear for the security of their savings. In banking circles, mistakes by individual managers rather than a structural crisis were held responsible for the turbulence that particular houses experienced.[6]

The continuous expansion of the financial sector in West Germany is in sharp contrast with the modest academic discussion of its background and the social implications of the incessant growth in economic power of financial institutions and insurance companies. Journalists and politicians occasionally refer to the "power of banks" in their opening statements in leading articles and at press conferences.[7] No journalistic headlines, however, can conceal the fact that at least within German-speaking countries there have been few substantial or only relatively

6. See Hanns C. Schroeder-Hohenwarth, *Banken im Wandel* (Cologne: Bank-Verlag, 1987), p. 33. The deposit guaranty fund of private banks to which all banks contribute for the protection of customer deposits provides a means for coping with crises (ibid., p. 29).
7. See, for example, ibid., p. 309; Peter Glotz and Otto Graf Lambsdorff, "Zu mächtige Banken?" *Wirtschaftswoche,* nos. 14 and 15 (1987).

one-sided studies regarding the specific development and social implications of the financial sector since the publication of Andrew Shonfield's extensive analysis[8] of economic politics in Western Europe and the United States.[9]

Since the days of Rudolf Hilferding,[10] the theme of financial capital using its economic power to exert influence on the dynamics of other economic sectors as well as on the political situation has dominated the academic discussion. In the 1960s Shonfield's comparative study helped give lasting support to the theory of the financial sector's central role in economic and social development.

In particular, Shonfield praised the avant-garde role of the banks in the formation of a future-oriented economic and social structure that led to economic recovery after the collapse of Hitler's Germany. West German banks did much more than the civil bureaucracies in drawing up planning perspectives and estimating demands of modern economic and social dynamics. The creation of large civil plans, as in France, was superfluous because the banks carried out a much more efficient administrative role.

In their adoption of Shonfield's theories many analysts call the management levels of the large West German banking and insurance houses the true power and steering centers in the economy and society. Some authors (for example, Fach and Esser in this book) assume that banks exercise their growing economic power to develop future-oriented concepts for branches in a crisis such as that experienced by the steel industry. In doing so, traditional operation and market structures are as rigorously eliminated as the presumed and real workplace surpluses.

In 1974, Ulrich Jürgens and Gudrun Lindner indicated the need for additional perspectives when they wrote, "We believe that the current discussion on the power and influence of banks bypasses the central problem. Proxy voting power, share-holding and personal involvement in the board of directors (of large industrial companies) are considered here as sufficient evidence; the informative value of these factors is not further expounded."[11] This observation is still relevant in the second half of the 1980s. From Shonfield to the *Spiegel* editors who released a magazine in 1985 with the cover article "Deutsche Bank World Power"[12]

8. Andrew Shonfield, *Geplanter Kapitalismus. Wirtschaftspolitik in Westeuropa und USA* (Cologne: Verlag Kiepenheuer und Witsch, 1968).

9. Since the days of Rudolf Hilferding hardly any theoretical and systematic works on the political economy of the credit superstructure have been written (cf. the editorial on Probleme des Klassenkampfs [*Prokla* 63], 16th ed. [Berlin: Rotbuch-Verlag, 1986], and Ulrich Jürgens and Gudrun Lindner, "Zur Funktion der Macht der Banken," *Kursbuch* 36, "Geld" [Berlin: Kursbuch-Verlag, 1974]).

10. Rudolf Hilferding, *Das Finanzkapital* (Cologne: Europäische Verlagsanstalt, 1968).

11. Jürgens and Lindner, "Zur Funktion der Macht der Banken," p. 121.

12. *Der Spiegel* 39 (2 November 1985): 40.

one view has prevailed. The economic power and political influence of banks and insurance companies, however, has reached a new dimension at the end of the 1980s that can no longer be analyzed using traditional concepts of political influence in industry. We consider an expansion of the previous discussion necessary for two reasons that are a result of the structural changes in the financial market.

First, changes in the relationship between financial institutions and industry have remained largely unconsidered in the previous discussion. Pertinent statistics have shown that West German industrial and commercial firms have created a large pool of liquid funds for which in the last years there have been no lucrative investment options. Such customers therefore appear to banks and savings banks not only as applicants for loans but also as potential depositors. Furthermore, these enterprises are increasingly in a position to finance their own growth by accumulating their own surplus reserves, as well as make use of differentiated financing possibilities through international financial markets and extensions of contractor loans. Their ability to do so suggests the banks' limitations in the shaping and organization of capitalism.[13] In a study that has been published only in the United States, Philip A. Wellons[14] has inferred that West German banks and insurance companies can no longer be considered equivalent to economic and social power development as was generally done by Shonfield and his followers. He also inferred that the relationship between the credit business, industry, and state must be understood in a more discriminating way today than twenty years ago.

Second, it is not possible to comprehend the significance of the changed social function of banks and insurance companies in the last twenty years. In discussing the background and social significance of the economic power of financial institutions and insurance companies, more consideration must be given to the enormous expansion in the last two decades primarily because of the systematic growth of the bulk business with private households (loans, savings, and financial transaction services). Managers of banks, savings banks, and insurance companies unanimously agree that this is where their money is made. Business with private customers has been expanded to such a degree[15] that financial institutions now play a decisive role in fulfilling individual customers' financing requirements. This dimension was missing in previous discus-

13. See Jürgens and Lindner, "Zur Funktion der Macht der Banken," p. 146. Welzk emphatically confirms this trend. The importance of the banking industry for direct credit financing, especially of larger amounts of trade and industry capital, has accordingly continued to decline over the last decade and a half (Stefan Welzk, *Boom ohne Arbeitsplätze* [Cologne: Verlag Kiepenheuer und Witsch, 1986]. See also John Zysman, *Governments, Markets and Growth* [Ithaca: Cornell University Press, 1983]).

14. Philip A. Wellons, *Passing the Buck: Banks, Governments and Third World Debt* (Cambridge, Mass.: Harvard Business School Press, 1987).

15. Schroeder-Hohenwarth, *Banken im Wandel*, p. 23.

sion of the power of banks. Private customer business has contributed to the banks' and insurance companies' present position in regulating and controlling a substantial fraction of the populations' financial transactions. The credit business has thus become a direct social power that contributes to the steering and redistribution of private life prospects.

The comparatively early and massive attention given to private customer business by West German banks and insurance companies is explained in the next section of this chapter. We will describe the conditions that led to the generalization of the banking system (Universalbanken) in West Germany since the end of the 1960s as in no other Western industrial country and question this development with regard to the changes in market strategies and enterprising concepts of banks and insurance companies. The massive expansion of private customer business is based on the broad use of electronic data-processing and modern communication techniques as well as on structural changes in recruiting and employment of personnel. The financial sector has mobilized considerable energy to modernize itself, and it is now considered one of the leading branches in the use of new techniques and working concepts.

THE BEGINNING OF NEW MARKETS IN THE 1960S

Since the founding of the Federal Republic of Germany, the country's financial institutions have changed their outward appearance very little. There are three central institutional groups: private banks (including large commercial banks); savings banks, regional banks, and cooperative banks; and a relatively small group of leading insurance companies. A structural change, however, has led to basic changes in the business activity and internal job division within the branches of the financial groups. This process was already under way in the 1960s.

The division of spheres continued throughout the postwar period until the mid-1960s. At that time the private banking houses' view of a "practically unlimited, ideal world" was destroyed. Up to that time "the banks virtually had a stable, national set of economic factors which were advantageous in having a large degree of predictability: low inflation rates, minimal interest-rate fluctuations, stable exchange rates, an economy oriented to expansion. Economic and therefore business-policy forecasting was not a dangerous game. The then prevailing traditional spheres of job division between the three large groups of the banking industry,[16] the interest rate cartel to safeguard the interest spread and

16. Since the middle of the last century, the division of labor within the various financial groups has been relatively clearly defined. *Private banks* include large banks such as the Deutsche Bank, the Dresdner Bank, the Commerzbank, and also private regional banks, as

also the virtually nonexistent foreign operations, allowed the life of the banker to be predictable."[17] In the mid-1960s, three major factors emerged which provoked the financial sector to resurvey market potential and to reorganize.

First, by the end of the first phase of reconstruction, basic consumer needs had been generally satisfied. For private customers, there now arose new, more long-term investment and credit requirements. Second, the end of nearly twenty years of continual upward movement brought far-reaching problems and challenges. The banks' business policy had to adapt to fluctuating interest rates that were influenced by measures the Federal Bank undertook to fight inflation. Of special importance was the removal of interest bonding in 1967, a practice that had been introduced in the 1930s to tie lending and credit rates to discount rates, thereby offering banks a fixed interest spread. Third, with the increase in direct foreign investment by West German enterprises, the banks had to stop concentrating on the home market and, instead, build up and extend their capacity to carry out external transactions. New courses of action had to be developed following the unpegging of foreign exchange rates as a result of the collapse of the Bretton Woods system.

The reorientation of business policies was strongly stimulated by the vigorous expansion of business from private customers, which triggered changes in the division of labor within banks and in the organizational structure of each enterprise. By the second half of the 1950s, the government had begun to allow banks to expand their dealings with private customers. For example, in 1958, the public need test for founding

---

well as both large and small private banking institutions (Sal. Oppenheim, Trinkhaus, and Burghart). Traditionally these banks deal primarily with large industrial enterprises, wealthy private customers, and foreign banks (H. J. Runge, *Der Bankbetrieb* [Stuttgart: C. F. Poeschel-Verlag, 1961]). *Public savings banks*, which after 1815 emjoyed a boom, were structured in the manner of English savings banks. Their activities focused on their local economic areas. They dealt with the deposit and loan requirements of the local authorities and local businesses and also handled "small fry" savings accounts. By the middle of the nineteenth century concern for poorer classes slowly began to disappear. Henceforth, the savings banks aimed to attract savers from higher income brackets (H. U. Wehler, *Deutsche Gesellschaftsgeschichte*, vol. 2, *1815–1845* [Munich: Beck, 1987], p. 107). The savings banks formed an association with the public regional banks/giro centers, which are traditionally responsible for financing federal and state borrowing and for processing payments when these exceed the limits of individual savings banks. *People's banks and rural credit cooperatives* concentrate their banking activities on farming and agricultural trade customers, agribusinesses, and smaller establishments (trades). They based their business policy on the principles of self-help, responsibility, and organization; commercial orientation was purely secondary (Runge, *Der Bankbetriebe*, p. 17). Especially in the 1960s, the parts of cooperative branches were integrated under the name *Volksbanken* (peoples' banks). They cooperate on a regional level with the cooperative central banks, which play the same role as public regional banks in relation to savings banks.

17. Schroeder-Hohenwarth, *Banken im Wandel*, p. 24.

branches was removed, permitting banks to expand their territories. From 1965 to 1975, the entire Federal Republic was covered by a network of branches so dense it had no parallel in comparable industrialized countries.[18] In 1959, on the suggestion of the federal minister of economics, Ludwig Erhard, the *Kleinkredit*, a loan for personal use, was created. This was the first form of consumer credit. Up to that date, private customers were mostly granted loans for housing; subsequently diverse forms of consumer lending provided the banks with lucrative new markets. Last but not least, in the 1950s the savings banks introduced current accounts to deal with wage and salary payments for the crowds of customers who were now rushing to the cashier counters at local branches. In ten years 80 percent of the working population had become dependent on private current accounts.

Thus by the end of the 1960s, German banks and savings banks had become the central handler of private consumers' financial affairs. Wage and salary payments were credited, and rent and bills for water, electricity, and other local services were debited.[19] Banks had a quasi-monopoly with the vast majority of private transactions in the form of transfers, standing orders, and automatic direct debit authorizations through current accounts. This has been an extremely lucrative business for banks. Because all private monies are at their disposal for a few days at least (usually for much longer), banks can take advantage of investment opportunities; the increasingly high fees for services charged by the banks since the mid-1970s have become a central part of the profit account in banking.[20]

With the expansion of private customer business, all groups within the West German banking industry became "universal banks," a metamorphosis that has also occurred in other comparably industrialized countries over the last few years.[21] One difference exists, however, in that the traditional division of work between the three big institutions in the Federal Republic had been more or less replaced by the mid-1970s.

The universal banking system stems from the previous century,

18. "Although the number of banks themselves was reduced by half from 1967 to 1980, the number of branch offices as a whole rose to almost 45,000, so that today there is one for every 1,400 inhabitants in the Federal Republic" (ibid., p. 26).

19. The expansion of business from private customers also characterizes many credit institutions in other industrialized countries. Compared to similar institutions worldwide, West German banks and savings banks started to cultivate this sphere of business much earlier and on a branchwide basis. The savings banks and credit cooperatives were soon joined by the big commercial banks in serving private customers; little place was left in this segment of the market for specialized institutions such as credit card companies, and even the installment sales financing institutions that specialized in consumer credit were in no position to compete for new customers (see *Manager Magazine* 17, 3 [March 1987], p. 180).

20. See Baethge and Oberbeck, *Changes in Work Patterns.*

21. See Olivier Bertrand and Thierry Nayelle, *Human Resources and Corporate Strategy: Technological Change in Banks and Insurance Companies* (Paris: OECD, 1988).

though mainly only for large private banks, which overcame the split into investment banks and commercial banks in the 1890s, categories that still exist in Anglo-Saxon countries today. These banks integrated long-term investment and security business dealings (issues and trade) and also more short-term trade credit and deposit banking.[22] When they began to provide services for customers in the mid-1960s, they created a third support for their business policy. At the same time, customers' deposits gave these institutions a broader refinancing basis within their own houses. The expansion of private customer business helped increase the steadiness of their business policy and their corresponding profitability. The universal banks were therefore able to employ highly diverse instruments to compensate for fluctuations and crises in various market segments.

With the expansion of the private customer business, the way was open for savings banks, public regional banks, and credit cooperatives to join the universal banking system. The short- and long-term acquired savings and the spread of noncash payment transactions, including deposits from foreign banks, greatly expanded the volume of deposits at a local level (savings banks and people's banks) and at a regional level (regional banks/girocenters and cooperative central banks), which in turn widened the margins for credit transactions. Savings banks and people's banks could then provide medium- and large-scale enterprise customers with loan and financial services. They were able to discard their image as primarily institutional collectors of capital and grant credit to nonbanks.[23]

Today more than 75 percent of all companies in the banking sector act as universal banks.[24] Both private and commercial customers can receive more or less all of a given bank's services at a branch office or at a main office. This development has led to a general homogenization of products and service functions in the banking industry, whereby certain local activities have remained with each institution.[25] In addition, it

22. See C.-L. Holtfrerich, "Zur Entwicklung der deutschen Bankenstruktur," in Deutscher Sparkassen- und Giroverband, ed., *Standort-Bestimmung* (Stuttgart: Deutschen Sparkassen-verlag, 1984), p. 13.

23. Ulrich Semmelrogge, in an analysis on the part savings banks play in the qualitative growth of employment initiatives, complained that the savings banks had decreased their traditional role of carrying out public, socially oriented business on local markets. Today they base the granting of credit on purely market economy decisions, adopting the guidelines of the rest of the banking business. Thus they have thrown away margins for the financing of new employment ("Kassensturz?" *Sozialismus* [1986]: 58).

24. Mortgage banks and savings and loan associations do not operate as universal banks but deal mainly in special savings agreements and loans for construction projects. They are subsidiaries in the strategies of the larger universal banks and insurance concerns.

25. Private banks still have a much larger market share than savings banks and cooperative banks, especially in international business and investment banking (see *Manager Magazine* 18 [1988]: 180).

Table 10.4. Market share of banking groups, except mortage banks and specialized industries, 1960–1984 (in percent)

Year	Business volume[a]			Savings deposits[b]		
	Savings banks	Private banks	Credit cooperatives	Savings banks	Private banks	Credit cooperatives
1960	23.8	26.9	6.0	63.3	15.8	14.1
1970	23.0	24.8	7.7	58.8	17.3	18.2
1975	22.1	24.5	9.4	53.4	17.9	22.2
1980	22.1	23.6	10.9	52.0	15.7	25.2
1984	22.0	22.2	11.4	52.8	14.4	25.5

[a]Without trading establishments.
[b]Without bank savings bonds.
SOURCE: German Federal Bank monthly reports.

Table 10.5. Market share in lending business, 1960–1984 (in percent)

Year	Savings banks			Private banks			Credit cooperatives		
	Short term	Medium term	Long term	Short term	Medium term	Long term	Short term	Medium term	Long term
1960	14.4			60.0			12.3		
1970	19.1	17.0	24.9	52.1	34.7	12.9	13.7	8.3	5.3
1975	20.5	21.1	23.0	49.4	29.6	11.7	15.4	11.0	7.1
1980	24.8	21.5	23.2	42.9	32.4	14.2	18.7	16.2	8.8
1984	23.9	19.9	23.5	43.4	28.9	13.0	18.1	17.1	9.6

SOURCE: German Federal Bank monthly reports.

brought about a new balance in the distribution of shares of the market (see Tables 10.4, 10.5, and 10.6).

Today, market decisions are no longer made only by the successors of Hermann Josef Abs and Robert Pferdmenges.[26] Representatives and managers from savings banks, regional banks, and credit cooperatives have long been included in the circle of pinstripe-suited bankers. And by the end of the 1970s at the latest, managers from the large insurance companies could take their place among the financial aristocracy.

The century-long relatively stable market division between banking and insurance was ended in recent years by life insurance companies, which began to sell their customers not only insurance against risk

26. Abs, speaker on the board of directors of the Deutsche Bank in the first two decades of the FRG, was seen as the leading banker in the Federal Republic for years. Even Shonfield was very impressed by Abs. Pferdmenges, connected with the Cologne banking house Sal. Oppenheimer, was considered an especially close associate of Adenauer. For many years he was also member and chairman by seniority of the German parliament.

Table 10.6. Tendency of the balance sheet total according to credit institutions

	Geschäftsvolumen					
	1978		1982		1985	
Institutions	Absolute in million DM	Percent	Absolute in million DM	Percent	Absolute in million DM	Percent
Large banks, regional banks, private banks	452,625	24.6	606,839	22.8	719,619	22.4
Savings banks and central clearinghouses	711,157[a]	38.6	1,019,779	38.4	1,223,200	38.0
Cooperative banks	259,428	14.1	396,843	14.9	496,134	15.4
Private banks specialized in mortgages, public real estate credit institutions under public law, special credit institutions, installment banks, branches of foreign banks	418,694	22.7	634,019	23.9	777,348	24.2
All banking groups	1,841,904	100.0	2,657,480	100.0	3,216,301	100.0

[a]Compared with the following years without balance sheet total of central clearinghouses (increase in 1978–79 due to statistics DM 8.9 thousand million).

SOURCE: Deutsche Bundesbank, monthly reports, various volumes.

(death and accident) but also financial investment contracts.[27] By so doing they have been able to compete more effectively for the investment potential of private households (see Table 10.7). Of the annual share of the monetary wealth formation of private households in 1975 (DM 104 billion), only DM 15.27 billion fell to the insurance companies, but in 1985 their share had risen to DM 40.56 billion (from a total of DM 127.4 billion). At the same time savings deposits placed in banks were cut by half.[28]

"The battle over the piggy bank," as the press once described it, is thriving. Banks and insurance companies are increasingly searching for strategies that will appeal to the largest number of private customers. It is not surprising, therefore, that in 1984 certain banks offered "a savings product with insurance protection" in their attempt to compete with the insurance industry for customers' savings. When one considers that during the next decade vast sums of capital from accumulative life insurance policies will be set free (as contracts from the first boom at the end of the 1960s and beginning of the 1970s terminate; experts speak of capital amounting to double billion figures), the future importance of private customers for banking and insurance institutions becomes clear.[29] Both universal banks and big insurance companies are developing market concepts that focus on providing customer services for *all* financial service matters—an "all-finance concept."[30]

Today some insurance and banking companies are signing cooperation contracts for the joint marketing of corresponding products. Insurance products are sold by banks, and specific forms of financial investments and loan financing which insurance companies are not allowed to sell are offered by insurance field organizations.[31]

The picture of the structural change in West Germany's financial service sector is completed by consideration of the role of concentration processes. Apart from the big commercial banks, the banking industry in the Federal Republic in the 1950s and 1960s consisted mainly of small and medium-sized institutions. Since then savings banks, people's banks, and rural credit cooperatives have gained much power through merg-

27. Financial services that were normally given by banks and savings banks are now given by life insurance firms, which also include in their business line policy loans, mortgage loans, and investment funds.

28. See Gesamtverband der Deutschen Versicherungswirtschaft (GDV), ed., *Die deutsche Versicherungswirtschaft-Jahrbuch 1986* (Karlsruhe: Verlag Versicherungswirtschaft, 1987), p. 39.

29. See Baethge and Oberbeck, *Changes in Work Patterns.*

30. See Congena, ed., *Bank-Entwicklung.*

31. See H. Oberbeck, R. Oppermann, and E. W. Osthues, with L. Beyer, K. Bischoff, and W. Rettberg, *Die Veränderung von Dienstleistungsqualität durch Informations- und Kommunikationstechnik.* Interim research report (Göttingen: SOFI, 1986).

Table 10.7. Trend of the gross premiums of the private insurance companies' direct business between 1950 and 1983, split up according to insurance branches

Insurance branch	1950		1960		1970		1980		1983	
	In million DM	Percent	In million DM	Percent	In million DM	Percent	In million DM	Percent	In million DM	Percent
Life insurance[a]	854	36.9	3,539	37.9	10,781	38.9	32,652	41.3	40,850	41.9
Health insurance	453	18.9	1,256	13.4	4,040	14.6	9,836	12.5	12,662	13.0
Insurance against damages/accident insurance	1,061	44.2	4,546	48.7	12,876	46.5	36,441	46.2	44,052	45.1
of which										
Fire, *Feuerbetriebsunterbrechungsversicherung*	304[b]	28.7[b]	708[b]	15.6[b]	1,735[b]	13.5[b]	3,562	9.8	3,606[c]	8.2
Liability insurance (third party insurance)	86	8.1	418	9.2	1,294	10.0	3,917	10.7	3,917	11.1
Accident insurance	53	5.0	230	5.1	918	7.1	2,938	8.1	3,866	8.8
Motor traffic insurance	360	33.9	2,086	45.9	5,788	45.0	15,459	42.4	17,688	40.1
All insurance branches	2,398	100.0	9,341	100.0	27,697	100.0	78,929	100.0	97,564	100.0

[a]Including pension and death benefit funds.
[b]Household contents and building insurance during 1950, 1960, and 1970 are included in fire insurance.
[c]From 1983 onward without building monopoly insurance.
SOURCE: Dieter Farny, *Die deutsche Versicherungswirtschaft. Markt-Wettbewerb-Konzentration* (Karlsruhe: Verlag Versicherungswirtschaft, 1985), Table 2, p. 24.

ers.[32] Among other results, this concentration has led to the creation of professional management structures within most enterprises. Whereas in the past a few individuals headed the small and medium-sized establishments, today most banks have departments whose primary concern is the strategic and conceptual leadership of the company.

Increasing concentration also characterizes the insurance sector. Since the beginning of the 1970s, there has been a trend toward providing multibranch insurance under the one parent concern. Having diversified their range of offers, the bigger insurance companies have an improved portfolio balance and can employ their field service divisions more effectively. A trend that further suits this policy is the establishment of subsidiaries offering noninsurance services such as building society and investment businesses. Today seven insurance groups control approximately 45 percent of the market. The leading position of the market is held by the Allianz-group, which controls approximately one-quarter of the market.[33]

The expansion of the private customer business within the financial industry can be appropriately interpreted only within the framework of massive government initiatives for the cultivation of general prosperity and government measures for the protection of this market segment. Here the typical West German modus operandi concerning the conflict over the distribution of income comes into play. Banks and private insurance companies are united in a political strategy that, independent of specific governments, accommodates conflicting interests between capital and labor and regulates the accommodation of these conflicting interests by establishing measures to secure and increase the long-term reproductive needs of private households. The social and economic policy implemented by the government has always been designed to mitigate the social conflicts between capital and labor. With tax benefits on long-term and (since 1959) premium-aided savings agreements, the government strongly promoted the citizens' ability to save money.

All these measures led to an increase in most people's income and, until the mid-1970s, to a delay in the reaccumulation of capital within the economy as a whole. "The tendency for accumulation of private means to exceed the declining quota figures of companies and the government first appeared in 1965. The decreasing self-financing in the business sector and the growing government debt could only be rescued

32. The number of independent savings banks and credit cooperatives was reduced by half during the last two decades as a result of concentration. At the end of the 1980s there are still roughly 590 savings banks and about 3,500 cooperative banks (*Manager Magazine* 18 [September 1988]: 43).
33. See Dieter Farny, *Die deutsche Versicherungswirtschaft. Markt-Wettbewerb-Konzentration* (Karlsruhe: Verlag Versicherungswirtschaft, 1985).

by increasing private savings activity."[34] Thus banks and insurance companies found comparably favorable conditions for the expansion of private customer business. Private households were discovered as new potential partners, and the financial industry was able to secure this promising market sector under the government's protective wing. Having been twice bitten by the experiences of complete loss of private savings and monetary assets because of hyperinflation (1923) and currency reform (1948), bank customers have demanded legislation to protect their deposits against bankruptcy. This aim was achieved by curbing competition and especially by closing the market to foreign competitors.

Unlike in the United States, for example, where the government guarantees the safety of deposit accounts and protects the public from losses sustained as a result of the collapse of banks, the Federal Republic takes the indirect method of decreeing the stability of the banking business.[35] Thus in 1967, by government decree, the number of banks and branches that could be established was reduced and a limit was set on the interest rates for credits and deposits. Following this, deposit guaranty funds (in private banks) and joint and several liability funds (in savings banks, regional banks, and cooperative banks) were given the responsibility for keeping new competitors out of the thriving financial business. The members of these funds alone decide which new companies to accept into their ranks. The established banks, savings banks, and insurance companies therefore monopolized the lucrative business of dealing with the savings of private households.

There is a broad consensus in West German society that restrictions should be imposed on the handling of private customers' deposits and that speculative deals should be checked. Therefore it is certainly possible that the management policy in banks and insurance companies is becoming increasingly conservative with expansion of the private customer business.[36]

34. Bernhard Schramm, "Der Wettbewerb um den privaten Kunden," in Landesbank Rheinland Pfalz, ed., *Banken* (Frankfurt: Fritz-Knapp-Verlag, 1983). Private households took a dominant role in the refinancing of banks, savings banks, and insurance companies. More than two-thirds of the total economic savings fall into the category of private households since the mid-70s (GDV, ed., *Die deutsche Versicherungswirtschaft*, p. 37).

35. See Volker Ronge, *Bankpolitik im Spätkapitalismus*, Starnberger Studien 3 (Frankfurt: Suhrkamp, 1979), p. 96.

36. In the last few years, politicians have increasingly complained about the conservative, past-oriented business policy of the West German credit business. In particular, the present minister of research and technology, Heinz Riesenhuber, criticizes the lack of innovation and willingness to risk or lack of courageous, structure-oriented business policy. Loans have been given only against the security of the past, never of the future. "Until now, banks have only been willing to make loans if one could guarantee that one no longer needed it" (quoted in Schroeder-Hohenwarth, *Banken im Wandel*, p. 227).

THE FUTURE OF BANKING

Although the work and occupational structure of employees in banks and insurance companies have changed, employees in most modern market-related service sectors are not heading toward the far-reaching gloomy future forecast by Fordism and automation. Inasmuch as Fordism stands for the strict separation of supervisory and executive activities as well as the strict division of action sequences, it plays a minor role in the financial sector and mostly concerns the back-office employees. The major trend today is toward computerizing the once separated back-office activities as much as possible and combining the remaining ones with more qualified activities.[37]

Today nearly all personnel activities in the offices of banks and insurance companies have been affected by the application of computer-generated communications technologies. In addition, as the continuing development of newer, more sophisticated technologies demonstrates, rationalization strategies within enterprises have advanced to the highest executive and management level. This development, however, is not a confirmation of the forecast of an age of empty offices as a result of computer-generated communications technology or of the assumption that the rationalization of service sector activities has to follow the same "Taylorized" pattern that dominated in production for a long time.

The expansion of rationalization in the financial sector does not obscure the fact that especially in market-related specialized departments firms are being selective in the technologies they use. Rather than automation at all costs, specific forms of technological support and technological control of work procedures determine the rationalization strategies in companies.[38]

Since the end of the 1970s in the upper echelons of banking, as in other sectors of the service industry, a fundamental change in perspective has occurred with regard to the use of computer-generated communications technology and the design of company work processes. We have called this *system rationalization,* a term that refers to the new quality of rationalization of internal service activities and external service relations.

System rationalization within the service sector means that the application of computer-generated communications technology is used not for single functions within enterprises but for the integrated technological and social transformation of work, companies, and market struc-

37. We have considered this discussion at more length in Martin Baethge and Herbert Oberbeck, *Zukunft der Angestellten* (Frankfurt: Campus, 1986).
38. We have formulated this thesis on the basis of extensive empirical research in more than a dozen financial service companies (see ibid.).

tures. Such an expansion of the rationalization concept has brought about increasing changes in rationalization strategies in the service industry. Opportunities for maintaining market strength and maximizing productivity are no longer seen principally as replacing personnel by automated processes and computerized customer self-service, a concept that dominated the pattern of rationalization in enterprises during the 1970s. An ever-increasing number of service enterprises are realizing that to focus exclusively on reducing personnel can prove counterproductive for marketing service products. Many customers want highly skilled assistance, especially when faced with complex services, including many monetary, credit, and security transactions. In addition, the amortization of the concept of automation seems less secure than ever. Nevertheless, individual banks and insurance companies also focus on capturing a niche in the market when designing their respective concepts of automation, self-service, direct selling, service reduction, and so on.

The new rationalization perspective has replaced ideas about technology applications and task organization to eliminate manual back-office functions. To cope with increasing business, most banks centralized back-office functions in the 1960s and early 1970s. Most affected by this change were the procedures for payment transactions (sorting of vouchers and preparing vouchers for data processing). Vigorous efforts were made to introduce central mainframe computers to build up data files for all types of accounts, thus enabling the first forms of remote data processing to be used.

To cope with bulk business with the aid of new data-processing developments, banks and savings banks have had to agree on technical and organizational processing methods for payment transaction forms. Within nearly ten years, they had introduced several methods of automating payment transactions. A single machine-legible printing style was adapted for all forms required for payment transactions. By the end of the 1970s nearly all forms, for instance, debit, transfer, and check forms, were standardized. A standard bank code system was implemented. Agreement had to be reached on the organization of individual banks according to regional location and also on facilitating the identification of individual banks according to their respective banking group. This system has been functioning since 1979. Finally, regional computing centers were established in the savings bank and cooperative bank sector which operate and develop further the data-processing systems within companies. The result was many synergy effects in application of new technologies and the planning of new projects of technological support.

As part of these efforts to provide more favorable conditions for the increased use of data processing in companies, considerable rationalization effects in coping with payment transactions and bulk business were ensured. Thus fewer personnel were needed for back-office departments. In 1972, for example, around one-third of all bank employees still worked in back-office areas, compared to about 20 percent in 1976 and 10 percent in 1986.[39]

The removal of personnel from back-office areas as a result of automation did not lead to a reduction in staff numbers in banks and insurance companies. Instead, the personnel structure was rearranged. The aim of this restructuring is to place more and more personnel in the area of customer assistance and to intensify business relations.

Such changed staffing concepts are representative of the restructuring of the entire business policies of banks and insurance companies since the 1970s. Banks and insurance companies have seen the improvement of market forecasting and control as a prime means of optimizing business strategies for market penetration. With the aid of computer-generated communications technology, the behavioral dispositions and desires of customers, suppliers, and merger partners should become more evident, enabling more accurate analysis of market potential. Such increased market control, however, still depends on the prevailing forms of transactions on the service market and on the cooperation between technological applications and qualified personnel. Therefore, the determining principle of rationalization in the offices of the banking industry is not automation and the ousting of personnel but, rather, the principle of technology selection which benefits employees. Employees are seen not as adjuncts to the work processes of the dominating technology but as in a position actively to create market relations.

The automation of entire administrative complexes is limited to back offices. In areas of the enterprises that advise customers and agree on conditions, the line followed throughout is to use technology to support qualified staff. This means that the technological potential available from suppliers is not fully used in the market areas of financial enterprises. The same is true in the majority of banks in which mainly customer consultants and clerical personnel use the integrated data-bank system for preparing for consultations with customers and for making decisions about contractual conditions. Customer consultants are responsible for finding gaps in the market for individual customers and preparing their consultations with customers.

Undoubtedly, there are other technological possibilities in market areas and loan departments. Some clerical activities seem too tightly

39. The widespread automation of payment transactions is also evident in the high degree of payment procedures carried out mechanically. According to experts from the savings bank organization, a third of all payments could be dealt with fully automatically by the second half of the 1970s (Baethge and Oberbeck, *Changes in Work Patterns*).

controlled by highly complex software programs. Clerical personnel seem pushed into occupational roles in which they perceive themselves as simply cogs in the wheel of programmed technological operations. In general, however, computer-controlled task processing has less to offer than computer-supported task processing. The majority of company representatives who affirm the present combination of technology and consultation by qualified personnel obviously see their opportunities for growth best served when customers are bound to the company by competent specialist personnel. In contrast, customer consultants and clerical personnel who are too obviously controlled by data processing when assessing subject-specific business procedures and customers' inquiries are seen as detrimental to marketing. Banks are also skeptical about self-service terminals, viewing them mainly as an additional service, not a replacement of services provided by qualified personnel.[40]

The implementation of the computer support strategy for clerical tasks in banks and insurance companies depends on the creation of centrally organized data-bank systems for all accounts and contractual relations. To do this, however, requires a high-performance mainframe computer with high storage capacity. The bigger enterprises in the financial sector have supported the development of such integrated customer and contract data-bank systems over the last ten years. They support the concept of high-performance central data-processing computers because they see such computers as the best means for optimizing business policies and planning and for achieving optimal procedural processing effectiveness (no procedure would be processed twice) and performance quality (customers' inquiries would be handled immediately).

With strengthened strategic-conceptual management control, the service enterprises focus on external relations and the dynamics of the market. Internal business operations should be organized as efficiently as possible to cope with existing externally fixed market data. The strategic-conceptual planning and control of business policies attempts to anticipate and influence developments in market structures. Improvisation and exclusive time-related acting on the market, the credo of an ever-increasing new generation of managers, are good; the system-

40. The high investment and costs that would be necessary to install self-service terminals contradict a strategy of increased automation. In many companies it is becoming obvious that technological costs have caught up with personnel costs over the last ten years. Managers are increasingly doubting whether rationalization investments will amortize. The idea that "one can exactly measure electronic data processing costs but not that of its benefits" can be increasingly heard in the credit and insurance business. Investments of 20 to 30 percent ten years ago achieved an effect of 70 to 80 percent, but this relation has reversed, underlining the growing need for technological selection (see Baethge and Oberbeck, *Changes in Work Patterns*).

atic analysis and planning of potential development processes of market dynamics are regarded as being even better.

So far, this strategy has been used chiefly for dealings with private customers and with small and middle-sized firms for which primarily local branch offices are responsible and for which growth targets and sales strategies are outlined with ever-increasing perfection by the management levels in the banking industry.

When today banks and insurance companies not only assess business success according to overall net profits but also as far as possible the profit to be made from each single business activity, central management control is increasing at the cost of specialized departments and branch offices. The range of services offered, the forms of product presentation, the time spent in consultation, and the concluded business transactions are all examined down to the minutest detail. Profitability and strategic importance for company policy are further assessed to allow conclusions to be drawn on consultation and sales strategies and product and group selection on the market.

The future qualified employee needed by the financial industry to help implement the new business policy and work organization will be characterized by good technical skills, intellectual flexibility in the face of changing situations, well-developed analytical abilities in interpreting information, and communicative competence. All in all, this means an increase in, and more perfection of, the skills that good bank and insurance sales personnel have always had.[41]

Routine work and dequalification on a large scale do not determine the direction of development today. On the contrary, a work organization strategy focusing on task integration and expansion for individual clerical employees and leading to more complex work profiles is in evidence in the market-related services in banks and insurance companies. This is not inevitable, however, and is not being followed in all areas that operate on the market and in which it makes sense to take the individual customer by his or her hand. The employees occupied in these fields might be described as winners of the rationalization process.

Besides these employees, however, less qualified personnel will be needed in back offices well into the future. Changes that are regarded as positive in the task profiles for customer consultants, field service personnel, and clerical employees have negative consequences for the work

---

41. In contrast to the development in production, in the service sector, the skilled worker involved in high-tech production procedures is not especially concerned with "warranty" or "secondary production work" and, as Kern and Schumann describe it, has nothing in common with the classical skilled craftsman. Rather, the highly skilled employee has to deal on a wide level with sales-administrative tasks such as customer consultancy, market observation, and bargaining over conditions.

and occupational situation of low-level workers in this area. The exclusion of this group of employees from specialist customer consultancy and the limiting of their job responsibilities to simple routine activities and follow-up processing tasks relating to business transactions have reduced the content of their task spectrum. The accelerated computerization of these processing functions is reducing the content of these tasks and creating a work situation that offers little incentive to learn. These employees are the losers of rationalization in the financial sector.[42] Even if in the long run these jobs are rationalized out of existence, a relevant group of employees will continue to hold them for the next five to ten years, 10 to 20 percent in banks and 20 to 40 percent in insurance companies. The vast majority of such employees are women.

In the financial sector, therefore, the emerging personnel spectrum has at one end an ever-decreasing minority of low-qualified employees, the vast majority of whom are women who have no occupational future in the company and whose position is threatened by technological rationalization. At the other end of the spectrum there is a growing group of highly qualified experts at the managerial level and in the performance and control positions who normally have university degrees in economics, law, or computer science and who so far have had relatively exclusive occupational positions with good career prospects. Between these poles lie the majority of the staff, most of them clerical employees with many years of occupational training and, increasingly more often, extra qualifications that they have received in occupational training courses. Although their tasks may be interesting, their chances for promotion to upper-level company positions have been diminished by the large numbers of academics moving into managerial departments. More than ever before they are dependent on higher training certificates.

Most employees are not facing the dawn of a golden age. Despite an increase in the importance of individual skills, the position of an employee within the company and his or her individual career prospects will become irreversibly weaker following the introduction of computer-generated communications technology and because of changes in the structure of the labor market. The internal balance of power between management and employee has shifted to the benefit of management, though neither side would readily admit it. More possibilities of controlling the flow of work, the increased clarity of business and market processes, and the new form of electronic data storage and data switching make management less and less dependent on experienced em-

---

42. The computer industry in West Germany, specifically Nixdorf, benefits from this development. By 1988 Nixdorf was claiming that the computerization of routine functions in the credit institutions represented one-third of total sales in 1987 (see the chapter by Junne in this volume).

ployees. Such knowledge is easier to transfer today and can be made more readily available than in the past.

In addition, this new potential for control provides companies with a labor market that contains many well-qualified applicants who possess a high school or university education and, in many cases, professional training. Faced with a situation that will not change to any great extent in the near future, qualified middle-level employees are under great pressure, and it is difficult to forecast how they will cope, both in their occupation and in society. Will they act collectively to win back terrain that is threatening to disappear from them for good, or will they continue to seek further training to increase their competitive performance? At present there is much to be said for individual adaption. Further training and education support and can strengthen the individual pattern of social integration which has had a long ideological tradition in the service sector.

This ideological tradition also influences both the union's ability to act and its authority. There is hardly an occupational field in which the union has such a low organizational level as in the financial sector. Only about 20 percent of bank and insurance company employees are members of a union. The major reasons why the unions in banks and insurance companies have difficulties getting a foothold are high incomes, ideological reservations, image, and a high proportion of female employees. Tough wage negotiations cannot be conducted with weak battalions. In the last few years, wage increases and negotiation margins have decreased in the financial sector, and there were isolated "warning strikes" in the last round of contract negotiations. This does not, however, signal a turning point leading to a strengthening of the union's position or to increasing social class conflicts.[43]

Finally, in the future there will be fewer jobs in banks and insurance companies than in the past. Even though rationalization has not yet led to large-scale redundancies, our findings leave no doubt that the rationalization projects have already limited personnel requirements. Companies are employing fewer people, yet their business yields are increasing. We predict that this trend will continue. As long as business yields continue to increase, the sinking demand for personnel will not be viewed as a problem in the financial sector. But as a societal problem it can no longer be overlooked. Meanwhile, the results of rationalization are evident in the core areas of the service sector, banks, and insurance companies, less in the form of redundancies and more in the form of nonemployment of new personnel despite increasing business yields. Employees are aware of this and can consider themselves the beneficia-

43. These are estimated numbers based on membership figures of the different trade unions in this sector.

ries of rationalization, maintaining an income and social prestige that allows them membership in a conservative aristocracy among white-collar workers.

AN IMMOBILE FINANCIAL GIANT ON THE INTERNATIONAL PARQUET?

As this chapter has shown, a thorough structural change in the West German credit business has been accomplished in the last twenty years. Its most important characteristics are generalization of the universal banking principle and elimination of the large banking groups' focus on confined market segments; stronger competition among financial institutions which opens the way for dissolution of the boundaries between banks and insurance companies; and promotion of broad bulk business with private customers.

This structural change has given the financial sector new dimensions and has brought about the internal reorganization of work procedures and the use of new technology. A new horizontal division of labor (today one usually distinguishes only between banking business with professional customers and with private customers), new work concepts that have led to an elevation of employees' qualification levels, and the investment in modern information and communications techniques have given a totally new profile to the work landscape of banks and insurance companies. In customer service there is increased automation of processing and improved quality of technical assistance for advising customers.

Overall, West German financial institutions seem to be well equipped as they enter the 1990s. The characteristics that indicate a relatively stable situation for the West German financial companies at the end of the 1980s are good prospects for a continuing prosperous development in business volume, a continual although cautious concentration of power, and increased use of modern techniques as well as mostly professionally trained personnel. The situation is, however, not without problems.

Structural change and internal reorganization are not only economic affairs. The financial sector's social role and power has been redefined. The economic power of West German banks and insurance companies is greater than ever before. This power is less than in the past determined by the control of big industry and the financial institutions' role in international economic affairs, although the press has sometimes maintained otherwise.[44] In our opinion, the financial industry's control over

44. Hilferding, *Das Finanzkapital*; *Der Spiegel* 39 (2 November 1988).

a substantial fraction of the population's financial transactions is of greater importance.

In addition to the economic influence on big enterprises through mandates on their board of directors, the financial sector has gained social power in the redistribution of personal incomes. This new social power is based on the monetarization of all social exchange relationships and is supported by the control of the financial transactions, credit, and investment interests of private customers by the German universal banks. Their monopolistic position in this segment of the market is protected by a variety of national measures, directed particularly against foreign competitors. There is every reason to assume that the financial institutions use their social power in a very one-sided manner to promote a redistribution from the bottom to the top.

This redistribution effort can be demonstrated first by the interest policy. In the last few years private customers have had to accept a greater difference between active and passive interest because the banks and insurance companies reaped considerable earnings through private customers' business.

Second, the use of new technology for the achievement of a qualitatively high level of market control provides a much clearer view of market structures and expansion potentials than was possible in the past. The companies are the first to profit from the information gained. Although the range of services offered at banks and insurance companies has so far increased rather than decreased, the mechanisms of control are less evident and less subject to influence by the average customer. This process has been vigorously pursued by banks. For decades, free services, especially in the regulation of all forms of payment transactions, have been increasingly subject to a move to charge fees. Customers are not always aware of this policy, therefore, it is almost impossible for them to take advantage of competitors on the market. The financial institutions say that the adoption of new technology necessitates this charge policy. Wherever expensive automation technology has been installed, it is intended that customers should be attracted to its use through a differentiation in charges (for example, standing orders in payment transactions).

Third, the value of personal consultation and service is being questioned now that, with the aid of new computer-generated communication technology, extensive customer group profiles and profitability calculations are available to each subsidiary. For example, a bank might consider eliminating long-term financial consultative services in a branch in urban areas with an above average number of pensioners as well as employees near retirement.

Fourth, today specialist brokerages are located where they can best provide complete consultant services for insurance institutions and banks. West Germany is experiencing a phenomenon similar to that which is occurring in the United States, where within a few years independent investment firms have taken over the management of nearly 40 percent of the volume of invested assets in pension funds.[45] Computer-generated communications technology is applied here as a consultative technique to illuminate various offers and product alternatives.[46] Only financially strong customers such as doctors and university teachers profit from the offers made by these brokerages; with these groups of customers either legally prohibited consultation fees are individually agreed on or lucrative follow-up contracts are drawn up. Most average customers have little chance to take advantage of these strategies. Banks and savings banks are finding policies such as "customer group-oriented consultancy services" more and more attractive. It is thus becoming increasingly difficult to satisfy the growing needs for consultation of the socially weaker groups of the population to prepare for the material security of old age.

When consultative know-how and attractive service offerings are increasingly tailored to social groups from which lucrative follow-up deals are expected, banks, savings banks, and insurance companies tend to use their power in that segment of private customers to manipulate and redistribute social wealth and opportunities in life. They turn particularly to customers who already possess property and income derived from a privileged social position. And they turn away from socially deprived customers. There can be no doubt that wielding such a power of redistribution in a situation of declining expenditures of the welfare state and of shifting responsibilities for social security to the individual must have an effect in shaping the social structure, especially when the redistributive policy of the financial institutions is accompanied by a corresponding tax policy of the government.

It seems that the different spheres of influence of the financial institutions do not coexist without conflicts concerning their internal organization and their capacity to expand in different markets. Even though the majority of German banks and insurance companies claim to operate universally in all segments of the national and international money market, many institutions seem to be limited in their ability to meet the necessary requirements. If our view is correct, the strong expansion of the private customer business in a large number of banks and insurance companies (with the exception of the large private banks) has led to a relatively one-sided allocation and concentration of company resources

45. See Congena, ed., *Bank Entwicklung*, p. 77.
46. See Oberbeck, Oppermann, and Osthues, *Die Veränderung von Dienstleistungsqualität durch Informations- und Kommunikationstechnik.*

in the domestic market. If true, this would confirm doubts about the future prospects of banks and insurance companies as powerful branches of industry. One could hypothesize that German banks and insurance companies determine market conditions in the provinces (local and regional markets with their various small and medium-sized businesses and private customer sectors) using the full range of modern management instruments. But they are not able to play a similar dominant role in international markets despite their increasing world expansion in recent years.

Whereas for a long time German banks were considered the avant-garde of the industrialization process, often taking the offensive in breaching national frontiers, today they tend to avoid taking great risks in international markets. Consequently, German banks are foregoing involvement in larger direct business activities abroad. Thus "the share of banking activity within the Federal Republic (including branch banks and subsidiaries of foreign banks) concerning the amount of foreign lending of all foreign loans granted worldwide, sank from 7.1 percent in 1975 to 3.9 percent in 1985."[47] The market share of banks operating in the United States and Japan has increased, however. Moreover, the subsidiaries and branch banks of Western banks have expanded in centers abroad, where they receive tax relief and supervisory benefits. This development has contributed to the Federal Republic's fall to sixth place among the leading banking nations.[48]

In view of the importance of the Federal Republic in other world economic areas, as one of the nations leading world trade and as a nation with the second most important reserve currency, West German financial houses are minimally involved in the internationalization of economic relations. Even the Deutsche Bank, which was described by the *Spiegel* as a "world power," is not one of the leading big banking houses in the world market. In foreign activity, West German banks are in fifth place behind the Japanese, American, French, and English financial institutions. The West German banks are cautious regarding the development and application of innovative financing techniques. "In these cases they nearly always left the leadership in the hands of Japanese, American or British management and were satisfied with underwriting or with the role of co-managers."[49]

47. See Helmut Hesse and Horst Keppler, "Die Internationalisierung der Finanzmärkte und die Einbindung deutscher Banken und Börsen in diesen Prozess," in C. P. Claussen et al., eds., *Zweihundert Jahre Geld und Brief* (Frankfurt: Fritz-Knapp-Verlag, 1987), p. 103.

48. The United Kingdom takes first place, then the United States, Japan, France, and Luxembourg (ibid.). See Winfried Wilhelm, "Der tiefe Sturz der Hochfinanz," *Manager Magazine* 18, no. 1 (1988): 102.

49. Hesse and Keppler, *Internationalisierung der Finanzmärkte*, p. 123.

The reservation shown by West German banks on the international market contrasts to the increased activities of West German trade and industry concerns regarding the transference of capital (foreign investments and acquisition of blocks of shares in foreign companies). German financial institutions are lagging behind the large trade and industry concerns, leaving the influence on economic matters in the hands of the captains and crews of trade and industry, who include many nationally and internationally well-versed financial experts. Banks and insurance companies follow the industrial penetration of previously closed and still unapproachable markets and attempt to organize the resulting necessary financial arrangements. Whether this alone is sufficient for the active future design of branch development remains a question.

Various authors have indicated that the reservation on the part of West German banks toward innovative financial engineering cannot be assessed simply in terms of a deficit in their business policy. Obviously, this recalcitrance also reflects the relatively liberal financial market regulations in the Federal Republic and the structural features of the universal banking system, which freed West German banks from having to devise methods to circumvent administrative restrictions on particular financial markets, as, for example, lending and securities businesses had to do. Likewise, the banks have been free to arrange their own terms for credit and deposits since 1967 so that no new instruments had to be created to circumnavigate restrictive regulations.[50]

Nevertheless, according to economic journalists, West German financial institutions seem to have "slept through the radical change on the international financial markets." When the dark storm clouds of the great stock market crash in 1987 had withdrawn and account had been taken of new possibilities and developments on the international capital market, the "severed German artery" was reported everywhere. Although a few banking houses operating worldwide suffered only a light bruising from the stock exchange crash, having been protected by skilled business constructions (a mixture of universal banking principles and specialized investment know-how), an extensive computer system, and a worldwide network of experienced dealers, dozens of West German institutions were seen as big losers. Even though institutions from the United Kingdom and other countries had similar experiences, this event proved that some specific structural deficits are present in the business policy of West German banks. Last but not least, in specialist circles some of the blame for the West German losses is put on the shoulders of its own banking system. Accordingly, investment banking remains only

50. See Uwe Traber, "Neue Formen des Geldes. Innovationen auf den internationalen Finanzmärkten," in *Prokla* 63, p. 89.

one line of business among many. The management and control structures in the headquarters are considered too stolid in their attitudes toward high-priced commercial market sectors, both national and international.[51]

Even if the universal banking principle concerning the expansion opportunities of domestic private customer markets has proven itself to be a strong engine for motivating business, it does not seem to provide automatically flexible competences for action in internal business. In addition, despite all the training efforts over the last twenty years, German financial houses have still not managed to overcome existing deficits in employees' mobility and qualifications, especially at the middle-tier level (subject knowledge and languages); the lack of qualified employees has hampered banks' international financial business.[52] Presumably, far too long a time was spent meeting challenges created by the expansion of private customer business. This could also have reinforced fundamental psychological barriers against a more venturesome international business policy. If we hear increasing complaints today that there is conservativism in the financial sector's business policies and less willingness to be involved in future-oriented and risky undertakings in national and international financial markets, the reason could be an overall one-sided focusing on the special interests of the private customer market, whose highest priority, in the light of recent West German history, is security and stability of money investments.

51. See Wilhelm, "Der tiefe Sturz der Hochfinanz," p. 111.
52. See Baethge and Oberbeck, *Changes in Work Patterns*.

PART IV

CONCLUSION

CHAPTER ELEVEN

Stability and Change in the Emerging Third Republic

PETER J. KATZENSTEIN

Three changes are transforming the context of West Germany's Third Republic in the 1980s: new currents in international politics, new social movements in national politics, and new production technologies in industrial plants. This book has sought to characterize these changes and to examine their consequences for diverse sectors of West Germany's political economy. The analysis points to a conclusion which I seek to analyze further in this essay. Different sectors of the West German economy are experimenting with new practices to respond to the new challenges that confront them at home and abroad. At the same time West Germany's emerging Third Republic is tied to its predecessors by remarkable institutional and political continuities in national politics.

This convergence between experimentation and continuity is the most striking political characteristic of West Germany in the 1980s. The big change which Chancellor Kohl and his new government called for in 1983 has not occurred. But innumerable small changes are transforming West Germany's economy and society. If there is one predominant tendency in the bewildering array of changes in West Germany in the 1980s, it is a trend toward decentralization. Because change is occurring largely within existing institutions rather than outside of them, and

For their comments, criticisms, and suggestions on several drafts I thank the authors in this volume as well as Michael Goldfield, Peter Hall, Jeremy Rabkin, Sidney Tarrow, and the members of the Seminar on State and Capitalism since 1800 at the Center for European Studies at Harvard University. An excerpt of this essay was published under the title "The Third West German Republic: Continuity and Change," *Journal of International Affairs* 41 (Summer 1988): 325–44, and an earlier draft was included as number 9 in Harvard's Center for European Studies Working Paper Series.

because change occurs on a small rather than a large scale, it is easy to overlook the cumulative effect of many small-scale changes over time. But for the foreseeable future we must emphasize the major empirical findings of this book: the convergence of flexibility and stability.

The subtitle of this book, *Toward the Third Republic,* emphasizes that the 1980s is a decade of transition for the Federal Republic. The pattern of change identified here, experimentation and change within a stable institutional framework, has not yet become fully established in politics. In 1984–85 the elites of the major interest groups and political parties confronted the possibility of instituting large-scale change at the cost of substantial domestic political conflict and considerable losses in international competitiveness. In the end they chose instead to steer developments into well-established institutional channels. It is important to point out that political interests did not succumb to the institutional pressures of West German politics. Rather, they chose not seriously to disrupt those institutions. As of this writing, the summer of 1988, the situation remains unchanged. Because no compelling new political strategies have been articulated in any political quarter and because of the very considerable achievements of West German institutions in responding to a variety of changes, the most important political and social actors have chosen to continue supporting the existing institutional arrangements in national politics. With every passing year that choice is becoming more unalterable, but only a self-conscious acceptance by the political elites of existing institutional patterns in times of multiple changes would securely implant the Third Republic.

This book covers the main sectors of West German industry as well as a central segment of its service industries. The industries included are core sectors that have been the economic backbone of West Germany as well as the main source of its success in the international economy. This is not to argue that all important sectors have been included and that all of them share in the pattern of response described here. Agriculture is an obvious example.

Furthermore, the focus on industrial sectors magnifies the achievements and disguises the costs of the West German way of renewing its international competitiveness. This bears underlining at the beginning of an essay that seeks to interpret a set of empirical case studies that cast a light on West Germany's political economy which is decidedly more optimistic than an interested reader of the American press may be accustomed to. The most visible of these costs is the rise in West Germany's unemployment rate from 2 to 3 percent in the 1970s to 8 to 10 percent in the 1980s. The implications of substantial unemployment for West Germany over the next five to ten years receive special attention in the concluding section of this chapter.

There are other costs not highlighted by this book. Because of the sharp increase in structural unemployment, West Germany no longer welcomes foreign workers. Among foreign workers residing in the Federal Republic, the Turks, as the largest group, are experiencing many forms of discrimination, primarily because of unemployment among West German workers and the social and political difficulty of assimilating Islamic and Central European cultures. Although it is difficult to generalize about the extent of political discrimination the Turks suffer, it is clear that political authorities have been slow to respond to often deplorable conditions and that the federal government seeks to stem the growing influx of refugees from Third World states.

West German social policy also reflects significant adjustments to the economic conditions of the 1980s. Virtually all major programs have been pruned, with the poorest sectors suffering most. But it would be wrong to mistake fiscal frugality and a recalibration of the West German welfare state for an all-out attack on the principle of an active social policy. Demographic changes now transforming West German society will make some fundamental policy changes, especially in the structure of the social security system, almost inevitable after the year 2000. But until the end of the century, and perhaps a few years beyond, the existing programs can be financed. West German industry has been successful in the 1980s within a broader social setting based on a strong consensus on the principle of the social welfare state.

How do we gauge the performance of West Germany in the 1980s? In the analysis of political economy the concept of success or failure raises the thorniest of all problems. It is easy to talk about the economic success or failure of individual firms in adapting to change. It is somewhat harder, though still possible as the case studies in this book show, to talk about the economic and political success or failure of different segments or sectors of industry. But it is virtually impossible to talk with precision about the political success or failure of West Germany or for that matter of any political order. Each state distributes the benefits and costs of its policies in particular ways. We lack a measure for comparing, for example, the benefits accruing to the craft producers of machinery with the costs of unemployed Turkish steelworkers. Successful political regimes are admired because they are effective in concealing the costs of their policies, not because they are not incurring any costs. West Germany is no exception. Its continued industrial prowess is inextricably linked to the most difficult conditions experienced by the weakest and most marginal sectors of West German society.

INDUSTRY AND CHANGE

West Germany in the 1980s is affected by three different changes. The chapters in Part I of this book described these changes and suggested some of their possible consequences for West Germany's political economy. The industry case studies in Part II focused on the relationships between these three changes in specific sectors of the West German economy.

Three Changes

In her chapter Joanne Gowa argues that the international economy is anchored in a stable, bipolar international system. In contrast to the unpredictabilities of the multipolar system of the interwar years, in the 1980s the members of the Western alliance form a stable core for the trade, monetary, and investment regimes that link states. In contrast to the 1930s, the interests of the major capitalist states are fundamentally compatible; each ally has a major stake in the security and welfare of its partners. The military alliance, as well as the character of the welfare capitalism that emerged after 1945, implied that nation-states would absorb, at least in part, rather than merely export some of the costs of economic adjustment in the 1970s and 1980s. Despite the waxing and waning of superpower conflicts in the 1980s, this basic structure of the international system is unlikely to change in the foreseeable future. Ironically, the continued division of Germany is one of the essential ingredients of that stability. Since the international economic order rests largely on the distribution of capabilities in the international state system, the prospects for West Germany having continued access to liberal international markets remain good.

But within that stable order there remains ample room for change. Three sources of change in particular stand out. Since the 1960s, the United States has demanded with increasing insistence that its major allies, including West Germany, abandon their strategies of free riding and instead actively support the postwar international economy. West Germany remains vulnerable to U.S. pressures and is thus likely to continue to fill the role of the "honest broker"[1] mediating conflicts over issues such as macroeconomic policy, trade conflict, and East-West export controls. This role is well served by the low profile the Federal Republic has adopted in the 1980s. In contrast to Japan's export-oriented firms, West German corporations were better prepared for the sharp appreciation of the deutschmark in 1985–86. In response to a similar experience in 1978–79, West German firms adopted strategies (less expansion of market share, more liquidity, more product innovations) that now permit them to absorb substantial losses for several years

---

1. Peter J. Katzenstein, "West Germany's Place in American Foreign Policy: Pivot, Anchor or Broker?" in Richard Rosecrance, ed., *America as an Ordinary Country: United States Foreign Policy and the Future* (Ithaca: Cornell University Press, 1976), pp. 110–35.

without undue strain. Similarly, the European Monetary System (EMS), which Chancellor Schmidt helped set up in the late 1970s, provided an effective buffer. It created quasi-fixed exchange rates in Western Europe and thus sheltered about two-thirds of West Germany's exports from extreme currency fluctuations. And since the West European market was partly protected from foreign competition, the EMS contributed to a dynamic improvement in West Germany's economic position. West Germany is doing nothing to divert attention from the trade conflict between the United States and Japan. Neither by temperament, inclination, nor ability does Chancellor Kohl seek to emulate Chancellor Schmidt's forceful leadership style; and thus he reinforces the low profile of the Federal Republic in the international economy. For a variety of reasons, West German demands for policy change are more muted than those of the United States or even Japan.

Whether this low political profile will be adequate in the long term for diverting the demands of the United States within a changing international economy remains to be seen. Robert Gilpin, for one, argues that the Bretton Woods system of multilateral liberalization is being supplanted by a new system that mixes mercantilist competition, economic regionalism, and sectoral protection.[2] While acknowledging that a low profile has served West Germany well in the 1980s, even optimists are likely to concede that different international or domestic circumstances, including a more protectionist administration in Washington or a SPD-Green coalition government in Bonn, might quickly force West Germany into the hot spot of U.S. political attention reserved in the 1980s largely for Japan and the newly industrializing countries. West Germany is unlikely to remain deaf to strong demands that it actively maintain as well as exploit the free-trade system. Should these demands aim, as they have with a more pliant Japan, at greater reliance on domestic expansion rather than on West Germany's preferred strategy of export-led growth, the political ramifications for national politics could be very substantial. The conflict with the United States over interest rates which preceded the crash of October 1987 serves as a useful reminder of how quickly the Federal Republic can find itself at the center of a major international controversy.

A second source of change within an overarching stable bipolar state system derives from the potential instabilities of the international financial system. The overhang of Third World debt has created the potential for chain reactions of bank failures. Pending a change in U.S. policy, this continues to be true even after American banks began in 1987 to follow the policy of West European banks of writing off as bad debts a substan-

2. Robert Gilpin, *The Political Economy of International Relations* (Princeton: Princeton University Press, 1987).

tial proportion of their outstanding loans to Third World states, which is likely to shift rather than eliminate the debt crisis. Tougher rescheduling negotiations between private banks, now less vulnerable to threats of default, and Third World states will probably lead to more restrictive economic policies of Third World debtor states and thus, indirectly, to smaller markets for U.S. exports. This will prolong the substantial trade deficits of the United States as the largest debtor country in the world. In short, the fragility of the international financial system is likely to continue as a possible source of change that could affect dramatically West German access to international markets. The rapid shifts in financial power which in the 1980s are favoring Japan and, to a lesser extent, West Germany make it plausible to assume that a reorganization of the international debt regime, should it occur, would probably involve substantial West German financial resources.

Finally, a third source of change lies in the social and political upheaval in the Soviet Union and throughout most of Eastern Europe. Gorbachev's political reforms are spurred by an acute sense of the economic and political failings of socialism. The new emphasis on the principle of market competition in socialism promises to open the Soviet Union and Eastern Europe to more economic contacts with the West. The Federal Republic is likely to seize a sizable share of the new opportunities for increases in trade, foreign investment, and technology transfer. Although a renewed economic opening to the East will do little to alter the Federal Republic's overwhelming reliance on trade with the West, it may accord it a somewhat more active role in East-West relations. More important, a renewed economic opening to the East may become a source of tension between the Federal Republic and the United States should American-Soviet relations sour. The conflict over the gas pipeline and technology transfers which split the Western alliance in the 1980s portends the magnitude of possible future diagreements.

Jost Halfmann argues that changes in the institutional structures of the Second Republic opened up some political space for new social movements. Although their salience and political impact are particular to the Federal Republic, the new social movements are signs of a normal rather than of a crisis politics. Halfmann stresses the concurrence of old and new social movements and the effect they have had on West German politics. "Rights" movements, like the unions, articulate the traditional demands of social equality and citizenship. "Reciprocity" movements with a strong egalitarian bent cluster in the main urban centers. They express the changing contours of industrial society: new patterns of work, an individualization of lifestyles in some social strata, and the growth of postmaterial values among selected social groups and age cohorts. These movements or movement segments are typically opposed to the "productivity coalition" uniting business, unions, and the major West German institutions around the objective of export competitiveness. "Risk" movements, finally, focus on the harmful consequences of technological changes such as nuclear power. These movements aim at nothing less than control over decision-making processes in both the public and the private sectors. The political relations between these three types of social movements are exceedingly complex. They do not represent mutually exclusive groups or group claims. Rather, they provide interpretive lenses through which we can view the rise and fall of West Germany's new social movements and the different demands they make.

Many of these movements are marked by a clear antiestablishment character, especially among their younger supporters. This phrase needs to be understood broadly. It includes not only strong criticism of prevailing political practices in the Federal Republic but also, as the peace movement showed in the early 1980s, an ill-defined sense of restlessness with West Germany's place in the Western alliance and its position at the fault line of the East-West conflict in Europe. Expressed as anti-Americanism, this restlessness concealed a growing national consciousness which a conscientious reading of the evidence shows to be West German rather than German.[3] The goal of reunification has not been renounced by any significant segment of the West German population, but Joanne Gowa's analysis shows that a vast majority acknowledges reunification to be unobtainable in the foreseeable future. This recognition does not lead, as once feared, to an irredentist German nationalism among the young in the Federal Republic but their acceptance of the Federal Republic as their normal state.

The new social movements have had a substantial adverse effect on the relative strength of the SPD and thus a notable impact on the entire West German political system. These movements grew in the late 1970s because the major political parties and interest groups no longer controlled fully all of the political space. Halfmann argues that economy, society, and politics became less tightly coupled in the late 1970s and 1980s than they had been before. Niches for mobilizing social constituencies and for surviving periods of demobilization existed in local and regional politics. Forty years after the fall of the Third Reich this reconstitution of West Germany's civil society has brought democratic participation more in line with democratic theory than had been true for the first two West German republics.

Only some of the links between social movements and new production technologies are direct. At the fringes of the West German economy one

3. Gebhard Schweigler, "Normalcy in Germany," paper presented at the Wilson Center European Alumni Association Conference, Dubrovnik, Yugoslavia, 20–27 May 1988.

can find in agriculture, the crafts, and industry small firms or groups organized by followers of one of the new social movements. But these alternative economic forms of organization are very small and rarely involve any new production technologies. Instead, the most important direct links are ideological. They exist, for example, between social movements and the unions. Ecological and peace groups and the unions are constantly skirmishing over who is most entitled to press ecological or peace issues, but they may also cooperate within the new social movements.[4]

More typical are two indirect effects linking social movements to new production technologies. The first link operates primarily through the party system. Social movements force new issues, such as ecology or nuclear power, on the political agenda. They have caused the emergence of a new party, "the Greens,"[5] which both reflects and accelerates the process of electoral realignment.

The international system is a second link. If West Germany's new social movements have foreign analogs, the pressures they exert may well create growth markets for new industrial products, for example in the area of antipollution technologies such as the catalytic converter. But if West Germany's social movements are exceptional in their political prominence, they will burden West German producers with new costs, thus diminishing their international competitiveness. The scant evidence available to date suggests that the truth lies in the middle. Social movements are typical of developments in some societies and atypical of developments in others. West Germany's industrial profile may eventually differ somewhat from that of countries that have no social movements, but this does not necessarily mean that the Federal Republic will be condemned to a loss of international competitiveness.

The third set of changes is the new technologies that are beginning to transform the process of industrial production. Horst Kern and Michael Schumann emphasize in their chapter the specific skill bases of the work force which are favorable to the introduction of new production technologies in West Germany in the 1980s. These technologies broaden the spectrum of adjustment strategies of individual firms, industry segments, or industrial sectors. The new technologies have important con-

4. Heinrich Siegmann, *The Conflicts between Labor and Environmentalism in the Federal Republic of Germany and the United States* (New York: St. Martin's, 1985); Herbert Kitschelt, "Left-Libertarian Parties: Explaining Innovation in Competitive Party Systems," *World Politics* 40 (January 1988): 194–234; Jan C. Bongaerts, "Was ist Chemiepolik? Versuch einer Synopse der Positionen," *Discussion Paper* IIVG (Wissenschaftszentrum Berlin, 1987).

5. Michael Grewe, "Environmentalism and the Rule of Law: Administrative Law and Movement Politics in West Germany and the United States," diss., Cornell University, 1987. Herbert Kitschelt, *The Logics of Party Formation: Ecological Politics in Belgium and West Germany* (Ithaca: Cornell University Press, 1989).

sequences for the relative position of different groups of workers ("winners" versus "losers"), different industries, the deployment of labor, and the linking of products and production. New production technologies have complex consequences. Depending on their context, they can encourage the reskilling of workers and can enhance the power of labor on the shop floor. Alternatively, these new technologies can lead to the deskilling of workers, the segmentation of the labor force, and the decline of labor's power. In either case established strategies of mass production are being sacrificed as new technologies make human work not less but more important to the economic success of individual firms in most sectors of the West German economy. Some declining industries, such as shipbuilding or mining, are largely unable to introduce new ways of organizing production. Here rationalization often means the destruction of industrial capacity. But this is not the typical development in West Germany. Instead, this era of transition is marked by two trends, a shrinking in the quantity of work and an enhancement in its quality.

The political implications of these divergent trends are far from clear. Their relative magnitude is not only technologically but politically determined. At the extremes we can think of two political models. First, divisions within the labor force might become so deep that the political basis for constructing new social alliances between rationalization "winners" and rationalization "losers" simply would not exist. Alternatively, changes in production technologies might lead to the persistence of protest among a reinvigorated labor movement, which could create the political basis for reforms supported by both the losers and the winners of rationalization. The segmentation and the artichoke models are hypothetical constructs that define the range of political possibilities. The reality of West Germany's future political economy will probably be found between these two extremes. This at least seems to be the lesson of the 1980s. The West German labor movement is not fully politicized on questions of new production technologies. Traditional union support is strongest among the "tolerators" or "losers" of technological change. Yet West German labor has typically welcomed rationalization and modernization. The structural ambivalence of labor is also illustrated by the divergent experiences of different industries. For example, on questions of new production technologies unions intervene forcefully in the automobile industry but play a very low-key role in the chemical industry. Yet the unions must win the support of rationalization winners if they want to retain their power on the shop floor.

These international, national, and plant-level changes are not restricted to West Germany. Changes within the liberal postwar economy, the rise of new social movements, and the development of new production technologies can be observed throughout the advanced industrial world. The relative importance of these changes may differ from one state to the next, and their effects will differ depending on a state's position in the international system as well as the character of its domestic and industrial structures. Nothing in the analysis of the three chapters in Part I suggests that we are dealing with idiosyncratic changes affecting only the Federal Republic.

Furthermore, only the analysis of production technologies points to the conclusion that the 1980s may indeed have brought something substantially new and different. But even in this instance the emphasis is on the effects of the microelectronic revolution on the increased importance of human work rather than on the prospects for automation and robotization. By contrast, the analysis of a liberal international economy embedded in a relatively stable bipolar system and of the convergence of rights, redistribution, and risk as the catalysts for old and new social movements both point to substantial political continuities. Finally, and closely related to the question of continuity, are the observable rates of change. The chapters in Part I suggest a descending order of magnitude as we move from plant-level to national and international sources of change. These patterns are summarized in Table 11.1.

West German Industry

What has been the pattern of industry response to the three different changes affecting West Germany? I use the term *pattern* rather than *strategy*. In this era of transition, change and its consequences are not fully understood. Businessmen, workers, interest group officials, party politicians, and state bureaucrats have grafted recently acquired coping mechanisms onto established historical practice. The term *strategy* would dignify a bewildering range of responses in different parts of West Germany's political economy with an intellectual order and a self-consciousness that do not exist.

At the same time the pattern of industry response is very clear. As Gerd Junne points out in his chapter, the distinction between sunset industries such as steel and shipbuilding, sunrise industries such as microelectronics, telecommunications, and biotechnology, and core manufacturing industries, so common in our interpretation of American history, is of limited use in understanding the West German economy. West Germans do not think in terms of sectors rising and falling. Instead they conceive of new technologies which are diffused throughout industry. Similarly, typically they do not view services such as banking and insurance as part of a postindustrial economy, a set of activities independent of and separate from manufacturing. Rather, they see services as an

Table *11.1.* Three sources of change

| | Sources of change | | |
Type of change	International	National	Plant
Particular to West Germany	No	No	No
Discontinuous development	No	No	Yes
Observable rate of change	Low	Medium	High

integral and growing part of a modern industrial economy.[6] These views make the similarity in the response across a broad spectrum of West German industries less surprising than one might expect at first. West German industry modernizes not through epic struggles between industries that rise and fall but through the quick and quiet diffusion of core technologies throughout all of the major industrial sectors.[7] Furthermore, the growth of new information technologies and other services typically is not a process that occurs apart from changes in manufacturing but is linked intimately to them. This is not to argue that no industrial sectors or sector segments are being closed down. In their chapter Josef Esser and Wolfgang Fach, for example, refer among others to shipbuilding as a noteworthy case precisely because it differs so greatly from the experience of all the other major sectors discussed in this book.

For the purpose of presentation only, the discussion that follows will group the three core industries (autos, chemicals, and machinery) and compare them with other sectors (steel, shipbuilding, semiconductors, telecommunications, biotechnology, and banking) not as often regarded as West Germany's economic core. The data point to widespread experimentation in distinct industrial settings.

The pattern of response is broadly similar in each of the three core industries: a combination of flexible specialization grafted onto the existing pattern of either mass production (in autos and chemicals) or traditional crafts production (in machinery). In automobiles this process occurred, as Wolfgang Streeck's chapter shows very clearly, in two distinct ways. Mass producers like Volkswagen moved to high-volume, specialized production in the 1970s to avoid competition at the low end of the market, and specialist producers such as Daimler-Benz increased

6. Stephen S. Cohen and John Zysman, *Manufacturing Matters: The Myth of the Post-Industrial Economy* (New York: Basic Books, 1987); Eberhard von Einem, "Dienstleistungen und Beschäftigungsentwicklung," *Discussion Paper* IIM/LMP (Wissenschaftszentrum Berlin, 1986).

7. Henry Ergas, "Does Technology Policy Matter?" in Bruce R. Guile and Harvey Brooks, eds., *Technology and Global Industry: Companies and Nations in the World Economy* (Washington, D.C.: National Academy Press, 1987), pp. 191–245.

their production considerably. In chemicals the distinction between mass and crafts production was also blurred, if for different reasons. Because of its great capital intensity and the high rate of product innovation, this industry had, as Christopher S. Allen argues, always approximated incompletely the model of mass production. New developments in "high chem" (new materials) and "fine chem" (pharmaceuticals) are moving the industry further away from the production of bulk chemicals into market segments less threatened by volatile shifts in energy prices and worldwide overcapacities. The emergence of biotechnology promises diversification and future growth. Lacking a tradition of mass production or science-based innovation, the machinery industry, as Gary Herrigel shows, is reaching a new synthesis of traditional and high-tech craft production.

The institutional order in which the spread of new production technologies occurs varies across these three industries. In the automobile industry our attention is focused almost exclusively on West Germany's stable, cooperative industrial relations system. The relation between the union (IG Metall) and the works councils inside the plant is subtly shifting to favor the latter, especially on questions that arise in the application of new production technologies. But the relation between unions and councils remains symbiotic on many crucial questions: a long-term perspective geared to success in international markets, support of energetic measures to train and retrain an already highly skilled labor force, and a willingness to exploit the opportunities of technological change as well as suffer the costs it imposes. In the chemical industry since the early 1970s, relations between management, union officials, and works councils have been even tighter than in automobiles, but the relative importance of the works councils has been greater. Furthermore, a far-reaching internal decentralization of the three dominant chemical producers provides for a large number of relatively autonomous centers run by scientists which collaborate with central laboratories. The flexibility in research and development and the adaptability and innovation that this form of organization encourages are matched in other parts of the industry by the existence of a large number of specialized, medium-sized firms and their ancillary subcontractors. This system reproduces the competitiveness that the large firms gain through their internal decentralization. Finally, the machinery industry features, in Gary Herrigel's words, two industrial orders: an autarkic order in which centrally administered workshops are vertically integrated and remain isolated from their regional setting, and a decentralized order consisting of loose confederations of independent firms that rely on extensive networks of private and public institutions. Changes in international market and production technologies are encouraging further concentration of firms in the autarkic order as well as a decentralization within firms; and they are leading to extensive shifts in subcontracting in the decentralized order as well as rearrangements within and among the supporting private and public institutions that provide technical information, marketing assistance, and capital.

West Germany's social movements have had no noticeable effect on the machinery industry. Some of the issues championed by the new social movements—the construction of an extensive interstate highway system, the issue of a general speed limit, and the peril to West German forests stemming from automobile pollution—have had only a small effect on the evolution of the auto industry. The chemical industry, on the other hand, has been a prime target of ecology movements first and the Greens later. In 1985–87 the Greens and the SPD formed a coalition government in Hesse. A prominent leader of the Greens became state minister for the environment in Hesse, a traditional area of concentration of the chemical industry. This political experiment might have provided a serious threat to established ways in which the industry governs itself and interacts with public officials, but the coalition was short-lived. The primary effects of the Greens and the ecology movements thus are likely to be indirect through the political agendas they set for the established parties or through their reliance on the courts or popular mobilization around ecological issues such as the massive chemical spill in the Rhine in 1986.

With the exception of the decentralized order in the machinery industry, state policy primarily affecting these three core industries is indirect. Even in the greatest crisis for VW, West Germany's largest automobile producer, Chancellor Schmidt insisted that the private sector solve the grave problems the company faced in the mid-1970s. In the chemical industry the regulatory framework set by the state is based on the principle of self-regulation which is deeply entrenched in Germany's political history.[8] Only in the decentralized part of the machinery industry can we find a general acceptance of state support to facilitate the adjustment of small and medium-sized firms to changing market conditions. The exception is noteworthy because it generates conflicts about the proper role of state intervention. Baden-Württemberg's governor, Lothar Späth, favors state intervention to strengthen the regional economy of southwest Germany. But his activist conception is shaped by the French statist tradition of intervention rather than the concertation model favored by West German small business which seeks support from a variety of public and private sector institutions.

At the international level technological change and international com-

8. Peter J. Katzenstein, *Policy and Politics in West Germany: The Growth of a Semisovereign State* (Philadelphia: Temple University Press, 1987).

petition interact in such complex ways that their effects cannot be sorted out cleanly. In all three sectors West German producers are encountering new competitors from Japan as well as other parts of Asia, the Mideast, and the Third World. This new competition has led to renewed efforts throughout the advanced industrial states to enhance competitiveness. The role a more integrated European Community might play in the future thus is of great importance. For the automobile industry, a more integrated Europe might become a possible solution should Japanese competition seriously threaten the market segments into which West German producers are now moving. West German producers could easily endorse the more protectionist stance of French, Italian, and British producers. The European market is already of overwhelming importance for West German automobile firms, and the history of the catalytic converter shows that the West German producers are very aware of the strategic importance of Western Europe. For the chemical industry, however, with its enormous investments in the United States and its global outlook, closer Western European integration might become a problem. Although the European market is important, cartel-like arrangements among European firms are likely to be costly for West German producers who are confident that they can face the competitive pressures on European as well as world markets. For the machinery industry, finally, with its highly specialized and decentralized production profile, Europe is neither a possible solution nor a possible problem. Rather, it is part of a global market in which the industry competes.

Complementing mass-production systems, flexible specialization, made possible by the emergence of new production technologies, has become an important element outside of the core manufacturing industries. Wolfgang Fach and Josef Esser argue in their chapter that through specialization, diversification, mergers, and other means, West German steel producers for many years have adopted policies that have moved them out of crude steel production. In contrast, in the shipbuilding industry, management mistakes in the 1970s, particularly efforts to compete for too long in the market for large bulk carriers and tankers produced much more cheaply in South Korea and Japan, have virtually closed down the industry. The current production of specialty ships and the possible future development of new marine technologies are on so small a scale that the contrast with steel is overwhelming. West Germany remains today the largest and most efficient steel manufacturer in Western Europe precisely because it adopted early and far-reaching programs favoring specialization. Gerd Junne shows that in high-tech industries such as electronics and telecommunications, flexible specialization takes other forms. Nixdorf, for example, is an excellent example of a relatively small and dynamic firm that succeeded by finding profitable market niches such as the provision of in-house, integrated computer systems for the banking and insurance sectors. The West German giant Siemens shows its own variant of flexible specialization. Behind some of its Japanese, North American, and European competitors in the development of hardware, it seeks to specialize in the construction of integrated systems that require expertise and market presence in both electronics and telecommunications. In this instance flexible specialization benefits from large firm size. West Germany is not first in the adoption of new core technologies but it is a close second. For the quick and efficient diffusion of technology the Federal Republic relies on a host of rarely noticed institutions, especially on a regional basis, to assist small and medium-sized firms. American-style venture capitalists, spin-off firms, or technology parks are relatively unimportant.

Finally, service industries also illustrate the convergence of flexible specialization, as in banking, and with mass production, as in insurance. In contrast to manufacturing, Martin Baethge and Herbert Oberbeck argue, services illustrate with particular clarity a point acknowledged explicitly by Horst Kern and Michael Schumann in their chapter. New production technologies can enhance central control over organizations rather than decentralization. And they can increase rather than decrease stressful work.

Across these industries variable institutional mechanisms have shaped West Germany's plants as they were affected by new production technologies. The main institutional innovation in the steel industry has been a move to reorganize corporate structures so as to isolate as fully as possible the traditional, unprofitable steelmaking operations from the profitable parts of the business. The shrinking scope of the parity provisions of the codetermination legislation governing coal, iron, and steel is only one political consideration among a host of financial, economic, and political ones that pushed the managers of the steel industry in this direction.[9] Although corporate reorganization such as the setting up of small, independent, innovative firms funded by industrial giants such as Siemens remains the exception in West Germany, new production technologies have consequences for how established institutional mechanisms work. Collaborative arrangements in collective problem solving or in the application of new technologies bring teams of middle management and skilled workers together. These teams have ambiguous relations to both top management and the works councils as the traditional representatives of business and labor. Furthermore, while acknowledging that the individual's job situation and job satisfaction may well improve, Gerd Junne lists in his chapter a range of possible adverse

9. Ibid., pp. 125–48.

effects of new production technologies on West Germany's system of codetermination. We lack at present adequate empirical evidence to reach firm conclusions. But the argument recurs in Martin Baethge's and Herbert Oberbeck's chapter, based on substantial empirical data in a wide range of service industries. It also resonates with the argument about the trade-off between the quality and the quantity of work which is a central point in the essay by Horst Kern and Michael Schumann.

The importance of West Germany's social movements for these industries has varied a great deal. In the steel and shipbuilding industries social movements have played only a minor role to date. But since the mid-1980s the Greens in particular are attempting to press ahead with some of the union demands for a "national solution." For the Greens nationalization would become part of a new economic strategy oriented more toward domestic than foreign markets, focused on ecologically sound regions, and concentrating on retraining labor for innovative ecological products. Politically these programmatic demands have been without practical consequence. In the two main steel-producing regions, North-Rhine Westfalia and the Saar, the Greens failed to get 5 percent of the popular vote necessary to gain representation in the state parliament. In high-technology industries, on the other hand, the new social movements act as a constraint in some instances and provide possible opportunities for future growth in others. The nuclear industry, like chemicals, has been a central focus of the opposition of West Germany's social movements and the Greens. In microelectronics and biotechnology social attitudes are more ambivalent. Clear-cut opposition exists only to the increased potential for controlling or manipulating the population, as in the case of broadband telecommunications or genetic engineering. Social movement supporters are, as Gerd Junne argues, an important segment of society consuming new electronic products. Often they favor opening up possibilities for more decentralized and less polluting forms of production. Furthermore, the strong opposition of social movements to other high-risk, polluting, high-technology industries may intensify the support for microelectronics and biotechnology among members of the economic and political establishment. Direct constraints imposed on some high-tech industries may lead to indirect opportunities for others. Finally, the effect of the new social movements on the service industries appears to be slight at best. Traditionally close relations between employees and employers appear to be loosening in the banking industry, but it is implausible, given the scanty evidence, to attribute this to the rise of social movements.

The form of state policy also varies across these industries. In steel we encounter cases in which a succession of different forms of state intervention have been tried to assist in the shrinking of overcapacity and the elimination of jobs. Corporatist models of concentration were tried in the 1970s in the Saar and in the 1980s in the Ruhr steel regions. Because of the determined opposition of individual states and corporations to any central solution, the effort to reorganize the industry on a national basis, under the guidance of West Germany's banking community, failed in 1982. Since 1983 government subsidies totaling about DM 3 billion have provided the context in which each corporation has tried to adapt modernization programs best suited to its particular situation. Since 1987 there have been renewed efforts by the federal government, in cooperation with business and labor, to seek a national solution. And the experimentation with corporatist crisis management at local and regional levels has continued. Because the shipbuilding industry was of less economic importance the failure of corporatist methods of crisis management at the regional level, in contrast to steel, never led to efforts to develop a national political solution. In the high-tech industries the shift in policy by and large has been from direct subsidies to a few large firms like Siemens in the 1970s to indirect forms of assistance in the 1980s granted to medium-sized and smaller firms aiming at an acceleration in the diffusion of new production technologies. Finally, state policy affects service industries like banking or insurance indirectly, through the regulatory framework it provides. In the domestic economy government oversight follows a familiar German pattern of self-regulation by the industry, whereas in the international economy government policy has provided the industry with a substantial degree of protection.[10]

International competition and technological change are closely related in shaping an industry's competitiveness. This at least is the pattern suggested by West Germany's core and high-tech industries. Yet it was primarily the competition of less efficient but heavily subsidized West European producers, as in steel, or the competition of low-cost, government-subsidized shipyards in Asia, as in shipbuilding, that accelerated the decline or demise of these two industries. In sharp contrast, in banking and insurance the primary factor affecting competitiveness was technological change.

Finally, at the international level Western Europe plays a role in the variable fortunes of West German industry. The West German steel industry, for example, has been severely hampered by the far-reaching subsidization of its less efficient competitors in Western Europe. But because of West Germany's dependence on open export markets for its other industrial products, including the exports of manufacturing products of other divisions of West Germany's major steel producers, political demands for protectionism have remained muted. Indeed, in the

10. U.S. Congress, Office of Technology Assessment, *International Competition in Services*, OTA-ITE-328 (Washington, D.C.: U.S. Government Printing Office, 1987).

steel trade conflicts between the European Community and the United States, the West German government has typically chosen to play the role of banker. For reasons of both interest and ideology West Germany can at best, as in the case of steel, act the role of a "soft" protectionist. Europe and the larger world beyond are becoming increasingly important as markets for banking and insurance, but to date they have neither been a particular problem nor a possible solution for West German business in these two service sectors. This situation is likely to change as the American pressure for free trade in services is bound to grow. In the area of high-tech industry, on the other hand, the European option is a valuable way of diminishing West Germany's technological dependence on certain U.S. products. The link-up of Siemens and Philips for the joint production of a megabit chip is a good example. Because West German producers like Siemens specialize in the production of high-tech components and systems rather than individual products, they are to some extent sheltered, as Gerd Junne argues, from the creeping protectionism with which other European states support their own national producers.

The message of the six sector studies is clear. West German industry has come through the turbulent 1970s and 1980s remarkably well. Success was neither preordained nor inevitable. In each case reasons for concern exist. Now that market share is no longer easily gained at the expense of other European producers, will West Germany's automobile industry be able to compete against the advantages Japanese producers may have in design? Will West Germany's chemical industry succeed in mastering the new research and product development requirements of biotechnology? Can a modern industrial economy succeed in the long term without a world-class, competitive semiconductor industry? Is West Germany's machinery industry alert enough to avoid a disastrous repeat of the misjudgment of market trends as happened in the machine tool industry in the early 1980s? Only a few years ago, in the early 1980s, answers to these questions were often pessimistic. And even today apparent success stories in machinery, automobiles, and chemicals record some shortcomings of West Germany's industrial order that could prove very damaging in the future.

Yet these studies also show that rapid changes in production technologies, the rise of new social movements, and volatility in international markets have done little to undermine the comparatively strong performance of West Germany in the 1970s and 1980s. As Table 11.2 demonstrates, given the deterioration in the performance of all major capitalist economies since 1960, compared to the other major industrial states West Germany's policy of a "middle way" has held its own,[11] particularly

11. Manfred Schmidt, "West Germany: The Policy of the Middle Way," *Journal of Public Policy* 7 (1987): 135–77.

compared to the United States, the Reagan revolution to the contrary notwithstanding. This is indicated by a sharp deterioration in the American trade balance, inflation, and unemployment rates that exceeded corresponding West German figures and no superior growth performance as measured by real GDP per capita. Compared to Japan, however, between 1979 and 1985 West Germany lost ground. But the sharp appreciation of the yen since 1985 and the projected dramatic decline of new entries into the West German labor market in the early 1990s make it likely that the Federal Republic will do comparatively better in the 1990s. Since they are influenced by many factors, economic performance measures are difficult to evaluate cross-nationally. But the figures in Table 11.2 clearly sustain the minimal claim that the Federal Republic has done reasonably well in the 1970s and 1980s when compared to its major capitalist competitors.

Examining the recent past offers no special insight into what may happen in the future. When asked about the future, John Maynard Keynes is reported to have paused for a long while and then answered, "the future will come." While this book is prospective rather than retrospective, none of the authors pretend to have magic foresight. What they offer is evidence from the recent past that shows convincingly that West German industry has coped very well with multiple sources of change in the 1970s and 1980s, certainly better than the average reader of the American press might suspect.

Table 11.3 summarizes the responses of West German industry to the three sources of change. The central point of this schematic summary as well as the discussion that preceded it is to underline the differences in the pattern of response of different industries. At the plant level distinctive responses combine established industry practices with new ways of coping with change. The institutional mechanisms that are triggered by the convergence of mass production with flexible specialization vary a great deal. At the national level the importance of social movements for different industries also differs, as does the form of state policy. And at the international level the relation of international competition and technological change varies across industries as does the role of Europe.

No single factor or small set of factors—regional setting, corporate characteristics, strength of the labor movement, technological aspects of production, concentration of industry, position in world markets, influence in national politics to name but a few—provides an adequate and parsimonious explanation for the pattern summarized in Table 11.3. Instead, the central point of this table is to emphasize the variability of conditions and patterns of response in specific industries. Widespread experimentation in meeting change is visible everywhere. We are watching a fluid system of industrial production. In myriads of smaller ways that do not make front-page news multiple changes are affecting West

325

Table 11.2. Economic performance of major industrial states, 1960–1985

Country	1 Change in the consumer price index		2 Unemployment as percent of total labor force		3 Change in real GDP per capita		4 Trade balance as percent of GDP		5 Sum of ranks of columns 1–4	
	Rank	Percent	Rank	Percent	Rank	Percent	Rank	Percent	Rank	Sum
West Germany										
1973/74–79	1	4.7	2	3.5	2.5	2.5	1	2.4	1	6.5
1979/80–85	2	4.2	2	6.5	2.5	1.4	1	1.7	2	7.5
1960–85	1	3.9	2	2.8	3	2.7	1	2.1	1.5	7
Japan										
1973/74–79	3	10.0	1	1.9	2.5	2.5	2	0.4	2	8.5
1979/80–85	1	3.6	1	2.4	1	3.3	3	1.4	1	6
1960–85	3	6.4	1	1.7	1	5.7	2	0.8	1.5	7
United States										
1973/74–79	2	8.5	5	6.7	5	1.4	4	−0.4	4	16
1979/80–85	3	6.8	3	8.0	2.5	1.4	5	−1.6	3	13.5
1960–85	2	5.3	4	6.0	4	2.1	5	−0.2	3	15
France										
1973/74–79	4	10.7	4	4.5	1	2.6	3	−0.2	3	12
1979/80–85	5	10.2	4	8.3	5	0.6	4	−1.1	5	18
1960–85	4	7.4	n.d.	n.d.	2	3.1	3	0.1	n.d.	n.d.
United Kingdom										
1973/74–79	5	15.6	3	4.2	4	1.5	5	−1.0	5	17
1979/80–85	4	8.9	5	9.8	4	1.1	2	1.5	4	15
1960–85	5	8.4	3	4.2	5	1.9	4	−0.1	4	17

SOURCE: Organization for Economic Cooperation and Development, *Economic Outlook: Historical Statistics/Perspectives* (Paris: OECD, 1987), pp. 39, 44, 68, 83.

Table 11.3. Industry responses to change

Three sources of change	Shipbuilding, steel	Autos	Chemicals	Machinery	High-tech	Services
Plant level						
Flexible specialization or mass production	Both	Both	Both	Traditional crafts and high-tech crafts	Both	Both
Institutional mechanism	Variable	Variable	Variable	Variable	Variable	Variable
National level						
Importance of social movements	Low	Medium (opportunity)	High (constraint)	Low	Mixed (opportunity/constraint)	Low
Form of state policy	Direct	Indirect	Indirect	Partly direct Partly indirect	Partly direct Partly indirect	Indirect
International level						
Competitiveness affected primarily by international competition or technological change	Primarily international competition	Both	Both	Both	Both	Primarily technological change
Role of Europe	One source of the problem	Possible solution	Possible problem	Unimportant	Possible solution	Unimportant

Germany in the 1980s. Individuals, institutions, and industries are experimenting in new ways to respond to these changes. The Kohl government may have failed to bring about the decisive big change in national politics, but small-scale change and experimentation are nonetheless pervasive in the Federal Republic.

Institutions and Change

The convergence of experimentation with stability is distinctive of West Germany's movement toward the Third Republic. This is in sharp contrast to the politics of the First and the Second Republics. Then as now one could observe dynamic social and economic change. The 1940s and 1950s witnessed, for example, the influx of more than 12 million ethnic German refugees, first from Eastern Europe and later from the German Democratic Republic. In the 1950s West Germany, like the rest of the OECD states, lowered its tariffs substantially and reestablished free convertibility. In the 1960s guest workers began to arrive in large numbers. And in the 1970s in growing numbers West German corporations began to move some of their operations abroad and rationalized their production facilities at home. These and other changes affecting the very base of West Germany's economy and society were accompanied by major institutional changes. This of course was very evident in the prelude to the First Republic when, after 1949, the institutions of postwar Germany took shape in intense battles, for example, over the character of federalism, codetermination, or the role of the social welfare system. But it was also characteristic of the "second founding" of the West German Republic in the mid- and late 1960s. Cooperative federalism, the universities, the system of labor market administration and the consultation among the major political and economic actors about economic policy all represented important institutional changes initiated to address what was then perceived as a pressing agenda of social reform and economic modernization. In contrast, movement toward the Third Republic has not witnessed any analogous major institutional transformations. In contrast to other industrial states, by and large there existed a broad congruence between politics and markets. Getting the state back out of markets simply was less important. And pervasive change has not led to blockages, violent eruptions, and a crisis politics. In West Germany, pervasive changes provide instead an opportunity for recalibrating institutions piecemeal rather than acting as a catalyst for more fundamental institutional change.

Changes in the Relative Position of Institutions

Change occurs within existing institutions rather than through their dismantling. It does so in three different ways.[12] A new context can empower institutions that before had been less central politically; it can disempower institutions that had been central; or it can transform the role institutions play in the larger political economy.

The change from the First to the Second West German Republic in the 1960s illustrates how a new context can empower institutions that had been less central before. In the 1950s the overriding questions for many actors in and analysts of West German politics involved the similarities and differences between Bonn and Weimar. Attention was riveted on the formal institutions of West Germany's young democracy: parliament, the executive, the judiciary, federalism, and the party system. Would these institutions take hold in an authoritarian society defeated in war, suffering through the trauma of national partition, bloated by a refugee population which at any moment might turn to an irredentist politics, and harboring millions who had been committed Nazis? The "economic miracle" of the 1950s, everyone recognized, promised an answer too easy for many of these troubling questions. Indeed, the fear, still lingering in the 1970s, was that West German democracy might be no more than a fair weather democracy. Without the inducements of a prosperous economy, the Germans would probably turn, as they had before, to a nondemocratic politics.

At the center of the Second West German Republic was a second set of institutions. The peak associations of business, a centralized labor movement, centralized professional organizations, and a wide range of parapublic institutions were critically important components of "model Germany." West German democracy was no longer feared to be unstable; rather, it was criticized at times for being too stable. Neocorporatist politics was viewed as centralized, secretive, and technocratic. Suiting well technical criteria of efficiency, it was viewed uneasily as lacking in democratic participation. As the West German economy outperformed most of its competitors after 1973, political unease began to focus on the evident limits of a neocorporatist politics to attract the political loyalties of the young and other members of oppositional social movements.

The pattern of institutional stability and widespread experimentation which distinguishes the 1980s invites us to shift attention once again from the formal institutions of a liberal democracy and the peaks of the institutional oligarchies of West Germany's neocorporatist democracy

12. I am indebted to Gary Herrigel for his incisive comments on an earlier draft of this section.

to other institutions such as the works councils and the vocational training system dispersed throughout West German society. The acceleration of technological change, the reinvigoration of civil society through new social movements, and the changes and competition imposed from abroad are providing a new impetus for change within existing institutions.

Over time a new political context can also lead to institutional atrophy. Fringe political parties are an excellent example. Refugee parties in the First Republic were always suspect as potential supporters of an undemocratic politics. The center of such a political challenge to West Germany, it was feared, was a succession of neo-Nazi parties as well as political splinter movements to the left of the SPD. In the 1950s extremist parties were outlawed and refugee parties garnered just under 10 percent of the national vote. During the first postwar recession of 1966–67 the votes for the neo-Nazi party in several state elections approached 10 percent. The party missed by a hair receiving 5 percent of the national vote in 1969 and thus entering the Bundestag. But the sharp economic downturns of the mid-1970s and early 1980s have not led to a revival of extremist parties. West German society has absorbed and assimilated the overwhelming majority of former refugees. Neo-Nazi and Communist splinter parties received less than 1 percent of the national vote in the 1980s. The passing of time, the dynamics of electoral competition among the large established parties, and state policy all have helped in bringing about this atrophy of the radical political parties of the 1950s and 1960s.

The fate of institutionalized policy conversations among the political and economic leadership of West Germany is a second example of institutional atrophy. Convened by the economics minister, the "concerted action" was a quarterly meeting of the leaders of the major West German institutions. The meetings were voluntary. No votes were taken, and no minutes were kept. The main purpose of the open-ended discussion was to share information on the condition and likely future of the West German economy. Rather than creating an institutional forum for coordinating central decisions, the concerted action was designed to avoid or limit unnecessary distributional struggles based on faulty economic projections. Its heavily technocratic and secretive character did not withstand the pressures of the economic turmoil of the 1970s. When the Federation of Employers challenged the constitutionality of an extension of the principle of codetermination before the Constitutional Court, the unions decided to withdraw in 1977. Chancellor Schmidt proceeded to orchestrate other discussions serving similar political objectives. In the Third Republic such meetings have occurred very rarely, and they serve largely the symbolic purpose of signaling the existence of open lines of communication between a center-right coalition government and West Germany's trade unions. Secret, all-embracing, top-level policy conversations are not central to running the political and economic affairs of the Third Republic.

Third, and finally, besides empowering or disempowering institutions, a new context can also affect the role institutions play in the larger political economy by altering their relative positions. West German federalism and regional economic policy are cases in point. In the First Bonn Republic federalism centered largely on the jurisdictional and constitutional struggles between the federal and state governments. Of all the issues this had been the most contentious one the Parliamentary Council confronted while drawing up the Basic Law, West Germany's constitution, in 1948–49. The states were jealous of their strong position and ultimately opposed to any encroachments by the federal government. But in the 1960s awareness grew rapidly that the states often lacked the resources necessary to cope with economic and social change and to live up to the constitutional mandate of assuring equal social and economic opportunities for all citizens, irrespective of their place of residence.

The institutional overhaul at the outset of the Second Republic thus included provisions for the cooperation of federal and state governments in a number of "joint tasks," including regional industry policy. West Germany's system of "cooperative federalism," it was originally thought, would lead to stronger influence and control of the federal government. Instead, in numerous policy arenas, including regional industrial policy, a carefully calibrated system of distributive politics prevailed that defied quick adjustment through centralized control. Economic and social pressure eventually shifted away from the underprivileged, marginal rural areas in the 1960s and 1970s toward the congested urban areas and old manufacturing regions suffering in the 1980s from a crucial shortage of moderately priced housing and often double-digit unemployment. Thus state governments in the growing south and in the declining north have expanded their role in economic management. Lothar Späth, governor of Baden-Württemberg, built his political reputation on having managed aggressively and successfully a deliberate policy of regional industrial modernization.[13] In neighboring

13. Charles F. Sabel et al., "Regional Prosperities Compared: Massachusetts and Baden-Württemberg in the 1980s," *Discussion Paper* ICM/LMP (Wissenschaftszentrum Berlin, 1987); Christopher S. Allen, "Regional Governments and Economic Policies in the Federal Republic of Germany: The 'Meso' Politics of Industrial Adjustment," paper presented at the 1987 Meetings of the Southern Political Science Association, Charlotte, N.C., 5–7 November 1987; Hans E. Maier, "Das Modell Baden-Württemberg. Über institutionelle Voraussetzungen differenzierter Qualitätsproduktion—Eine Skizze," *Discussion Paper* IIM/LMP (Wissenschaftszentrum Berlin, 1987).

331

Bavaria, the CSU has followed for decades a strategy of decentralized, rural industrialization, supplemented by the political efforts of CSU leader Franz-Josef Strauss of concentrating some of the major high-tech armament and aerospace manufacturers around Munich.[14] Between 1979 and 1984 North-Rhine Westfalia funded an ambitious program of regional industrial development thus hoping to revive its declining centers of heavy industry in the Ruhr valley. And farther north the city-states of West Berlin, Hamburg, and Bremen are trying to make themselves once again attractive especially for investments by high-tech industries.

The upshot of these different developments has been the same everywhere. Small and medium-sized firms in particular are relying increasingly on institutional support cultures—university research institutes, technical universities, vocational schools, local and regional Chambers of Commerce providing consulting services for marketing and sales, and a variety of technological assistance institutes—that are designed to help them in the transition from artisanal to high-technology production. In addition, the federal government is assisting with sectoral policies designed to accelerate the spread of new production technologies. West German states have clearly become more important actors on questions of industrial policy. Their initiatives rather than what remains of the cooperative federalism of the Second Republic mark the politics of the Third Republic. As in many other instances, the signals point here to decentralizing tendencies within political and economic structures that are stable at the national and international levels.

Three Stabilizing Factors

Why does the widespread experimentation and change affecting West German industry in the 1980s not result in large-scale institutional transformations? The reason is threefold. It lies in the enduring international structure that circumscribes West German choices, in the institutional continuities of West Germany's semisovereign state, and in the tight institutional links between the industrial arenas that are experiencing change and national institutions.

West Germany has been the clearest demarcation line in the bipolar postwar world order that Joanne Gowa has analyzed. Germany's division and the political relations between the two superpowers have been part and parcel of the same bipolar structure. Over time international

14. Aline Kuntz, "Regional Differentiation in the Federal Republic: Conservative Modernization in Bavaria," *German Studies Newsletter* 8 (July 1986): 16–20; Kuntz, "Conservatives in Crisis: The Bavarian Christian Social Union and the Ideology of Antimodernism," diss., Cornell University, 1987.

tensions along the border between the two Germanies have lessened. Berlin no longer is a serious international trouble spot as it had been in the 1940s and 1950s. The Western alliance is no longer absolutely essential to the self-definition of all West Germans. Other international political arrangements in Europe have become imaginable, especially as long as the winds of political and economic reform blow strongly from the East. Western Europe, for example, might eventually emerge as a potential buffer for and supporter of West Germany. But major institutional and political change in West Germany would probably require more than an intensification of intra-European relations. A neutralist West Germany or an isolationist United States is possible, though hardly probable, as an alternative future. But short of these or some other dramatic changes in the structure of the international state system, institutional and political continuities in West Germany are reinforced by the very slow rate of change in the international system.

A second reason for the stability of the institutions in West Germany's Third Republic is the strong legacy of a dense network of parapublic institutions.[15] They bridge the public and private realms and facilitate a relatively quiet process of formulating and implementing public policy. Many of these institutions date back to the nineteenth century; others were created only after 1945. They include corporate bodies, foundations, and institutes that typically are organized under public law. Examples include Chambers of Commerce and Industry, professional associations, and public radio and TV stations. These institutions express a general German principle of organization: independent governance of social sectors under the general supervision of the state. The political intent is to marshal the expertise of the major social and economic sectors under the auspices of state authority and thus to make the exercise of state power both technically more informed and politically less oppressive. Parapublic institutions act like shock absorbers. They induce stability both directly and indirectly. Political controversies are typically limited in the process of policy implementation. And the very presence of these institutions limits the scope of policy initiatives. This distinctive institutional structure dates far back in German history and covers most policy sectors since 1945. Political conflict among different social interests finds precious little open space in the Federal Republic.

A third major reason for the stability of West German institutions is intimately linked to the second. There exist tight links between numerous changes in West German industry and stable institutions in national politics. In the automobile industry, to name but one example, adjustment to change was facilitated by the close links between a voca-

15. Katzenstein, *Policy and Politics in West Germany.*

tional training system and a skilled labor force, between engineering schools and middle management, between factory councils and unions, and between thousands of small suppliers and the major car producers. Technological, economic, and social changes are thus filtered into existing institutions rather than bypassing them and pressing for fundamental institutional change. I shall illustrate this political feature of the Third Republic with reference to West Germany's system of industrial relations and vocational training.

West Germany has a dual system of industrial relations in which unions are responsible for collective bargaining and participation in codetermination in the boardroom while elected works councils help organize working conditions inside plants and at the workplace. The relation between unions and works councils is symbiotic. Eighty percent of the elected works councillors are union members. Modified and extended in the 1970s, both institutions together have resulted in a cooperative management of the conflictual relations between labor and business. The legal protection that codetermination has granted West German labor has made manpower policy a permanent objective of corporate management and has maintained corporate flexibility in the face of technological change.[16] The strong role of the works councils in recruitment, dismissal, and assignment of workers within the plant has similarly encouraged a long-term approach to manpower policy that has been conducive to accommodating technological change. On the other hand, new production technologies have shifted the relative power from the unions to the works councils. The entire system of industrial relations is becoming more decentralized and based around individual enterprises. National unions, however, still remain important actors, offering organizational support and expertise to works councils rather than defining uniform regulations covering entire industries.

West Germany's vocational training system provides for a different dualism. The young are educated in schools and trained in firms.[17] The

16. Wolfgang Streeck, "Co-determination: The Fourth Decade," in Bernhard Wilpert and Arndt Sorge, eds., *International Perspectives on Organizational Democracy* (New York: Wiley, 1984), pp. 391–422; Wolfgang Streeck, "Industrial Relations in West Germany, 1974–1985: An Overview," in Everett Kassalow, ed., *Unions and Industrial Relations— Recent Trends and Prospects—A Comparative Treatment*, special issue of *Bulletin of Comparative Labour Relations* 16 (1987): 151–66; Streeck, "Industrial Relations in West Germany: Agenda for Change," *Discussion Paper* IIM/LMP (Wissenschaftszentrum Berlin, 1987); Streeck, "The Uncertainties of Management in the Management of Uncertainty: Employers, Labour Relations and Industrial Adjustment in the 1980s," *Work, Employment and Society* 1 (1987): 281–308; Arndt Sorge and Wolfgang Streeck, "Industrial Relations and Technical Change: The Case for an Extended Perspective," in Richard Hyman and Streeck, eds., *New Technology and Industrial Relations* (Oxford: Blackwell, 1988).

17. Josef Hilbert, Helmi Sudmersen, and Hajo Weber, "Selbstordnung der Berufs-bildung. Eine Fallstudie über die Evolution, Organisation und Funktion 'Privater Regierungen,'" Universität Bielefeld, Arbeitsberichte und Forschungsmaterialien, no. 18,

system centers around West German business in providing an adequate number of vocational training positions to absorb successive generations of youngsters who enter West German labor markets each year. But it also involves the peak associations of business and the trade unions in cooperatively defining the school curriculum and job qualifications of a large number of occupations and trades. Finally, it requires the backing of the state to sanction as public policy the agreements hammered out by the various groups. This elaborate system of organizing this very important feature of West Germany's political economy links individual firms to top-level institutions. When, as in the 1980s, the number of potential apprentices exceeds the number of open positions, the reverberations are felt right up to the office of the chancellor. The expected severe apprentice shortage in the 1990s will probably also link grass-roots and national-level institutions in ways that are hard to foresee today. Technological like demographic change also links the different levels of the system. The adoption of new production technologies requires a respecification of the qualification requirements of a skilled worker. This is an elaborate and slow process involving all of the major actors, including the unions, and resulting in new state regulation only when a consensus solution acceptable to all has been found.

West Germany's system of industrial relations and vocational training serve here only as examples of the tight links between changes in industry and national institutions that are a crucial political feature of the Third West German Republic. Together with a deeply rooted system of parapublic institutions and West Germany's position in the international state system, these tight links help to account for the absence of large-scale institutional change despite widespread experimentation.

Political Interests in Institutional Stability

The flexibility of West German industry and the experimentation with which business and labor seek to adjust to new economic conditions is to some extent reflected in the political conflicts and programmatic debates over the future course of West German politics. But even these conflicts and debates within and between the major political parties, the business community, and the unions show that large-scale institutional change was in the end politically unobtainable and unappealing. It was unobtainable for the simple but important reason that the constitutional

1986; Stephen F. Hamilton, "Apprenticeship as a Transition to Adulthood in West Germany," *American Journal of Education* 95 (February 1987): 314–45; Wolfgang Streeck et al., *The Role of the Social Partners in Vocational Training and Further Training in the Federal Republic of Germany* (Berlin: European Centre for the Development of Vocations Training, 1987).

provisions are such that only a solid majority in the Bundestag and a two-thirds majority in the Bundesrat would have given the CDU/CSU the power to legislate far-reaching institutional changes without taking account of the policy preferences of either the F.D.P. as its coalition partner or the SPD as the major opposition party. As is true of the United States, in its own ways West Germany's political and constitutional order tends to disperse power, and this necessarily inhibits effecting large-scale institutional change.

In the 1980s important social groups and political parties made a decision against a fundamental overhaul of the institutional order that defined West German politics in the 1970s. But they have not yet made a self-conscious decision to embrace that order. Instead, one has the impression that interest group leaders and party elites are looking for concepts that help them better understand and respond to the conditions of the 1980s and 1990s. The exhaustion of the economic policy approaches of the 1960s and 1970s had become evident to the leading party theoreticians of economic policy, Kurt Biedenkopf for the CDU, Wolfgang Roth and Oskar Lafontaine for the SPD, and a group of authors for the Greens. Yet confronted by structural unemployment, ecological crisis, and international competition, in their different ways the books they published reflect a convergence between cautious traditionalism and radical reorientation.

Biedenkopf's book is noteworthy because it seeks to find a political solution for a low-growth society that no longer relies on the pushing and hauling among interest groups and political parties.[18] For Biedenkopf that solution centers around the "ordo-liberalism" which Ludwig Erhard, the economics minister of the First Republic and briefly its chancellor in the 1960s, had made popular in the 1950s. Society is a self-regulating mechanism that uses both market competition and general state regulations to maintain freedom, justice, and order. But Biedenkopf's traditionalism is compatible with policy prescriptions to which the mainstream of the CDU does not respond naturally, for example, a shorter workweek or vigorous protection of the environment. Furthermore, Biedenkopf accuses his own party, rather than the SPD, of having traded, in the late 1950s, Erhard's version of liberalism for an electorally popular social welfare state funded by the temporary dividends of economic growth.

Wolfgang Roth's book also exemplifies a fundamentally traditional orientation.[19] Roth defends a growth-oriented economic policy that

18. Kurt H. Biedenkopf, *Die Neue Sicht der Dinge: Plädoyer für eine freiheitliche Wirtschafts- und Sozialordnung* (Munich: Piper, 1985).

19. Wolfgang Roth, *Der Weg aus der Krise. Umrisse einer sozial-ökologischen Marktwirtschaft* (Munich: Kindler, 1985).

seeks to eliminate unemployment. Significantly, Roth is silent on how to reach an objective in the future which scores of special state programs failed to address in the past when the SPD controlled the levers of power in Bonn. Yet the book is explicit in defending market institutions, acknowledging the need for rationalization investments by business, and courting business to support state industrial policy. Roth also seeks to integrate the protection of the environment into his economic program. Codetermination of capital and labor in the running of West German industry is to be enlarged to accommodate representatives of ecological interests. And new environmental technologies and products should be fostered as areas of future economic growth. Roth's "social-ecological" market economy is tailor-made to build a bridge to the Greens, which have undermined the political prospects of the SPD more directly than those of other parties. Whether such a bridge might become a viable structure for future coalition governments is one of the central questions in the evolution of the Third West German Republic.

Oskar Lafontaine is by far the youngest member of the SPD's top leadership and a possible candidate for the office of chancellor in the years ahead. Although on questions of foreign policy he is to be counted as a prominent member of the party's left wing, Lafontaine's views on economic and social issues are well to the right of the mainstream of the party and especially the labor movement.[20] Because of the growing internationalization of the West German economy, Lafontaine regards the objective of full employment as unobtainable through national policy. Instead he proposes to redefine the concept of work by including socially useful, unpaid employment. This enlarged concept of work should be secured for all citizens through a variety of social policies including social security, social assistance, unemployment compensation, and state subsidies for education and vocational training and retraining programs. At the same time Lafontaine favors a further reduction in the workweek even at the cost of sacrificing wage increases. The assertion of individual identities and changes in collective solidarities within existing institutions for Lafontaine evidently is not only a challenge for established union policies but also offers an opportunity for the SPD to end its political isolation through a renewed coalition with the F.D.P.

Because of their heterogeneous character the Greens do not have one economic policy program.[21] But the demand for the forceful implementation of long-term objectives, such as defense of the environment, the

20. Oskar Lafontaine, *Die Gesellschaft der Zukunft* (Hamburg: Hoffman and Campe, 1988).
21. Frank Beckenbach et al., *Grüne Wirtschaftspolitik—Machbare Utopien* (Cologne: Kiepenheuer & Witsch, 1986).

337

yearning for smaller-scale forms of organizing social and political life, the preference for combating unemployment through a "green industrialization" policy, and the attempt to transcend partial perspectives on emerging policy problems appears to be central to any Green program on how to manage a rapidly changing, modern industrial economy. These tenets overlap with parts of the programmatic writings of Biedenkopf and Roth. The convergence between traditionalism and reorientation thus is noticeable in the 1980s even among the most radical critics of West Germany's political and economic practices.

These programmatic discussions are to some extent reflected in the conflict within political parties. Lothar Späth, CDU governor of Baden-Württemberg, and the late Franz-Josef Strauss, leader of the CSU and governor of Bavaria, exemplify different forms of state intervention. In Baden-Württemberg's decentralized regional economy state activity is geared primarily to assisting medium-sized and small firms. Bavaria, by contrast, features in addition large corporations active particularly in the defense and aerospace industries, which require stronger and more direct forms of state intervention. These differences between the CDU and CSU are, however, small compared to the shrinking of state influence demanded vocally by the right wing of the F.D.P. To the small numbers of West German supporters of supply-side economics and deregulation, state intervention from the Right has as few redeeming features as does state intervention from the Left. After 1983 this led to a celebrated confrontation between the F.D.P. and the CSU over the partial privatization of Lufthansa Airlines, which has been stalled by the adamant opposition and skillful maneuvering of Bavaria's Governor Franz-Josef Strauss.

Within the SPD the rifts over economic policy are concealed by the search for a political alliance strategy with the Greens. But the party represents in fact three different positions. One group favors a mixture of nationalization, tripartite industrywide consultation or investment planning, and aggressive development of high-technology industries. Looking for possible alliances with the Greens, a second group seeks, as do the Greens, to develop a decentralized modernization strategy around pollution-free industries. Finally, a third and probably the largest group prefers a more centrist course of modified Keynesianism that focuses on the elimination of unemployment and accommodates technological change.

These political debates and conflicts also occur in the business community and in the labor movement. Large corporations and small firms are pressing for greater flexibility, particularly in the deployment of labor and in the allocation of work time. But in contrast to small and medium-sized businesses, big corporations need to take into account the position of the unions in West Germany's social market economy. Weakening organized labor too much might foster union irresponsibility and undermine an essential pillar of West Germany's economy. As Wolfgang Streeck argues in his chapter, the "old" social movement of capitalism aims at transforming West Germany's political economy perhaps more than do the "new" social movements and the Greens. Although this conflict within the business community surfaced in 1984, during the prolonged strike for a shortened workweek, it is built into the technological changes and political character of the emerging Third Republic.

The labor movement suffers from other strains stemming from the same new context. Technological change, as Kern and Schumann argue, is empowering some groups of workers but not others. More significant, the growing importance of labor markets within the major firms has strengthened the position of the works councils and skilled workers at the expense of the unions and semiskilled or unskilled labor. Traditional working-class solidarities are naturally threatened in an era of fundamental structural changes involving entire industries and regions of the country. The unwillingness of important actors to tear asunder the fabric of national institutions as well as the convergence between traditionalism and reorientation in the programmatic discussion explain the absence of sustained political pressure for fundamental institutional or political change at the national level.

Because their stability is so impressive, at first glance the national institutions of the Third Republic do not appear to respond to economic and social change. The remarkable continuities between the Second and the Third Republics reinforce this impression. But this is only one part of the story. The structure of the international state system and the legacy of its semisovereign state do not easily permit large-scale institutional change. But national institutions are open to more subtle changes that give expression to the experimentation occurring in economy and society. Change is occurring within institutions rather than bypassing them. And the relative importance of these institutions shifts gradually over time. Put differently, change is not blocked. It occurs in small doses that make West Germany's political life fairly predictable.

Tendencies toward Decentralization

The convergence between institutional stability and widespread experimentation creates decentralization tendencies within existing institutions. I shall try to support this argument by briefly looking at the more centralized response of industry and politics in two sectoral crises, coal in the 1960s and textiles in the 1960s and 1970s. Furthermore, government policy affecting especially high-technology industries also favored a more centralized approach in the 1960s and 1970s.

When the world coal glut finally hit West German producers in 1957, it was the beginning of a prolonged structural crisis for one of West Germany's key industries. For political reasons the allies decentralized the industry after 1945 and, in the form of the Schumann Plan, made it part of the cornerstone for a more integrated Western Europe. Finally, as in iron and steel, the unions won the right for parity codetermination in the coal industry, thus assuring themselves of half of the votes on the supervisory boards of coal corporations. Between 1957 and 1967 a variety of halfhearted government assistance programs failed to stop the shrinking of the industry, especially in employment. The economic recession of 1967 finally triggered forceful action of the federal government. A special law passed in 1968 provided for the concentration of most of the industry in one large national economy, the Ruhrkohle AG. A new federal commissioner for coal mining was appointed. Under the auspices of the Bundesrat a Coal Advisory Council was set up which included all of the relevant actors. And the industry became the first training ground for developing an active labor market policy providing for more generous separation pay as well as retraining and moving allowances. These changes were possible politically because of the strong position of the unions in the industry as well as the growing role of the SPD in national politics and its prominent position in North-Rhine Westfalia, West Germany's largest state and home of most of the mining industry. The overall response thus was to centralize control largely in the hands of the federal government, to share power with the unions in the key decisions, and to assist business by offering a guaranteed stream of income instead of uncertain future profits. Concentration and concertation aptly summarize the response to the coal crisis.

West Germany's textile and garment industries also experienced a serious structural crisis in the late 1960s and early 1970s.[22] An intense labor shortage rather than foreign competition was the primary impetus for a far-reaching investment program favoring rationalization, capital deepening, and a strategy of mass production. To reduce labor costs further West German producers opted for a strategy of outward processing, leaving the most labor-intensive stages of production to Eastern European or Mediterranean producers who would ship the product

22. Folker Fröbel, Jürgen Heinrichs, and Otto Kreye, *Die neue internationale Arbeitsteilung: Strukturelle Arbeitslosigkeit in den Industrieländern und die Industrialisierung der Entwicklungsländer* (Reinbek: Rowohlt, 1977); Fröbel, Heinrichs, and Kreye, *Umbruch in der Weltwirtschaft: Die globale Strategie: Verbilligung der Arbeitskraft, Flexibilisierung der Arbeit, Neue Technologien* (Reinbek: Rowohlt, 1986); Wayne Brooke Nelson, "Maintaining Competitiveness: Lessons from the West German Textile Industry," M.A. thesis, Massachusetts Institute of Technology, 1987.

back to West Germany for finishing. As a result, employment declined by a third. The federal government was not involved in this program of structural adjustment but West German banks were. West Germany's leading textile firm at the time, Delden, invested DM 200 million in less than six years. A long-term investment perspective and access to capital markets were thus provided by banks intent on modernizing the industry and making it again competitive in world markets. By the mid-1970s the experiment appeared to have succeeded. The export value of textiles and garments rivaled that of iron and steel. And between 1975 and 1982 the annual growth of exports of textiles and garments was above 10 percent, thus making it one of the most successful export industries.[23] West Germany's "private" policy became a model for its West European competitors. Adjustment had been timely, and its international dimension, outward processing, eventually became part of the policy model advocated by the European Community. West Germany's defense of liberal market solutions to the problems the textile and clothing industry has faced since the late 1970s would have been less plausible had it not experienced a successful restructuring of this industry with the help of its centralized, private banking sector.

In the 1980s neither public nor private interventions have been as centralized in addressing crisis conditions in particular industries or of particular firms. In both steel and shipbuilding the federal government has studiously avoided getting too deeply entangled. Instead it has preferred delegating responsibility either to individual states, as in shipbuilding, or to advisory councils which were charged, as in steel, to prepare reorganization plans. Similarly, the failure of West Germany's banks in the early 1980s to rescue AEG, West Germany's second largest electronics firm, was an important signal indicating that the era of a centralized private industrial policy was over. This is not to argue that the federal government or the banks could never be drawn directly into sectoral crises. But the threshold for centralized public or private crisis management has risen substantially.

Past government policy seeking to influence the evolution of West Germany's high-technology industries also favored a more centralized approach than appears to be distinctive of the Third Republic.[24] The putative technology gap between the United States and West Germany

23. Werner Väth, "Konservative Modernisierungspolitik ein Widerspruch in sich? Zur Neuausrichtung der Forschungs- und Technologiepolitik der Bundesregierung," *Prokla* 14 (1984): 83–103.

24. Frieder Naschold, "Technological Politics in the Federal Republic of Germany," *Discussion Paper* IIVG (Wissenschaftszentrum Berlin, 1983); Väth, "Konservative Modernisierungspolitik"; Ergas, "Does Technology Policy Matter?"; National Science Foundation, *The Science and Technology Resources of West Germany: A Comparison with the United States*, Special Report NSF 86-310 (Washington, D.C.: National Science Foundation, 1986).

spurred efforts in the mid- and late 1960s to give general indirect aid not only for basic research in the universities and research institutes like the Max-Planck Society but to focus indirect aid on specific projects in four areas: nuclear energy, aerospace, data processing, and marine research. In the 1970s a more interventionist-minded SPD government created the Ministry for Research and Technology to meet the challenge of modernizing the West German economy. The federal government adopted a sectoral approach to problems of industrial structure aiming, among others, at the support of technology diffusion through direct government subsidies for individual projects. At the same time the federal government developed programs and political structures for a socially oriented technology policy which involved the labor movement in devising programs to avert some of the negative consequences of technological change for workers.

State-centered or corporatist-style technology policy has become less important in the 1980s. The growth in government programs has slowed down dramatically from 7.4 percent in 1975–79 to 2.4 percent in 1983–87.[25] And the allocation for the largest and most centralized research program, the nuclear industry, has been slashed in half.[26] Support for production technologies is increasing disproportionately, but in 1987 this area accounted for only 1 percent of the total federal research and development budget. Although the federal government continues to be concerned over the international competitiveness of West German industry, it has discontinued direct funding of product development and has adopted instead a comprehensive plan for the development of communications technologies administered by different ministries and agencies. Although there exist strong continuities in government policy from the Second to the Third Republics, a tendency toward decentralization is also evident.

The telecommunications industry is a case in point.[27] Changes in technology and deregulation in the United States since the late 1970s

25. National Science Foundation, *Science and Technology Resources of West Germany*, p. 14.
26. Väth, "Konservative Modernisierungspolitik," p. 93.
27. Marcellus S. Snow, "Telecommunications and Media Policy in West Germany: Recent Developments," *Journal of Communication* 32 (Summer 1982): 10–32; Karl-Heinz Neumann, "Economic Policy toward Telecommunications, Information and the Media in West Germany," in M. S. Snow, ed., *Marketplace for Telecommunications: Regulation and Deregulation in Industrialized Democracies* (New York: Longman, 1986), pp. 131–52; Douglas Webber, "The Politics of Telecommunications Deregulation in the Federal Republic of Germany," University of Sussex, School of Social Sciences, Government-Industry Relations Project, 1986; Kevin Morgan and Douglas Webber, "Divergent Paths: Political Strategies for Telecommunications in Britain, France and West Germany," *West European Politics* 9 (October 1986): 56–79; Webber, "The Assault on the 'Fortress of the Rhine': The Politics of Telecommunications Deregulation in the Federal Republic of Germany," paper presented at the Conference of the Council of European Studies, Washington, D.C., 30 October–1 November 1987.

have provided the context for several government reports and public debate of the monopoly position of the German Post Office in this crucial industry. Significantly, the West German telecommunications regime has remained very stable. The Post Office continues to be part of the system of public administration. Attempts to turn the Post Office into an independent public corporation have failed. Privatization appears to be out of the question. And the trend to opening the domestic market to foreign suppliers has been slight. The institutional stability in this industry is striking. Yet significant changes are nonetheless occurring. Deregulation in the terminal equipment market is enhancing limited competition. And even in the core telecommunications equipment market relations between the Post Office and its traditional suppliers are changing as more competitive bidding procedures for telecommunications equipment have been adopted. Decentralizing tendencies are altering relationships that for decades had been very tight.

THE THIRD REPUBLIC IN COMPARATIVE PERSPECTIVE

Three Republics

The pattern of policy change characteristic of West Germany in the 1980s raises the intriguing question of how movement toward the Third Republic in the 1980s compares to the first two republics.

Most of the major innovations in foreign and domestic policy were made in 1949–52, the prelude to the First Republic, and in 1966–69, the prelude to the Second. Even though the final capstone was laid only with the Paris Agreements in 1955, in the first three years of his chancellorship Konrad Adenauer basically put into place the framework for his policy of Western integration. Similarly, the years 1966–69 were an essential preparatory phase for Chancellor Brandt's successful completion of his Eastern policy in 1969–72. In Adenauer's case the initial three years were more important; Brandt's Eastern policy, on the other hand, was primarily executed between 1969 and 1972. Yet in both instances West Germany's two major foreign policy initiatives were condensed into two five-year periods.

The same is true of domestic policy. Central to the first period was a great struggle over the character of West Germany's industrial relations system. In 1951 labor won a big political victory, equal representation on the supervisory boards of firms in the iron, coal, and steel industries. The Works Constitution Act of 1952, however, was a major defeat. It extended the principle of codetermination to the major corporations outside of these three industries but granted labor only one-third of the seats on supervisory boards. This subtle yet decisive change set the

343

agenda for the labor movement for the next three decades. The prelude to the Second Republic (1966–69) was defined politically by the formation of the Great Coalition between the CDU/CSU and the SPD. These few years saw major innovations in economic policy, in the budget process, and in a variety of institutions linking federal and state governments which permitted reform and innovations in fields such as regional, labor market, education, and administrative reform policy.

In sharp contrast in the 1980s, neither in foreign nor in domestic policy have there been any dramatic breaks. This would in any case have been unlikely in 1980–83, when the SPD was gradually losing its grip on power. But significantly it did not occur either after Chancellor Kohl won a resounding victory at the polls in 1983. In 1984–85 some segments of the CDU/CSU, the F.D.P., and the business community discussed the desirability of a fundamental change in West Germany's political order. Conflict with the labor movement increased sharply in a bitter strike over the thirty-five-hour workweek in 1984 and changes in the legislation covering strike actions and lockouts. But in the end the important actors preferred not to disrupt well-established political relations and institutions.

The remaining years of the First and Second Republics, as well as the movement toward a Third Republic that we are witnessing in the 1980s, have been utterly devoid of dramatic political gestures or substantial deviations from well-tested policies. Political problems do of course exist. But they are broken up and factored in an orderly manner within the dense institutional policy network distinctive of the Federal Republic. This institutionalization of virtually all political problems into a mold that generates a centrist politics explains the frustrations critics on the political Left and Right have experienced throughout the postwar era. West German neo-Marxists often point to the latent crisis of West German capitalism. To some extent this is the political credo of neo-Marxism everywhere. But in the case of West Germany, one might argue that neo-Marxists are correct in sensing movement and change underneath the secure institutional blanket that distinguishes West German politics. But though they are correct in sensing movement, neo-Marxists mistake the process of experimentation, of breaking political and policy problems into smaller components, for a process of social fermentation and the onset of large-scale political change. Analogous frustrations exist on the opposite side of the political spectrum. West German conservatives often express the desire to deal with political problems through direct action that would tear asunder the densely woven institutional fabric of West German politics. Because they inhibit forceful political leadership, the density and multiplicity of West Germany's rich institutional life is anathema to many conservatives. Somehow West German conservatives feel robbed of the deeper meanings of political action and political life in a system that makes it difficult to raise the arm and virtually impossible to wield the ax.

Why, we may ask, was large-scale institutional change possible only in the prelude to the First Republic and in the transition to the Second Republic? Why did political incrementalism prevail in the remaining three decades? In particular, why has movement toward the Third Republic been marked by a fundamental continuity in the big political picture? In the West German case, two factors in particular appear to determine the incidence of large-scale institutional change: fundamental changes in the international system and basic realignments in West Germany's party system. The shift in American foreign policy that occurred in 1947 was reinforced dramatically by the outbreak of the Korean War. This made possible Adenauer's strategy of Western integration rather than the SPD's preferred policy of neutralism and unification. Similarly, the nonproliferation treaty of 1967 and the détente policy pursued by the two superpowers after Richard Nixon's election to the presidency created an international constellation favorable for the preparation and implementation of Chancellor Brandt's Eastern policy. In the realm of party politics the early years of the First Republic saw dramatic movement toward the consolidation of the position of the CDU/CSU. Its electoral share increased from 31 percent in 1949 to 45 percent in 1953, while the SPD's strength stagnated just under the 30 percent mark. And the Great Coalition, which the CDU/CSU and SPD formed in the years 1966–69, gave the government total control of the Bundestag and the entire federal policy machinery.

In contrast to these earlier periods of large-scale change, the early 1980s witnessed not structural changes in international or domestic politics but merely a deterioration in the international climate and a change in the composition of the government. The deterioration of American-Soviet relations and the decline in the international economy seriously affected the political capacities of the Schmidt government to sustain itself in power. They did not, however, amount to a break in the structure of international constraints and opportunities in which the Federal Republic had moved since its inception. The existence of American deterrence and a liberal international economy were questioned by some segments of the population on both sides of the Atlantic. But political support for a continuation of the Western alliance system never was in doubt. The Schmidt government was toppled by the decision of the F.D.P. to realign itself with the CDU/CSU rather than see its electoral prospects damaged, perhaps irretrievably, by the evident crisis of the SPD. Although the rise of the Greens has affected the position of the SDP more adversely than that of the other major parties, the electoral

345

majority of the CDU/CSU and F.D.P. continues, as did the SPD-F.D.P. coalition in 1976 and 1980, to hover around the 55 percent mark. In sum, the conditions that made possible large-scale changes in the preludes to the First and Second Republics did not exist in the 1980s.

But this argument conceals a more important theoretical point. The relatively optimistic conclusion of this book written by political scientists and sociologists points to an intriguing suggestion. The very condition that economists, especially in North America, often point to as the most serious impediment to West Germany's economic growth, the case studies in Part III identify as the key to West Germany's international competitiveness. West Germany has prospered because of the density of its institutional life that for the economist's taste seems to encroach too much on markets. This has not led to the institutional arteriosclerosis economists fear, brought about by four decades of peace and prosperity.[28] The advantages of these institutions for reducing uncertainty and risk (or what economists call transaction costs) apparently are greater than their disadvantages for efficiency. We may hope that in the coming years institutional economics will develop better ways of locating the point at which the benefits of institutions reducing uncertainty equals the cost measured in diminishing economic efficiency. This book suggests until that time we should remain skeptical about the zealous claims of some neoclassical economists who study markets to the exclusion of all other institutions.

Recognition of the importance of institutions for West Germany's market economy harbors its own risk of overgeneralization. A large number of institutions exist in the local and regional economy that have proven essential to the adaptability, for example, of the machinery industry in southern Germany, in northern and central Italy, and in Japan. This much we know from existing studies that criticize conventional economic analysis.[29] But describing that institutional richness at the microlevel is not the same as explaining the pattern of West German, Italian, and Japanese adaptation to change in economics and in politics. Instead, the task at hand is to specify the particular West German pattern of adjustment emanating from a distinctive institutional and political configuration in national politics. To some extent industrial sectors have their own life in local and regional economies as well as in the international division of labor. But the contours of that life are largely defined politically by the national patterns of politics and policy.

28. Mancur Olson, *The Rise and Decline of Nations: Economic Growth, Stagflation, and Social Rigidities* (New Haven: Yale University Press, 1982).

29. Michael J. Piore and Charles F. Sabel, "Italian Small Business Development: Lessons for U.S. Industrial Policy," in John Zysman and Laura Tyson, eds., *American Industry in International Competition: Government Policies and Corporate Strategies* (Ithaca: Cornell University Press, 1983), pp. 391–421; David Friedman, *The Misunderstood Miracle: Industrial Development and Political Change in Japan* (Ithaca: Cornell University, 1988).

Three Capitalisms

The politics of West German industry can be compared to that of other capitalist states. West Germany resembles most closely the stable corporatist politics and flexible economic policy distinctive of the smaller European democracies.[30] This is no surprise. Germany's partition after 1945 made the country smaller and enhanced its perception of vulnerability and dependence on world markets. A consensual style of politics came to prevail over the political extremes. Centrist political parties and centralized interest groups fashioned a democratic style of politics. Over time the question of national reunification receded in importance while questions of economic productivity and social welfare assumed central importance.

In a broader perspective West Germany's major economic rivals, the United States and Japan, typify liberal and statist political arrangements that respond differently to economic and social change.[31] Liberal states like the United States press for international liberalization and at the same time often seek to export the costs of change to other countries. Because they lack the political means for selective intervention in their own economies, they often adopt a variety of limited protectionist policies. Such action normally creates a temporary breathing space for producers hard-pressed by international competition, but it rarely addresses long-term structural shifts in international competitiveness. Conversely, statist countries like Japan are endowed with the means and institutions to preempt the cost of change by seeking structural transformations in their economies. Because it seeks to meet head-on structural changes in the world economy this strategy often requires protectionist policies, at least in the short and medium term.

Liberal and statist adjustment strategies result from distinctive political structures. American's liberal regime is shaped by a strong business community that has become politically less secure since the 1930s. The feeling of insecurity is not a function of objective political circumstance but derives instead from the erosion of a position of unquestioned primacy which business had enjoyed between the Civil War and the Great Depression.[32] Industrial unionism in the United States emerged late and never succeeded as much as did most European labor movements in making its presence felt as an independent political force on the national scene. In addition, the American state is politically frag-

30. Peter J. Katzenstein, *Corporatism and Change: Austria, Switzerland, and the Politics of Industry* (Ithaca: Cornell University Press, 1984); Katzenstein, *Small States in World Markets: Industrial Policy in Europe* (Ithaca: Cornell University Press, 1985).
31. Peter J. Katzenstein, ed., *Between Power and Plenty: Foreign Economic Policies of Advanced Industrial States* (Madison: University of Wisconsin Press, 1978).
32. David Vogel, "Why Businessmen Distrust Their State: The Political Consciousness of American Corporate Executives," *British Journal of Political Science* 8 (1978): 45–78.

mented. It may even be labeled weak if we consider the apparently contradictory heavy-handed legal intervention in economic and social affairs to which the U.S. government often is driven for lack of other instruments of power and control. An arms-length relationship between industry and finance exists as a result of the structure of America's capital markets.[33] Government-business relations tend to be distant and adversarial rather than integrated and cooperative. And the U.S. labor movement basically is excluded from the crucial decisions affecting investment and employment both in national politics and at the level of the plant.

In Japan's statist regime business plays the central role in what one book has called a system of creative conservatism.[34] Business, especially big business, is at the center of the political coalition that has sustained the Liberal Democratic Party in power for three decades of uninterrupted rule. After a brief period of explosive growth in the immediate postwar years, Japan's labor movement has since not succeeded in escaping from the relative political isolation in which the Left in postwar Japan has found itself. The Japanese state, on the other hand, has been a strong and important actor in the evolution of Japan's postwar economy.[35] In contrast to the United States, the network linking the different actors in Japan's political economy is relatively tight. Japan's financial system is based not on autonomous capital markets but on a system of administered credit which accords the state a prominent role in influencing investment flows in the economy. Government-business relations are integrated and cooperative by U.S. standards. And labor, excluded from the corridors of power at the national level, is incorporated into decision-making structures at the plant level, not uniformly to be sure, but in ways that differ significantly from the exclusion of U.S. labor at both national and plant levels.

Distinctive of West German politics is the relative equality in the distribution of power among different actors.[36] No great disparities exist, by the standards of U.S. and Japanese politics. In West Germany business and labor are politically so well entrenched that they can accommodate themselves with relative ease to changes in government control by successive center-right or center-left coalition governments.

33. John Zysman, *Governments, Markets, and Growth: Financial Systems and the Politics of Industrial Change* (Ithaca: Cornell University Press, 1983).

34. T. J. Pempel, *Policy and Politics in Japan: Creative Conservatism* (Philadelphia: Temple University Press, 1982).

35. Chalmers Johnson, *MITI and the Japanese Miracle: The Growth of Industrial Policy, 1925–1975* (Stanford: Stanford University Press, 1982); Richard J. Samuels, *The Business of the Japanese State: Energy Markets in Comparative and Historical Perspective* (Ithaca: Cornell University Press, 1987); Friedman, *Misunderstood Miracle.*

36. Katzenstein, *Policy and Politics in West Germany.*

The organizational strength and institutional presence of both business and labor, though variable, is impressive by U.S. and Japanese standards. These actors are relatively closely linked to one another, thus resembling Japan more than the United States. The relation between industry and banks is close, based on a system of competitive bargaining rather than of private capital markets or credits administered by the state. Government-business relations are stronger than in the United States, and government-labor relations are more closely knit than in Japan. Tight links between interest groups, political parties, and state bureaucracies create an inclusionary politics.

These broad characterizations of the political strategies and structures of "liberal democracy" in the United States, "productivity democracy" in Japan, and "industrial democracy" in West Germany offer an essential reference point for understanding the distinctiveness of the West German response to change in the 1980s. In the United States and Japan industrial sectors are typically viewed as growing and declining, either autonomously through shifts in market competition or under state guidance; West Germany with its stable industrial structure emphasizes renewal and change within existing industrial sectors. The United States and Japan think in the categories of a "big power," either in military-political domination or economic-technological preeminence; West Germany thinks like a small state in terms of the exploitation of market niches in a favorable political environment. Finally, strong segmentation tendencies in the labor force exist in the United States through deskilling and wage differentiation and in Japan through a selective solidarity that encompasses a minority of the total labor force; in West Germany these segmentation tendencies are gathering strength in the 1980s but still remain much weaker.

Fault Lines for Potentially Seismic Changes

An examination of the changes likely to affect West German politics in the 1990s forces us to make explicit two contrasting images of historical change that often inform our judgments on daily events. According to the first image, the political, social, and economic universe is fluid and permissive of small adjustments and changes. In this view change in history is unobtrusive and comes in small doses which over time will redefine how political actors conceive of their interests as well as gradually reshape the structures in which they move. The second image emphasizes not the fluidity but the stickiness of political, social, and economic arrangements. In this view continuities, especially institutional continuities, are a central fact of political life. Institutions will have

349

a substantial effect on how interests are defined and pursued. West Germany in the 1980s and 1990s, I have argued here, supports both images of historical change. Widespread experimentation points to the fluidity of political, social, and economic arrangements while the absence of large-scale institutional change serves as a useful reminder of the enduring qualities of West Germany's institutional life. Which of these two facets of West German politics we judge to be more important depends not only on the questions we ask but on the unspoken assumptions that inform our analysis of West German politics. Those who have lived through the horrors of the 1930s and 1940s are likely to emphasize that the big political picture in West Germany has remained stable in the 1980s. Oblivious of the heavy legacy of Germany's past, young students of West Germany point to the pervasiveness of many small changes as the most important development in the 1980s. As a member of the middle generation, I am trying to steer a middle ground between reading all West German developments back into German history on one hand and being altogether uninterested in the history of the Federal Republic and of Germany on the other.

The argument of this chapter seeks to account for the convergence between a myriad of small-scale changes throughout West German industry and the institutional and political stability of the Federal Republic. This analysis must therefore be especially sensitive to pointing out political developments or conflicts that might lead to dramatic changes in West Germany's political economy. Domestic labor markets, international capital markets, and the cumulative effects of incremental changes favoring decentralization of political practices and institutions are three areas that might effect dramatic changes in the political economy of the Third Republic.

Developments in West German labor markets are one possible course of large-scale change. The reduction in the quantity of work (a net loss of 1 million jobs between 1973 and 1986 as compared to a net gain of 24 million jobs in the United States) and a sharp expansion in the number of long-term unemployed among the total number of unemployed workers (an increase from 14 percent in 1977 to 31 percent in 1985 as compared to a 2 percent change in the United States from 7 to 9 percent) are posing serious challenges to the labor movement.[37] Early retirements and a shortening of the workweek did not prevent the unemployment rate

37. Lindley H. Clark, Jr., "Why Unemployment Stays So High in Germany," *Wall Street Journal*, 22 May 1987, p. 18; Frieder Naschold, ed., *Arbeit und Politik: Gesellschaftliche Regulierung der Arbeit und der Sozialen Sicherung* (Frankfurt: Campus, 1985); Heidrun Abromeit and Bernhard Blanke, eds., *Arbeitsmarkt, Arbeitsbeziehungen und Politik in den 80er Jahren* (Opladen: Westdeutscher Verlag, 1987); Manfred G. Schmidt, "The Politics of Labor Market Policy: Structural and Political Determinants of Rates of Unemployment in Industrial Nations," in Francis G. Castles, Franz Lehner, and Manfred G. Schmidt, eds., *Managing Mixed Economies* (Berlin: deGruyter, 1988), pp. 4–53.

from increasing sharply to about 8 to 9 percent in the 1980s. One consequence of this change is the creation of a group of politically disaffected younger West Germans, now between about twenty and thirty-five years of age. This group currently has great difficulties finding attractive, well-paying positions; once they have found a job members of this group will be heavily taxed to finance West Germany's generous social welfare programs; and upon retirement thirty to forty years from now this group is likely to receive much less in return. A more immediate consequence is, as Kern and Schumann argue, a reduction in the quantity of work accompanied by an improvement in the quality of work for at least some segments of the skilled working class. The result has been to strain the solidarity of labor as well as weaken its political position. Growing unemployment has encouraged firms, backed by their works councils, to impose tougher criteria for recruitment. The intent is to stabilize a company's work force and to make its disposition, both in job allocation and working time, as flexible as possible. Qualification redundancies of employed workers and government policy favoring greater flexibility illustrate the growing importance of "internal" rather than "external" labor markets.[38]

The tendency toward social segmentation is not easily countered by the union movement. Politically the DGB has found itself on the defensive. Its relations with the CDU-F.D.P. government are strained. It has suffered severely from internal scandals that have led to the sale of the majority of shares of its own bank. And though it backs a "technological offensive" to take advantage of new production technologies, the unions have so far not succeeded in developing a program through which they could hope to receive the firm support of the works councils and workers favored by the need for new skills and qualifications at the workplace. Compared to virtually all labor movements in Europe, the political position of the DGB remains strong. But it is facing a process of quiet erosion of former beachheads of strength. The dramatic decline in the number of young workers entering the labor market for the first time in the 1990s will undoubtedly increase the market power of labor. But it will not eliminate the need for developing political concepts and strategies for strengthening worker solidarity and a broader social consensus on the role of labor in a rapidly changing economy. If such concepts and strategies are not developed, the trade-off between the quantity and the quality of work will remain a potential source for political mobilization and demands for large-scale institutional change.

The fragility of international capital markets is a second area that throws a pall over the international trading system on which West Ger-

38. Hans-Willy Hohn, "Interne Arbeitsmärkte und Betriebliche Mitbestimmung-Tendenzen der 'Sozialen Schliessung' im 'dualen' System der Interessenvertretung," *Discussion Paper* IIM/LMP (Wissenschaftszentrum Berlin, 1983).

man industry depends so heavily.[39] Since the Mexican crisis of 1982, however, the international debt regime has proven remarkably resilient. Relations between the IMF and the private sector have become closer. The banking industry has evolved institutional practices that so far have responded successfully to the great difficulties of potential defaults and debt rescheduling. The decision of the U.S. banks to write off a significant proportion of their outstanding loans as bad debts in 1987 has consolidated their position and the stability of the international financial system. Furthermore, domestic intervention mechanisms exist that make unlikely the recurrence of a 1930s-style collapse.

But it would be foolish to mistake a decade-long effort in successful crisis management for the existence of stable markets. No durable international debt regime has emerged in the 1980s. And changes in international financial markets are occurring at a dizzying speed. Technological changes and deregulation are pushing toward the creation of one global capital market. Financial power in that market is shifting with great rapidity to Japan and, to a lesser extent, to West Germany while the United States, should it refuse to change its economic policies, will continue to accumulate substantial foreign debts well into the 1990s. It is too early to gauge the consequences of these changes for a liberal international trade system. Japan has a strong interest in unrestricted access to U.S. markets, but American politics may be turning more protectionist. Threats to a liberal international economy might stem, as in the 1970s, from creeping protectionism or, as in the 1980s, from the possibility of financial collapse. In the 1990s destabilizing links between trade and finance, especially in U.S.-Japanese relations, may assert themselves. Because West Germany depends more on its exports than does Japan or the United States, it would suffer more from such instabilities in the global economy. The plan for the creation of a fully integrated European market by 1992 and the discussion about the future evolution of the European Monetary System indicate that the Federal Republic would probably seek to shelter itself from such instabilities through a further deepening of its European ties.

Finally, there is a third possibility for potentially larger-scale change in the politics of the Third Republic. It would be less spectacular than dramatic developments in the structure of domestic labor or international capital markets. The cumulative effect of the small changes that are creating pressures toward decentralization in the political institutions of the Third Republic might at some undeterminable threshold lead to large-scale institutional change. The structure of West German federalism which I discussed above is one example. Possible changes in the structure of the West German party system are another. The rise of

39. Miles Kahler, ed., *The Politics of International Debt* (Ithaca: Cornell University Press, 1986).

the Greens on the left of the political spectrum and of a small wing of free market advocates in the F.D.P. and CDU on the right are evidence of a broadening spectrum of political positions in the centrist politics of the Third Republic. The SPD's potential for change should not be underestimated. The party repudiated Chancellor Schmidt in the stationing of Pershing missiles in the early 1980s. It embraced a number of the political demands of the Greens in the mid-1980s. And the SPD appeared to be poised to engage the labor movement in a serious discussion about employment in the late 1980s. A wider political spectrum and a gradual recalibration in political weights eventually might have dramatic effects on the domestic balance of power that has assured export industries, the banks, and the labor movement a central position in West German politics since 1949.

The institutional logic of West German politics in the 1980s continues to embody the political consensus of the first two republics: social welfare and economic efficiency are not antithetical but mutually reinforcing. Each passing year reconfirms that consensus implicitly by giving these institutions further room for play. The public demonstrations of steelworkers threatened by a further layoff in the fall of 1987 did not constitute a potentially serious crisis, as had the demonstrations of 1984–85. The demonstrations were no less militant, but they occurred in a period in which the major political groups had implicitly agreed not to challenge fundamentally established political institutions. This stabilizes the social and political fabric of the Federal Republic. And each passing year makes clearer how difficult West Germany's political elites find it to think of large departures from the institutional networks in which they act. The Third Republic may not implant itself securely because, after a period of intense searching for new political concepts, West Germany's political elites self-consciously embrace the existing institutional order. Instead, that process of implantation may occur by default as the effort to think of new ways of organizing politics is stymied by the heavy hand of West German institutions which make "thinking the unthinkable" so difficult.

The evidence presented in this book and the argument of this chapter suggest that, short of unforeseeable major upheavals, pervasive small-scale change and experimentation in industry is compatible with a large measure of stability in national institutions and politics without sacrificing West Germany's international competitiveness. National institutions are stable because they accommodate changes occurring in the factory, in national politics, and in the international system. Political affirmation of these institutions would transform movement toward the Third Republic into an acceptance of its existence.

353

Index

Cornell Studies in Political Economy

EDITED BY PETER J. KATZENSTEIN

Library of Congress Cataloging-in-Publication Data

Industry and politics in West Germany : toward the Third Republic /
   edited by Peter J. Katzenstein.
      p.   cm.—(Cornell studies in political economy)
   Includes index.
   ISBN 0-8014-2357-0 (alk. paper).
   ISBN 0-8014-9595-4 (pbk.: alk. paper)
   1. Industry and state—Germany (West) 2. Industrial management—
Germany (West) 3. Competition—Germany (West) 4. Germany (West)—
Industries. I. Katzenstein, Peter J. II. Series.
HD3616.G35I54   1989   338.943—dc19   89-31033